Animality and Colonial Subjecthood in Africa

NEW AFRICAN HISTORIES

SERIES EDITORS: JEAN ALLMAN, ALLEN ISAACMAN, AND DEREK R. PETERSON

David William Cohen and E. S. Atieno Odhiambo, *The Risks of Knowledge*

Belinda Bozzoli, *Theatres of Struggle and the End of Apartheid*

Gary Kynoch, *We Are Fighting the World*

Stephanie Newell, *The Forger's Tale*

Jacob A. Tropp, *Natures of Colonial Change*

Jan Bender Shetler, *Imagining Serengeti*

Cheikh Anta Babou, *Fighting the Greater Jihad*

Marc Epprecht, *Heterosexual Africa?*

Marissa J. Moorman, *Intonations*

Karen E. Flint, *Healing Traditions*

Derek R. Peterson and Giacomo Macola, editors, *Recasting the Past*

Moses E. Ochonu, *Colonial Meltdown*

Emily S. Burrill, Richard L. Roberts, and Elizabeth Thornberry, editors, *Domestic Violence and the Law in Colonial and Postcolonial Africa*

Daniel R. Magaziner, *The Law and the Prophets*

Emily Lynn Osborn, *Our New Husbands Are Here*

Robert Trent Vinson, *The Americans Are Coming!*

James R. Brennan, *Taifa*

Benjamin N. Lawrance and Richard L. Roberts, editors, *Trafficking in Slavery's Wake*

David M. Gordon, *Invisible Agents*

Allen F. Isaacman and Barbara S. Isaacman, *Dams, Displacement, and the Delusion of Development*

Stephanie Newell, *The Power to Name*

Gibril R. Cole, *The Krio of West Africa*

Matthew M. Heaton, *Black Skin, White Coats*

Meredith Terretta, *Nation of Outlaws, State of Violence*

Paolo Israel, *In Step with the Times*

Michelle R. Moyd, *Violent Intermediaries*

Abosede A. George, *Making Modern Girls*

Alicia C. Decker, *In Idi Amin's Shadow*

Rachel Jean-Baptiste, *Conjugal Rights*

Shobana Shankar, *Who Shall Enter Paradise?*

Emily S. Burrill, *States of Marriage*

Todd Cleveland, *Diamonds in the Rough*

Carina E. Ray, *Crossing the Color Line*

Sarah Van Beurden, *Authentically African*

Giacomo Macola, *The Gun in Central Africa*

Lynn Schler, *Nation on Board*

Julie MacArthur, *Cartography and the Political Imagination*

Abou B. Bamba, *African Miracle, African Mirage*

Daniel Magaziner, *The Art of Life in South Africa*

Paul Ocobock, *An Uncertain Age*

Keren Weitzberg, *We Do Not Have Borders*

Nuno Domingos, *Football and Colonialism*

Jeffrey S. Ahlman, *Living with Nkrumahism*

Bianca Murillo, *Market Encounters*

Laura Fair, *Reel Pleasures*

Thomas F. McDow, *Buying Time*

Jon Soske, *Internal Frontiers*

Elizabeth W. Giorgis, *Modernist Art in Ethiopia*

Matthew V. Bender, *Water Brings No Harm*

David Morton, *Age of Concrete*

Marissa J. Moorman, *Powerful Frequencies*

Ndubueze L. Mbah, *Emergent Masculinities*

Judith A. Byfield, *The Great Upheaval*

Patricia Hayes and Gary Minkley, editors, *Ambivalent*

Mari K. Webel, *The Politics of Disease Control*

Kara Moskowitz, *Seeing Like a Citizen*

Jacob Dlamini, *Safari Nation*

Alice Wiemers, *Village Work*

Cheikh Anta Babou, *The Muridiyya on the Move*

Laura Ann Twagira, *Embodied Engineering*

Marissa Mika, *Africanizing Oncology*

Holly Hanson, *To Speak and Be Heard*

Paul S. Landau, *Spear*

Saheed Aderinto, *Animality and Colonial Subjecthood in Africa*

Animality and Colonial Subjecthood in Africa

The Human and Nonhuman Creatures of Nigeria

∽

Saheed Aderinto

OHIO UNIVERSITY PRESS

ATHENS, OHIO

Ohio University Press, Athens, Ohio 45701
ohioswallow.com
© 2022 by Ohio University Press
All rights reserved

Printed in the United States of America
Ohio University Press books are printed on acid-free paper ∞ ™

Paperback ISBN: 978-0-8214-2476-6

31 30 29 28 27 26 25 24 23 22 21 5 4 3 2 1

Library of Congress Cataloging-in-Publication Data
Names: Aderinto, Saheed, author.
Title: Animality and colonial subjecthood in Africa : the human and nonhuman
creatures of Nigeria / Saheed Aderinto.
Other titles: New African histories series.
Description: Athens : Ohio University Press, 2022. | Series: New African histories |
Includes bibliographical references and index.
Identifiers: LCCN 2021031167 (print) | LCCN 2021031168 (ebook) | ISBN
9780821424698 (hardback) | ISBN 9780821447680 (pdf)
Subjects: LCSH: Animals—Nigeria—Colonial influence. | Animals—Social
aspects—Nigeria—History. | Human-animal relationships—Nigeria—History. |
Nigeria—Colonial influence. | Nigeria—Politics and government—To 1960.
Classification: LCC DT515.75 .A34 2022 (print) | LCC DT515.75 (ebook) | DDC
966.903—dc23
LC record available at https://lccn.loc.gov/2021031167
LC ebook record available at https://lccn.loc.gov/2021031168

For
Chuku and Lekewogbe (dogs),
Jubilee (a horse),
Aruna and Imade (gorillas),
Alagba (a tortoise), and
Oni Ile Delesolu (a crocodile)

Praise Poem of Lékèéwọ̀gbẹ́, a Nineteenth-Century Yoruba Dog

Lékèéwọ̀gbẹ́!
Ajá Túgbẹ̀ẹ́
Ajá tíí forí ọ̀kẹ́rẹ́ jẹ̀kọ
Ajá tó mọ ọmọ rẹ̀ fún lọ́mú
Tí ń ki ọmọ odù òyà mọ́lẹ̀

Lékèéwọ̀gbẹ́ tó gborí ogun wáyé!
Ọ̀jọ́-kan-òjọ́kán
Ọ̀jọ́-kan-òjọ̀kàn
Tí Lékèéwọ̀gbẹ́ tẹ̀lé ògáa rẹ̀ rogun
Ó ṣojú Kújẹ́nyọ̀ olórí awo
Ó ṣojú Òjóòkegbè olórí ìmùlẹ̀!

Bí Túgbẹ̀ẹ́ ṣe ń gbé ẹbọ lọ n'wájú
Bẹ́ẹ̀ ni Lékèéwọ̀gbẹ́ ń gbó tẹ̀le
Ó di kìrìkàtà
Ó di kàràkìtà
N làwọn òkété bá bẹ́ jáde
kúrò ń'sà, lọ́sàn-án 'gan
Lékèéwọ̀gbẹ́ gbá tele wọn!
Ló bá kì'kan lórí mọ́lẹ̀

Ńjẹ́ kó bẹ̀rẹ̀ sí ní jẹ ẹ̀ ni Túgbẹ̀ẹ́ pariwo mọ́ọ
Ó ní "Págà!
Ṣé ìwọ ti gbàgbé ni
Pé ìran ajá kan kìí j'òkété
Ẹbọ l'Oníkòyí ń fi wọ́n-ọ́n rú
Ẹbọ l'Èṣọ́ Oníkòyí ń fi wọ́n bọ!

TRANSLATION

Lékèéwògbẹ́!
Túgbẹ̀ẹ́'s dog
The dog that knows how to care for his puppies
But mauls a grasscutter's

Lékèéwògbẹ́ is a destined warrior!
One fateful day
Lékèéwògbẹ́ accompanied his master to the war front
It was in the presence of Kújẹ́nyọ̀, a revered priest,
Òjóòkegbè, a revered priest, also witnessed it

As Túgbẹ̀ẹ́ marched on with the sacrifice
Lékèéwògbẹ́ followed behind, barking
The bush rats rushed out of their burrows
In broad daylight
Lékèéwògbẹ́ chased them

And as he was about to devour one
Túgbẹ̀ẹ́ screamed
Abomination!
Have you forgotten?
That a dog does not eat the pouched rat
It is Onikoyi's, the warrior's, sacrificial animal
It is for the gods and goddesses!

Contents

Illustrations

TABLES

Acknowledgments

An idea for an academic book is not a magic spell, occurring miraculously and without a process. In most cases, it is a product of encounters with related knowledge, unfinished business from previous projects, a search for new frontiers of knowledge, and access to a dense trove of data. All these gave birth to *Animality and Colonial Subjecthood in Africa*. I first began to think, academically, about animals while I was working on my book on the history of guns in Nigeria, published in 2018. Writing about the use of guns for hunting first introduced me to environmental history and human-animal affairs. But it did not take long for me to realize that hunting was just one of the numerous sites of human-animal encounter. To write a book solely on hunting, either local or imperial, or the history of nature conservation would amount to reproducing similar scholarships, especially from eastern and southern Africa. But I did not have to look far for ideas to situate the book in extant literature. My sources all point explicitly to the central thesis of this book—animals, like humans, were colonial subjects in Africa.

My appreciation goes to archivists, friends, and colleagues who aided this work in one way or the other. This is the third monograph I will have completed while benefiting directly from the kindness of Gboyega Ade-lowo of the Ibadan National Archives. At the Kaduna and Enugu offices of the Nigerian National Archives, Magaji Ikara Dalibi and Anthony Nwaneri, respectively, placed their decades of experience in the repository in service of my work. Researching a book that covers the entire country of Nigeria exposed my African-language limitations—besides English, I speak only Yoruba and a West African pidgin English. However, a text message or a phone call was all I needed to acquire the help of Chijioke Azuawusiefe, Ngozika Obi-Ani, Patrick Chukwudike Okpalaeke, and Chi-jioke Kizito Ona for translation and clarification of non-Yoruba words. Hu-zaifa Dokaji and Prince Vincent-Anene helped break the cultural hurdles in northern and eastern Nigeria during my fieldwork there and took many trips to the archives on my behalf. In the southwest, Victor Olaoye, Tolani Onike, Sikiru Yusuf, and Oluwaseun Williams procured authorization to use the repositories at the Obafemi Awolowo University and the Lagos High Court (Igbosere) and ran errands, collecting and depositing materials for shipment abroad to me. Williams also made the illustrations in chapter 4 into collages, thus preserving space and allowing me to keep visuals that aid the text of this book. Printing the praise poem of Lékèéwògbé, a nineteenth-century war dog in the epigraph of this book, required more than a single person's effort. Because the poem was originally collected in the 1950s but rendered in English by Horst Ulrich "Ulli" Beier, the absence of the original Yoruba version posed a significant challenge for me. I first translated it from English to Yoruba and then, with the help of Yoruba linguists Rasaq Malik Gbolahan, Olusegun Soetan, and Kola Tubosun and of Williams, transliterated and translated the poem back to English.

One needs more than access to data to write a book—a community of scholars and professional associations willing to listen to premature ideas as they develop is fundamental. In June 2017 Samaila Suleiman invited me to Bayero University in Kano to present the overview of this project. I publicly performed the praise poem of Lékèéwògbé at the Obafemi Awolowo University in June 2019 because Shina Alimi invited me there. As I completed the first draft of the manuscript, I received an invitation from Jane Desmond to give the plenary lecture of the Human-Animal Studies Institute at the University of Illinois Urbana-Champaign in July 2019. This event allowed me to speak to non-Africanists about the "animal turn" in African history and receive meaningful feedback. A week after submitting the manuscript to the Ohio University Press (OUP) for external review in October 2019, I gave a lecture focusing on animals in African urban locations at the University of Pennsylvania at the invitation of David Amponsah. Different versions of book chapters were presented at the panels sponsored by the Lagos Studies Association (LSA) at meetings of the African Studies Association (Chicago, 2017; Atlanta, 2018; and Boston, 2019), at a meeting of the African Studies Association of the United Kingdom (Birmingham, 2018), and at an LSA conference (Lagos, 2018). After delivering a talk, facilitated by Nancy Jacobs, to the American Society for Environmental History on October 27, 2020, and presenting at a seminar titled "Animal (Pre)History, Agency, and Legacy," organized by Stephanie Zehnle and Shumon Hussain in May 2021, I saw additional need to strengthen the contributions of this book to African environmental studies.

Animality and Colonial Subjecthood in Africa sees the light of the day because OUP acquisitions editor Ricky S. Huard, series editors Jean Allman, Allen Isaacman, Derek R. Peterson, and Carina Ray, and anonymous readers thought it is important. I have enjoyed working with other members of the OUP (Laura André, Tyler Balli, and Sally Welch) and copyeditor Don McKeon as this project transformed from computer text to a real physical book. At Western Carolina University, where I work, graduate student assistants Marilyn Goble and Michael Beam helped to copy materials. Interlibrary loan staff member Daniel Wendel procured crucial items at short notice, while Department Head Mary Ella Engel helped secure funding for travel and research. Until 2020 the Nigeria Office of the French Institute for Research in Africa augmented the cost of research by providing free accommodation in their guesthouse whenever I was in Ibadan. My appreciation goes to former director Elodie Apard and Deputy Director Emilie Guitard.

For the past twelve years, I have been privileged to have Bob Fullilove, one of the few people who read the book manuscript word for word, as my copyeditor. I thank him for challenging me to improve the manuscript through his thought-provoking comments. The Nigerian Nostalgia Project, with over seventy thousand virtual members, has been a blessing to many professional and amateur historians who enjoy the public history of Nigeria through visuals. Images from this virtual platform formed the basis of some of the narratives and illustrations in this book. Special appreciation goes to project administrators Debo Adetula, Etim Eyo, and Kehinde Thompson for their dedication to Nigerian history and for blessing the country with a platform that aids academic research in significant ways.

In writing a book that crosses disciplinary boundaries, I was compelled to rely on scholars who know more than I do on specific topics. For the chapter on animal cartoons and visual arts, I am grateful for the guidance provided by Bukola Gbadegesin, Dele Jegede, Ganiyu Jimoh (Jimga), Babatunde Lawal, Sylvester Ogbechie, Moyo Okediji, and the late Tejumola Olaniyan. Veterinary doctors Akintunde Alamu, Fatai Adebayo, and Olawale Oni helped me understand some of the scientific considerations that shaped the narratives in colonial documentation about cattle, horses, and donkeys. In addition to granting me access to every part of the University of Ibadan Zoological Garden, zoologists Adekunle Bakare and Akindayo Sowunmi explained the transformations of zookeeping in a language accessible to a layperson like me.

I am lucky to have a family that supports what I do as a scholar without any reservation. It is impossible to quantify the love of Olamide, my wife, and Itandola and Itandayo, my teenage children, and the sacrifice they make to aid my work. Olamide is the most consistent and the most generous funder of my research—she has continued to allow me to use family money in pursuit of my endless quest for knowledge. For me, the dichotomy between "home" and "work" does not exist, not only because I do 100 percent of my book writing from my home office but also because my family is at the center of my entire existence as a scholar.

Abbreviations

AG	Action Group
ComCol	Commissioner of the Colony Office, Lagos
DAO	Diseases of Animals Ordinance
DMSS	director of medical and sanitary services
DVS	director of veterinary services
LRC	Lagos Race Club
LTC	Lagos Town Council
MOH	medical officer of health
NAAS	Nigerian Animal Aid Society
NAE	National Archives of Nigeria, Enugu
NAI	National Archives of Nigeria, Ibadan
NAK	National Archives of Nigeria, Kaduna
NAUK	National Archives of the United Kingdom
NCNC	National Council of Nigeria and the Cameroons
NDT	*Nigerian Daily Times*
NEPU	Northern Elements Progressive Union
NRSPCA	Nigeria Royal Society for the Prevention of Cruelty to Animals
NYM	Nigerian Youth Movement
ProF	Province Files

RSPCA   Royal Society for the Prevention of Cruelty to Animals
RUGA   Rural Grazing Area
TUC   Trades Union Congress
WAP   *West African Pilot*
WAPO   Wild Animals Preservation Ordinance

Introduction

The 1956 royal visit by Queen Elizabeth II to Nigeria, a grandiose endeavor and show of imperial might that consumed an estimated two million pounds' worth of Nigerians' money, will remain in history books forever.[1] The colorful spectacle of colonial subjects across racial and social class lines vying to catch a glimpse of the head of a fast-crumbling British Empire left an indelible imprint on human memories.[2] Nigeria gave the queen what she came to see (civilization and modernity)—the so-called gains of a century of foreign domination that manifested in the tarred roads, hospitals, factories, social clubs, hygienic-looking schoolchildren waving the Union Jack in a show of patriotism to the empire, and a European-style public arena, among other carefully curated sites and symbols of imperialism. The guard of honor and militarization of every location she visited produced an ambivalent taste—it reinforced the military might of the British Empire in an atmosphere of superfluous merriment.[3]

Yet the dominion of imperial subjecthood and public ritual of power extended beyond humans to include respectable animals like the cattle that produced the milk that the queen and her contingent drank during their stay in northern Nigeria. Photojournalism gave meaningful coverage to the nonhuman creatures of the empire as it featured the queen "admiring" the milk-producing cattle for their service to the empire.[4] She also met another respectable animal named Burtu, a hornbill and the mascot of the First Battalion of the colonial military unit—the Royal West African Frontier Force (RWAFF)—who participated in the guard of honor staged normality, orderliness, and modernity. That a dog could be hanged, like a human, for contravening colonial regulations speaks volumes about how imperialism conceived biological bodies and affinity between its human and nonhuman subjects. The imposition of a dog or cattle tax was not just about materiality of animals—it also entailed obligation and protection derived from performing the civic duty of increasing the colonial treasury through levies. Colonial animals, like humans, were placed in the service of the empire. The donkey, the number one transport animal of British Nigeria, helped the invaders to achieve their capitalist expropriation. The horse became the insignia of imperial spectacle on the turf, performing power that fractured the tenor of interhuman politics. The idea of "animals and other Nigerians" simply suggests that "Nigerianness" (like ethnic categories) transcends the human factor. There were animal as well as human Nigerians.

COLONIAL SUBJECTHOOD AND ANIMALITY

African historical scholarship has come of age. From a discipline that focused on the history of men, written by men and for men, the theoretical breadth and discursive length of the field has expanded tremendously since the 1950s to accommodate new topics across lines of gender, race, location, and power configuration. We now know that a narrative of state and empire building that excludes women is incomplete and that the history of children, sexuality, and material culture, including guns, can help us to understand the past more fully. A history of Africa that excludes an ethnic group simply because it is categorized as a minority is as flawed as one that does not recognize core accidents of history, such as how location shaped the pattern of external contact and religious and ethnic identities. Today academic research on Africa prides itself on inclusion—that is, its capacity to write neglected communities and architecture of knowledge into mainstream history. Aided by the decolonization paradigm, scholars have continued to search for new ways of presenting old ideas in a manner that resituates people and knowledge in provocative ways. Writing about neglected communities empowers scholars to move from stale narratives and familiar cultural and political lexicons in an unending drive to reshape the landscape of knowledge.

One such community that has escaped the purview of Africanist historians is the animal inhabitants of the continent. In coming to terms with the limited attention given to animal history and human-animal entanglement in Africanist scholarship, one is drawn to the foundation of academic history of Africa, which is deeply influenced by Western historical methodology and a knowledge system that viewed history as simply humans' past activities; therefore, human agency is central to historical research. Yet neither indigenous African knowledge systems nor colonial archives, with their barrage of prejudice, conceived of the past as an exclusively human realm, devoid of nonhuman agency. Animals have been an integral part of Africa's past—making history and shaping narratives—with significant implications for major historical events. African history was not made by humans alone.

The tendency to treat history as exclusively about humans has resulted in a paucity of scholarship on animals in African history. As Sandra Swart opined in 2016, "As a distinct and self-baptized 'turn' or 'sub-discipline' within African History writing," animal history "is there—but little studied and elusive, a creature of the liminal spaces, nibbling at the edges of the conferences and journals." But, "as a living, breathing beast, it has been grazing in full sight of everyone in the historiographical field for as long as African history has existed and the locals have often caught and consumed it."[9] Swart attempts to establish a delineation between the scholarship on pastoralism, hunting, and conservation, which began to appear from the 1940s or earlier and recent ones "focusing on the animals themselves—and reflecting upon their role as subjects, rather than objects."[10] Examples of older and newer works include Robin Law's *The Horse in West African History* and Nancy Jacobs' *Birders of Africa*, respectively.[11] The geographical imbalance of newer works, written either from the perspective of environmental history or from animal studies, is clear. They have come from southern and eastern Africa and have focused mostly on wildlife, imperial hunting, and the politics of nature conservation.[12] A few monographs on single species of animals (such as dogs, horses, and birds), also from eastern and southern Africa, have appeared in the past two decades in response to the call for historians to write animals into African history.[13] As important as these works are, they tend to focus on humans' understanding of nature and the nonhuman world—the dynamics of the relationships between humans and animals are grossly neglected or underrepresented. The "animal turn" in African history is still in its infancy.

When placed in the right perspective, humans' historical trajectory was dictated not only by intrahuman affairs but also by their engagement with nature, including animals. In writing animals into Africa's past, a historian is compelled to address the question of historical agency. If we go by the conventional definition of history as humans' past activities alone, we will eliminate nonhuman agency and narratives in historical processes and social imaginaries. But historical agency transcends human action—animals were political actors too. Scholars may never agree on the extent of agency that animals wielded in the past, but it is undeniable that animals shaped the tenor of political and social processes, directly and indirectly. As I will show in this work, animals have taken independent actions (as they searched for social connection, water, food, shelter, and sex) that created a chain of reactions that then formed the basis of turning points in human history. Animals resisted human encroachment of their domain, violated human-made laws that undermined their livelihood, reshaped landscapes that reordered human existence, and served as subject of significant debate across multiple strata of the imperial society. From the British tabloids and Parliament in the metropole to village meetings in the colonies, animal affairs notched a place on the agendas that historians of Africa have ignored. The proanimal humanitarianism that made the question of cruelty to Nigerian animals a subject of discussion in the British Parliament and media was informed by the "savior" mentality that shaped responses to "barbaric" culture by metropolitan critics of imperialism.

Animals obviously do not document their own experience; writing about them from the text and narratives composed by humans is an effort to give them voice. In writing animals into human history, a historian must think about what animality constituted in the framing of humans' everyday interaction with the natural and built environment. It is my hope that the animal-centered narratives, ideas, and events described here indicate clearly that writing about nonhuman creatures is worthwhile—for expanding the frontier of knowledge, mainstreaming neglected narratives and colonial subjects (i.e., animals), and shaping contemporary discourse about the enduring legacies of imperialism. Instead of focusing on a specific animal, as many of the existing scholarships tend to do, *Animality and Colonial Subjecthood in Africa* broadens the historiography of animal studies by putting many species (from cattle, goats, and pigs to dogs, horses, donkeys, and even wildlife) into a single analytical framework. The thematic breadth of the book varies from the story of rabies, the animals Nigerians ate, and the discourse of cruelty to entertainment, wildlife conservation, and the representation of animals in literature and visual arts. The dynamics of race, ethnicity, class, disease and imperial science, resistance to colonialism, environment, identity formation, and urbanization (among other themes) flow through the book. No other work on human-animal relations in twentieth-century colonial Africa has attempted this.

Colonialism and colonial subjecthood are the foundations on which this book is built. Right from the early 1950s, when academic study of Africa began, scholars have been preoccupied with what it means to be a colonial subject. Early scholarship on colonial subjecthood engages with the politics of indirect rule, which Mahmood Mamdani termed "decentralized despotism," that succeeded in British Africa "by tapping authoritarian possibilities in culture, and by giving culture an authoritarian bent" and association to underscore the creation of institutions and laws that defined political obligations and rights.[14] Embedded in colonial political systems are the principles of law and order, classification of "tribes" into "friendly" and "unfriendly," "civilized" and "primitive," and "docile" and "martial," among other uncanny indexing.[15] What constitutes subjecthood and citizenship of the colonies vary across location. Yet they are united by their insistence on positioning colonialism as benevolent to Africans. The early scholarship on African colonial subjecthood was later complemented by studies focusing on colonial capitalism and expropriation. Labor and taxation were central to the running of the colonial state,[16] but they also extended to control of human's reproductive and productive power. This accounts for why some of the biggest resistance to colonialism started as labor and tax unrest.[17] The rise of social history, which uses marriage, gender, women, and sexuality as points of analysis, considerably expanded the studies of colonialism. Matters like marriage and sexuality that colonial subjects would consider private, scholars have argued, have significant public ramifications on how colonialism framed morality, labor, and capitalism.[18]

When carefully appraised, the paradox of colonial subjecthood that scholars have studied with specific focus on humans is also evident in the experiences of animals. I posit that all the core dichotomies of human colonial subjecthood—indispensable yet disposable, both good and bad, violent but peaceful, saints and outlaws—are embedded in the identities of Nigeria's animal inhabitants. If class, religion, ethnicity, location, and attitude to imperialism determined the pattern of relations between human Nigerians and the colonial government, species, habitat, material value, threat, and biological and psychological character (among other traits) also shaped imperial attitudes toward animal Nigerians. Aside from being colonial subjects and "natives," nonhuman Nigerians were also ethnic bodies. What does it mean to be an Igbo, Yoruba, Tiv, Idoma, Hausa, or Fulani dog? In what sense do animals take on the unstable ethnic, racial, class, and other modulated identities of their human owners or their environment?

Service and labor are among the peculiarities of colonial subjecthood or what it means to be a colonial subject. In maximizing the gains of foreign domination, imperialism redirected the roles of animal colonial subjects. Precolonial roles either became obsolete or were expanded in new directions. Thus, the horse and donkey, who played an active part in the conquest of Nigeria as symbols of military expansion, became the primary means of transportation needed for the establishment of colonialism as well as insignias of leisure and athletic power among Africans and Europeans. The donkey, Nigeria's commonest pack animal, was integrated into the colonial labor force in a different fashion. While the direction of precolonial trade was northward, connecting humans and goods with the Saharan and Sudanese worlds, the colonial donkey's movement was mostly within the region that would later become northern Nigeria. Donkeys helped to courier the colony's wealth to the railway lines for onward shipment abroad. This same redirection of importance and role to meet the demands of capitalist enterprise also happened to cattle, which became the chief meat of the colonial state needed to feed the expanding population and generate wealth. The story of how beef changed Nigeria's history is being told for the first time here.

Animality and Colonial Subjecthood in Africa goes beyond a material analysis of what animals did in one of Britain's most important colonies. It encompasses a symbolic and textual analysis of animal lives shaped by facts, ideology, and materiality. It is a multispecies and interspecies study of animals' encounter with colonialism in Nigeria from both micro and macro perspectives. It reaffirms that animals have their own history both independent of and deeply intertwined with human stories. Beyond writing a history that engages with animal lives and fills obvious lacuna in the historiography of twentieth-century colonial Africa, this book offers an innovative paradigm for understanding the place of nonhuman creatures in colonial Nigeria. I conceptualize Nigeria's nonhuman creatures as "colonial subjects" and "modern" animals. This approach is useful for mapping out the unstable identities of animal inhabitants of Nigeria of various species as they adapted and responded to the colossal sociopolitical, economic, and structural changes ushered in by British colonialism. It transcends the notion of subjectivity; rather, it engages with the ways in which animals negotiated, dictated, resisted, and fractured new regimes of power under imperial rule. Being a nonhuman colonial subject does not automatically translate to lack of agency or powerlessness—rather, it is a state of existence and identity of a creature under foreign domination. Much of the acrimony about wildlife invading farms and settled communities and cities stems from the criminalized beasts. It was a form of resistance that reaffirmed or reclaimed agency over ecosystems that humans tried to monopolize through their unending desire for towns and built environments.

Humans and animals experienced colonialism in similar ways. Laws were enacted to regulate not only the activities of humans but animals' lives across changing physical and cultural landscapes. Yet animals' experience under colonialism was also shaped by the natural environment as well as by all the socially and historically constructed identities of their owners. Because animals were influenced by both nature and humans, their experiences tended to be complex and wide-ranging. Colonialism involved governance of and through nature; colonial possessions included not just the human inhabitants but also the nonhuman creatures and the environment as a whole. It is not possible to write the history of humans under colonialism without reference to the environment; the discourse of nature is all the more inevitable in a study that places animals at the center of human history. While humans only had to deal with standards and obligations imposed by fellow humans, animals as colonial subjects had to negotiate relations among similar and dissimilar species in their own "kingdom" as well as with fellow human colonial subjects and with the British invaders. Aside from transcending and crossing figurative and literal borders of the colonial state, conceptualizing animals as colonial subjects places them at the center of imperial ideology. It both challenges and reinforces the meaning of colonial power for nature.

Colonial animal subjecthood thus involves oscillating between the wild and the tame, culture and nature, order and disorder, and everything in between. It entails defining what animal power and agency mean and then attempting to reconcile political contradiction — one of the numerous planks on which colonialism rested. For instance, horsemen at a durbar, an equine-centered spectacle of imperial power through which colonialism enhanced its self-proclaimed legitimacy, knew that the success of the event would be determined by the conduct and cooperation of their gorgeously dressed horses as much as by the quality of their horsemanship. In this way, colonialism created new sites through which the horse affirmed its significance as a respectable colonial subject. So, too, is the racehorse, whose performance on the turf helped solidify racing as a national sport and exposition of imperial might. While colonialists considered it decent for horses to perform power at durbars and in racing, they viewed as dishonorable their ritual sacrifice by Africans for spiritual cleansing. British colonialists thought that the horse, as a colonial subject, should be protected from "primitive" religious and cultural practice, while they simultaneously exploited its physical and biological identities for events they favored.

What is true about the contradictory existence of the horse as a colonial subject is correct about the conflicted place of the dog in colonial Nigeria. A thoroughbred canine, who complemented humans' lives as a pet and received justice from the colonial courts when her owner's neighbor beat her with a stick, would be an outlawed body if found in the street during an outbreak of rabies, a disease that imperiled humans. One must view canines as colonial subjects to understand the contradictions in how the colonial state perceived them as creatures to be protected by law if unjustly treated by a fellow (human) colonial subject or as criminals to be punished by death if found in the street suspected of carrying disease. What is more, modern animal husbandry that increased the production of livestock to feed expanding human populations may be viewed as humans' material exploitation of animals for meat, milk, and skin; it also affirmed the significance of livestock to human survival. When colonial officers and leading African elites published in the newspapers a photograph of themselves with a massive bull, a product of imperial science and experimentation aimed at improving livestock yield, they depended on the beast to support their political credibility. Visual images of animal or agricultural shows served to highlight the gains of foreign veterinary science—just as those of then-popular baby shows emphasized the superiority of Western biomedicine and maternity care.[19]

THE MODERN ANIMALS OF NIGERIA

The idea of imperial modernity in African historical scholarship is clear to scholars. At the center of the colonial enterprise was the notion that imperial modernity would help obliterate the backwardness of Africa's institutions and political processes. Thus, civilization was expected to create modern societies and people. Scholars may not agree on whether Africa was already modernizing before the second half of the nineteenth century when colonialism began to take root, but few would disagree that the vocabulary of modernization was central to colonial propaganda—it justified and legitimized imperialism.[20] Modernity was ubiquitous in mainstream rhetoric and the practice of power and identity formation. Its artifacts and symbolism were everywhere—in particular schools, hospitals, communities, and neighborhoods, as well as in the general political economy. The outcome was the modern African—a new breed of human who epitomized or was expected to uphold all the positive gains of colonial domination. African nationalists opposed the notion that Africans could not rule themselves and thus were in need of foreign domination; however, they never underestimated the significance of modern infrastructures, biomedicine, urban planning, market economy, and political processes bequeathed to them by their colonial overlords. To a large extent, political decolonization was never packaged as a complete return to precolonial institutions and power structures; critiques of colonialism of the 1950s and 1960s acknowledged this was impossible. Rather, decolonization was about selective appropriation of the colonial heritage to meet an African-centered agenda of progress and development to benefit Africans.

Colonial modernity, this book argues, was not just about humans; it encompassed animals. It operated at two overlapping levels: colonialism sought to produce modern animals while also using the notion of modernity to shape human-animal encounters. Animal bodies and identities were sites and symbols through which modernity found expression as a viable alternative and solution to African "primitivity." Animals, like human colonial subjects, were also expected to be modern. New urban sanitation laws, which became inevitable because of the transformation of precolonial settlements into colonial cities and modernist ideologies of "proper" urban planning, changed the habitat, ecosystem, and sociolegal constructs of the public presence of domesticated animals. The notion of desirable and undesirable urban animals drew parallel lines between pets and livestock and domestic and wild animals. While the domestic/wild distinction insisted that the true wild is beyond city boundaries, the pet/livestock division saw the city as the natural home of pets and undervalued the significance of livestock in humans' everyday survival.[21] Urban "rewilding"—that is, the occasional "straying" or "intrusion" of wild animals into the built environment of the city designed only for human habitation—criminalized their bodies in response to the real or imagined danger of competition for space. Yet livestock found in the inner-city tarred roads would be impounded or "arrested" for disobeying the law aimed at turning them into a modern being, because the farm, not the modern street, was their "rightful" home.

I argue that city, one of the citadels of colonial modernity in Africa, is more than human. The colonial city, no doubt, was a quintessential human achievement and a product of human desire, preference, bias, obsession, and impression. However, animals were omnipresent, shaping how humans defined failure and progress. Some of the biggest debates about modern urban planning and aesthetics of everyday life in the city were defined by humans' contradictory impression of the material and symbolic roles of a wide variety of animal species. The opposing notions of "good" and "bad," "loyal" and "rebellious," "ugly" and "beautiful," and "clean" and "dirty" animals were framed by how humans would like to see and enjoy urban modernities. From public health and pollution consideration (which informed slum-clearance schemes), extermination of rats, and rearing of goats to how dog fancying defined social class and racial hierarchy, the story of city animals should be an important theme in African urban studies. Colonial urban planners disliked the presence of domestic and wild animals, even though modern human settlements were built on the latter's natural habitat. Modernist notions about what constitutes desirable and undesirable urban animals were a weighty domain of tension, as Chapter 1 demonstrates. This tension itself should be seen beyond humans' consistent attempt to challenge draconian colonial policies. Rather, it must be viewed from how animals' symbolic and material value shaped the inconsistent notions of urban desirabilities.

Even the dog, the most beloved urban animal across societies, was expected to be modern. In the diction of proper bodily conduct, urban dogs held a unique place in modernist notions of utility and companionship. They were, like urban humans, expected to be more intelligent, law-abiding, and "clean" than their rural counterparts. They were closer to "civilization" because urban communities were the bastions of advanced modernity. The stereotype of the street dog, an outlaw animal that declines control, and lives in peripatetic savagery, was only applicable in the city. Rural dogs could not be a "street" or "ownerless" dogs, not only because the modernist metaphor of the street—site of danger and disrespect toward order—was essentially urban, but also because they had a well-defined utility value as hunters in close-knit rural communities. The debate over dog taxation was vociferous partly because rural dwellers and urbanites tied dog utilitarianism to conflicting notions of modernity.

What is correct about the dog is correct about the emotional consideration that shaped the agitation led by some Europeans in Lagos against fellow foreigners who shot at birds in flight, which the former considered a "delight and pleasure to watch." Nothing like this happened in the villages, not because village people were indifferent to the destruction of nature but because of modernist framing of birds as among the beauties of the urban skyscape.[22] Hence, the fact of "senseless destruction of large number of harmless" beautiful birds by the "predatory instincts of unscrupulous and irresponsible individuals," all of whom were Europeans, gives a racialized dimension to the idea of savagery that framed the elastic conception of cruelty to animals. The suggestion that the entire city of Lagos be declared as a "game sanctuary" to end the shooting of birds—but not leopards, lions, or dogs—fit the prioritization of animals in accordance with a skewed imagination of danger; the concern was less for animals in their ecosystem than for little White children playing in Turnbull Park of Ikoyi, a Europeans-only neighborhood in Lagos.[23] Flexible notions of nature conservation, urban aesthetics, livability and safety, and moral sensibilities to nonhuman creatures have historically occupied a contradictory status in humans' construction of positive, responsible, and safe modernities.[24]

The dichotomy between the city and villages was just one out of the countless ways of viewing modern animals. Even a beast, living deep in the wilderness, maintaining an intimate relationship with the "purest" manifestation of nature, can also be modern. There is a certain modernity in wildness. A modern lion, elephant, or leopard, among other wild animals, was both a beneficiary and a victim of the integration of Nigeria into global capitalism. These animals' material and symbolic values increased as liberalization of guns and of trade in live animals and trophies commodified their existence. Yet they would also become creatures to be protected from wanton destruction, through legislation informed by a "scientific" conservation ethos. The savior ideology that shaped wildlife conservation, which denigrated Africans as poachers for killing animals in their domains while praising Europeans who carried out the same act as "scientists," "conservationists," and "naturalists," operated within the frame of a colonial double standard. The modernist dimension to conservationism involved the affirmation that nature, as one of the gains of imperialism, can be "scientifically" preserved by creating sanctuaries for animals to breed in peace far from human molestation. Scientific conservation, like every domain of colonialism, was arrogant in its conception of sanitized progress and order for the colonial subjects of the wild.

Ethologists and naturalists developed new concepts to differentiate African animals from their counterparts in other parts of the world. To be African was to be primitive; to be an African animal was to be ultraprimitive. In animal behavior discourse, a modern racehorse was an award-winning thoroughbred equine exposed to the modern turf constructed by the British across the country and being groomed and trained and ridden by modern jockeys under the close watch of a European-trained veterinary officer. A modern dog was a "trainable" animal that does not socialize with the filthy street dogs and instead lives within the territorial delimitation of its owner's abode. When colonial officers decried the lack of trainability of African canines, they neglected the power of language and social mores in dog-human relations. Uncritical of or neglecting the dogs' ethnic background, they blamed them for not responding to commands and instructions in their own language. This prejudice toward indigenous dogs mirrors that toward Africans. In everyday dealings with their human colonial subjects, the British associated language with intelligence. Not being about to speak or take instruction in English was framed as a sign of cranial predevelopment. The most modern of animals, like humans, were therefore those with constant contact with Europeans and educated Africans, who epitomized the best of civilization. The distinction that the cat, regardless of its breed or pedigree, of a European possessed was not limited to the beauty of its abode or the "healthy" diet offered in government stations but was the effect of its constant contact with the agents of modernity.

The moral sensibilities that turned animals into creatures to be protected by colonial laws can best be understood by the notion that modern and civilized humans must threat animals with respect. Civilized humans must have compassion for animals. Even African modernist artists understood the status of the colonial animal as a modern creature. Animal cartoons—a modern medium of expressing visual arts—was one of the most consumed protest arts in colonial Nigeria because animal iconography gave artists the aesthetic flexibility to express modern notions of power. The modern animal as a speaking creature in cartoons stood in for humans in expressing the ambivalences of colonial subjecthood.

A modern animal was both a beneficiary and a victim of colonial veterinary sciences. Its body, physiology, and biological character would form an integral part of scientific experimentation aimed at placing the human and nonhuman creatures on the path to modernity. With the improvement of colonial science and veterinary medicine, modern animals would survive in places far away from their original habitat. Humans introduced animals to new communities where they had not existed before. Their presence in new abodes would transform landscapes and ecosystems. The central philosophy of colonial medicine—to keep subjects healthy for the benefit of colonial capitalist expropriation—is evident in veterinary medicine, which was a purely capitalist science. Efforts to control epidemics, among animals and humans, were therefore targeted toward maximizing the materiality of the colony and its subjects. Western animal biomedicine was arrogant, not only by disrespecting vernacular science but also by constituting itself as another arm of colonial law and order. It complemented physical infrastructure that changed how humans consumed meat as well.

Movement and mobility within and across colonial boundaries also defined the modern animals of colonial Nigeria. The life history of cattle in colonial Nigeria could undergo multiple migrations that precolonial cattle would never experience. By 1950 a calf born in Kano might be herded across thousands of miles, from northern Nigeria to the South, in response to seasonal supplies of forage or to avoid animal diseases, finally to be slaughtered four years later at the municipal abattoir in Ibadan, processed into sausage at the Nigeria Cold Storage Company in Lagos, and then loaded into airtight boxes and transported back to Kano in refrigerated railway cars for sale in supermarkets. Similarly, a lion cub born in the forest of Lokoja might be captured by locals, presented to the British monarch as a gift, transported to Britain and exhibited for entertainment at the London Zoological Garden, only to become a laboratory animal, serving the scientific community. At death, the lion could assume a new life as an embalmed species exhibited in perpetuity at the Natural History Museum. The unprecedented "legal" and "illegal" transportation of colonial animals to private and public menageries outside Africa during the twentieth century challenges scholars to rethink diaspora beyond the human. Animals, I argue, were part of colonial diasporic experience.

What is more, modern animality did not represent a complete disengagement from precolonial or "traditional" identities. Rather, modern conceptions of animals coexisted with the traditional, creating a host of contradictions. Much of the animal-induced conflict between Nigerians and the colonialists is attributable to the conflicting identities that animals assumed under British imperialism. The modern animal was both a biological and sociohistorical being. The desire to expand the practical and symbolic value of domesticated animals led to the expansion of intraspecies breeding by private individuals (Africans and Europeans alike) and by the colonial government. The importation of foreign breeds of animal, as well as plants, was part and parcel of imperial expansion and carefully nurtured at veterinary and experimental stations across the country. The appearance, shape, size, and even behavior of modern animals was remarkably different from their precolonial counterparts. When urban Nigerians began to keep exotic European and mixed-breed dogs, they depended on the canine to boost their image of being modern. The history of dog fancying among educated Nigerian urbanites points to the capacity of animals to transform human experience.

AN INTEGRATIVE HISTORY OF AFRICAN ENVIRONMENT

Writings about the African natural environment predates the imposition of colonial rule. For centuries, travelers and explorers have registered their fascinations in a dense trove of reports, memoirs, and travelogues, which remain some of the earliest written accounts about Africa's flora and fauna.[25] These works, as problematic as they are for laying the foundation of some of the stereotypes about Africa, have served as veritable template for debating controversial subjects, including but not limited to spatiality and origins of communities, precolonial military culture, and the impact of the Atlantic slave trade, to mention but a few. Contentious debates, such as the one on the authentic birthplace of Olaudah Equiano (also known as Gustavus Vassa) have relied on documentation of precolonial geography, landscape, and place names.[26] And when African archaeology and historical linguistics emerged as academic fields, they built on the narratives of movements, settlements, and environmental changes to engage with provocative debate over origins of civilizations, indigeneity of African technology, and invention of traditions.[27] Precolonial African environment narratives go beyond the descriptions of the fauna and flora to include how geography shaped ethnicity, religious contact, and Africa's relations with the external world.[28]

But foreign explorers and travelers were not the only nonacademic writers of African environment and nature. From the 1920s, indigenous African-language creative writers produced novels, which have been adapted into famous epic films.[29] From the creation legends to myths on origins of cultural networks, the representations of nature in these folklorist and fictional writings established a core fact about Africans' understanding of the inseparability of the human and the nonhuman worlds. These two worlds, in the imaginations of indigenous nature writers, are always in a state of flux, not just because all humans have an animal totem but also because the human soul could manifest in trees, mountains, and even in ocean waves. Arguably the most famous local nature novelist in colonial Nigeria was D. O. Fagunwa, who published Ògbójú Ọdẹ Nínú Igbó Irúnmalè (The Forest of a Thousand Daemons) in 1938.[30] By 1963, when he died in a river accident, Fagunwa had published over a dozen novels deeply influenced by nature, wildlife, and the environment.[31] Although written in English, another notable work, My Life in the Bush of Ghosts, among other books by Nigerian writer Amos Tutuola, belongs to the same genre of local writings on the complex manifestations of souls and spirits in human and nonhuman bodies.[32]

A shift in documentation on the African environment took place from the 1960s, when academic historians entered the scene. The historiographical essays on the subject by William Beinart and Vimbai Kwashirai established two lines of thought on the African environment.[33] First is the anticolonial approach, which followed the apocalyptic version of global environment history based on the ecological disruption caused by colonial conquest. Population displacement and land sequestration altered African ecology as diseases and pathogens ravaged the land. These genres of writing criticized scientific conservation, arguing that anxiety over the "extinction" of natural endowments, which justified game laws and forest exploitation rules, was part of the broader institutions of colonial violence—the savior mentality that stood at the center of colonial paternalism. The "degradation" narrative, as this is also called, has since been complemented by scholarship that privileges African-centered vernacular science and indigenous practice of nature conservation, which deployed tradition, spirituality, and local technology for land and disease management.[34]

A common trend is discernible in academic research about the African environment: they either focus on the living creatures (animals and humans) and wildlife conservation or on agriculture, landscape transformation, and disease and pathogens. Or they follow the two discursive frames outlined by Beinart and Kwashirai. In the pages that follow, I put all these into a single analytical framework in offering what I call an "integrative approach to Africa's environmental history." This approach seeks not to compartmentalize nature and environment but to see them as constitutive and interrelated. I have treated the living and nonliving endowments of nature as a system in understanding the past. It is not enough for scholars to emphasize that the ecosystem is a web of interrelations and interdependency of all the endowments of nature. Proving this through concrete narratives and examples is more germane.

The experience of the cattle and donkeys justifies the value of an integrative approach to environmental history. After the imposition of colonial rule, the old donkey caravans connecting northern Nigeria with northern Africa disappeared, giving way to new ones connecting the region to modern southern Nigeria. Cattle trade routes, distinct from donkey caravans, also emerged. New commercial and agricultural activities sprang up along the new donkey caravan and cattle trade routes, transforming landscape in unimaginable way, as the commercial breeding of donkeys and cattle for purely economic gains intensified. The movement of these nonhuman creatures, in response to changes in human-animal relations, directly impacted land use and the ecosystem. Conflicts emerged over animal movement, not just because animals destroyed farm produce but also because land, rivers, mountains, and other endowments of nature were more than economic assets in many communities—they are also abodes of the gods and goddesses.

The discussions of animal diseases in this book underscores the spread of pathogens in response to transformations in human-animal relations. New animal diseases appeared across the country as old ones found homes in places where they did not exist before. Humans learned and unlearned everything they knew about zoonotic ailments, while a brand-new arm of colonial power—veterinary medicine—surfaced to improve animal health for the purpose of maximizing their materiality and to protect humans. Control over human and animal movement, in response to pathogenic agents, became grafted onto the colonial practice of policing the body. New ideologies of urban spatiality aligned with urban racial segregation to put nature at the center of urban governance and policing racial boundaries. In another vein, forest conservation operated at two overlapping plains: in addition to delimiting human settlement, it impacted agriculture and animal husbandry with its focus on preserving trees for commercial logging. I have written about big-game hunting within the context of small-game hunting because the narratives of wildlife conservation are inseparable from local communities' dependency on small animals for their daily food supply.

An integrative approach to Africa's environmental history hones inter- and intraspecies coexistence and independency on nature. The diversity of voices, ideas, and representation about environment is a product of the divergent understanding of people across race, gender, religion, ethnicity, and class on humans' responsibility towards nature. What constitutes indigenous perspectives on the environment was not homogeneous across the country, just as how Islam and Christianity did not agree on how to define animal cruelty and protection. What passed for "primitive" exploitation of animals in one part of the country was permissible in another. The attack on indigenous African worldviews on animals was a constant site of tension between Nigerians and the British colonialists and their Nigerian collaborators because the former had a much more complex understanding of animals beyond their observable identity as part of nature.

A book covering the entire country of Nigeria—from the arid lands of Bornu in the North to the swamps and creeks of the Niger Delta in the South—is bound to present a much more complex understanding of the environment by thousands of ethnicities cohabiting with millions of animal species. From Muslims and Christians to "pagans," African elites to White European officers, large-game trophy collectors to small-game hunters, ruralites to urbanites, farmers to herders, forest officers who conserved trees to game officers who protected wild animals, science to superstitions, and textual and oral evidence to art and literary representations and everything in between, this book's integrative approach to Africa's environmental history has excavated myriads of voices and perspectives to the fullest possible degree. In the pages that follow, readers will encounter animals in their diverse habitats—aquatic creatures like the manatee, which the government attempted to protect because of "extinction" but which the riverine communities depended on for a protein supply; land animals like leopards, which threatened livestock; and birds that enhanced urban landscapes and complement the modern dialectics of viewing the cities. The environment discussed in this book includes both the physical one that has well-defined boundaries and parameters of encounter and the figurative boundaryless that gave artists like Akinola Lasekan unlimited flexibility to position human-animal encounter in unimaginable ways.

METHODS AND SOURCES

Having been born and raised in Ibadan, in southwestern Nigeria, I had my closest encounters with animals while rearing a ram and goat a few weeks before Muslim festivals and family occasions. I also helped a family member raise rabbits for two years after graduating from high school. These animals were then slaughtered for food. I did not see a donkey until my first visit to northern Nigeria in 2003 and rode a horse for the first time when I celebrated the completion of my study of the holy Quran at the age of ten in 1989. It was symbolic for Muslim parents to hire horses—the animal that played a strategic role in the spread of Islam—to celebrate their children's milestone in mastering the tenets of the religion and Arabic literacy. But horses were not part of daily life in Ibadan. Up until 2005, when I moved to the United States, the entire city of more than five million people could not boast of fifty horses. With the exception of local families like that of Basorun Ogunmola, who kept a "pet" horse, most of these horses belonged to the local polo club.

and depth of sources about the past often reflect the relative value placed on agents, objects, and subjects of history in shifting contexts. Historical data are never comprehensive. In the case of human-animal relations, this is especially true. Those who documented Nigeria's past preserved their impressions of certain types of animals while leaving others out of the picture, depending on the value they derived from them or how the animals shaped their lives. Thus, a certain imbalance in the historical treatment of animals is inevitable, being a function of the quantity and quality of data. Nonetheless, some research trajectories hold bright promise beyond a multispecies study such as the present work.

In writing this book, I combed the major National Archives of Nigeria located in Ibadan, Kaduna, and Enugu. The sources I consulted on such topics as rabies, cruelty to animals, racing, bylaws for impounding animals, and wildlife provided clues to the importance of animals in the framing of coloniality, subjecthood, and modernity. The Ibadan archives include correspondence and reports by colonial officers, among other colonial records, giving voice to the administrators of imperial power and to political entities across southwestern Nigeria. The Enugu and Kaduna archives contain perspectives of colonial officers and Nigerians from the eastern and northern parts of the country, respectively. Documents from the United Kingdom's National Archives, not surprisingly, represent the perspectives of metropolitan power but also shed critical light on the intersections of proanimal welfarism and the so-called civilization mission in the colonies. As one would expect, the perspectives of Nigerians include petitions, which historians of Africa have argued are valuable sources for understanding the colonial encounter from local and intimate perspectives.

Another documentary source utilized in this book was the array of expert reports on animals in the records of the veterinary, agriculture, and animal husbandry departments. This book is the first study to make use of these massive stocks of records. Without them, it would have been impossible to show how cattle became a symbol of colonial capitalism, how cattle capitalism related to colonial progress, decolonization, and nation building, and how veterinary medicine shaped public health in colonial Nigeria. Dozens of scientific reports compiled by imperial fact-finding missions on fish farming in the 1950s are still untapped and waiting to be explored. The founding of the Nigerian Field Society in 1930 brought to a much wider audience the writings of British foresters, conservators, zoologists, ornithologists, botanists, and naturalists who self-identified as "Anglo-Nigerians" interested in nature and game. The society's journal, the *Nigerian Field*, debuted in 1931 as Nigeria's first fauna-and-flora, country-life magazine, carrying articles and engrossing photographs and illustrations of game hunting and trophy collecting, scientific conservation, horticulture, and expansively diverse animal species, including insects such as butterflies.[35] Although the readership of this magazine was primarily European nature enthusiasts, whether in Africa or abroad, its content is valuable for understanding the imperialist mind-set on environmental exploitation. In 1948 the Nigerian Field Society initiated an ambitious project, the Natural History Survey of Nigeria, harnessing the strength of its members, who had strong knowledge of botany, entomology, mammalogy, meteorology, ornithology, ichthyology, cartography, photography, and geology, among other fields related to natural history.[36]

In addition, the increasing presence of digital photos and videos on the internet is changing how historians do research, bringing us much closer to events of the past and in many cases telling stories in ways that textual evidence would never be able to do. Yet it also raises key concerns about continued access and copyrights. This work has also benefited from the public and private video and photo archives digitized on the websites and social media platforms of the Nigerian Nostalgia Project, Reuters, and British Pathé, among others.[37]

One of the core arguments of this book, that animals were colonial subjects, is easy to prove through the gamut of laws governing virtually all animals in Nigeria. The Annual Volumes of Laws of Nigeria are widely available in research libraries, but colonial laws must be placed in proper historical and sociopolitical context. Official court proceedings—massive stacks of records in their original bound form—as well as accounts published in newspapers may put a human face on colonial statutes. While the court records covering northern and eastern Nigeria are deposited at the Kaduna and Enugu National Archives, those of southwestern Nigeria can be found in the central library of the Obafemi Awolowo University, Ile-Ife. The colonial Lagos court records were deposited at the Igbosere High Court on Lagos Island, but may have been destroyed during the October 2020 protest against police brutality. In all, the conditions of Nigerian archival collections and the years covered vary widely, but they reveal the real working of imperial institutions.

Historians of colonial Africa traditionally depend on oral interviews and accounts in African-run newspapers for the perspectives of Africans on the colonial encounter. This book conforms with this norm. However, the geographical spread of the interviews and newspaper sources used was determined largely by the animals being researched. I carried out extensive interviews in northern Nigeria, visiting private and community horse stables and polo and race clubs, some of which had existed since the colonial era. Stories about favorite durbars, polo matches, and racehorses have not disappeared from public memory and have even been archived in oral literature. It is only in eastern Nigeria that one can learn about the so-called ritual horses used for burial and chieftaincy ceremonies. What the British painted as a barbaric culture receives a new meaning in the narratives of senior men who shared their recollections of a horse culture that defined notions of superior masculinity and "bigmanship." In southwestern Nigeria, families like the Basorun Ogunmola of Ibadan have kept a white horse since the mid-nineteenth century. Talking to the custodians of the present white horse unmasks generation after generation of previous horses and their exploits as the community "pet" through which local history is told and manifested on a daily basis. At the University of Ibadan Zoological Garden, which came into existence in 1948, I learned about famous captive wildlife, their beloved caregivers, and their relations with the public they entertain. Whether learning about prominent dog breeders in southern Kaduna or the life and times of sacrificial dogs in Ondo, one thing is clear—animals, like humans, shared common experiences, even though the location, breed, and ethnicity of their owners and place of origin varied.

If animals are largely invisible in mainstream Nigerian history, it is because historians are not asking the right questions or digging deeper for nuisances. One does not have to spend countless of hours mining data in the archives to come to terms with the role that animals played in colonialism. Such popular texts as the autobiographies of politicians and nationalists like Obafemi Awolowo, Ahmadu Bello, and Nnamdi Azikiwe, which generation after generation of Africanist scholars have read, contain references and, occasionally, detailed narratives about animals.[38] It was a dog-bite incident that forced Azikiwe to relocate to Lagos in 1915 at the age of eleven. Nigerian history would have taken a different turn had he not moved there when he did.[39] Another dog-bite case in 1954 fractured the tenor of race relations and decolonization.[40] The trial judge in this matter, Mason Begho, lived the rest of his life with the nickname "the dog-bite magistrate."[41] Through the memoirs of Europeans, we learn of dogs that were also part of the colonial adventure or were, in a way, colonizers themselves.[42] Frederick Lugard, the most famous colonial officer in Nigeria, left for what would later be known as northern Nigeria in 1894 with a grand bull terrier.[43]

From this variety of sources, I have sifted out animal-centered narratives. While it is possible to read a two-hundred-page report on modern animal husbandry and not get a critical perspective on the animals, the same document makes better sense when viewed from an animal-conscious mind-set. The same applies to the documentation on rabies and durbars. As I processed these materials, I asked a simple question: Would this event or debate happen without animals? How did the ecosystem and pattern of relations humans maintained with animals shape the matter being discussed? Would these sources help explicate my core argument that animals were colonial subjects and creatures of modernity? This, among other approaches, is my way of mainstreaming animals in African history.

CHAPTERS IN BRIEF

This book is divided into two thematic sections. Each chapter then follows a chronology that maps out the evolutions and transformation of relations between humans and animals. The foundation for most of the ideas engaged in this book—cruelty, disease, aesthetics, materiality—were all laid from the late nineteenth century to the 1920s. As in other colonial sites, the interwar years were characterized by the firm establishment of colonial rule. All the manifestation of colonial power began to have significant implication for Nigerian humans and animals. This explains why the documentation and narratives increased tremendously from the 1920s through the 1950s.

Part 1, "Loyal Companions, Tasty Food, Distinguished Athletes, Political Beings," is concerned with the materiality and symbolism of a variety of animals in addition to the ways they transformed ideals of leisure, companionship, and the display of imperial might. Chapter 1 explores how the population expansion in the first half of the twentieth century impacted the natural environment. As villages gave way to cities and large administrative towns, animal husbandry underwent a reconfiguration, which served multiple human and material purposes. Unavoidably, food pathways and nutrition changed, allowing beef to become a staple in Nigerian diets. But this transformative experience was also a direct consequence of the colonialists' carefully curated agenda that turned the cattle trade into a potent arm of British capitalism. The chapter examines how domesticated animals that Nigerians ate (goats, sheep, pigs, cattle) became a subject of modernist discussion. Debates about food shortages, rearing of livestock in the cities, and modern veterinary medicine and animal-fattening stations were inescapably shaped by notions of progress and civilization. From the construction of modern abattoirs to acrimony over the adoption of the "humane killer" device for slaughtering livestock, the experience of the animals that Nigerians raised for food found clear expression in modernist rhetoric.

Without the donkey, the colonial Nigerian economy would have suffered a major setback. In chapter 2, I focus on the technology and landscape of animal transportation. The movement of solid minerals, humans, and agricultural products that sustained imperial capitalism was made possible by the donkey, whose biological features supported heavy weight-lifting. Not even the introduction of motorized transportation would drive the donkey out of its prime position as Nigeria's primary means of transportation. The donkey's identity as a faithful laborer contrasts with that of the horse, which occupied a prestigious place in elite colonial culture. In explaining how horse racing became the national sport and a symbol of colonial modernity and why the donkey became the "official" pack animal of the colonial state, I turn my searchlight on ecological transformation, improvements in veterinary science, and new ideals of recreation.

Perhaps no other animal in Nigeria has had a closer relationship with humans than dogs. Chapter 3 treats the history of Nigerian canines from the perspective of changing human-dog relations. With colonialism came the diversification of the Nigerian dog population. Foreign breeds of dogs were brought by colonial officers and expatriates of many nationalities. The dogs of colonial officers were coimperialist interlopers—modern canines that enjoyed the privileges of their owners. They biophysically transformed their new habitat, and their influx paved the way for a new era of dog fancying. No other animal shaped the tenor of race and class like the dog. Such fluid social indexing of dogs as "pet," "utility," "taxable," and "stray" were not only contradictory—they were also informed by the idea that dogs should adhere to Eurocentric practices of a modern society.

The representation of modern animals in the modernist art of Akinola Lasekan (1916–72), a pioneering Nigerian cartoonist, is the main theme of chapter 4. Lasekan conceived of the colonial Nigerian state as a zoo, a modern menagerie with a well-defined border where chaos and order maintained a delicate balance. At the center of his politics of representing the colonial state as a zoo are all the features of modernity. The modern animals in Lasekan's cartoons wore European dress, spoke English, and were lawyers, expatriates, and educated elites who emphasized the significance of enlightenment in the drive toward self-representation. Of course, they were also colonial bodies, manifesting all the features of imperial subjecthood, including resistance. Lasekan's characters were speaking nonhuman creatures who expressed complex ideas about politics, empire, and self-representation. The central idea in this chapter is how Lasekan domesticated nature and wilderness for modern political conversation during the last two decades of the British imperial presence in Nigeria. The shifting identities he gave to dissimilar animals aligned with their intrinsic biological character. In representing the colonial government as a predatory carnivore and the populace as sheep (its prey), Lasekan further emphasizes the status of real and fictional animals as colonial bodies.

The second section of this book features chapters on human-animal relations, with a concentration on fear, pathology, moral sensibilities, and animal welfare. It primarily focuses on situations, encounters, and events that configured politics of epizootics and zoonosis, material and symbolic exploitation, welfare, and wildlife conservation. By constituting a lethal challenge to the body politic, epidemics like rabies, the scariest of the zoonoses, gave colonialism the legitimacy to impose its narrow concept of public health, as chapter 5 illuminates. Although Africans and Europeans did not agree on the symbolic or practical importance of dogs, they acknowledged the existence of rabies, a deadly epizootic disease. The epidemiology of human and animal rabies is directly linked to unprecedented mobility of people across regional and international boundaries. If the disease came through colonialism as alleged, it would also be solved through modern veterinary science—or so the government was convinced. From the Dogs Ordinance, which aimed to protect animals and humans from rabies, to the manner of capturing "stray" canines during rabies outbreaks, the identity of Nigerian canines as colonial subjects is clear.

The scholarship on African wildlife has centered almost exclusively on eastern and southern Africa, leading to the common misconception that West Africa was not home to large animals. Ironically, there are significant historical parallels in the stories of wildlife in West Africa and those in eastern and southern Africa. Colonialists consistently turned African subjects into poachers on their own land, while representing Whites who engaged in indiscriminate plundering of wildlife as conservators and legitimate imperial hunters. However, Nigeria, being a nonsettler colony, presents an opportunity to go beyond this well-charted path to fully grasp the politics of wildlife conservation in a different way. I argue in chapter 6 that in both their formulation and implementation, wildlife conservation laws present interesting perspectives on indigenous or vernacular knowledge about the wild and nature. While emphasizing that colonial conservation policies were informed partly by the conviction that both the human and nonhuman inhabitants of Nigeria are governable, I place regional distribution of Nigerian wildlife in conversation with the changing cultural landscape to shed light on the contradictions of wildlife conservation. The founding of private and government zoos and the export of Nigerian wildlife to zoos beyond the continent operated within the framework of transforming animal lives to meet modern notions of conservation. The dialectics of seeing wild animals in captivity changed under colonial rule. Unlike in the precolonial times when the domestication of wild animals was an integral part of ritual power relations and religious identities of communities, the modern zoo took a secular bent, in its professed philosophy of saving animals from "extinction," its built environments for viewing captive animals, and the projected pattern of relations humans maintained with the tamed beasts.

How moral sensibilities toward animals changed under colonial rule is the primary focus of chapter 7. In bringing animals under the purview of the laws for protection against ill-treatment, the colonial government introduced a new regime of modernist thinking about progress and civilization. Civilization would no longer be defined as acquisition of Western education and entrenchment of Western biomedicine alone—it would also be measured by how humanely animals were treated. The circumstances under which the government assumed the role of protector of domesticated animals against human cruelty, while also possessing the power to kill stray and unlicensed dogs, dovetails with the asymmetries in power—the hallmark of imperialism. Unlike other elements of the modern animal welfare movement spearheaded by British colonialists, educated Nigerians contributed an audible voice through such charitable organizations as the Nigeria Royal Society for the Prevention of Cruelty to Animals (NRSPCA). Like the colonial government, these Nigerian elites believed the majority of their fellow Nigerians were unkind to animals because they were "ignorant" and not "enlightened." What constitutes cruelty was a fluid concept and varied across animal species. Animals became subjects of legal tussles in colonial courts, which decided the gravity of offenses and the corresponding punishments.

The final chapter uses the experience of the donkey and horse to further tackle the question of animal rights and welfare. If the horse did not deserve to be badly treated because, as an athlete and royal personage, it featured in events that helped uphold imperialism, the donkey, Nigeria's most important transport animal, needed to be treated right because of its economic significance. The growing presence of worn-out former racehorses in the streets of provincial capitals, the doping that racehorses suffered, and the use of horses for ceremonial sacrifices in eastern Nigeria, critics argued, signified a disservice to the animal that brought so much joy to the people. The campaign to end cruelty to the horse and donkey borrowed heavily from the rhetoric of measuring humans' progress by how well they treat their animals. But, more importantly, it pitched Western civilization championed by the British colonialists against Islamic traditions that were practiced in northern Nigeria where much of the equine population resided. The book concludes with an epilogue that reflects on the status of human-animal relations in postcolonial Nigeria.

PART 1

∽

Loyal Companions, Tasty Food,
Distinguished Athletes, Political Beings

1 ⌐ A Meaty Colony

Nigerians and the Animals They Ate

Please do not think we are kind to our animals or that in this we were
actuated by the love for the dumb beast. No. What we want is more meat
and to see it wasted in sweat . . . is more than we can bear.

— G. G. Briggs, legal secretary of Eastern Region, 1952[1]

It is surprising to note that Shomolu is now the home of pigs. It is pigs
everywhere—in your kitchen, in your parlour, in your bedroom and
even, among the bolder ones, on your dinner table.

— A. Mpama, "Home of Pigs," *West African Pilot*, August 24, 1957

IN 1906 two English bulls named Bungay and Prince were imported
from Great Britain for a farm in Onitsha, in southeastern Nigeria. But
the farm "was not a success," and regrettably the animals did not "leave
any issue [offspring]." A year later, the governor of Lagos Colony, Walter
Egerton, presented Prince and Bungay to two local chiefs—the Emir of
Ilorin and the *Alaafin* (king) of Oyo, respectively. Neither animal lived
long with its new owner. Bungay died in 1907, followed by Prince, who
was much younger, in 1908.[2] Why were Prince and Bungay brought to
Onitsha, even though Nigeria already had a large cattle population? The
answer to this question is not far-fetched. Animals and plants were an integral part of British ecological imperialism, which transformed the natural
environment of the colonies to meet the material, symbolic, and aesthetic
proclivities of the colonialists through importation of metropolitan stock.[3]
All animals and plants were not of equal material value in the colonial
ranking of livestock. Metropolitan livestock and plants ranked higher
than their colonial counterparts because they were products of a highly

advanced human society, the colonialists believed. One of the earliest concerns of the British in Nigeria (as in many parts of the continent) was the "small" size of local livestock, whose utilitarian value was considered limited. Veterinarians and agricultural experts thought the introduction of the English bulls would initiate a genealogy of prize cattle that could serve as draft animals, meat and milk producers, and sources of hides and skins. Imperial animals and coagents of imperialism like Prince and Bungay were also victims of empire building. Their lack of immunity to African pathogens largely accounts for their early deaths.

This failed experiment did not end the attempt to modernize Nigerian animal husbandry to maximize capitalist expropriation. In May 1954 *West African Pilot* (WAP) photojournalists introduced their readers to Sule, a half-bred Zebu calf born through artificial insemination in Vom, the epicenter of colonial veterinary science in colonial Nigeria. Praised as an example of "the wonders" of animal medicine, Sule weighed 52 pounds at birth on February 2, 1953, and had amassed the significant weight of 453 pounds by May 1954.[4] The story of Sule was not an exception—many mixed-breed calves were raised in veterinary stations in Nigeria. However, instead of importing exotic bulls from Britain or elsewhere or producing mixed-breed calves like Sule in commercial numbers, colonialists established a form of veterinary medicine that focused mostly on local trade cattle—that is, animals raised mainly for meat. It was scientifically and economically wise, veterinarians thought, to devote more attention to securing the health of local breeds in response to the elastic terrain of African livestock diseases, especially rinderpest and trypanosomiasis. Throughout the colonial period, over 90 percent of Nigerian livestock were of local West African breeds, raised by the independent Fulani herders according to their ancient nomadic pastoral culture; the form of land sequestration practiced by Europeans in eastern and southern Africa for private and public ranches being uncommon in Nigeria.[5] The country did not achieve the goal of raising working cattle in commercial numbers.

In turning precolonial livestock into modern beasts, colonial science envisioned them as colonial subjects and legitimizers of imperialism. Animal or agricultural festivals that showcased the fruits of agrarian labor, including animals, were part of the annual veneration of royalty and the worship of ancestors and gods in most West African cultures in precolonial times; however, these pageants became secularized under colonialism, taking on new names, such as "agricultural shows," that aligned with the use of spectacle to affirm colonial legitimacy (see fig. 1.1).[6] Animal bodies

FIGURE 1.1. Prize-winning cow at the Birnin Kebbi Agricultural Show (1958). *Source: Nigeria Magazine*, no. 59 (1958).

became politicized in colonial agricultural shows, where the success of agricultural policies was now measured by the extraordinary size, weight, and yield of livestock produced by local farmers, who were encouraged to foster the "spirit of rivalry and healthy competition" in animal husbandry. Printed in Nigerian newspapers in 1957, a photo of Queen Elizabeth II admiring huge prize-winning cattle at the Royal Agriculture Show in England—like other symbols of modernity—was intended to remind nationalists of an ideal conception of progress in a decolonizing society that still depended on its erstwhile colonizers for modernist inspiration.[7]

The lives, bodies, and materiality of modern livestock were always under threat. The frequent outbreak of livestock diseases altered their core identity from essential economic assets, aesthetic exemplars of imperial power, and symbols of colonial progress to outlawed bodies whose carcasses must be carefully handled to safeguard human and animal health. For cattle, the line between indispensability and undesirability was thin.

This chapter is about modern livestock, whose story is inescapably bound up with colonial veterinary medicine, a purely capitalist scientific endeavor in Nigeria. While most scholars may ignore animals in the narratives of human medicine, it is impossible to exclude humans in any discussion of animal medicine. This partly explains the intersections of modern animal husbandry and the discourse of nation building. In inserting animals into African urban studies, this chapter examines the contestation over space by humans and animals within the framework of urban mobilities, technology and infrastructure, sanitation, town planning, public health, and abattoir politics. Beef became the number one protein in Nigerians' diet during the first half of the twentieth century owing to the rise of colonial urban centers that went hand in glove with carefully designed animal husbandry policies that increased dependency on large animals to feed ever-expanding populations. The narratives and historical circumstances underlying the first epigraph of this chapter, a reinforcement of the economic significance of beef, could not have happened before the twentieth century.

A MEATLESS DAY FOR IBADAN

Natural or artificial scarcity of a commodity can reveal its indispensability.[8] In May 1958 a thousand Ibadan butchers went on strike to protest an increase in the slaughterhouse fee from 5s to 15s by the Action Group, the ruling party in the old Western Region of Nigeria.[9] What appeared to be an industrial action had significant political and security implications, as rumors filtered through town that the butchers would direct their idle knives, normally used for preparing beef for human consumption, on innocent people. Impressions of the role that butchers played in the French Revolution circulated through the minds of some high-ranking political officers of the time who could not jettison fears that Ibadan butchers might act similarly, since both situations had the trappings of class conflict and discontent toward the prevailing power structure.[10]

Nonetheless, the strike temporarily changed the foodways and nutritional habits of residents. The "rush for fish in the markets was so great that, within a few hours, all available stock was sold out," the WAP reported on its front page.[11] The increase in demand for fish in this episode was not an exception. The scarcity of goat meat, mutton, and beef led to an increase in requests for other classes of protein, such as chicken, which also became an inflated or scarce commodity due to excess demand.[12] Strikes by butchers were a recurring development in the colonial labor force. Seven years earlier, in April 1951, when the Lagos Town Council (LTC) increased the cattle lairage fee from £104 to £3,650 per annum, a range of economic life in the city came to a halt, exposing the economic vulnerability of the colonial state and its dependency on beef and cattle wealth.[13] Similarly, in August 1958, when A. Y. Ojikutu, president of the Lagos and Colony Butchers' Union, declared that all meat markets would be closed in honor of the passing of an elite market woman, Aminatu Oja, WAP editors penned a rebuttal titled "Meat, Meat, Meat" to register displeasure over hardship caused by the scarcity of an essential item due to the action of the union leader.[14]

Better understanding of how the butchers' strike and meat market closure elicited political, security, economic, and dietary concerns requires making sense of some ecological changes that occurred under colonial rule. Livestock were historically part of household social capital, serving as a means of currency and exchange, while also providing direct products such as food, milk, hides, and skins. A typical household was therefore a breeder of food animals. Yet pastoralism, which stood in contrast with agrarian culture, gave humans a different encounter with animals as mobile assets and capital. While pastoralism had been practiced for centuries in the place that would later be known as Nigeria, its scope changed under British imperialism to meet the demands of colonial capitalism.[15] Colonialism expanded the meaning of pastoral life and led to an unprecedented increase in the livestock population used to feed the expanding human population. Imperial legislation superseded any local grazing rules.[16] Therefore, modern cattle had greater access to grazing land and water sources across the country than did their predecessors. Herders transported them from the northernmost tip of Bornu Province to the southern tip of the Niger River delta to search for livelihood and commercial opportunity or to avoid livestock diseases.

The expanded access that modern livestock had to pasture came at a cost. Ancient tensions between nomads and agriculturists over grazing and arable land and water resources intensified.[17] Livestock diseases became virulent as pathogens were introduced to places where they had not existed, causing high mortality for animals that lacked immunity. For example, herders seasonally relocated their trade cattle in response to the menace of the tsetse fly, a dark-brown or black fly varying in length from six to thirteen millimeters and the biological vector of trypanosomiasis. The herders' moves to the highlands during the wet season and to the farm and lowlands during the dry season had attendant implications on land tenure.[18] The acting director of veterinary services summed up how nature and animal care shaped human movement: "They [herders] move across the country, not so much where their fancy takes them as where the [herd's] demands of food and water, warring with the prevalence of the tsetse fly, insist that they go."[19] As trade cattle moved across cities and rural communities, they were forced to adjust to a myriad of laws governing their physical presence in these locations.[20]

The cattle trade, like most commercial activities, defied artificial colonial boundaries by adding important layers of identity to the animal populations of West Africa. Northern Nigerian cattle one day could become Fernando Po or Niamey cattle the next, as different regimes across colonial possessions shaped economic, cultural, medical, and political obligations and perceptions toward the animals.[21] The fact that the neighboring French colony of Niger had just two European veterinary officers to care for about two million cattle in 1931 worried colonial authorities in Nigeria. Due to the slow pace of colonial modernity in Niger, the medical condition of animals in that colony, which often moved across the imperial borders, threatened the livestock within Nigeria.[22] And although Nigerian and French authorities signed animal quarantine agreements in the early 1930s, they did not end occasional tensions over the danger that animal pathogenic agents posed to the environment and public health.[23]

Scientific cooperation through the exchange of technical knowledge was also vital. This kind of cooperation increased over time, with the expansion of funding from colonial development schemes in the 1950s. In January 1957 the inaugural meeting of the West African Committee on Epizootic Diseases, comprising members from French Togoland, French Cameroon, French Equatorial Africa, Portuguese Guinea, the Gambia, Sierra Leone, the Gold Coast, the Belgian Congo, Angola, Liberia, and Nigeria met at Vom to carry out regional recommendations of the Inter-African Bureau for Epizootic Diseases, an Africa-wide survey conducted in the early 1950s.[24] Yet, despite this intercolonial cooperation, occasional diplomatic scuffles over animal health took place. A few months after its independence from Britain in 1957, the new state of Ghana tested its diplomatic strength by banning the importation of cattle from Nigeria. It later rescinded its embargo, warning that "the ban would be re-imposed if there is evidence of infection of local cattle traceable to Nigerian origin."[25] As table 1.1 shows, Ghana was the largest recipient of Nigerian export cattle in 1959–60.

TABLE 1.1. ANIMALS EXPORTED FROM NIGERIA, 1959–60

Animal	Ghana	Sierra Leone	Europe	Other Countries	Total
Cattle	18,458	–	–	–	18,458
Sheep	32	–	–	–	32
Pigs	–	–	–	–	–
Horses	45	–	–	1	46
Goats	85	–	–	–	85
Fowl	–	40	–	–	40
Turkeys	7	37	–	–	44
Parrots	1	-	822	74	897
Other birds	2	-	18	18	38
Dogs	12	2	44	7	65
Cats	3	1	3	1	8
Monkeys	–	–	349	54	403
Other species	–	–	–	–	8

Note: All exported animals were accompanied by a veterinary certificate of health.

Source: Federal Department of Veterinary Research, Annual Report for Year 1959–1960 (Lagos: Government Printer, 1960), 65.

Urbanization is an important factor in the story of Nigerian cattle. Not only did it increase reliance on large animals to feed the exploding population; it also contributed to the destruction of natural habitats required for raising healthy cattle. The land on which cities and towns were built was formerly home to game animals. Dietary changes from game and fish to beef, even in riverine communities, thus became inevitable. The most reliable evidence of Nigeria's reliance on beef comes from the animal slaughter records compiled by sanitary officers who supervised government abattoirs in the big cities, towns, and provincial capitals. These data exclude food animals killed at home, in smaller communities where the government did not run an abattoir, in private ceremonies, and during public festivals such as the Eid-al-Kabir.[26] Even in big cities, private or illegal slaughtering of livestock took place in contravention of government laws. In 1938 the numbers of cattle, sheep, and goats slaughtered in government abattoirs in the core cities of the northern provinces were 238,278, 293,608, and 977,992, respectively. In Lagos alone, 17,481 cattle, 1,458 sheep, 653 goats, and 1,595 pigs were killed in that same year. In the remaining parts of southern Nigeria, 63,306 cattle, 9,506 sheep, 6,275 goats, and 2,190 pigs found their way to meat markets.[27]

Consumption of livestock for food increased along with population expansion and the increase in urbanization.[28] By the end of colonial rule in 1960, an average of 600,000 cattle were processed for meat on a yearly basis in Lagos.[29] Similarly, from January to September 1957, 50,422 livestock (29,223 cattle, 3,869 sheep, 11,584 goats, and 5,746 pigs) were slaughtered in abattoirs of Nigeria's Eastern Region.[30] In September 1955 alone, the Kano Emirate abattoir killed 26,981 livestock (7,251 cattle, 2,555 sheep, 17,110 goats, 20 camels, and 45 pigs).[31] In broader perspective, Nigeria in 1952 had a population of twelve million trade cattle.[32] This figure, derived from cattle tax records, was far below the actual census of cattle for several reasons, according to veterinary officers. While some cattle owners did not know the exact size of their herds or relocated their animals to remote areas to evade taxes, others entered into illegal agreements with tax collectors to exchange levies for other agricultural items. Some tax collectors also collected revenues without recording them.[33]

Beyond their obvious material value, the animals Nigerians ate were also political bodies, whose images were exploited by both colonialists and Nigerian nationalists. The newspapers performed their identities in myriads of literary, textual, and visual forms—all for political purposes. The expansion of photojournalism in the 1950s coincided with nationalists' push for modern animal husbandry as one of the cornerstones of economic development after independence. Photos of draft bullocks on farms, piggeries with giant sows feeding scores of piglets, and cattle-fattening stations were strategically framed as development projects in modern animal husbandry that would intensify under the leadership of ruling political parties (see fig. 1.2).[34] Carefully curated exhibitions of fat cattle during official tours of Obafemi Awolowo, Nnamdi Azikiwe (Zik), and Ahmadu Bello, the heads of the regional governments of the 1950s, exaggerated African-led social advancement as the Union Jack was gradually being lowered.[35]

The decentralization of animal husbandry from the early 1950s expanded competition for political control at regional and central government levels. As the regional governments took over the machinery of propaganda from the colonial state, they used regional achievements to justify why they deserved a greater share of power at the federal level. When Zik toured the Eastern Region under his control ahead of the general elections in 1959, he was presented with a "living thing . . . a fat bull."[36] In another instance of animal husbandry propaganda, Zik is pictured admiring a massive bull in the midst of his own admirers.[37] Similarly, the news headlines "East Collects £3,466 from Cattle Tax" and "East Makes 1st Export of 21 Cattle to Fernando Po" extolled the drive toward internal economic self-sufficiency.[38] News from other regional governments—like the report that ten thousand people had, in February 1960, attended an agricultural show in Sokoto where the winner of the "best pair of working bulls" was

FIGURE 1.2. British breed of large white sows at a privately owned farm in Kano (1959). Courtesy of Eliot Elisofon Photographic Archives, National Museum of African Art, Smithsonian Institution.

presented with a prize of a sword—points to a similar development in animal husbandry propaganda from the North.[39] Regardless, development discourse within the frame of decolonization did not see a difference between industrialization and modern animal husbandry. Mechanized agriculture, ranching, and animal experimental stations would, the nationalists insisted, produce agricultural products that would fetch foreign reserves for Nigeria, while also guaranteeing an abundance of food.[40] Trade cattle, with an estimated population of twelve million selling at a rate of from £7 to £12 per head in the early 1950s, were generating significant income—from cattle taxes to transportation and abattoir levies—that neither the British nor the Nigerian nationalists failed to overlook.[41]

"HOME OF PIGS"

How animals were raised for food was intricately connected with availability of pasture and fodder, climatic change, human settlement patterns, advancements in veterinary medicine, and the response of communities to changes in their meat supply. Creativity in maximizing animal yields in an era of meat shortage, caused by outbreaks of livestock disease or labor strikes, took place at different times across many communities. In no period did this become as serious a nationwide matter as during World War II, when veterinarians were compelled to rethink traditional methods of raising trade cattle through nomadism. To address a shortage of meat caused by emergency wartime regulations, the veterinary department established cattle-fattening stations, first in Vom in early 1940 and later that year in Agege (Lagos). Animals brought there from the North were, in addition to pasturing, placed on a special diet that included concentrates and medication to increase their size before they were slaughtered.[42] The general criticism of nomadic pastoralism was that trade cattle tended to become emaciated, lose weight, and even become diseased through the long North–South journey.[43]

After being given unusual access to the fattening facility, the Lagos press swung into action, writing detailed editorials praising the scheme and educating the public about its importance for the future development of animal husbandry. This is one of the few episodes where the progovernment *Nigerian Daily Times* (NDT) and antigovernment WAP and *Daily Service* would agree on the value of a specific government project.[44] While the NDT pointed out how the "rigours of war conditions have opened our eyes to certain industrial possibilities of this country which we never imaged before," the *Daily Service* waxed optimistic that the fattening stations would supply the public with "beef of very high quality" and called for additional stations to be established across the country.[45] Yet in some parts of the country (especially the eastern provinces), it was wartime import restrictions on stockfish that changed dietary habits in favor of beef consumption. W. Burke, one of the leading veterinarians of the 1940s, was confident that the temporary change could benefit the government in the long run: "It may be that after the War the people of these parts may have acquired a taste for beef and that it will not be necessary to import stock fish. This would be a happy result and one more step in the sound economy of this country."[46]

The cattle-fattening project went along with the campaign to encourage Nigerians to go into modern animal husbandry—through cattle ranching in the South. Agricultural and veterinary officers were convinced that southern Nigeria was not taking advantage of its lands for raising cattle and that if Nigerians there would do so, they could share in the kind of cattle wealth that the northern Fulani, whose entire existence revolved around livestock, possessed.[47] Newspaper editorials and articles established an unpopular fact—that the old, nomadic way of raising trade cattle could not sufficiently meet the beef needs of Nigeria's growing population. Not only would cattle ranching reduce the South's reliance on northern Nigeria and further help the southern economy; it would also ameliorate the incidence of zoonotic and epizootic diseases since the animals would not have to trek or be transported from the North. "One of the most important and most lucrative branches of agriculture is animal husbandry, especially the cattle industry," stated an *NDT* article, probably sponsored by the government, that touted cattle ranching to the southern public. It then spoke in a language that would have appealed to many business-conscious people: "Very few persons we think are aware that the Government Agricultural Department has been busy carrying out experiments with a view to establishing practical proof that development of the industry in the south on an economic basis is possible."[48] Another article gave this caveat, frantically insisting that unless the government gave loans or what it called "hire purchase" to prospective ranchers, the project would not achieve its desired outcome.[49]

However, this project remained largely on paper and in the imaginations of veterinarians, development experts, and agricultural officers. In the 1950s the regional governments of western and eastern Nigeria established ranches, which served as fattening and experimental stations for local and international cattle stock. One of these stations, the Obudu Cattle Ranch operated by the Eastern Region Development Corporation, measured more than ten square miles on a cloud-enveloped, grass-covered plateau, which rises some five thousand feet above sea level, and was valued at £230,000. In May 1958 the ranch cared for eighteen hundred head of cattle from the Cameroons and northern Nigeria, serving as "gigantic lair" for cattle to recover their "health and meat-yield" before moving farther south.[50] In the Western Region, the Fashola experimental station imported foreign breeds and actively experimented with crossbreeding to increase cattle product.[51]

The lack of private investment in commercial cattle ranching did not mean individuals were not raising livestock for commercial purposes on a small scale in response to high demand for meat in the city. Moreover, Muslims and practitioners of indigenous faiths who used animals in their observation of festivals and religious rites found raising their own livestock cheaper than buying from commercial markets. Urban livestock keeping was disadvantageous to the government, which derived income from every aspect of the livestock business and sought to police animal health in the interest of public safety. As a result of the intensification of regulations governing urban livestock keeping, the "Goat and Sheep Bye Law," as it was colloquially known, criminalized the raising of livestock and the "straying" or public presence of animals such as goats, sheep, and pigs in cities. The implementation of city livestock legislation varied widely, but common practice included impounding animals found on public roads or around public buildings and infrastructure.[52] Introduced first in Lagos in the second half of the nineteenth century and later passed in other Nigerian cities, urban livestock rules also found loud expression in the rhetoric of modern city planning. Lagos had the most stringent of the goat and sheep bylaws in that they prevented Muslims from raising animals for their festivals. Up to 1945 they could only keep a ram for religious rites up to five days before the festivals.

Modernist notions of the city insisted that livestock had no home there. Their natural home, the government insisted, should be in the rural areas where abundance of pasture, habitat, and settlement patterns support their existence. Veterinarians' conviction that urbanites could not raise healthy animals led to the criminalization of livestock raising that violated urban planning codes. Authorities were convinced that while domestic livestock represented social, economic, and cultural capital in rural communities, in cities they existed only as threats to sanitation and health. Only the dog—except in the event of an outbreak of rabies—befitted the city as security guard and companion.

City livestock legislation divided Nigerians across social class and religion. Some city people refused to acknowledge the colonialists' simplistic conception of livestock as urban nuisance. For these residents, animals were economic and social capital for their owner's household. The newspapers, the mouthpiece of the public, were alive in documenting dissenting voices. In the 1920s and 1930s two newspapers—the *Lagos Daily News*, owned by pioneering Nigerian nationalist Herbert Macaulay, and the bilingual *Eleti Ofe*—insisted that people should not be imprisoned for raising animals to meet a multiplicity of needs. While much of this criticism took the form of editorials and open letters, at least one article in *Eleti Ofe* published in August 1923 adopted satire in ridiculing the spectacle of shame that livestock brought upon the town council officers who impounded stray livestock.

However, a portion of the educated class supported the antilivestock policy. A. Mpama, in his newspaper petition, sarcastically labeled Shomolu, a district in Lagos, "Home of Pigs" and asked the government to act against the animal nuisance because the district's human residents paid taxes.[53] The abhorrence for pigs, even among lower-class Nigerians, seemed to be more common than for goats and sheep.[54] Aside from polluting the communal water supply, stray pigs destroyed home foundations, accelerating threats to human safety.[55] The gravity of pigs' threat to human livelihood and ideals of hygiene varied widely. In rural communities, like Aparaki in Ijebu Province according to a petition written by locals to the editor of the newspaper *Ijebu Review*, pigs caused "untold misery, unpleasantness, wastage of public funds and permanent removal [relocation] of many eminent citizens" to other parts of the country.[56] Another petition from Idanre made the exaggerated claim that damages caused by pigs led to a "dearth of food which has resulted into inevitable famine."[57] In the northern city of Kano, pigs and illegal piggeries constituted more than filth—they possessed "natural repugnance" for Muslims, in the words of the secretary of the Northern Provinces. Here, while the ruling elites disapproved of the section of the urban livestock legislation that forbade keeping of goats and sheep in the older part of town, they supported the prohibition against urban piggery.[58]

Urban livestock were to blame for an increase in accidents on inner-city roads, both government officials and some among the educated class insisted. "It is curious now that traffic is several times heavier than it was in those days," a newspaper editorial noted, in an attempt to place the matter in historical context to justify the firm implementation of urban animal legislation. Affirming the competition for city space between the human and nonhuman creatures, the editorial continued: "These animals seem to be made to enjoy absolute freedom of the road to the extreme annoyance and grave risk of motorists who very often have to dodge and swerve in order to avoid collision with them."[59] For others, it was the beautification of their neighborhood and the success of urban horticulture promoted by the government that was at the mercy of urban goats.[60] Perhaps no other criticism was as representative of the perspectives of noncolonialists than a newspaper petition by Henrietta Millicent Douglas, a Pan-Africanist, social worker, and journalist from the West Indies who had made Lagos her home:

> Yaba is called the "Garden City." This name has been more
> or less a misnomer owing to these destructive animals [goats].
> They even climb one's verandah, jump on to the bannister to get
> at the plants which are out of their reach. I have always lamented
> the fact that no sensible person would be so rash as to venture to
> cultivate plants, and so encourage Horticulture Society. The goats
> and also fowls are everywhere. They roam at will throughout Yaba,
> as if it were still a deserted estate.[61]

The ideological camp opposed to the keeping of livestock oscillated from total prohibition to regulation. Prohibitionists were die-hard urbanites who wanted to completely outlaw the keeping of livestock, while those who favored regulation believed "there is certainly no objection to anyone keeping livestock" provided they were kept in closed yards. In April 1945 the LTC revised its Goat and Sheep Bye Law to meet the transformation in the danger animals posed to vehicular movement and human safety, while also responding to criticism from the Muslim community that buying rams a few days before Eid-al-Kabir created artificial scarcity and inflation.[62] The revised regulation abolished year-round the keeping of sheep and pigs on the densely populated Lagos Island. Residents of this area and the mainland could keep a maximum of two goats or sheep one month before the Eid-al-Kabir without government permit. Those on the mainland could keep these animals in enclosed yards but had to receive permits from the medical officer of health (MOH). One *NDT* editorial gave a solid nod to this revised law:

> No one can reasonably disagree with the Municipal authorities taking steps to afford the members of the public a measure of safety particularly in Lagos where the traffic in recent years has become exceedingly heavy and the population abnormally large. The present situation with regards to traffic is such that motor drivers have to exercise the utmost care to avoid road accidents, and if these animals are allowed to roam about as it is often the case in the already congested streets of Lagos, a great inconvenience will be caused to users of motor vehicles and the lives and limbs of both pedestrians and motorists exposed to needless risk.[63]

This editorial and its supporters were uncritical about salient factors that caused accidents, which extended beyond animals' intrusion onto roads, including the overwhelmed public road network and disobedience of traffic rules by unskilled drivers in the 1940s and 1950s.[64] As with the debate over humane slaughtering in chapter 7, the goat and sheep law snowballed into religious stereotypical epithets describing Muslims as "unsophisticated elements" in a modern colonial society run in accordance with Western culture heavily influenced by Christian ideologies.[65]

The resistance of Muslims to the revised urban livestock-keeping legislation was not informed by notions of proper city planning, accident prevention, or sanitation; rather, it was shaped by the legal infringement on their religious freedom and livelihoods. While the *NDT* generally supported the government, one of its rivals, the *Daily Service*, the official organ of the Nigerian Youth Movement (NYM), penned critical antigovernment editorials under such headlines as "Scrap the Undemocratic Bye Law" to register its displeasure on behalf of the people.[66] The underrepresentation of Muslims in the Western-educated class reduced their visibility in the print media, which shaped perceptions among the reading public.[67] But the *Daily Service* did provide space for the expressions of a few, like the sanitary inspector simply identified as Ajao. In his petition Ajao educated readers about the importance of animal sacrifice to Islam, while minimizing the alleged public health implications of keeping household livestock within the city.[68]

Such newspaper advocacy complemented physical confrontations of government officials and elites by the Muslim community. On September 19, 1945, Muslim leaders mobilized their community for a mass meeting attended by about five thousand people where they further emphasized that the revised law discriminated against Muslims, while enriching the government and commercial livestock dealers.[69] They insisted that trade disputes, livestock disease, and inadequate transportation facilities, among other factors, led to inflation of animal prices, which justified the decision to raise sheep in the household.[70] Artificial scarcity could increase the prices of rams during the festival to as high as £10 to £15—the average price of a large bull.[71] What is more, the Ansar-ur-Deen Society, one of the Islamic sects in Lagos, started a £20,000 education fund in the early 1940s or earlier to be raised with the proceeds from hides and skins of Eid-al-Kabir's rams donated by Muslims.[72] This fund became necessary given the discrimination that Muslim children experienced when enrolling in schools run by Christian missions. The more expensive a ram was, the lower the quantity of hides and skins donated to the school fund. As with most colonial policies, the goat and sheep law favored one group of colonial subjects while jeopardizing the interests of other. Thus, it is easy to understand why cattle dealers and C. A. Williams, the manager of Lekki Poultry Industry, would support the law.[73] A business simply named Farmers, Traders, and Service, Co. advertised in the newspaper asking people to bring their animals for rearing in their government-approved facility for a "moderate" cost.[74] The mobilization of the Muslim community against the revised legislation was strong enough to compel the government to shift its position by increasing the number of rams that people could keep for their festival observation from two or more.[75]

Cattle, aside from humans, were the most mobile colonial subjects in Nigeria. While the largest number of trade cattle were raised nomadically, foraging over thousands of square miles to meet the demand for beef, many were transported via new mechanized technology, such as railways, lorries, and modern ferries, thus changing the nature of their mobility, with impacts on their nutrition and health. When the railway reached Kano from Lagos in 1912, it was expected to carry humans, solid minerals, and agricultural resources—not cattle. With time, the railway services discovered the economic imperatives of constructing special cars to transport livestock (see fig. 1.3). As the fastest means of transport, railways helped reduce emaciation of cattle due to long treks and circumvented the menace of the tsetse fly. A herd of cattle could start its journey from Bornu plying the government-approved trail, feeding and drinking, over weeks in order to arrive in Ilorin for shipment by rail to Lagos or Ibadan in the Southwest.

Nigeria's elaborate river networks also served the transportation of trade cattle. Loading docks across the Niger River and Benue River provided entry points for cattle from northern Nigeria to the Lagos Apapa cattle lairage, handling as many as seventy thousand cattle per year in the mid-1950s. As the cattle trade increased, the government was dissatisfied with the use of regular vessels that also transported humans for moving

FIGURE 1.3. Cattle cars crossing the Niger River (1954). *Source: Nigeria Magazine*, no. 44 (1954).

animals across the rivers. Accidents were also common in poorly made local vessels. By the 1920s the Public Works Department in these areas had established shipyards and staffed experts to design and build special cattle ferries, capable of transporting up to twenty tons of animals per trip. Humans' aesthetic concerns were a less important factor in the design and building of cattle ferries than the safety and behavior of the cattle themselves. Shipbuilders believed that the more they studied how animals behave under different river and ocean conditions, the higher the chances of making technological headway in building ships that would not capsize. A lower incidence of accidents meant a higher number of cattle transported and greater revenues accruing to the government and private businesses. However, accidents in government-run cattle ferries did take place, to the dissatisfaction of everyone involved in the cattle trade—from colonial officers, veterinarians, and Public Works Department engineers, to herders, dock laborers, and consumers. One such accident on the Katsina-Ala River in August 1956 claimed thirty-six cattle and led to a renewed effort to ensure cattle safety.[76]

Trade cattle's main source of food was forage, which existed naturally and in varying quantity across the country. Although the modern cattle of colonial Nigeria had expanded access to pasture because imperial land-use law overrode indigenous legislation on grazing, they also confronted challenges, including limited access to water, prolonged drought, and frequent outbreaks of epizootic diseases. All these natural constraints were intensified by the creation of government forest reserves, which were set up purely for the international lumber trade. The reserves denied humans and animals access to vital resources, such as wood for fire, forage, and land for agriculture.[77] Thus, the politics and language of forest governance were capitalist oriented and tailored toward preservation for the purpose of maximum expropriation.

Up to the mid-1930s, grazing was not allowed in the forest reserves. But the explosion of the Nigerian cattle population, the diminishing of pasture due to rapid urbanization, and the incessant conflict between herders and farmers changed this practice. The modus operandi of grazing in forest reserves become a heated debate. While "sound forestry," according to the chief conservator of forests (CCF), "demands that fullest use is made of all forest produce, major or minor, including grass," the fear of overgrazing, damage to tree roots and rhizomes/rootstalks by goats, and illegal egress of village and nomad stock created tensions between the colonial government and Nigerians who thought that forestry regulation violated their right to maximize the resources endowed by nature.[78] The CCF presented the dilemma of forest conservation: "Nomadic sheep and goats are undesirable in reserves but their value to the country is considerable and they must therefore be catered for."[79] However, the exclusion of goats and sheep in the proposed grazing regulation, according to the director of veterinary services (DVS), "mean[t] a virtual ban on nomadic herds of the cattle since no such herd is without its flock" of sheep and goats.[80]

While some forest officers thought that grazing should never be allowed in forest reserves, even though "illegal grazing" was common, others like the CCF believed that rotational and controlled grazing in forest reserves was inevitable. Those who kicked against grazing of forest pasture argued that herders might abuse the privilege to exploit forest resources. They preferred to criminalize grazing as a whole than expend scarce resources to monitor grazing in reserves whose sizes varied from ten to fifty square miles.[81] But the consequences of preventing forest reserve grazing were grievous—in 1950 in Kano, fifty thousand cattle died of starvation due to prolonged drought.[82] Other core questions included how long in a year forest grassland could be opened to grazing and how native authorities, whose perspective on forest utilization did not always align with that of the government, could possibly be involved in the proposed grazing rotational scheme.[83]

To maximize the materiality of cattle, an experiment in rotational grazing in forest reserves was carried out across northern Nigeria in the 1950s.[84] It required close supervision, given that herders, for disease-control purposes, would not kraal or keep their animals in one location for a long time, notably during the rainy season. Rotational grazing thus increased the work of the veterinary, agricultural, and forestry departments charged with ensuring that allotted plots were replenished after grazing and were disease free. But it also had an economic dimension. The native authorities, a ruling body composed chiefly of traditional African elites, would not benefit directly from cattle tax not paid to their coffers, so they were reluctant to approve the use of their forest reserve for the project. If properly managed, rotational grazing in forest reserves could serve as a "natural" experimental station for testing vaccines, veterinarians thought. For political officers, it could also make collection of the cattle tax and monitoring of the population of livestock easier in each area. Yet it would be a counterproductive project if restricted only to one, given that overpopulation of cattle would occur in areas where it was permitted. Up to the end of colonial rule, the status of grazing in forest reserves remained undefined—continually devised and redevised, often to the confusion of cattle herders. When the *Nigerian Citizen* reported the arrest and fining of one Malam Koreshi for grazing his cattle at the Penyam Forest Reserve in July 1956, a stream of correspondence among conservationists and colonial officers revealed the confusion over whether grazing was permitted in that reserve.[85] Koreshi, as gleaned from the correspondence, probably thought it was legal to allow his cattle to graze there.

KEEPING BEASTS ALIVE AND HEALTHY

The North was the birthplace of colonial Nigeria's veterinary science because it is the natural home of much of the country's bovine and equine populations. The first veterinary officers were appointed at the request of Frederick Lugard, the British administrator who created the colonial state of Nigeria by merging the northern and southern protectorates in 1914, to cater to the horses of the mounted infantry of the colonial army, the West African Frontier Force, in 1904. Veterinary service became an official government service in 1914 with the appointment of F. R. Brandt as the first chief veterinary officer in Zaria. The early years of veterinary establishment in Nigeria were characterized by isolated and uncoordinated developments, due in part to World War I. However, in 1924 a permanent veterinary station was built on 1,468 acres of land at an altitude of 4,300 feet in Vom, on the plateau in the Middle Belt. The location was specifically chosen for its proximity to the main nationwide railway line—thus, laboratory equipment, official correspondence, and vaccines could be transported across the country in a timely fashion. The location was also free of the tsetse fly and had ample access to grazing land for the station's animals. A powerhouse of scientists—from bacteriologists and pathologists to entomologists, virologists, parasitologists, and veterinary doctors—would turn Vom into a potent arm of colonial modernity with responsibility for proffering solutions to the unstable landscape of animal disease.[86] The veterinary department's annual budget of £192,520 in 1954 was among the largest for a single government department.[87] From Vom, European veterinary officers and their African assistants were dispatched across the country to track the epidemiology of livestock diseases and to release scientific reports, which shaped the lives of both humans and animals as well as their engagement with their environment.[88]

From the 1940s, efforts were made to popularize the work of the veterinary department among the public through newspapers. This project was carried on in tandem with the print media's role as promoter of colonial institutions deemed important or beneficial. A 1941 editorial in the *NDT* regretted the "unfortunate deficiency in public knowledge" (especially in southern Nigeria) about the veterinary department and called for a "fuller public recognition" of the "extremely valuable public service" of what it exaggeratedly described as the "most deserving branch of the Civil Service in this country."[89] Through the 1940s and 1950s, more and more articles, photographs, editorials, and news reports about the veterinary department would appear in the print media.[90] This expansion of public awareness also reflected the intensified activity of veterinary science—a direct consequence of the spread of zoonotic and epizootic diseases. Yet, as we have seen earlier, it also found expression in the well-curated attempt by powerful elites in the 1950s to use modern animal husbandry and agriculture to validate their claim to superiority.

A central element of veterinary work in Nigeria was the formalization of veterinary education. Africans had interacted with Western veterinary medicine from the dawn of colonial contact, providing local perspectives on livestock diseases. However, indigenous knowledge could only serve the animal population well if Western ways were fully institutionalized through formal and informal education and training, veterinarians argued. In 1944 the first set of Africans equipped with technical knowledge of Western veterinary medicine graduated from the Vom veterinary school and received the title of "veterinary assistants." They were lower-cadre staff whose work complemented that of European veterinary officers.[91] The 1954 report of the Department of Veterinary Research of Nigeria explained the anticipated outcome of this racialized position: "The better the Veterinary Assistant is trained therefore the nearer the services given directly by the Veterinary Officer."[92] In 1954, 514 Africans, predominantly northerners, received training in European veterinary medicine. This amounted to one veterinary assistant per 7,500 tax-paying cattle or one veterinary assistant for every 24,092 head of livestock.[93]

This acute shortage of veterinary officers led to a campaign to promote the animal health profession in the print media. "No matter how well qualified a man is, he should not think of applying for any post unless he is a genuine keen lover of animals. . . . Quite apart from that, unless you love animals you will be bored with the job." Veterinary officer Dr. R. Brewster described animal-centered prerequisites for becoming a veterinary assistant in a radio broadcast dedicated to veterinary science and titled "Broadcast on Careers" in late 1951.[94] After declaring that the prosperity of Nigeria "depends, without doubt, upon its two major industries, Agriculture and Livestock" in pontificating about career prospects in animal care, Brewster then painted the role of veterinary officers as vital to public health and as a rewarding profession capable of paying as much as £200 per annum.

But critics of the veterinary department would not agree with the beatification of the veterinary assistants. They accused the government of discrimination for not admitting graduates of the Vom veterinary school to membership in such prestigious international bodies as the Royal College of Veterinary Surgeons, despite the rigor of their three-year education; the graduates also faced discrimination in remuneration and conditions of work in general.[95] This, according to one James Oko, "caused much concern and spiritual depression to them."[96] Critics viewed veterinary assistants as another group of lower-cadre workers whose chances of upward professional mobility were restricted. A similar critique of the veterinary establishment by the WAP in November 1953 was part of the opposition to the expansion of lower-cadre positions for Africans and increase in expatriate Europeans.[97] The newspaper desired to see more African veterinary surgeons receiving a quality education in Britain and taking over from European expatriates—a proposal called simply "Nigerianization of the Civil Service."[98] Another open petition about the proposed conversion of Vom into an "institution" worried that it would "provide shelter for expatriates who have been adversely affected" by the increased replacement of Africans with European staff in other government departments. The author of the petition, Emmanuel Diji, worried that the proposed plan would "jeopardize the future of African staff" whose career advancement could be truncated by the presence of Europeans who occupied higher positions and were better paid.[99] The debate over the career of veterinary assistants was among the central issues of decolonization, which serves to highlight the importance of animals in 1950s Nigeria.

Western veterinary medicine produced contradictory outcomes: it both complemented and undermined indigenous animal science at the same time.[100] In demonstrating its superiority to African approaches, Western veterinary medicine gradually supplanted local ideas that had proved effective in managing animal health before its arrival. Western veterinarians were ready to learn from indigenous practitioners, as much as they could without contravening their alleged superiority. As multifaceted as colonial veterinary medicine was, its most elaborate undertaking was research into vaccines and their production for the inoculation of livestock. Therefore, the modern livestock of Nigeria were both the victims and beneficiaries of experimental serums, like the dried goat virus and the dried lapinized virus, used in fighting animal diseases. In designing and implementing inoculation regimens, colonial veterinary medicine took many factors into consideration, such as breed of animal, conditions of transport, nutrition, and even the ethnicity and class of owners. Thus, vaccination of cattle against such diseases as rinderpest was as much a study of social and environmental conditions shaping human and animal lives as an effort to find a scientific solution to the ravages of nature.[101]

Vaccination did not permanently solve cattle diseases. It was only effective if the animal had not contracted the virus, was under a year old, and continued to be separated from a sick herd. A combination of preventive and curative therapies had to be adapted to the history, breed, husbandry method, and movement of each herd (see fig. 1.4). Vaccination research had to keep pace with the speed of the transformation of the animal diseases themselves since a successful vaccine designed for a virus type in one year might not work when new pathogens of the virus emerged in

FIGURE 1.4. Cattle dip at the Obudu Cattle Ranch (1959). *Source: Nigeria Magazine*, no. 60 (1959).

subsequent years. For another thing, although colonial veterinary medicine originated in Europe, its deployment was dynamically shaped by the unique animals and environments of Nigeria.[102]

Most animal diseases were communicable ailments—hence the imperative to quarantine and restrict animals' movement during a disease outbreak.[103] Yet the movement of animals was inevitable, especially in search of food. The Diseases of Animals Ordinance (DAO), the nationwide regulation that served as the legal framework for controlling animal diseases, defined animals as only domesticated creatures, such as camels, dogs, ostriches, poultry, rabbits, antelope, cattle, donkeys, goats, horses, mules, oxen, sheep, and swine. The legislation made it mandatory for people to report outbreaks of disease to the government or veterinary facility. Sick animals were prohibited from moving in or out of a diseased area. Disposal of dead animals and disinfection of kraals had to be conducted under the supervision of sanitary and veterinary officers. Defaulters could be punished by imprisonment and fine.[104] A 1941 amendment to the DAO empowered any court in the country to punish defaulters, even if the offense was committed outside its jurisdiction. This unusual amendment recognized the fluidity of the landscape of livestock disease and human and animal movement.[105]

The DAO also spelled out the entire colonial veterinary establishment, including quarantine and vaccination camps. The camps shaped how animals encountered modern veterinary therapy, while also exploiting them in the name of sound medicine. Trade cattle were among the animals most commonly used for experimental biomedical research. After all, these animals, unlike those in the veterinary stations, lived in a largely "natural" or "uncontrolled" environment where they were exposed to the avarice of nature and unpredictable pathogens. By training herders in modern animal medicine, the veterinary establishment turned Africans into agents of Western biomedicine.[106] The level of trust in Western veterinary medicine varied among individual herders, some of whom combined Western and indigenous therapy (in varying proportion) to keep their beasts alive. Medical pluralism in animal science was inevitable, not only because Western biomedicine could not effectively cater to all of Nigeria's livestock but also because only herders who paid the cattle tax were mandated and eligible, regardless of their disposition toward Western veterinary medicine, to receive vaccines for their animals. Millions of domestic livestock owners knew little to nothing about Western veterinary science throughout the colonial era.

Colonial veterinary medicine focused predominantly on trade cattle for several reasons. First, they were food animals, capable of transmitting zoonotic diseases to humans. Second, they had an obvious economic impact on the colonial treasury, not only because their owners paid taxes on them but also because they fueled a long chain of interrelated commercial transactions, from abattoir and market stall levies paid by butchers to revenues from railway and vessel operators. Third, the epidemiology of trade cattle was easier to monitor because they were mandated to be transported along approved routes (trails, railways) and stationed in designated government quarantine camps for vaccination and inspection for disease. One such post in Kaduna in the mid-1950s was capable of accommodating about six hundred cattle at a time. As many as a hundred thousand cattle from Kano, Niger, Katsina, Zaria, and Sokoto Provinces en route to the southern provinces passed through it on a yearly basis.[107] Without the trail there, it would have been impossible to vaccinate a total of 46,057 livestock against trypanosomiasis and rinderpest from June to November 1959 in Bauchi Province alone. Quarantine camps enhanced the enumeration of the cattle population—a condition that shaped economic and medical policies.

But none of these precautions could stop an outbreak of disease. Medical failures did take place, either because of weak or poorly preserved vaccines or medical error by veterinary officers or their assistants, one of whom was described in 1956 as a young Vom graduate who "does not have the authoritative manner required for running [quarantine] camps."[108] Blame shifting between veterinary officers and herders was inevitable, partly because they were not always in agreement over the efficacy of vaccines and the proper procedures for inoculation. As a result, whenever an animal died after inoculation, veterinary officers sought social or environmental causes or tried to determine human error on the part of the herders. In the view of one provincial veterinary officer in Adamawa, herders who did not believe in the efficacy of Western biomedicine possessed an "outlook [that] can scarcely be described as one of scientific detachment."[109] Many herders saw vaccines not only as inefficacious but as capable of triggering death. "When we ask the owners, who have not been to a camp for a number of years, why," said the veterinary officer of Jos in relaying the perspective of local herders three years before Nigerian independence, "we usually get the same reply that they fear the losses connected with the dry goat vaccination."[110] Commenting on the "rumor" and "suspicion" of heavy mortality and debility that followed the administration of the dry goat vaccine for rinderpest, the DVS for northern Nigeria asserted in 1957 that attendants in immunization camps in the plateau "are decreasing and have now reached what may be a seriously low level."[111]

TABLE 1.2. DOSES OF VACCINES ISSUED IN NIGERIA, 1957–60

Vaccines	1959–60 (doses)	1958–59 (doses)	1957–58 (doses)
Dried goat rinderpest virus	2,183,200	1,633,325	1,516,525
Dried lapinized rinderpest virus	146,760	98,950	134,355
Fowl pox	119,100	116,500	52,700
Newcastle disease	1,097,540	1,038,750	420,150
Rabies	17,266	17,429	9,598
Blackwater	1,932,550	1,656,900	1,890,850
Anthrax spore	631,800	350,100	316,500
Haemorrhagic septicaemia	160,160	118,800	173,750
Fowl typhoid	220,450	242,300	147,350
Fowl cholera	208,850	242,250	144,350
Contagious abortion, S.19	1,100	1,997	712
Contagious bovine pleuropneumonia	315, 125	431,610	103,725
Contagious caprine pleuropneumonia	93,000	109,800	69,450
Total	7,126,901	6,058,711	4,980,015

Source: Federal Department of Veterinary Research, *Annual Report for Year 1959–1960* (Lagos: Government Printer, 1960), 63.

Aside from the production of vaccines and the process of inoculation, the modernization of the cattle trade involved creating and maintaining cattle trails to enhance quarantine service offered in the veterinary camps. The trails served more than veterinary purposes—they directly shaped landscapes and patterns of human settlement and other economic activities such as commodity trading and farming.[112] They became the yardstick for measuring distance, giving directions, and understanding topography. Cattle trails had political, economic, and medical values. From the political angle, they helped in resolving conflicts between herders and farmers, provided that the herders followed the designated routes. Economically, native authorities could charge levies on each head of cattle passing trails sited in their community. In medical terms, they aided monitoring in the event of a disease outbreak. Hence, for any native authority "lucky" enough to have cattle trails in its jurisdiction, maintenance was vital, even though the amount of taxation imposed on herders was always a subject

FIGURE 1.5. Cattle market in Abakaliki in southeastern Nigeria (1959). Courtesy of the Simon Ottenberg Collection, National Museum of African Art, Smithsonian Institution.

of disagreement among everyone involved. In all, the trails could be a lifesaver or a death trap—depending on the quality of maintenance.[113] In 1952 the Eastern Region government introduced a bill that imposed a levy ranging from 6d. to 2s. on every head of trade cattle entering or raised in the region to provide veterinary facilities, water, carriages, safer river crossings, and grazing land for cattle plying the trails.[114] The DAO, the government argued, was incapable of improving the conditions of cattle, many of which died or were debilitated by the bad conditions of the cattle trail (see fig. 1.5). It took another three years for this legislation to come into effect.[115]

TOWARD SAFE BEEF CONSUMPTION

On November 21, 1942, one Amodu Rufai Shitta, described in the press peculiarly as an "old man," was convicted of slaughtering a ram without a government permit in Lagos. Shitta had contravened a law in effect across major Nigerian towns that prohibited private slaughtering of livestock without a permit, except for during popular festivals like Eid-al-Kabir. During cross-examination, Shitta claimed that he bought the animal for Eid-al-Kabir but decided to kill it sooner because it was sick. Shitta's excuse for killing the animal was germane to the purpose for which the government had imposed the livestock slaughter law in the first place. To prevent the feared spread of zoonotic and epizootic diseases, slaughter or abattoir legislation led to the policing of private homes in search of contraventions that could undermine public health. In the words of MOH doctor I. Ladipo Oluwole, Shitta had committed a "serious offence" by disobeying a law that mandated reporting cases of sick livestock to the government. To worsen the situation, he had distributed half of the carcass by the time he was arrested.[116]

Shitta's case was by no means an exception in Lagos or other big cities and towns across the country; however, the religious dimension complicated his situation. It was inconceivable to many that an animal required for a religious rite and spiritual cleansing should be a subject of secular legislation driven by public health concerns. Not even the "general" permit allowing Muslims to slaughter their animals for Eid-al-Kabir was enough to lessen the tensions over government actions to moderate religious observances.[117] Yet adherents of indigenous faiths did not receive such accommodation, even though animal sacrifice was also important in their religions.[118] Ironically, chicken, which Christians used for celebrating Christmas, did not come under the ambit of enforcement of private slaughter rules. The tasking of sanitary officers to inspect the carcasses of privately slaughtered animals in homes, even where people had paid for permit to kill the livestock for whatever reason, was an extension of the state's power to name "desirable" and "undesirable" animals—in violation of core principles of spirituality and communal bonding.

Slaughtering laws had ramifications for public health at public abattoirs and meat stalls in the big cities and provincial capitals.[119] Abattoir laws empowered sanitary and veterinary officers to prevent the slaughter of animals deemed sick. Such animals had to be removed from the abattoir and safely disposed. But it did not end there. Even after a slaughter, a sanitary officer could declare beef unhealthy for human consumption and confiscate it. All butchers were required to undergo training in hygienic slaughtering, flaying, and dressing of carcasses and were required to possess a permit to carry out each of these tasks.[120] Aside from licensed butchers and their assistants, only veterinary, town council, and sanitary officers and police in uniform were permitted in government abattoirs. Yet neither abattoirs nor sanitary and veterinary establishments were cheap to run. In the 1940s a capital requirement for building a standard abattoir stood in the range of £12,000 to £15,000. As in other domains of colonial encounter, the drive for modernization of abattoirs did not match the financial commitment for their smooth running. Even high-ranking public health officers complained, such as the president of the LTC, who confessed in late 1933 that "the conditions under which animals are butchered in Lagos today are unworthy of a humane administration."[121] Similarly, veterinary officer J. H. B. Best described the Umuahia slaughterhouse in 1940 as in "shambles, no one is in authority, everyone seems to be his own authority. The method of slaughter is cruel and crude in extreme."[122]

The challenge of running an abattoir put infrastructural, environmental, and public health issues in conversation with one other. For example, veterinarians believed that the climatic conditions of Nigeria intensified bacterial contamination of meat, which could lead to gastrointestinal problems for consumers. "In a cold climate, bacterial contamination of the meat does not lead to the same rapid putrefactive changes as in the case of the hot humid" climate there, said the DVS in giving an environment-centered explanation for the bad condition of meat and abattoir alike.[123] But his familiar language of African exceptionality did not end there. He warned that it is wrong to assume that meat in any state of decomposition can safely be consumed by Africans. "This may be the case with certain tribes that habitually eat 'high' [decaying] meat," he qualified, before then concluding that "it is certainly not so in the case of other Africans, who are not more resistant to bacterial changes in meat than are the average European."[124] Other reports expressed worries that contamination was a product of unhygienic handling of carcasses in the abattoirs where "live beasts are being thrown down amongst their dead, dying, and butchered" on the slaughter slab. The blood, water, and viscera littering the slaughterhouse floors ended up smeared over the surface of meat meant for the market, which led to what the director of veterinary services described as "grossest contamination."[125]

A radical transformation in slaughterhouse practices aimed at reducing meat contamination appeared inevitable. Some sanitary and veterinary officers believed that if livestock were slaughtered in the evening and hung overnight, "they would have a better appearance and be more wholesome and palatable and have higher nutritive value" when consumed the following day.[126] But this contradicted abattoir law, which stipulated that animals should not be slaughtered between five o'clock in the afternoon and five in the morning. A debate over who was most qualified to monitor the abattoir also came to light, as agents of colonial modernity fought one another over their overlapping power. Veterinarians, the DVS insisted, not sanitary and town council officers, should oversee the abattoirs. He wanted all butchers to be direct employees of the town council to guarantee maximum compliance with sanitary rules.[127]

The colonial government no doubt possessed enormous power to make medical and sanitary laws in accordance with its own understanding of meat safety and sound public health. But the people affected—namely the butchers, cattle herders and dealers, and meat sellers—put up fierce resistance. For instance, the initial abattoir law stipulated that livestock must be slaughtered in the evening and allowed to "set" for sale in the morning of the following day. The government was forced to revise this legislation because butchers and meat sellers insisted that such practices were not economically viable because consumers declined to buy the meat of an animal slaughtered the previous day. This necessitated the slaughtering of livestock in the abattoir in the morning to be offered for sale at meat stalls by early afternoon. When the government attempted to revert to the old practice of slaughtering in the evening and selling the following morning, public criticism and anxiety mounted about the circulation of "rotten" meat in the public.[128] Although Lagos MOH doctor Oluwole believed that such "stale" meat was not "rotten," consumers and critics of the health department did not.[129] In shaping public anxiety toward the circulation of "poisoned" or "dangerous" meat in markets, newspaper editors positioned themselves as the people's mouthpiece opposing the lax public health policies that constantly put the wellness of the people in danger. "When therefore poisoning is traced to commodities which reached the homes daily," the WAP editorialized in August 1953, "the appeal to the sense of civic responsibility of the people of Lagos cannot but be welcomed with two aims in view." The editorial then went on to highlight government's failure to prevent the circulation of "bad" meat.[130] Other newspapers published open petitions by Nigerians against the unsanitary condition of abattoirs and their "unpleasant odour" as part of their general critique of modernizing society.[131] "Rumors" about dangerous meat compelled the government to take responsibility for issuing official statements distributed through multiple channels, including town criers and the newspapers. One such notice about an outbreak of anthrax published in the NDT in March 1943 presented the consequences of consuming unhealthy meat and offered a temporary solution.[132]

Veterinary science did not actually possess all the power that it professed. This limitation angered livestock butchers who trusted the veterinary assistants to certify an animal safe for consumption before slaughtering, only to feel betrayed when the beef of the same animal was condemned for destruction because some parts (such as the lungs) showed signs of diseases. "If veterinary officers and Malams do not know which of these animals has a disease while alive, how can we expect the butchers to know?" questioned an *NDT* editorial of September 28, 1950, pitching its support for Nigerian businesses while advocating for an insurance program to compensate "unfortunate butchers."[133] In October and November 1954, butchers at the northern city of Minna went on strike twice to protest the destruction of carcasses discovered by the sanitary inspector to have tuberculosis. They called for the removal of the sanitary inspector and allegedly threatened to kill him.[134] Not surprisingly, the response of the government to this kind of criticism absolved veterinary medicine of any failure, while downplaying the frequency of such occurrences and without addressing the core question of compensation to butchers for their losses.[135]

The growth of modern private butchery was a direct response to the fact that the government alone could not effectively supervise an adequate supply of healthy meat for public consumption. It was also promoted by the rise of Nigerian consumer culture that sought to replicate Western business models to meet the tastes of Europeans and the expanding class of educated Africans. Firms such as John Holt managed by both Africans and Europeans capitalized on the anxiety over "poisoned" meat to position themselves as the gateway to healthy nutrition. They would slaughter livestock in their private government-approved abattoirs, preserve the meat in their cold rooms, repackage and brand it with such attractive names as "Prime Agege Beef," and then sell direct to residences.[136] An advertisement by one such private meat company, Cold Store, owned by the United Africa Company and that claimed to have branches "throughout" Nigeria, included a line that racialized labor: "Butchered and dressed under expert European supervision, all our stocks are available in excellent condition."[137] Their efforts complemented foreign importation of tinned processed beef and dairy products from Europe.[138]

The raising of modern cattle transformed colonial Nigeria's economic, social, and political landscape, even necessitating the introduction of Western veterinary science. By focusing on the history of trade cattle, this chapter has highlighted the politics of representation, imagery, capitalism, and nation building that emerged in colonial Nigeria. From public health concerns, abattoir regulations, and urban livestock laws to trade union politics and nature-reserve management, both Nigerians and British colonialists contested the notions of modern society and the place of cattle in it. In the next chapter, our attention will move to the donkey and horse, whose existence unleashed a chain of events and identities that made nonhuman creatures an indispensable component of Nigerians' experience.

2 ⤳ The Living Machines of Imperialism

Animal Aesthetics, Imperial Spectacle,
and the Political Economy of the Horse and Donkey

In Ouadai, Nigeria, and all over the southern Saharan oases, the donkey is
the friend of the farmer. He does the bulk of hard work with a minimum
of expense and grumbling. One could not think of Northern Nigeria
without Neddy. For traveling and trek purposes in southern Sahara, and
Nigeria, the jackass is the most important part of a poor man's outfit. Jacky
can live and work where pack oxen die. He can bore through belts of
tsetse fly in safety without more than an odd wag of his tail, though strange
to say, he cannot live there. . . . Whenever you get angry and feel inclined
to shoot him for some trick he plays you, don't forget that you can't get
on without him. I can hardly call the donkey a dumb animal, for I am
reminded that Balaam's ass had the gift of speech, and even argued with
his master. Treat him like a lady, and Jacky will have the last word.

— Dugald Campbell, *On the Trail of the Veiled Tuareg* (London:
Seeley Service, 1928)

"Mutual Admiration," the caption of a *Nigerian Daily Times*
(*NDT*) photo featuring nationalist Adeyemo Alakija and Jubilee, his favorite racehorse who won the highly contested 1946 Victory Cup Race,
goes beyond a mere journalistic embellishment and fictionalization.[1] So
also is the caption, published in the *Daily Service*, of another photo of
the two that describes them as "holding consultation" three days before
the race.[2] During the shifting contexts of the first half of the twentieth
century in Nigeria, both humans and horses established a valid relationship of symbiotic respect. In exchange for human kindness toward them,
racehorses as colonial subjects and modern creatures performed power on
the turf, rewarding their owners and fans with financial success and leisure

satisfaction. Jubilee, a distinguished white racehorse, was among count-less first-class animal athletes that transformed humans' understanding of honor and stardom. Horse racing involved performance of power on two planes—the horse performed not only for itself but also for humans, who used it to wield influence. Newspaper and popular narratives about the exploits of racehorses humanized the beasts in a quest to blur the obvi-ous biological boundary between them and humans. Figurative expres-sions and idioms such as "backing the wrong horse," "jaded horse," "dark horse," "Trojan horse," and "Who will be at the rein?," among others, are not merely the abstract literary expressions of literate urbanites who wit-nessed horse racing on a regular basis. They have a practical implication for human-horse relations in the real world.[3]

To understand the circumstances under which Jubilee and Alakija re-ceived mutual respect through horse racing, one needs to place the seismic shift in horse identity and power in historical context. The imposition of co-lonialism ended military expansion, for which horses were predominantly used, and created new domains of relations, shaped by the notions of mod-ern and colonial subjecthood of both horses and humans.[4] The decline in the Nigerian horse population (due in part to the death of cavalry warfare) brought humans closer to horses and increased their personal knowledge of individual animals through equestrian spectacles and leisure-time events like horse racing. As the state sport in colonial Nigeria, horse racing attracted as many as thirty thousand spectators, who assembled at the racecourse for a multitude of reasons: to support their favorite racehorses, catch a glimpse of famous colonial officers and local chiefs, place bets to improve their finan-cial fortunes, socialize and network for personal and collective gain, or even reinforce established paradigms of colonial subjecthood. A host of com-plex social, political, and economic relations emerged and were sustained around the modern horse of colonial Nigeria. Equestrian sports and leisure activities shared the core features of political spectacle: human and animal bodies in motion, adhering to stagecraft and scripts decodable by spectators and performances aimed at influencing the public's political reality.[5] Thus, they went beyond entertainment and spectacle of colonial modernity, ex-tending into crucial sites through which the government shaped and re-shaped dominant notions of power, honor, and respectability.[6]

Equestrian sports captured the imagination of both ordinary people and aristocrats. So deeply enmeshed were they in the main fabric of co-lonial culture that locals and foreigners thought they were a European invention. In his autobiography, titled *My Life* and published in 1962, the premier of the Northern Region, Ahmadu Bello, corrects this historical fallacy, reclaiming the horse's identity from its colonial abductors. "After all, we were practically brought up on horseback and anything to do with horses comes as second nature to us," Bello recalls of his childhood in Rabah, near Sokoto.[7] Photographs of indigenous racing during Muslim festivals, among other visual evidence, support Bello's affirmation of equestrian sports' deep roots in northern Nigeria.[8] Despite their precolonial heritages, the modernization of racing, polo, and the durbar, which colonial officer turned historian Anthony Kirk-Greene appropriately described as "the heart of the North" under colonial rule, transformed the horse into a modern colonial subject.[9]

This chapter examines how the horse and donkey changed Nigerian history, underscoring their multifaceted roles as combatants, working animals, symbols of pride and power, and athletes. The horse and the donkey occupied a prime place in popular and elite construction of "good" modern animals and colonial subjects. The donkey became the "official" pack animal of colonialism because of its strength and patience under heavy loads, among its other biological attributes. Little or no training was required to maximize the value of this first-class working animal, without whose help modern colonial capitalism would have suffered a major setback. The horse, on the other hand, was the noblest of all animals to most people. It received human admiration for its celebrated elegance, grandeur, majestic and aristocratic stature, patience, and even courage. If daily distance was measured by the number of kilometers covered by the horse, units of economic goods and patterns of human settlements were defined by the quantity of merchandise the donkey carried and by its caravan trail. The movement of horses and donkeys thus transformed both landscape and environment, responding to the shifting configuration of political power within and between the colony and the metropole. While many of these features of the horse and donkey cut across cultural divides, how they manifested in specific local realities did vary. Straddling the fields of animal studies, sports, economic history, imperial spectacle, and entertainment, this chapter argues that in becoming a modern animal and colonial subject, the horse and donkey shaped and were shaped by realities unique to imperialism.

"THE HEART OF THE NORTH"

Unlike in southern Africa, where horses were the first domesticated stock imported by settlers in the mid-seventeenth century, in Nigeria the British invaded a country with a long equestrian tradition.[10] From the last decade of the nineteenth century, the third battalion of the colonial army, the

West African Frontier Force (WAFF), was a mounted infantry stationed in northern Nigeria. However, the "pecuniary loss" owing to the high mortality rate of military horses compelled the WAFF to consider importing horses from the Americas and Europe in 1899.[11] But this would soon change when the colonial army invaded the Sokoto Caliphate, which supplied it with thousands of horses seized from local communities and jihadists. The mounted infantry at this period was constituted into eight companies of one hundred men each and headquartered in Zaria, in the heartland of northern Nigeria. Military officer A. J. N. Tremearne, who came to Nigeria in 1902 after participating in the Ashanti expedition in what is now Ghana, described Nigerian military horses as "fairly tractable, strong, and swift" under command. Their sizes, he remarked, increased as one traveled northward and far from the tsetse fly belt.[12]

The casualties of the conquest of Nigeria therefore included military horses. While some died in the line of duty, many more lost their lives after being bitten by the tsetse fly, which Herbert C. Hall, a British army officer who joined the mounted infantry in 1903, described as "a great curse south of the Benue."[13] Trypanosomiasis causes neurological problems, anemia, lack of energy, and fever. In his memoir, *Barracks and Bush in Northern Nigeria,* Hall noted that his superiors did not foresee the difficulty and cost of "feeding and upkeep of such large number" of confiscated horses.[14] The misery of the war horses was compounded by a lack of suitable accommodation on the military base, which Hall labeled a "death-trap" for horses.[15] No day passed, he asserted, without the necessity of removing dead horses from the stable to a "respectable distance" where they were given "a perfunctory funeral."[16] He attributed the high mortality rate to the failure of the British officers, who were not acquainted with the geography of the tsetse fly, to learn from the locals. Indigenous medicine, which had helped saved horses for centuries, received little to no respect in the army. Constance Larymore, who accompanied her military officer husband to northern Nigeria in 1903, advised that the last resort in treating a sick horse or pony "is to employ a native horse doctor—he may know more about it than we do, and he certainly cannot well know less!" Her observation points to the efficacy of non-Western biomedicine for trypanosomiasis and epizootic lymphangitis at a time when Western veterinary science was nonexistent in the region.[17]

To reduce horse mortality, common practices of the era included covering up the animals during the months of July and August, preventing them from grazing in swampy lowlands or from mingling with local cattle herds, where cases of trypanosomiasis were large, and utilizing smoky fires to discourage flies.[18] Idiosyncratic mixtures of Western medicine and local

African knowledge combined in varying proportions as early colonial officers (most of whom were not horse experts) fought to keep as many horses as they could alive. Later the mounted infantry was spread out across northern Nigeria in Sokoto, Bornu, and Kano Provinces to improve the health of horses and deal effectively with local resistance to colonial rule. After World War I, feelings that the mounted infantry had outlived its usefulness increased within the military. Finally, in 1921 the last two companies of the mounted infantry were disbanded and merged with the regular infantry battalions, who could now be transported by truck, thus ending more than twenty years of war horses in colonial Nigeria.[19] However, they remained part of the military and police forces and were used for ceremonial parades and riot control throughout the colonial era.

While the horse ceased to be a combatant in the army by 1921, the donkey was employed as a beast of burden of the colonial state, playing an indispensable economic role throughout British rule in Nigeria. Although the southern railway project—undertaken to facilitate the movement of solid minerals and agricultural goods and humans to Lagos, the main port—reached the northern city of Kano in 1912, donkeys were still required for transporting merchandise from sites of production to the railway line. However, the donkey did not become Nigeria's most popular pack animal by accident but by clear physical advantages that other competing pack animals lacked. Not only was it well adapted to the savanna and the Sahara; it also could carry up to 120 pounds of merchandise over twenty-five miles per day and without water for up to five days (see fig. 2.1). Initially colonial officers, including Frederick Lugard, did not have confidence in the donkey

FIGURE 2.1. A caravan of donkeys at Lokoja (1957). Courtesy of Derek Miles Greening.

as a viable pack animal for their aggressive expropriation schemes—even though local communities had depended on it for centuries. In a 1904 report, Lugard described the donkey as slow, small, and not durable enough to be a serviceable means of transport. Therefore, he promoted other pack animals, like the oxen and mule. Unfortunately, oxen could not produce the desired outcome because they were costly and not easy to procure. They also could not withstand a long, arduous journey. Efforts to breed mules by importing some breeders from Argentina were not successful. Moreover, mules were four times the price of donkeys: in 1909 a mule was selling for £5 compared to a donkey offered at £1. 5s. From all indications, both mule and oxen did not satisfy the colonialists' economic model of achieving significant returns with minimal investment.[20]

By 1909 Lugard would change his negative review of the donkey with the following commendation: "Pack donkeys have justified their introduction. Their mortality is heavy, but this is fully compensated for by their low price, small amount of food required, and the little attendance necessary."[21] This was essentially how the donkey became the official pack animal of British imperialism in Nigeria. A northern Nigeria report of 1910–11 stated that "they have proved the most suitable of the pack animals."[22] In 1907–8, the administration of northern Nigeria hired more than three thousand donkeys. The gradual investment in veterinary medicine from the second decade of the twentieth century reduced the mortality rate of the donkey, which further increased its economic value.

Aside from its strength and low maintenance cost, other core features of the donkey enhanced its use. Unlike the horse and camel, the donkey was easy to maneuver and could climb mountains and hills with much ease. Although donkeys are afraid of large bodies of water and thus could not be used to cross deep rivers, they were easier to breed—virtually every farmer and household in northern Nigeria kept them as important social and economic assets. In addition, as colonialism intensified its grip on the means of production, so, too, did it control the dynamism of donkey breeding. Two categories of donkeys (household and commercial)—based on ownership, location, chores, and maintenance—had existed before the twentieth century, but they took an elaborate form under colonialism. Household or domestic donkeys were predominantly home-based animals who served their immediate owners, mostly farmers. Commercial donkeys were bred by farmers who leased them out to merchant companies, traders, and transporters engaged in the movement of goods such as cash crops and solid minerals. The need of African traders and foreign firms to maximize profits intensified this division between domestic and commercial donkeys such that more and more donkeys were bred for economic purposes. Their prices went up from around £1 in the first decade of the twentieth century to as much as £10 in the 1930s. Dugald Campbell, a fellow of the Royal Geographical Society and an early twentieth-century British author and traveler, wrote about the indispensability of the donkey, its emotional makeup, incredible perseverance, and advantages over other pack animals in a factual, albeit occasionally exaggerated, and poetic manner rarely found in most documented sources (see the chapter epigraph).

Aside from this documentation by a foreigner, local oral and literary traditions paid tribute to the exceptional patience of the donkey. Kirk-Greene recorded this Hausa proverb on the donkey in his book, first published in 1966: *Hakurin kaya sai jaki* (Only a donkey shows patience under a load).[23] Together, these physical and behavioral qualities of the donkey outweighed its occasional manifestations of discomfort and resistance to chores. As Campbell's impression and other sources suggest, donkeys did assert some resistance. If underfed or tired, they could refuse to carry the load and run at large until their handlers could bring them under control. Regardless, the donkey's economic role cannot be overemphasized. Even the emerging consumer culture recognized its utility in a depiction of competition between new and old technology of transporting economic goods. An advertisement for Hercules bicycles in the *West African Pilot* (WAP) in the 1950s tried to tarnish the donkey's long-standing reputation as a natural beast of burden, depicting it crumbling under heavy weight.[24] The horse and donkey played more than military and economic roles in colonial Nigeria. In addition to hammock litters carried by porters, equine technology was equally important as the means of transportation for colonial officers for their daily administration of the colony. Greater mobility translated to consolidation of political power. J. D. Falconer, who entered the colonial service in 1908, clearly established the importance of the horse to British imperialism when he stated in the preface of his appropriately titled book *On Horseback through Nigeria* that "the journey as described, however, is by no means an impossible one for an experienced traveler, able to obtain fresh horses and carriers as required throughout the course of his travels."[25] Horse riding was also popular among Europeans who worked as miners and representatives of large trading companies. Numbering around fifteen hundred in Jos in 1926, many of them kept horses, and "riding was popular."[26]

The story of the horse and donkey allows a historian to engage some contrasting dynamics of colonial modernity, shaped by location, environment, and ecology. Motor transportation, which was already a dominant symbol of modernity among elite Africans and Europeans in Lagos by the second decade of the twentieth century, did not become a feature of elite life in northern Nigeria until the late colonial era. Hall was right that "until the arrival of the motor, the horse was the rich man's mode of getting about" in northern Nigeria.[27] When Kenneth J. Bryant arrived as a colonial officer in Lokoja in 1920, there were only two motor vehicles, a lorry belonging to the government and a car, which he described as "ancient," owned by a "very large man" in the Prisons Department. Reflecting in 1959, after serving in the region for more than thirty years, Bryant saw no incentive to own a car in the 1920s. Not only were the cars of the era unreliable in a country with very few mechanics; they also had "narrow tyres, which were quite useless in sand or soft going."[28] The entire country had from two thousand to three thousand road miles, few of which were tarred in the mid-1920s.[29]

A year before Nigeria's independence from Britain, the country had about thirty thousand miles of roads, which fueled an increase in both commercial and private car ownership. Yet this did not end the culture of horse ownership for business and leisure in the North. From colonial masters and local chiefs to the new educated elites like Bello, the possession of a stable of beautiful horses was a sign of ancient tradition in a society that was also open to the benefits of modernity, including driving a beautiful Jaguar or Rolls-Royce. Up to the late 1950s in northern Nigeria, horsemanship for colonial officers was a necessity and virtue, despite the growing popularity of motor transport. In one of his tours of northern Nigeria, which Kirk-Greene described as a "horse-happy" region, the last British head of the colony, Governor-General James Robertson, demanded that all district officers escort him on horseback and in full uniform. However, one "horse-shy" district officer confided in his resident officer that "he could not trust himself to stay in the saddle." The resident excused him, only to remove his name from those invited to the dinner with Robertson.[30]

The advice given to prospective officers on horse keeping in the memoirs of colonial administrators should be read as an extension of the significance of the equine to imperialism. The biggest problem regarding horses in Nigeria, these memoirs established, was not finding a suitable one for hire or outright purchase but keeping it alive. Even the few colonial officers who owned horses in Europe had to be reintroduced to equine culture in Africa, so different were the medical, environmental, and sociological conditions that shaped human-horse relations. Hence, maintaining the sound health of privately owned horses was considered as part of the infrastructure of comforts and conditions required for the proper administration of the colonies. Larymore's full-length chapter in her memoir on horse care more than any other colonial writing that I have seen deserves special attention, including for reasons touching on the gendering of colonialism. "My feminine readers may feel inclined to 'skip' this chapter with the remark: 'Well, the stables are not in my department'" — so she opens her chapter predicting what readers may think about caring for horses, a practice that was masculinized in Britain. Her advice on how to supervise the stable boys and feed, groom, and protect the horses from disease fits into the bigger narrative that seeks to problematize the daily life of wives of colonial officers in the colonies. Larymore asked prospective wives of colonial officers to take her advice seriously because it would be their primary responsibility to look after the horses since their husbands would spend much of their day working in the office. If most colonial officers simply thought of their horses as mere tools of imperialism, Larymore's narrative treats the equine as a pet and a component of everyday life that requires some emotional investment:

> For she naturally loves horses, and cannot but be fond of her wiry little thirteen-hand ponies in Nigeria; because they are, as a rule, sweet-tempered, willing, honest little souls, whose mistress will, in almost every case, have reason to remember how gallantly they carried her on such and such march, and how cleverly they limbed and negotiated the nasty places, and forded uncertain-looking rivers. This alone will give them a strong claim on her loving care, and will admit, after a time at all events, that it is worthwhile to learn all she can on the subject. . . . For ourselves, I hardly think we could sleep in peace unless we had paid our usual visit to the stables to satisfy ourselves that all was well there.[31]

THE PRIDE OF THE TURF

As noted earlier, equestrian sports, which many viewed as a colonial invention, had been in existence for centuries in the areas that would later be called Nigeria. The transformation of equestrian sports from precolonial to colonial or modern leisure events from the late nineteenth century went closely along with the changes in the identity of the horse and the consolidation of imperial power. In Lagos, horse racing started as early as the 1860s when a piece of land was mapped out as a racecourse. Viewing fast-moving horses in competition for speed fired the imagination of most Lagosians, who were experiencing racing for the first time. By the 1890s horse racing had become an annual event attracting thousands of spectators. A Lagos journalist wrote admirably in 1898 that "whenever Englishmen are to be found, there will you also find a Cricket Club and a Race Course."[32] The popularity of racing continued into the early twentieth century. In 1903 and 1907, respectively, the *Lagos Standard* described horse racing variously as "the great annual event in the local world of sports" and "the greatest sporting event of the year [attended by a] large and motley crowd which assembled at the Race Course, and which might be numbered by the tens of thousands."[33]

If modern horse racing in Lagos was introduced by the city's civilian European population, in northern Nigeria it should be traced to the military camps that sprang up during and after the British conquest of the region.[34] The mounted infantry attracted European commissioned and noncommissioned officers (NCOs) because it gave them unlimited access to military horses for recreational purposes. Different battalions met at different locations to compete for prizes. In Maiduguri, the first colonial polo club in the region (the Lake Chad Polo Club) was established around 1912 on the military base. The paucity of Europeans meant that racial segregation in sports would not be possible, as White European officers and Africans formed integrated teams. The highly skilled African NCOs even taught some Europeans the game—further validating Bello's insistence that equestrian sports predated colonial rule.[35] With time, and the increase in the European population, polo teams were organized along racial lines. Black teams and White teams met two to three times a week. The opinion of Langa Langa (H. B. Hermon-Hodge) that the Black teams "had the best eye, and hit the hardest, but lack[ed] the brain-play and combination; so, that the sides were pretty even" extended racial prejudice, especially in terms of intellect, to sports. His other assertion that African NCOs were "taught the game—as far as we, ourselves only learners, could teach them" speaks effectively to how colonialism expanded and complemented "indigenous" methods of playing.[36]

Memoirs of colonial officers provide some insight into the conduct of the early incarnation of equestrian sports.[37] Although West Africa was dreaded as the "White-man's grave" by early visitors and adventurists, it featured "plenty of open orchard bush, park-land, horse-trekking and the chance to play polo," among other opportunities, that pulled colonial officers to northern Nigeria, noted Kirk-Greene.[38] Hall and his fellow veterans, whom he described as "the very best fellows," joined the mounted infantry after serving in South Africa because of "the possibilities of active service, and the prospects of sport, when weighted against the monotony of home duty."[39] In Sokoto, Martin Kisch and his colleagues played polo for one hour on each Monday, Wednesday, and Friday in 1908.[40] The unusual sketches of equine actions in his book directly reflect the central role of horses in multiple economic and cultural contexts.[41] In another portion of his memoir, Hall explains the importance of horses in military recreation after enumerating the natural and logistic challenges his unit faced: "But all these trials did not in the least daunt our O.C. [officer in charge] or those under him who were all old campaigners, well used to rough it. Sport of every sort was the order of the day: what better opportunity could be imagined—with about 400 horses to be kept in exercise?"[42] Hall also gave a short description of the course, conduct, and impact of steeplechasing on the health of the soldiers. Introduced by his superior officer, who had participated in the Grand National race in Britain, steeplechasing gave soldiers "green horses out of the latest mob that had arrived from somewhere."[43] He mentioned that the Lokoja steeplechasing course of two miles and eighteen fences rivaled the legendary one at Aintree in Britain.[44]

As colonial officers recounted their leisure experiences, they also gave their impressions of the conduct of the horses. "Perhaps the most wonderful thing that struck me about these horses," Hall relates of his encounter with Nigerian equines, which he described as all locally bred, "was the way that most of them took to polo and jumping."[45] He attributed this to the fact that Nigerians began to ride horses as young as two years old—thus, the horses grew up mastering jumping. However, he felt that their backs were ruined by the time they were nearly fully grown. He was surprised that many "raw horses," which had never seen a White man before or used a European bit, went into polo with "greatest kindness. . . . I have seen them go round the jumps without once refusing."[46] Yet some of the horses showed an interest in polo at the beginning, only to detest the game later—to the point that they would not want to come near the field. Hall had an ankle fracture that kept him in the polo camp clinic for three months after forcing himself on a horse that seemingly expressed a sudden dislike of the sport.[47] In some ways, Hall's description of the consequences of trying to forcefully ride one of his horses could be read as a form of agency demonstrated by the animal. It is one of the few references to how horses attempted to prevent human imposition. Be that as it may, as equine sport enhanced colonial military culture, it seeped into literature, including a poem in a 1911 collection titled *Lyra Nigeriae* by E. C.

Adams (alias Adamu). Titled "The Old MI," it paid tribute to the lost military glory of the mounted infantry in Zaria, the importance of equestrian sports to military life, and the horses that made all this possible.[48]

In northern colonial Nigeria, racing and polo would leave their original homes in the military barracks and become civilian sports, open to the public—namely, European nonofficials and local aristocrats within the broader colonial administration. Equestrian sports were promoted in part by colonial culture that emphasized sportsmanship for its officers, regardless of their background. Indeed, a good colonial officer was part politician and part sportsman. But beyond this, sports provided what Kirk-Greene described as a "first-class opportunity" for social networking that "could be a bit of an obsession" for district officers in northern Nigeria.[49] At the polo grounds, they played alongside local chiefs during off-duty hours, discussed political matters, resolved conflicts, and received advice from colleagues.[50] So important was polo to the elite culture of northern Nigeria that not only was it played "to a high standard," in Kirk-Greene's words, but local chiefs also achieved remarkable success in the game.[51] Of the northern elites' polo careers, those of Muhammad Dikko dan Gidado (r. 1906–44) and Usman Nagogo (r. 1944–81), both of Katsina, stood out clearly.[52] The latter's handicap (+7) was the highest in the history of polo in Nigeria until his death in 1981.[53]

But horse racing, not polo, was the most important state-sponsored sport in colonial Nigeria. As previously stated, horse racing was a crucial site through which the government shaped and reshaped dominant notions of power, honor, and respectability. The pavilion "gaily decorated" with such motifs of imperialism as the Union Jack, accompanied by musical performances from the army and police bands, and featuring opulent appearances by colonial officers and their wives, as well as traditional elites (in their free-flowing robes and gowns and magnificent hats and turbans), who sat in the order of their power within the colonial hierarchy at racing events—all served to enhance the dialectics of seeing and being seen in colonial Nigeria.[54] Even educated elites like "moderate" nationalist Adeyemo Alakija and "collaborator" Kitoyi Ajasa, described in 1932 by the administrator of the colony as "perhaps the gentleman . . . with the greatest knowledge of all forms of sports" in Lagos, were popular dignitaries at the racecourse.[55] At racing events, colonial officers made vital political statements and provided justification for British colonialism in the presence of heavily armed police and military forces. The staging of races to commemorate key events, such as a change of leadership in the colony and birthdays and coronations of British monarchs, fused the rituality of imperial politics with leisure. The role of the governor of Nigeria as the patron of race clubs was a nuanced sociopolitical signifier that translated into real power.[56]

As colonialism solidified across the hinterland, so also did urbanization intensify with the creation of provincial capitals, which attracted Europeans who started race clubs. From Enugu to Kano to Ibadan, the mortality rate of horses declined as veterinary medicine expanded to deal with trypanosomiasis and the tsetse fly, its biological vector. Race clubs mushroomed in the interior of the country, continuing the tradition of showcasing trends from the metropole and Lagos to display the gains of "civilization."[57] With advancements in colonial science, what began as an irregular occurrence in the nineteenth century later became a regular event, featuring hundreds of horses in each race meet across the country. The expansion of railway transportation meant that racehorses could be kept in the North, far from the tsetse fly during the rainy season in the South, and brought back just in time for the race meets, which lasted from one to four days in the 1940s. Similarly, racehorses were transported to Nigeria by air from across the world by the late 1940s.[58] This development represented a climax in the long history of movement of animals for sports and entertainment in Nigeria.[59]

The popularity of racing increased in relation to the creativity of its organizers—that is, race clubs. If the mainstream European and African elite culture promoted racing events organized during Christian festivals (such as Easter and Christmas) above other religious observances in the South, northern Nigerian race clubs organized theirs during the Islamic festivals of Eid-al-Fitr and Eid-al-Kabir.[60] By the late 1940s the Lagos and Kano race clubs met at least six times per year over three to four days each time. "Some racing enthusiasts are of the opinion that even if these meetings become a monthly feature they will still be as popular as they are now," reported a promotional article in the NDT, which further established the popularity of racing in Lagos.[61] Another claim by a racing report in August 1947 that the Lagos turf "compares favourably with any in England" does not appear to be an exaggeration, given the massive investment in the sport by private bodies and the government.[62]

Racing was not immune to the discourse of race and race relations, partly because of its diversity that reflected the unequal distribution of power, while it also presented unusual opportunities for ordinary Africans. The Lagos Weekly Record emphasized that racing was "the one and only great sporting event which brought all sections of the community together on a level of platform" and that it created an atmosphere where "colour prejudice was more in the background and the true English love of sport brought into being a mutual feeling of good fellowship"; this emphasis was informed by a comparison with other sports and the degree of involvement of a spectrum of people.[63] Unlike in most organized sports (e.g., rifle shooting, boxing, tennis) that were deeply racialized and popular only among a section of either the White or Black populations, in racing racial intercourse (to use the language of the era) was inevitable because a diverse group of Africans and Europeans played complementary roles as horse owners, trainers, grooms, jockeys, and spectators. Although horse owners were predominantly Europeans, Lebanese, Syrians, and educated African elites (mainly because it was expensive to maintain horses), racing attracted a diverse group of middle- and upper-class Nigerians, regardless of education status, who performed support services that included covering the sport in the newspapers. At racing events, the critics of colonialism, such as nationalists, traditional chiefs, and the public, could temporarily set aside their differences as they cheered their favorite horses to victory. Popular local chiefs, whom a race report in 1941 favorably described as "a galaxy of the leading lights of the local society," promoted racing and enjoyed the privilege to share the pavilion with the White colonialists.[64] After racing, all would return to their segregated neighborhoods and spheres of political and economic power where the color of their skin shaped their engagement with the colonial state.

Arguably, no educated elite Lagosian of the 1940s could match Alakija in his passion for racing. If Ajasa's Periwinkle was the star horse in the 1890s, Alakija's Remembrance Day, Thank You, New Star, Jubilee, and Thousand Bombers were the pride of the Lagos turf in the 1940s.[65] Alakija's ascendancy to the chairmanship of the Lagos Race Club (LRC) in July 1946, through a unanimous vote, represented a turning point in the involvement of African elites in horse racing.[66] For one thing, it demonstrated that a Nigerian, after considerable investment, could occupy the premier position (previously held only by high-ranking British military and political officers) in a colonial sport. Praised in the press for his "simplicity of nature, direction of purpose, inflexible courage, and above all his tranquil indifference to praise or blame," Alakija was the African face of horse racing in the 1940s; he even wrote newspaper articles to defend objectionable actions of the LRC (see chapter 8).[67] His wife, Ayodele, like the wives of European colonial officers, also participated in performative elitism at horse races by distributing prizes and trophies to winners. Ayodele was also a proud owner of popular race-winning horses such as Rosemary and Juno, the latter of whom made a "successful debut by winning her first two races in a most decisive and convincing manner."[68]

Alakija's rise to the upper echelon of White-dominated and state-sponsored sport should be seen more as an example of Whites using Africans to promote a popular entertainment than as complete tolerance for Black bodies in an inherently racist colonial society. Those who claim that racing promoted "racial intercourse" rarely acknowledge that the pavilion, a crucial site of display of power, was open only to Europeans and a few elite Africans. The positive sentiment expressed by the *Lagos Weekly Record* that racing brought the "community together on a level platform" was referring to the entire racecourse space, not segregated sections like the pavilion.[69] Hence, racial segregation found in European communities and public facilities did extend to racing in varying ways. The contention that racing promoted interclass and interracial solidarity neglected the fact that forty-five hundred unpaid prisoners cleared the racecourse ahead of racing events in 1932.[70] The racial spectrum in racing was inevitable because it derived its strength from the diverse roles played by a lot of people. The constant reminder by the LRC that it was a "public institution . . . represented by every class and community in Lagos" sought to retain the public's investment in racing (in the form of betting) to keep it economically viable to investors.[71]

The idea that racing promoted racial and class harmony ignored criticism of nationalists like Nnamdi Azikiwe. Indeed, individuals like Alakija and Ajasa were tolerated in racing partly because they had a "liberal" perspective on colonial domination or were "moderate" nationalists who also loved horses. Alakija was on the management board of the *NDT*, the de facto organ of racing and the LRC and the most important progovernment newspaper. The near absence of racing news in the rival *WAP*, among other newspapers owned by Zik, was not an accident at all. It reflected the disagreement over the role of racing in colonial hegemony. Instead of carrying racing stories and editorials, the *WAP* focused on athletics and soccer, among other sports, which Zik (himself a big fan of track and field) supported. Not only did the *WAP* criticize the government for spending public money on horse racing at the expense of other sports; it also argued that the racecourse, occupying a big expanse of land at the heart of the colonial capital, could serve a better public good. The newspaper argued that racing created a "hotbed" of entertainment "which is adverse" to the people. It criticized the government for benefiting "immensely from the flow of money at the turfs," even as the sport "consistently drain[ed] people's pockets" through betting. Here, as in other sites of colonial encounter, the

WAP extended its role as the mouthpiece of the masses while also attempting to shape the notion of "good" versus "bad" sports. The newspaper's critique that horse racing "does not add to our national character" probably explains why the sport began to decline from the 1960s.[72] After independence, Zik, among the first generation of the leaders of the country, abandoned racing. The Lagos racecourse would later be renamed Tafawa Balewa Square to honor the country's first prime minister, all in a bid to decolonize an edifice of colonial domination.

Like most organized sports in British Nigeria, horse racing was male-centered. While elite African women like Ayodele could own racehorses, they were not allowed to be jockeys. I have not come across any African woman professional jockey in colonial Nigeria. However, the lone White exception was a woman named G. Winterbottom.[73] To be sure, White women in colonial Nigeria, as Helen Callaway has noted, scaled many of the hurdles of imperial masculinity because they were considered to be higher than Black men and women in the racialized ranking of personhood.[74] They were more likely to be granted entry into privileged spaces in the colonies than in the metropole because of the status of their husbands, most of whom were political officers or expatriates. Described by the press as a person "whose expert jockeyship has become a matter of common knowledge and admiration," Winterbottom disrupted prevailing gender norms and attempted to expand women's participation in horse racing beyond their conventional roles as spectators, horse owners, or wives of colonial officers and African elites.[75] She "most beautifully" rode famous horses, including Trophy, to victory, causing the "greatest sensation" of the LRC's 1945 Christmas race meet.[76]

However, Winterbottom's success became a subject of controversy within the racing community. "Those who would not admit equality of men and women in the sport of the Kings are on purely sentimental grounds," opined a *Daily Service* front-page story criticizing the LRC for suspending Winterbottom because she was a woman. The remaining portion of the critique underscored the male-centeredness of colonial culture and the expectations it placed on women: "No Woman jockeys, they say, take part in horse racing elsewhere in the world. It is too masculine a job for women, whose dignity should be preserved."[77] I have not found any evidence contrary to the *Daily Service*'s critique that Winterbottom was suspended because her success on the turf challenged the male-centeredness of horse racing. Yet the "press war" between the *NDT* and the *Daily Service* over Winterbottom was just one of the numerous episodes of conflict over women's participation in strength sports in a colonial society where conflicting notions of "normative" gender and body shaped what is defined as "respectable" appearance and performance.[78] Equestrian sports enhanced honor for jockeys and trainers beyond the turf. In this way, what humans could not achieve by themselves, horses gave to them. Successful African and European jockeys and trainers would use their fame to gain access to the colonial establishment for upward mobility, as John Smith explained in the case of northern Nigerian youths in public schools in his *Colonial Cadet in Nigeria.*[79]

While all the social, political, and economic relations discussed above emerged and were sustained around horse racing, the true heroes of equestrian sport were not the jockeys, horse owners, and trainers but the horses themselves. Racing would not have existed without the horse.[80] Racing gave horses new identities as athletes, entertainers, and superstars who determined the fortunes of their owners and fans who bet on them. Their observable physical qualities, such as color, facial markings, height, speed, and breeding, were enhanced by the names given to them by owners, trainers, and even fans (see fig. 2.2). Hence, racehorse names were not

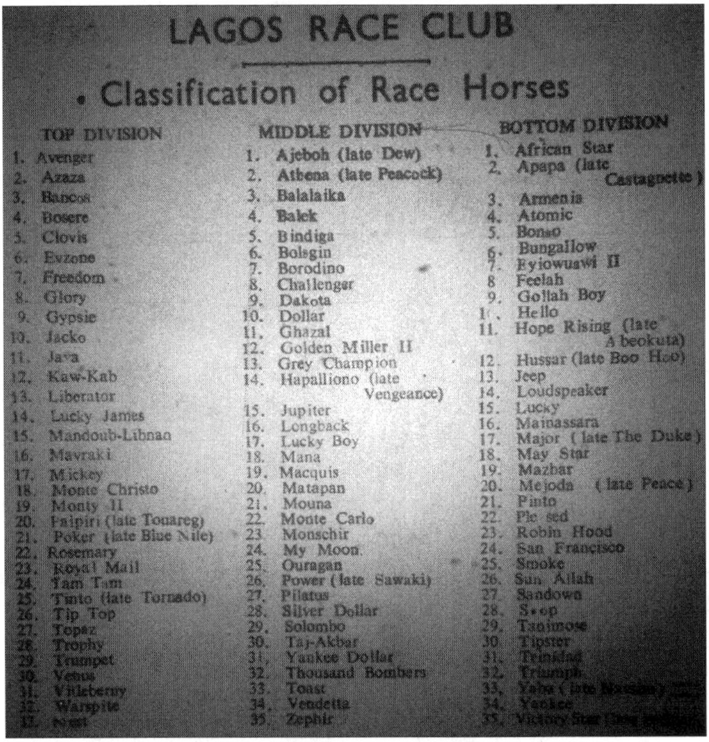

FIGURE 2.2. Classification of Lagos racehorses (1946). *Source: Nigerian Daily Times*, September 13, 1946.

a mere nomenclature of identification. Indeed, race enthusiasts identified more with the name and success of the horses than with their breed—even though breed was an important decider of success on the track. Regardless of whether they were bred in Nigeria or abroad, racehorses were given either African or European names. These mirrored urban cultural intersections, Atlantic cultural exchange, linguistic creativity, and the human quest to appropriate the natural world. Through their names, horses were expected to assume the real, imagined, and aspirational identities of their owners, jockeys, trainers, grooms, or even fans. In this way, a horse gave new meaning to humanhood.

The photos of racehorses and their owners and jockeys printed in the newspapers broadened the geography of celebrating success.[81] The expansion of photojournalism in the 1950s allowed humans to better document racecourse action, capturing all the features of power exalted by the beast amid the cheering crowd. If Nigerians paid to have the newspaper cover important life milestones (such as weddings, birthdays, the birth of a child, or the return of a student from abroad after completing an education), horse owners would also celebrate racehorses in the newspaper to assert respectability for themselves and their animal. Such newspaper headlines as "Record Crowds Watch Zouzou Carry Off Open Miles Purse," "Golden Miller Creates Sensation in Maiden Four Furlongs Race," "Trumpet Wins Open Mile Race," and "Poker Wins Race for Chairman's Prize," among others, served the complementary purposes of integrating horses into the established culture of stardom and of promoting racing for economic and political ends.[82] The published obituary of horses (like Ferris George's Big Game in 1943) beseeched the public for a moment of shared grief for a hero, whose presence on the turf would be missed.[83] If the image of the horse would not have appeared in the print media without humans, their owners and jockeys would not have achieved additional social and financial gain without the horse.[84]

The carefully written reports of race events in the *NDT* gave enthusiasts who were not spectators the opportunity to imagine a missed spectacle. Rendered in a language that humanized the equine, newspaper commentaries recognized significant agency on the part of the horses themselves. They contain such information as the horses' origin, ownership, physical features, and even temperament.[85] With descriptions oscillating between humans' and horses' appearance and level of enthusiasm, happiness, and success on the racecourse, newspaper commentaries are a dense trove concerning the colonial lifestyle made possible by horses.[86] As "turf-enthusiasts" debated the performance and classification of horses and other racing rules, a real and virtual community of horse lovers was created at home, in public, and in the workplace.[87] By petitioning race organizers to place their favorite horses in the right category or division, Nigerians helped the animals to assert their agency. In one case, when Maquis, described as the "greatest favorite" of the race, failed to place, a petitioner identified simply as "race-goer" did not mince words in expressing the financial consequences of the animal's failure: "The public whose money has thus been thrown away due to what may be described as a questionable transaction wish to know what has accounted for" Maquis's failure.[88]

The identity of Nigerian horses transcends naming and all the social constructions attached to it. Deeply embedded in their names is their ancestry, which remained in a constant state of flux due to active cross-breeding. One of the major consequences of racing for breeding was the emphasis placed on speed, required for success. Horse experts began to search for "fast" and "hot" blood in horses who must also be leaner, longer legged, and of lighter weight for maximum performance on the turf. However, many of the local breeds (measuring about fourteen hands and of Barb/Dongola ancestry) were considered too short by European racing standards. Yet what they seemed to lack in height, they made up for in being "serviceable," "hardy," of "good constitution," and possessing "remarkable staying power."[89] With the intensification of racing came the entrenchment of dichotomies between racehorses, specifically picked for their speed, and ceremonial or leisure ones, adored for size, height, and color.

Racehorses in effect created elite status, beyond being themselves a signifier of it. Horse ownership became a primary identifier of people, family, and communities. In 1944 the Association of Race Horse Owners was established in Lagos to protect the interests of investors in racing.[90] Local and metropolitan horse breeders and owners amassed wealth from trading in horses whose worth ranged from £100 to £2,000 or more. Therefore, financial transactions involving racehorses were part of the global trade in animals, which many race enthusiasts believed should be effectively pursued. "Can anyone doubt that horses of class and known ancestry would not lead to better racing and consequently bigger crowds and bigger prizes?" asked one racing enthusiast, F. R. C. Darcher, who described the LRC as the "wealthiest" race club in the country. In 1946, he envisioned the economic impact of a well-coordinated crossbreeding program capable of unleashing a West Africa–wide horse-trading enterprise with its hub in Lagos.[91] Darcher's reference to the failure of a project of crossbreeding

Nigerian mares with Arab stallions in the early 1930s suggests that his proposal was not new. But the central focus of his criticism that Nigerian horses were slower than their counterparts from Britain neglected such factors as training, jockeyship, and turf condition. Indeed, some of the most respected racehorses, such as Evzone (arguably the most expensive racehorse in 1940s Nigeria, with a worth of £3,000), were of local stock, not of English thoroughbred bloodlines.[92] Darcher's criticism of homebred horses sounds paternalistic—an attempt to look to Europe for a solution to what is framed as colonial deficiency. Modern colonial racing in Africa definitely had its origin in Western culture, but it was the homebred equine, not the foreign thoroughbred, that Nigerianized it.

"WHO WILL BE AT THE REIN?"

Sport and pleasure were not the only values that the horse added to human life. The magnificent animal also possessed symbolic power that complemented the aesthetics of respectability. The physical appearance of horsemen moderated social and political relations, enhancing notions of their invincibility and superior masculinity. Hall gives a vivid textual description of the intersections of horse riding, hierarchy, and the framing of elite power when he asserts that the "opulent" or "big" man preferred tall horses "so that he could look over other men's heads."[93] There is more to horse riding than this observable power relation between a rider and people on the ground. The horse seeped into cultural and political references in linguistic and artistic metaphors of social relations even in societies far from where horse riding was a vital part of daily life. The common colonial Nigerian idiom "To be on the horse" means to be powerful, boastful, and influential. In his memoir, nationalist Obafemi Awolowo described the editor of the *NDT*, C. C. A. Titcombe, while Awolowo worked as a trainee with the newspaper, as "every inch an aristocrat, always riding his high horse." Continuing, he criticized Titcombe as "distant and not easily accessible to people at our level," thus framing him as a person unwilling to associate with "ordinary" people due to his higher status.[94] Horse riding was also dialectical. The Yoruba saying *Aki ya go fun mo g' esin ri* (One does not give way to a former horse rider) reinforces the temporality of power—if sitting on horseback represents attaining power, to dismount and be unable to ride again denotes the reversal of fortune.

The horse inhabited the creative imagination of artists who tried to understand human existence through equine power and agency. During the era of decolonization, artists like Akinola Lasekan used the image of the horse, often in contrasting form, to reify interparty politics and the discourse of nation building, representing modern political discourse as precolonial cavalry warfare. If in one cartoon the horse (depicting Nigerian Public Support) would cooperate with its rider (Zik, the Nigerian St. George, and the National Council of Nigeria and the Cameroons [NCNC], his party) as it fought colonial domination, a horse in another cartoon (labeled the Western Region, which the NCNC sought to control) would resist being led into a perilous journey by its rider (the Action Group, the rival political party of NCNC).[95] In both contexts of visual art in colonial Nigeria, the horse was a tool for achieving human ambitions but had its own agency and could cooperate or resist in accordance with its own assessment of the projected success or mission of a campaign. "Who Will Be at the Rein?"—the title of another cartoon by Lasekan featuring a horse (the House of Representatives) waiting to be ridden by Zik, Awolowo, and Bello, the heads of the three regional governments on the eve of independence—continued the conversation of the equine as a tool for achieving political leadership of the evolving Nigerian nation-state.[96] The practice of presenting horses to political leaders as gifts during rallies borrowed from an ancient martial tradition, anachronistic in 1950s Nigeria but symbolically relevant for interparty politics and the independence movement.[97]

Quality horsemanship was an art, a performance, and a virtue that Nigerian ethnicities developed through the creation of indigenous chieftaincy titles to curate and nurture it. What constituted the peak of quality horsemanship would be influenced by location and the purpose to which the horse was kept. "The height of graceful horsemanship was to be able to dash off at the gallop and suddenly rein in so abruptly as to bring the horse right up on to its haunches," Hall described one equine performance in a nonmilitary setting. "At all fetes, religious and secular, this accomplishment was indulged in by all the 'dan sarakuna' (nobility). . . . The mob reveled in this play," he explained further.[98] Hall was describing the *jahi* royal horse greeting, conscientiously staged and performed only for royals and important visitors and during state ceremonies.[99]

The dominant image of the horse in colonial Nigeria was almost synonymous with imperial masculinity, even though women had been equally distinguished horse riders in precolonial times. As the Nigerian horse population declined due to the death of cavalry warfare, a reconfiguration of the gendered character of horse riding took place. Horse riding became more and more masculinized as the colonialists and

African male elites monopolized and redirected its symbolism in their favor. However, during the period covered in this book, a few women challenged the status quo. When Queen Elizabeth II visited Nigeria in early 1956, political activist Adunni Oluwole showed up to greet her on horseback.[100] Only the horse, not any other animal, would enhance her pride and imbue her with a deserved visibility and respectful presence. Knowing that the queen herself was an avid horse lover and rider, Oluwole probably wanted to make a political statement by using the horse to affirm her dignity as a colonial subject. What is more, riding on horseback allowed her to "honorably disrespect" the protocol of throwing herself onto the ground (as everyone, including the male elites, did) in greeting the head of a fast-crumbling empire. The founder of the Nigeria Commoners Liberal Party, Oluwole would ride on horseback during political rallies instead of riding in expensive, beautiful cars like male nationalists (see fig. 2.3).[101] Even on regular days, she would ride pleasurably around Lagos, "chin up and looking straight ahead without caring." "Taunted by men, she was unmoved. . . . It took a woman of unusual courage to do this in Nigeria of that period," biographer G. O. Olusanya submits.[102] Collectively, Oluwole and Winterbottom challenged the iconographic symbol of imperial male authority, each in her context and domain. For them, equine power was real power.

FIGURE 2.3. Adunni Oluwole (1947). *Source:* WAP, February 17, 1947.

Arguably none of the displays of equine power, ebullience, and royalty discussed in the preceding sections was a match for the durbar (see
fig. 2.4). So enchanting was it that attempts were made by the British to
attribute the durbar's origin to "the Arabian Nights or the stirring days"
of Shah Jahan, a sixteenth-century Mughal emperor, in furtherance of
their agenda to deprive Africa of its own cultural achievement and so-
phistication. Having witnessed a durbar in India, where she lived for four
years before coming to Nigeria, Larymore misguidedly thought the horse
extravaganza could not have been original to northern Nigeria.[103] Liter-
arily translated as "door of admittance" from its Persian origin, the durbar
was the formal ceremony in India and Afghanistan staged for welcoming
important visitors and announcing crucial political decisions.[104] However,
in colonial Nigeria, it had both internal and external, religious and secular genealogies.[105] Centuries before the British colonial conquest of the
northeastern corridor of Nigeria, horses played crucial roles in the military success of a great polity, the Sefawa dynasty, whose power reached
its peak in the sixteenth and seventeenth centuries. Even before the ad-
vent of Islam around the twelfth century, horse-centered ceremonies were
part of the rituals of power and installation of leaders, among other public

FIGURE 2.4. The Katsina Sallah durbar (1959). Courtesy Eliot Elisofon Photographic Archives, National Museum of African Art, Smithsonian Institution.

functions. The ceremonies of *bata* and *tawur*, which were carried out before a military expedition in Bornu, fused martial arts with entertainment and rituality to boost the morale of soldiers.[106] After helping to create the Sokoto Caliphate, the largest theocratic society until the early twentieth century in West Africa, the horse featured in important Islamic festivals (such as Eid-al-Kabir and Eid-al-Fitr) through which religious authorities institutionalized their ideology.

The colonial durbar was thus an invented tradition that appropriated and transfigured precolonial Islamic culture, military authority, and equine spectacle to meet imperial ideals of submission and post-Victorian pageantry. The repackaging of the precolonial durbar under colonial rule did not end precolonial horse-centered performance because horses continued to feature in royal processions, acrobatic displays, and reenactments of precolonial cavalry power during countless coronation ceremonies and public religious festivals. Rather, the colonial government strategically created and curated a form of durbar to place indigenous expressions of loyalty and statecraft at the center of imperialism by expanding old and creating new venues, dates, and honorees.[107] Consequently, one can identify two overlapping types of durbar in the first half of the twentieth century—"indigenous" and "colonial" durbar—based on the degree of involvement of the colonial masters and local chiefs and the manifestation of imperial might.[108]

The royal durbar of 1956 held in Kaduna to commemorate the visit to Nigeria by Queen Elizabeth II and the Duke of Edinburgh was by far the most spectacular of all durbars held throughout colonial Nigeria.[109] Taking place on February 2 and witnessed by sixty thousand people, it was also the most documented—thanks to the modern media technology employed by local and international visitors and journalists who recorded their impressions in detail.[110] The fame of the 1956 royal durbar traveled across the world, providing opportunity for Europeans to see a rare image of northern Nigeria. "What image does the average newspaper reader or cinemagoer abroad retain of all he saw and read three years ago?" asked Kirk-Greene, attempting to reconstruct the thought of the British people. "The unhesitating answer of millions overseas is: Durbar."[111] The publicity given to the journey of the 1956 durbar horses to Kaduna mirrored similar coverage given to people directly involved in the royal visit. In documenting the journey of durbar horses and their handlers across northern Nigeria to Kaduna, the *Nigerian Citizen* newspaper, under a headline "Preparing for the Durbar: The Great Trek Begins in North," stated that "never before in the history of Nigeria has there been anything quite like it." The paper then attempted to place the massive event within the context of similar imperial spectacles held in other parts of the British Empire: "Indeed, it is probably true to say that this is the first time that a trek of such magnitude has formed part of preparation for Royal Tour celebration in any country in the British Commonwealth." The newspaper prediction that "the Great Trek of 1956 will be spoken of and remembered for many years to come" indeed came to pass.[112] The appearance and orderliness of horses were truly important to the success of colonialism, which the queen came to witness. In total, 2,456 horses mounted by "well-dressed Nigerians" were mobilized from across northern Nigeria.[113] A temporary veterinary post was erected in each region to ensure the animals were "robust, healthy and among the finest" and free from "infection, disease, debilitation, and lameness."[114] Because some of the horses had to travel through the tsetse fly zone, another temporary veterinary post was set up close to the venue of the durbar to do a final check to ensure that the equine contingent arrived under safe conditions.[115] The vets checked for sores and any symptoms of physical degeneration that the horses may have suffered during a trek that, for some, lasted weeks, depending on the distance of their travel to Kaduna. The northern Sokoto contingent comprised five hundred horses and twelve hundred handlers who journeyed more than four hundred miles; their Adamawa counterparts from the northeastern part of the country made a journey of about five hundred miles over an entire month.[116]

Prisoners were mobilized to cut and dry hay for placement along major roads leading to Kaduna. In addition, Mallam Halilu Kano, a third-class veterinary officer with proven knowledge of horse behavior, was commissioned to head a group of marshals, who were "well dressed in their most picturesque riga [loose-fitting robe]." They stood in front of the royal box to guide the horsemen as they wheeled before the stand to give the royal salute.[117] European veterinary officers and their African assistants were on standby at the starting line, to ensure that horses that developed last-minute sickness received care, while dozens of cobblers repaired harnesses as needed. Bello, who dedicated an entire chapter to the royal visit in his autobiography, noted that one "would not think at first sight that veterinary officers would be particularly involved" at the royal durbar.[118] Rex Niven, a colonial officer who was actively involved in the planning, described the veterinary arrangement as "complicated"— apparently for lack of an appropriate word for the thoroughness of veterinary care for the horses.[119]

The horses gathered at the royal durbar of 1956 were not nameless or anonymous colonial subjects. Archival materials provide some interesting biographical information about them. They all belonged to high-ranking chiefs of the native authority who felt honored to have their best horses pay homage to the most important person in the British Empire. The ages of a group of two hundred from Sokoto ranged from six to fourteen years. While Shettima Zana Kari, belonging to the Sultan of Sokoto, was the youngest horse, the oldest, Zakaria Jajari, belonged to an unnamed district chief. The most expensive horse, Mastaf Dauro, was worth £100, while the least expensive, Aba Kari, was valued at £30. Their colors included liver, bay, brown, chestnut, black, white, and silver gray. Only five of the houses were assessed to be in "fair" condition by the European veterinarians' judgment; the remainder were rated either good or very good. None was classified as bad or lame. Their facial markings were representative of the kinds of equines found in northern Nigeria—blaze, stripe, star and snip, star and nose, and star and blaze.[120]

The royal horse salute, or jahi—the peak of horsemanship—was rehearsed several times before the durbar day. Bello, like other local and foreign observers and journalists, characterized the jahi charge as the "most exciting incident," the "climax of the unforgettable day," a "distinguishing feature," the "most hair-raising method of paying respect," an "unforgettable sight," "breathtaking," "incredible," the "most stupendous" aspect of the entire durbar spectacle.[121] Led by the *Shehu* of Bornu, the jahi royal salute of 1956 was described as "a wave of galloping horsemen who in their enthusiasm ignored white lines and stewards swept in, and a wildly cheering mass, waving swords and spears right up to the steps of the dais."[122]

There was more to the royal jahi salute than the galloping of horses and the threatening charge of the cavalry toward the dignitaries. The dialectic of seeing and being seen fed into a reconstruction of wartime bravery—not for the old indigenous rulers, for whom it was created, but for the new colonial power. The trading of political space and the dialectic of recognition were beyond mere performance of horsepower. In all practicality, the Crown replaced the Turban as commander of the faithful, with all the indisputable authority to wage war, appoint Emirs, and reconfigure the local power structure. The fierce charge of arrow- and lance-bearing horsemen brought to a halt just a few feet from the royal pavilion where the queen was seated simulated and reproduced the act of rebellion, which ended with ultimate fealty. It ritually recognized the possibility of revolt while also affirming submission to authority through a well-choreographed mock face-off.[123]

The conduct of the jahi charge mirrored similar ones held for important people, yet the queen missed what both Africans and Europeans thought was the peak of it all—the sudden rearing of the horse to its haunches with forelegs in the air. The government deliberately prevented this display, which many believed was an act of cruelty to the animal, for it involves the application of excessive force on the bit, which causes sores in the horse's mouth. As the queen was a patron of the Royal Society for the Prevention of Cruelty to Animals, it would be inappropriate for her to witness a practice that the animal welfarism movement in Nigeria opposed. The conduct of the horses, like that of humans, must be made to conform with ideals of civilization and the achievement of British imperialism that the queen had come to celebrate. She seemed to appreciate the spectacle of the durbar when she remarked, "This great concourse of men and horses has brought home to me the respect which you have for your ancient traditions."[124]

The royal durbar of 1956, thanks to the colorful photography and film preserved, provides historians the opportunity to go beyond the enchantment of the jahi salute to view how horse costumes mirrored the power structure and reflected local aesthetics and artistic ingenuity.[125] Being a durbar horse meant more than being ridden by elites or being well groomed; it also extended to the quality of the costume worn at important events. The durbar horses wore livery made of silk, leather, and velvet and designed with varying artistic details around the head, feet, and loins. In addition to individual horses' costumes, which reflected the taste and hierarchy of their owners, some contingents (like that of Bornu that wore trousers on their forelegs) also adopted a uniform motif aimed at creating a distinct appearance.[126] Horse costumes added a compelling layer of meaning to horse's physical appearance. For the British, a fine horse for a durbar was a healthy one, free from back sores, and ridden respectfully with humane bits; for the locals, physical fitness was as important as the gorgeous appearance. Unbeknown to most colonial officers, the horse contingents appeared at the durbar grounds prepared to engage in a stiff competition for the best-dressed horses. If expensive turban and riga served as the visual iconography for indexing local chiefs in accordance with the power they wielded in the colonial structure, horse costumes expanded the prestige of horse ownership, enabling rich personages to make political statements through their horses. Such statements were expected to result in political actions, privileges, and access to exclusive opportunities. Here, as in many other sites of power and self-fashioning, horses helped humans to define and redefine their own humanity.

A colonial Nigeria without the horse and donkey would have evolved in a different way. Durbars and horse racing with all the transformations they unleashed would not have existed. The pace, process, and administration of the colony would have taken a different turn. But historians do not study what would have happened—they are concerned with what did transpire and the consequences thereof. We know that the horse and donkey contributed to the making of a new world for Nigerians, deploying their biological attributes while responding to the new roles humans required them to play. They were colonial subjects in that they served imperialism first as instruments of conquest and later as tools of domination. They were also modern beings because their attitudes, behavior, and presence produced or conformed to core features of civilization and colonial progress. In the next chapter, we will turn our gaze on another animal—the dog—whose story as "man's best friend" complements that of the horse and donkey.

3 ⌒ "Dogs Are the Most Useful Animals"

A Canine History of Colonial Nigeria

Besides being amusing and interesting, dogs are the most useful animals. They help their masters in various ways, dogs assist them and protect the house free from the sharp practice of the night robbers all over Yorubaland. They increase the pleasure of the farmers by providing for them edible bush meats during the dry season of each year. . . . Dogs are often more faithful and helpful to their masters than human beings are to one another.

—S. S. Oyetunde et alia, 1942[1]

Recently I took my dog to the Cinema theatre. Then suddenly, at the crack of a gun-shot, it started up and barked. I managed to coax it into silence, but from that time it kept up a constant expression of its emotional re-action to the performances of the actors—groaning when the "desperado" was chained to a tree, grunting as if in jealousy when the damsel was kissed and whining when the damsel slapped her assistant.

—Oye Shobo, "Emotional Dog!," *Daily Service*, July 17, 1954

In 1959 Horst Ulrich "Ulli" Beier, one of the few European residents of colonial Nigeria truly qualified to write about Africa from the perspective of Africans, wrote an interesting account of dog-human relations titled "Yoruba Attitude to Dogs." A proud breeder of multiple generations of local dogs and a distinguished African art promoter and culture enthusiast, Beier helped found the literary magazine *Black Orpheus* and the cultural group Mbari Club, which initiated a turning point in transnational cultural production and circulation of African artistic talent. His account—a deconstructionist posture on European attitudes toward African canines—contributes a voice to the broader Afrocentric discourse that supplied the intellectual weapon for decolonization by integrating animals into the repertoire of knowledge that was mostly about humans. Beier was essentially decolonizing the Yoruba dog.

"At first sight, it might seem that Yoruba people care little for dogs," Beier writes, setting the tone for his cross-cultural discourse of dogs in the opening sentence of his account. He goes on to state observations of dogs in everyday life: "[They] seem to run astray in the village and, except for children, nobody seems to play with them. Frequently one sees them being chased away and lorry drivers kill them recklessly. Worst of all, they are eaten!" While not disputing the obvious fact that "Yoruba do not pamper their dogs as Europeans do," his further statement that "it is wrong to conclude that the Yoruba 'do not care for dogs' merely because they fail to turn them into lap dogs" invites readers to think about emotional sensibilities and physical bonding with animals from an African viewpoint.[2]

From religion, spirituality, founding of communities, and social cohesion to hunting, sanitation, security, and human companionship, Beier puts historical and ethnographic narratives in conversation with each other in highlighting the many roles of dogs among the Yoruba. He recounts the biography of a famous war dog named Lekewogbe in 1840s Yorubaland, reprints a praise poem, and argues that the Yoruba canine had a place in the popular conception of heroism.[3] In another account, "Dog Magic of Yoruba Hunter," Beier delves deeper into humans' fondness for animals, describing the Yoruba dog as "attractive and intelligent" and "excessively affectionate and attached." Yet he was convinced that "attachment to animals" observable among Europeans was a unique "kind of dog fondling and dog sentimentality."[4] He narrated two separate stories involving two of his dogs (named Tantolorun and Eefinniwa) to explicate the spiritual dimension of dog-human relations.[5]

Beier's audience was definitely not the Yoruba or any indigenous Nigerian ethnicity that would accept all the material and symbolic roles of the animal. Rather, he was writing as a European with a privileged African-centered perspective on an animal whose identity was embedded in colonial prejudice. Beier did not explain why he focused on Yoruba dogs alone or if he thought that the behavior of these dogs differed from that of dogs living among other ethnicities. He was probably aware that the experience of Yoruba dogs must be different from that of dogs of other geoethnic enclaves. And like any ethnically conscious ethnographic account, his avoids generalizations, instead focusing on the immediate geocultural space of the dogs he observed and lived among. Arguably, Beier was convinced that dogs were also "ethnic" bodies—in addition to possessing other identities imposed on them by humans.

This chapter explores the social history of dogs in colonial Nigeria. The indigenous dog population of colonial Nigeria expanded tremendously as humans' impact on the environment intensified demographic transformation. New breeds of foreign dogs brought from Europe and North America, in particular, led to diversification of the canine population (both biologically and culturally), creating a major expansion in the symbolic and practical importance of dogs as "man's best friend." If it was scientifically tasking to produce mixed-breed cattle, it was relatively easy to breed dogs of local and exotic parentage. Dogs' identities were constructed by both colonialists and Africans in ways that aligned with divergent understandings of canines' place in the natural order and in relation to human life. Hence, such fluid categories as "pet," "utility," and "taxable," in addition to ethnic-centered designations, reflected the complex pattern of dog-human relations in a racialized colonial society where social class, power dynamics, ethnicity, and location (among other paraphernalia of identity) determined the place of both human and nonhuman creatures. Dogs have thus adapted to the myriad of roles that humans have allowed them to play. From memoirs of colonial officers to petitions and newspaper articles written by Nigerians, Africans and Europeans documented their experiences with their dogs.

Yet all dogs (regardless of breed, ownership, or place of abode) were also modern animals and colonial subjects. They were expected to conform to the ethos of a modern society in their social behavior, bodily habits, public presence, and observable mannerisms. Most of the discussions about the dog tax, dog fancying, and crossbreeding were informed by humans' framing of how dogs should exist as subjects of a colonial state. Even indigenous cultural practices that placed dogs at the center of daily spiritual life were affected by the practical and symbolic ideologies of dog modernism. During the first half of the twentieth century, many people thought that all local African dogs belonged to the same breed or ancestry. We now know that they were in fact genetically diverse, even though the idea of a "pariah" dog, "pye-dog," or "village dog" (i.e., one living on the margins of the wild and the tame) has been around for a long time. The modern dog emerged in Nigeria, socially, when Nigerian city dwellers began to reassign "conventional" roles to dogs, turning them into parlor animals and companions in new sites of imperial power and modernity such as cinema houses. A new culture of dog fancying emerged as part of

Africans' quest to be "modern." The central idea that shaped dog taxation was also precipitated by elastic notions of modernity. Thus, being a modern dog was not just about living in the city but also responding to imperial ideology about economic obligation, regardless of location. Colonialism produced both modern animals and modern humans.

THE UTILITY DOG

During the period covered in this book, dogs continued to play the roles they were known for in precolonial times (guard, hunter, companion), while also adapting to the changes wrought by colonialism. African dogs appear in the history of colonial conquest even though scholars have all but ignored this. They were loyal combatants at war as well as victims of the violence that made colonialism possible.[6] One of the best-known canine victims of colonial conquest was Chuku, who was rescued during the Aro Expedition (1901–2) into the heartland of Igboland (see fig. 3.1).[7] After the "pacification" of the country, African dogs became colonial subjects. Their experience under colonialism was determined by such factors as the socioeconomic class of their owners and the impression on the part of the British of the level of "civilization" of the community or dominant ethnicity where they lived. As they moved from one part of the colonial state to

FIGURE 3.1. Chuku (ca. 1902). *Source:* Constance Larymore, *A Resident's Wife in Nigeria* (London: George Routledge, 1908).

another, they enjoyed or suffered opportunities and limitations informed by humans' unstable perceptions toward them.

A dog, in mainstream African discourse of the canine, could only be a utility or practical animal (as food, hunter, collateral, currency or means of exchange, ritual being, watchdog, travel companion, scavenger); it could not be a pet, for a pet dog was a "jobless" and fancy animal.[8] Hunting, as a cultural and economic activity, placed dogs at the center of everyday life in rural and suburban communities.[9] The end to civil unrest after the imposition of colonialism reordered the domestic economy, diverting the energy of precolonial warriors and empire builders into economic activities such as hunting. The intensity of hunting was shaped by environment and season.[10] As this chapter's first epigraph establishes, hunting increased during the dry season when thinner vegetation enhanced visibility and movement of humans and animals. The soil was also drier, improving dogs' quick pursuit of game such as cane rats and small antelope (see fig. 3.2). In another instance, the paucity of gunpowder used for firing a Dane gun increased reliance on dogs. In all, for hunting with dogs to

FIGURE 3.2. Hunters, their dogs, and their prey at Okene (1957). Courtesy of Derek Miles Greening.

be successful, a close relationship must exist between the hunter and the dog. This cordial relationship involves significant trust built around mutual respect and developed over time. Hence, prospective hunting dogs were usually acquired young and gradually socialized into the hunting culture.[11] And the practice of sharing the hunt with the dog further solidified human-animal relations. The Yoruba saying "We must greet the dog: he is the only animal that kills other animals for us to eat" pays tribute to a unique service rendered by dogs.[12] Dogs, like their hunter owners, were also occasional victims of hunting—they could be mauled by a dangerous beast. The *Nigerian Pioneer* reported in May 1916 that some young boys who set out to kill cane rats lost fifteen of their eighteen hunting dogs to a "full grown" leopard in Abeokuta. The leopard in question was later killed by an "intrepid young man."[13]

The nutrition and bodily habits of dogs placed African and European conceptions of filth at odds. If Europeans believed that allowing dogs to eat feces was unhygienic, Nigerians did not. Thus, a "feral" dog to the government was a valued "sanitation" utility dog to the people. The statement "Dogs help us in the sanitation of the town by eating up the excreta of our babies" by the *Deji* (king) of Akure in a 1948 petition gave the canine an important agency in public hygiene.[14] In addition, military officer A. J. N. Tremearne, who joined the colonial army in 1902 and who held mostly prejudiced attitudes toward Africans, made an exceptional "compliment" that "there is very little refuse. . . . The remains of the night's food are usually eaten the following morning, or are given to the dogs or vultures, while any loose grain is soon picked up by the fowls and goats."[15] Yet this statement does not suggest that the dog's scavenging behavior was permissible from the Western point of view. Tremearne's observation seemed to be based on household waste management only. He believed that, outside the household, the filth in Africa, more than malaria, endangered Europeans' health. "But the quantity of dirt which Europeans eat and drink is easily surpassed by that which finds its way into the insides of the natives, some of whom seem to revel in it," Tremearne wrote. "Perhaps it is necessary to their digestion, as is, I believe, the case with dogs, but whether necessary or not, they certainly get it," he said, associating animal habits with humans in the familiar racist language of era.[16]

In another vein, some of what European writers defined as filth—"vile beyond description," in missionary G. T. Basden's words—were sacrifices, placed at locations across communities and consumed by dogs, among other domestic animals, through which the spirit world was believed to communicate with the living who prepared the sacrifice for a multiplicity of purposes.[17] Spiritual food or sacrifices must be consumed—as evidence that prayers and wishes were accepted by the gods and goddesses. Dog keeping therefore was tied to a much bigger experience of spirituality and natural order. Their nutrition was based on the ecology, as well as the food culture and settlement patterns, of their place of abode. Hence, the colonialists' assumption that they ate only waste or "filth" is incorrect.

Dogs, like other domesticated animals, were often sacrificial beings—they featured prominently in spiritual and religious observances.[18] Animal blood sacrifice was believed to strengthen the relationship between humans and the ancestral world, which had significant power over people. Yet certain spiritual attributes of the dog (which enhanced its use for indigenous medicine) open interesting narratives about human-animal relations coded in facts, legends, and myth that most communities take seriously. For instance, there are two complementary stories about why dogs are sacrificed to Ogun, the Yoruba god of warfare and hunting, worshipped by anyone who used implements made of iron.[19] One version stated that a dog once bit Ogun's penis, and to prevent the dog from swallowing, Ogun severed its neck. Thus, it became mandatory for Ogun worshippers to behead a dog for worship. Another stated that Ogun asked for dogs, the most useful animal to the hunter, to test humans' degree of commitment to him. The following are the names of other Yoruba deities and their dogs: Esu (Madigbolesu), Sango (Lube), and Erinle (Omidunsin).[20] The place of the dog in indigenous faith is further enhanced by metanarratives centered around the creation of communities, identities, and ethnicities. The dog featured in myths about origins of death among the Igbo and in turning points in the history of communities such as Ara in southwestern Nigeria, where a yearly dog festival named Mobo served "as a symbol, reminding them of their own weaknesses and the need to acknowledge and seek divine help."[21]

Like many features of traditional African spirituality, dog-centered sacrifices underwent a transformation that reflected cross-cultural contact. The motorcar was a Western technological development that came through colonialism. Yet Nigerian car drivers treated their vehicles as an emblem of Ogun because they contained an iron alloy, steel. A shrine to Ogun was a common sight in public parking lots in colonial southwestern Nigeria where annual celebrations of Ogun featured dog sacrifice. The El Khalil Motor Drivers Union slaughtered dogs to "appease the god of iron against sudden motor accidents" in the New Year, reported the *Daily*

Service in January 1952.[22] Indeed, the popularity of Ogun worship and dog sacrifice increased in the city due to the spiritual and practical explanation of causation of auto accidents. A successful driver would be loyal to Ogun and apply basic driving caution and rules to avoid accidents. During his visit to eastern Nigeria in 1960, German writer Janheinz Jahn observed that the driver of the lorry he wanted to board tied the head of a little dog and pieces of iron (two of the emblems of Ogun) to the steering wheel. When he asked the driver why he should trust him to take him safely to Lagos, he replied, "I make good driving. . . . I know all rules." Jahn's interpretation of the duality of using Ogun for protection and obeying traffic rules to avoid accidents is a correct representation of the ways the Yoruba perceived the danger of modern technology and the importance of indigenous faith and spirituality.[23]

Similarly, dog barking went beyond what the colonialists and some African elites defined as "noise." In addition to barking to ward off thieves and alert the household in the physical world, dogs were believed to be sensitive to the invisible world (responding with barks to avert spiritual danger).[24] Hence, dogs, in local cosmology, did not bark for no reason. Beyond their spiritual importance, dog barks and sounds of different animal species and human activities were part of the auditory rhythm of daily life in settled communities. Dogs also observed barking restrictions. Seemingly able to sense sorrow and solemnization during burials and ritual fetes, they joined the human community in maintaining silence in honor of the departed. Another benefit of the canine, according to an African worldview, was found in a local medicine for gaining access to the invisible world that was prepared from dog eye mucus—another benefit of the canine where Western scientific empiricism was inadequate to explain the complex reality of daily life.[25]

THE PET DOG

Writing about dogs compels scholars to think about colonialism beyond just human agency. For one thing, aside from humans, dogs were the second most important agents of imperialism in Nigeria. If we call the British who came to Nigeria in the service of the empire "colonial officers," it is not out of place to designate the dogs who came with them "colonial dogs." Timing is an important factor in the indexing of dogs; thus, the experience of dogs who accompanied their owners in the conquest of Nigeria was different from that of those brought after the firm establishment of colonialism and of colonial cities and in the wake of Western veterinary advances.

Collectively, the dogs (regardless of breed or genealogy) of both officials and nonofficials would be designated as "Whites' dogs." Why is this categorization necessary? Obviously, dogs did not make rules, nor did they oversee daily life in the colony, as humans did. However, in Nigeria, as in other colonial sites, the rights and privileges that each group possessed was based on race, gender, power relations, and position in the colonial hierarchy. The Westerners in Nigeria, whether British colonial officers, expatriates, or members of the non-African business community from Europe, the Middle East, and North America, extended their privileges to their dogs.[26] Dogs in Nigeria were, in a sense, racialized beings. They were frequently used as proxies—"a blow against them therefore serves as a blow against their owners."[27] Categories like "colonial" and "Whites" are fluid, socially and historically unstable, and problematic. In changing contexts, many non-Africans (including Lebanese and Syrians), and their dogs, enjoyed some of the privileges of Whites.

The diaries and memoirs of early colonial officers take us into the lived experience of dogs as imperialist coagents. Aside from basic supply materials such as food, medicine, and guns, early conquerors of African territories saw the dog as a vital tool and companion in their tropical adventures. The animals' experiences were thus deeply intertwined with their owners' as they voyaged across the seas and hazardous inland terrain, traveled aboard train coaches, and enjoyed the beautifully kept gardens of government stations and segregated neighborhoods. From Frederick Lugard, who sailed out of Liverpool on July 28, 1894, with a grand bull terrier, and Langa Langa (H. B. Hermon-Hodge), who came to the country in 1908 with Peggy, a spaniel, to Constance Larymore, arguably the first European woman to live in northern Nigeria, who brought Binkie (a fox terrier) and Timmie (an Irish terrier) in 1902—one sees the role of dogs as more than a mere travel companion.[28] Their experiences were laden with triumphs and affections, and their loss or death met with sorrow on the part of their owners. Like Joan Sharwood-Smith and Larymore, colonial officer's wife Lassie Fitz-Henry dedicated a portion of her memoir to the life of her pets (Horace the goat, George the grass monkey, several kittens, chickens, and dogs), whom she described as "animal friends," who were given to her in Oturkpo.[29]

While many colonial officers brought their dogs directly from Europe, some acquired theirs while in Nigeria. "As some sort of compensation" for leaving their two children behind in England, Sharwood-Smith and her resident officer husband, Bryan, acquired two dogs—Gogo, an English cocker spaniel, and Poppy, a fox terrier—when they returned to Sokoto in northern Nigeria after their leave in 1945.[30] In addition, Fitz-Henry and her colonial officer husband, Billy, who arrived shortly after World War II, became guardians of Mr. Perkins, an Irish terrier, and Beetle, a small black-and-white fox terrier, when their European owners went on leave.[31] Derek Miles Greening, who was hired by the Northern Region's Public Works Department as executive engineer in Kabba Province in 1955, did not arrive with a dog. He became owner of Trixie during his four-year stay in northern Nigeria when her former owner left the country (see fig. 3.3). "I had known her [Trixie] for some time before he [the previous owner] left, and as I moved into his house, it was a natural transfer. She was a very

FIGURE 3.3. Trixie (1958). Courtesy of Derek Miles Greening.

faithful dog and followed me everywhere, even on to the dance floor when we had such an occasion," Greening recollected. The distress of Greening's permanent separation from Trixie in 1959 contrasted with the joy of his first encounter with her in 1955: "I left her with my successor as district engineer, Bida, with some sorrow I should say."[32] How different ownership shaped human-dog life would be an interesting topic for further research.

The colonial service did not underestimate the significance of dogs as coimperialists. While it was difficult for British men to receive approval to bring wives to the colony during the early stages of the colonial project, there seems not to have been any restriction on bringing dogs. The restriction on bringing female partners due to lack of modern facilities and the demands of colonial service may in itself have increased the popularity of dog companionship. From all indications, the colonial service was a dog-friendly endeavor, partly because care for dogs did not interfere, in a meaningful way, with the daily work schedule and core principles of colonial service. Unlike animals such as horses, dogs required minimal traveling arrangements and space. Many vessels would allow dogs to share the same coach with their owners. Private and government rest houses and hotels tended to welcome dogs. This meant that upon arrival in the country, dogs could be quickly integrated into the life of the colony.

References to dogs in the memoirs of colonial officers connected personal life with colonial adventure. For one thing, prospective members of the colonial service were encouraged to imagine a life with their favorite pet, far away from home. "This collection of notes, which aims at giving assistance to English men and women in Nigeria, would, to my mind, fall miserably short of the mark if it failed to include within its scope practical suggestions for the provision of comfort and the preservation of health of their dogs," Larymore states at the beginning of a chapter on "Dogs, Poultry and Cows" in her massive memoir of life in northern Nigeria published in 1908.[33] Her prediction that "English dogs would continue to come [to the colony] as long as Englishmen do" did come true.[34] In the mid-1950s, dogs were the largest (in number) of pets imported into Nigeria from abroad.[35] Having seen various types of English dogs—from massive bull terriers down to tiny Yorkshire terriers—being brought to northern Nigeria, Larymore recommended that puppies, well over distemper, of about six to twelve months old (weighing less than thirty pounds), would suffer less than older and heavier dogs. Not only would they be more amenable to new food and the Nigerian climate; they also would be more easily carried on horseback or in a box by human portage instead of trekking.

Larymore did not want others to repeat her mistake—Timmie, her "dearly loved little" Irish terrier "who marched always on his own feet," died within three months of arriving in Lokoja in central Nigeria due to long hours of walking in hot weather. The dog had lived under "perfect health" for four years in India and "weathered" eight months in Sierra Leone only to die shortly after arriving in Nigeria.[36] Other portions of her pet-advice manual focuses on nutrition, medication, and general care. Deductively, if humans require creativity in adapting to the Nigerian climate, so also do their dogs.

Europeans and other classes of foreigners who did not write memoirs documented their life with dogs in still photography and moving pictures, some of which were circulated across the empire. C. T. Lawrence captured on camera such cherished moments as having a meal and listening to a gramophone with his dog in the first decade of the twentieth century.[37] A photo of Walter Egerton, the governor of Lagos between 1903 and 1906, and three others having a meal features three dogs larking about the lawn of the government house.[38] Greening's camera captured Trixie's life with his family in different locales—from the undulating landscape of the Gurara Waterfalls in Niger Province and the swimming pool in Kaduna to the smooth deck of the Kano airport, from 1955 to 1959. A rare clip of footage of Francis and Betty Humphreys's family in 1947–48 in Kaduna, the administrative capital of northern Nigeria, with their two puppies, brings a researcher closer to the lived experience of colonial dogs than does any photo. Larymore and Langa Langa and their dogs, who lived in makeshift tents in the same region during the first decade of the twentieth century, did not enjoy the quality of life of the Humphreys and their canines, who lived in a gorgeous one-story government house. Betty took one of the puppies in a car ride to a polo game and later carried it on a fishing trip. The look on the face of a small girl (probably the child of one of the African servants) as Betty dries one of the wet puppies with a towel suggests a local's amazement at a European's dog fetish.[39]

The diversity of Nigeria's physical landscape figured significantly in the experience of colonial dogs. This factor rarely manifests in the pet-advice manuals, which tended to assume that all prospective colonial officers and their dogs would experience similar life in the colony. For instance, Larymore probably thought that incoming officers would be posted to remote areas in northern Nigeria, where trekking or "marching" (in the language of the time) over hundreds of miles was a sine qua non. So also did Tremearne, who brought a fox terrier and three kittens to northern Nigeria in 1903. His remarks that it is "certainly" unkind to bring English dogs to Nigeria unless "you are prepared to pay a special boy to look after them" and that the misery of going up rivers and of mosquito bites "made me determine never to bring another" did not apply to all colonial officers.[40] Another bit of advice by a colonial officer, simply identified as Major H, that whippets are the best dogs to take to the colonies because they "can run without feeling the heat much, and also follow on any march, however long, without tiring" was uncritical of the rigors of the colony's physical landscape.[41] On the contrary, many colonial dogs lived in the cities and towns, where trekking over a long distance was not a requirement of daily life. Their experience was different from that of Piccin, whose owner, Langa Langa, bought a pony trap to save her from the "weary trek" of twenty-four days across Bornu in the northeastern part of the country.[42]

In general, trekking distances within southern Nigeria were not as long as those in the North, where settled communities were separated by hundreds of miles. The expansion of motorized transportation and the entrenchment of colonial rule reduced typical trekking distances covered by dogs and their owners in the North. As the century progressed, colonialists' worries about the diet of both urban and rural colonial dogs eased, as they consumed less of the "dangerous" local food, given the regular supply of commercial dog food imported from Europe. By the 1940s government and private veterinary medical practices would complement human medicine, thus improving the health of dogs and increasing their life expectancy. Dogs were the most frequent pet patient at government veterinary clinics. In 1954–55, a total of 877 dogs, mostly belonging to Europeans, received treatment at the vet office in Lagos. More than half of the 3,885 animals treated at the Vom veterinary clinic during the same period were dogs.[43] Larymore's statement that "West Africa is *not* a healthy country for English dogs" applied only to the early era of colonial rule in northern Nigeria.[44] In 1908, when her book was published, many Whites' dogs in Lagos lived a much better life than their counterparts in Europe.

Regardless, Larymore and her counterparts clearly articulated the importance of dogs in the colonial adventure. Dogs in Nigeria were cherished by their European owners for the amusement they created. Letting them loose to run after other animals lessened the feeling of boredom that accompanied long travels and life in remote communities. Lugard's grand bull terrier, which would "tackle every living thing," caught sight of some sheep and made a beeline for them, worrying one almost to the point of death. "I believe he would go for an elephant or lion," Lugard estimated of his dog's audacity in his diary entry for August 12, 1894. So active was Lugard's dog that he would put it on a leash while shooting.[45]

Dogs' deaths and the attendant mourning of their owners, as painful as they were, further illuminate the intimate relationship between canines and humans. To watch a dog die of sickness (often blamed on the inclement environment, disease-inducing insects, or unsanitary conditions of Nigeria) represented, in a way, a gradual degeneration in the life of its human owner. To lose a dog entailed losing a comrade in the war against "primitivity," fought with European civilization. Yet nothing seemed more emotionally devastating than killing or ordering the killing of a dog to put it "out of its misery," as W. R. Crocker described the condition of his dog Chuck, who fell ill from a tsetse fly attack in September 1933. Chunk went blind and had to be carried around, for his body swelled. Just before Chunk was silenced, Crocker gave him his favorite food, then took cover in the nearby bush while a local teacher followed his instruction to fire a revolver into Chunk's ear, before burying him in a seven-foot-deep grave. "Death was instantaneous," Crocker's aide, who witnessed the shooting, related to him about the final minutes of Chunk's life. "Vale [farewell] Chunk," Crocker wrote in respect to his companion.[46]

Writing about life during and after a dog's death elongated the period and medium through which mourning continued to manifest. "Even now I hate to dwell on it," Langa Langa wrote in the subsection of his memoir, appropriately titled "The Tragedy of Piccin," about how he lost his dog when she fell off a train during their trip to Bornu around 1910. Langa Langa did not expect everyone to understand the pain of his losing Piccin: "No one who had never become entirely dependent on a dog for company for months at a stretch in the lonely, depressing outposts of beyond can possibly realize what a shock this loss was to me."[47] In reminiscing of his life with Chunk, Crocker pays a deserved tribute to a "constant companion, as constant as my shadow, for the last two years." He was "as affectionate and vivacious as he was good-looking," Crocker recalled of his lost friend in his journal entry of September 7, 1933.[48] Larymore's tribute to Binkie, whose "devotion and faithfulness to the last was very touching," was carefully written to evoke the maximum feeling of loss and despair in her readers. "When he was too ill to walk," Larymore wrote about Binkie's final days, "he would painfully and slowly drag himself down the steps, across the gravel, and lie, exhausted . . . his head between his paws, watching the Resident's Office with wistful eyes for the return of his beloved master."[49] She then went on to reprint (verbatim) a mourning poem to a dead dog by a writer identified simply as G. W. F. G. in the *Spectator*, a British magazine on politics, art, and literature published in 1903, replacing the original title "Modie: A Fox Terrier" with "Binkie: A Fox Terrier." Acknowledging that "the unfortunate person who is not a dog-lover will simply skip" the poem, she asserts that any dog lover who has not read it will love it as she does:

> Not strange, perhaps, that, on her beat
> Nature should hush, by one wide law
> The patter of four fitful feet,
> The scrape of a persistent paw.
>
> And yet the house is changed and still
> Waiting to echo as before
> Hot bursts of purpose hard to chill
> And indignation at the door.
>
> No friendly task he left unplied,
> To speed the hour or while the days,
> The grief that mourned him when he died
> Spelt out his little meed of praise.
>
> They say he only thought in dreams.
> What matter! Lay the silken head
> Throbbing with half a world of schemes
> Under the silent flowers instead.
>
> The spring winds in the lilacs play
> Beside the old wall where he lies:
> The ivies murmur night and day
> Their tiny lisping lullabies.
>
> Then ask not if he wakes again:
> He meddled not in things too deep;
> And Nature, after joy or pain
> Gives nothing half so kind as sleep.[50]

The poem sets the context for the designation of Whites' canines as "pet" dogs in Nigeria. The origins of the social construction of Whites' dogs as "pet" dogs can be found in the observable roles of dogs within the racialized colonial society. To be a pet dog was to share almost the same living arrangement or space with the owner, enjoy limitless public attention and petting, stay mostly indoors, and eat "healthy." Pet dogs were part of the dressings of colonial power—they can be seen on the lap of their masters or roaming the gardens in the photos of official events that defined the daily life of the colony.[51] The physical presence of dogs at state events was no accident; neither was it a situation void of emotion. Dog owners did feel that their animals deserved to be represented—just like any faithful companion. The reciprocal respect colonial officers gave to their dogs went beyond mere verbal and literary expression in memoirs and other writings. If Whites in colonial Nigeria considered compulsory medical tests for themselves dishonorable, the same for their dogs was equally unacceptable. Therefore, Whites often refused to surrender their dogs for observation for rabies symptoms—a conventional procedure after a dog bite—until a superior power intervened.[52] "When he removed the indignant 'Piccin' from her chair at my side, I fear I became rude," Langa Langa expressed his feeling toward a fellow colonial officer, Dr. Thompson, who visited him without a prior appointment.[53] In another part of his memoir, he recorded his impression of a copassenger on a train about him and Piccin: "Mrs. Guggisburg, who had seen me sitting on the edge of my seat to make room for 'Piccin' to get comfortable, has chaffed me with the remark, 'I believe you'd do more for that dog than you would for a woman.'"[54]

Pet dogs were viewed by Nigerians and Europeans as not having any "practical" or "economic" role. They were rarely used for sanitation; thus, a pet dog could not be a "feral" canine, people thought. The few pet dogs that were used for hunting belonged to "bush" colonial officers, who engaged in recreational hunting to emulate European gentry. Most urban or city dogs would never take part in hunting but would help protect their master's home. The image of a European segregated community was partly that of an abode inhabited by "fox-looking" canines capable of unleashing violence on unwanted visitors. In fact, dogs were important bodies in policing the racial boundaries of colonialism. And the best-known case of race-based dog violence took place during the last decade of British rule in Nigeria. On June 29, 1954, Nigerian judge Mason Begho of the Lagos Magistrate Court sentenced Alexander Gregory, a British expatriate pottery inspector attached to the government's Department of Commerce and Industry, to either twelve months in prison or a £120 fine and three strokes of the cane for inciting his dog, Jane, a seven-year-old white bull terrier, to bite a Nigerian trader, Inua Gombe, who had gone to his quarters in Ikoyi, a Europeans-only neighborhood, to sell wares.[55]

Begho's judgment was informed by many factors, ranging from judicial fairness, Gregory's conduct before and during prosecution, and the medical and psychological impact of the dog bite on Gombe. In the first place, Begho thought that if Africans were flogged for similar offenses, Europeans, for the sake of "justice for all races," should also be caned. The second factor was deterrence. "On deciding to give him option of a fine," Begho wrote, "it occurred to me to add some strokes of the cane to deter him from trying such an offence again as fine alone would not have deterrent effect." Third, Gregory was accused of "not showing sympathy" for the injured Gombe but rather of kicking him "in the ground." Gombe incurred a dog-bite wound on his penis for which he received thirteen stitches.[56] According to the judge, "it was doubtful whether Gombe would ever be able to have full sexual satisfaction thereafter."[57] Begho, nicknamed the "dog-bite magistrate" by the press, made a medical, and to some extent male- and sexuality-centered, justification for including corporal punishment in his judgment.[58] When the matter was reported to the police, Gregory, who initially resisted arrest, had also refused to allow the Lagos Town Council to take his dog for a medical examination except by "written authority or warrant entitling them to remove it," while bragging about spending £100 to fly his dog from London.[59] The involvement of the highest-ranked colonial administration reflected in the decision of supreme court justice Olumuyiwa Jibowu, who overturned Begho's decision, removing the corporal punishment but keeping the fine.

What started as an action by the dog Jane, ostensibly protecting her master's house against an intruder in a colonial outpost, became a subject of debate in the House of Commons in the British Parliament, a press war between British and Nigerian media outlets, and, more importantly, a major issue in the politics of decolonization and racial justice.[60] It was not unusual to invite veterinary officers to court to comment on injuries sustained by humans or animals during a violent encounter. What was unusual in this case was how the defense and prosecution framed dog psychology and human factors in the dog's behavior. As multifarious as the legal questions were, the case would have taken a completely different turn if the defense could have proved that Jane was an angry dog. Generally, according to veterinary and sanitary officers invited to testify in the case, dogs would bite "either due to incitement or excitement."[61]

But Jane, the dog at the center of this prosecution, would not bite due to "excitement" but only due to "incitement." She was a healthy, rabies-free dog praised by veterinary officers and neighbors as "an extremely friendly animal"—not even the discomfort of pregnancy would make her bite in anger.[62] The dog's attitude was of vital importance in this case. Neither the veterinary doctors nor the prosecution believed Gregory's submission that "the dog in my opinion was startled by the sudden appearance of the trader and hence it jumped at him and bit him."[63]

From the foregoing, the common view that pet dogs lacked "utilitarian" value is incorrect. Such notions emerged, in part, out of the proliferation of puppies and small dog breeds that were unsuitable for hunting in European communities. In addition, the exotic appearance of Whites' dogs contributed to their construction as mere pet canines. This foreignness or uniqueness stood in contrast to indigenous dogs, most of whom were described by Europeans, including Basden and Tremearne, as "poor specimens" and as uniformly "pariahs," "curs," or "scraggy" dogs.[64] It would of course be misleading to accept the impression that all Africans' dogs belonged to one breed, for centuries of global contact had diversified the local African dog population. In Lagos and Kano, Europeans actively engaged in crossbreeding African and European dogs, for artificially constructed standardized looks rather than for utility. Yet carefully managed crossbreeding was inevitable and took place under a myriad of circumstances—well before male or female dogs from Europe arrived during the colonial era. This could have been the story of Piccin, the only surviving offspring of Peggy (a spaniel), whom Langa Langa brought from Britain. Described as a "gem" for surviving more than three hazardous tours in northern Nigeria, Peggy initiated a genealogy of mixed-breed dogs that Europeans in Nigeria in the 1920s and 1930s fancied.[65] Langa Langa was silent about the fatherhood of Piccin, but her photo suggests that she was a mixed breed.[66] Crocker said Chunk's pedigree included a dominant strain of Langa Langa's dogs (dating back to Peggy). "Several races were mixed in his blood, but all good," wrote Crocker, admirably describing the genetic background of Chunk, who was "black, touched, symmetrically and prettily, with tan and white; smooth hair; and an unusually fine head."[67] Poppy, one of Sharwood-Smith's dogs, was of "mixed African and European parentage."[68] Beetle, whom Fitz-Henry described as "near fox terrier whose ancestry always remained in doubt," probably had some African genes in her.[69]

Meanwhile, deliberate canine crossbreeding represents only a fraction of the diverse dog population. Dogs would not respect the color bar in love affairs and social networking. Even in a segregated European neighborhood, dogs of different ownership, age, and breeds socialized to have sex and share food and affection. The criticism of the "invasion" of European neighborhoods by "wild" and "feral" dogs of Africans was motivated by Whites' desire to prevent their dogs from having sex with Africans' canines, in addition to the fear of rabies.[70] Yet many Whites' dogs did not fit the profile of a pet dog; rather, they "degenerated" into pye-dogs, according to their owners. Hence, the notions that only an African dog could be a pye-dog or that all Europeans' dogs were pet dogs or that only Africans' dogs posed a medical threat to the Europeans are all incorrect. Timothy Johnson, who joined the Nigerian colonial service in 1936, rising after independence to the position of second in command to Ahmadu Bello, the premier of the Northern Region, made a good observation that corroborates this. In his assessment of the degeneration of his dogs, he remarked, "My pups have grown up into most revolting little pi-dogs and I have given them all away except one and I think he will follow shortly." He described the puppies' mother as "a nice old thing."[71] Breeding of large numbers of dogs to sell or keep as pets was only carried out by a small group of Europeans, most of whom were merchants or businessmen who had a fairly stable living arrangement in the cities, rather than colonial officers, who moved around a lot. One of the core features of European dog fancying was keeping just one or a few dogs, not only because it was expensive to keep many but also owing to the fear of their becoming pye-dogs, as Johnson's writing suggests. One practice of the era was to prevent female dogs in heat from getting pregnant by containing them or castrating the males. When their dogs had multiple births, Europeans would give away "excess" puppies or sell them. This practice was partly responsible for diversifying the local dog population with exotic genes.

Europeans' dog fancying did not stay within the bounds of their homes or well-tended lawns. From the 1920s or earlier, a constant attempt was made to integrate European ways into mainstream colonial culture of leisure through dog shows. Directly and indirectly, the shows fueled the proliferation of thoroughbred and mixed-breed dogs because the conditions for success were determined by physical features such as length of tail, style of hair, and other traits peculiar to exotic canines. To further popularize the dog shows, organizers, who generally were wives of colonial officers or expatriates, began to use them to promote social causes. Winners of one such dog show, which helped to raise money for the blind in Kaduna in July 1953, included Oscar, Fudge, and Tunkar, a black retriever.[72]

Similarly, dog racing in the European community was organized informally during regular social gatherings. Probably impressed by dog racing's increasing popularity among Europeans, two British veterans of World War II, R. Burns and L. F. Crossland, established a private firm, the West African Dog Racing Company, in Lagos shortly after 1945. The company built what may have been the first professional dog race track in Nigeria, near Ikoyi in Lagos. To generate public interest and make a profit, the company sought government approval to install a totalizator for betting. However, this was rejected because private establishments could not formally establish sports betting in Nigeria; only government-backed social clubs like the Lagos Race Club were allowed to operate a pari-mutuel.[73] Be that as it may, the company succeeded in placing dogs at the center of colonial sporting culture, not only by their entrepreneurial success but also by donating to social causes like education. Probably impressed by the success of the West African Dog Racing Company, a local business, owned by Matilda Soremekun, sought government permission to establish a dog-racing company in 1948.[74]

European dog fancying was infectious to the point that it transformed dog-human relations of urban Africans. In the cities, Africans, like Europeans, kept dogs as guards but rarely as a means of exchange or for hunting. Dogs played a limited role in the spiritual practices of city people, whose revolt against indigenous spirituality increased in tandem with the expansion of urban cosmopolitanism. To emulate Europeans, some urban Nigerians acquired exotic dogs who lived in many ways similar to Europeans' dogs—eating foreign commercial dog food, benefiting from regular access to veterinary doctors, and being fondled by their owners. Thus, pet dog culture also thrived within the urban African community (see fig. 3.4). "Strange things happen in Lagos day by day . . ."—so begins a *Daily Service* news item about a dog dressed in a jacket and trousers made from an expensive imported material locally called *olowondabira* (the rich performing wonders) and paraded around the main streets of Lagos on the eve of the Muslim festival of Eid-al-Fitr in July 1949.[75] It was a common practice for rich Africans to dress up domesticated animals, including some tamed monkeys, in expensive local attire as a show of wealth and to mock detractors. What is modern in this case was the suit the dog was wearing and the combination of indigenous and modern codes of respectability to demonstrate superior class. Similarly, urban Africans copied Europeans by taking puppies to public arenas like theaters and sports fields, thus expanding the space for their canines to encounter colonial modernity. In writing about his dog's reaction to movie actions, Shobo, in the second epigraph above, affirmed the agency of his dog to act independently. Documenting

FIGURE 3.4. *From left:* Adesegun Tunde-Olowu, Beautie the dog, and Adedapo Tunde-Olowu. Benin City (ca. 1969). Courtesy of Adedapo Tunde-Olowu.

the emotions of a dog for the public to read increased the repertoire of ideas consumed in the print media.[76]

THE TAXABLE DOG

The material and symbolic roles of canines in the economic, social, and spiritual lives of Africans and non-Africans, outlined above, convinced the government that imposing taxation on them would be a good source of revenue.[77] When colonial officers argued that they could address noise pollution by reducing the "native" dog population through high-priced dog licensure, they were reinforcing modernist notions of urban orderliness. Beyond generating income, dog taxation defined notions of citizenship, modernity, inclusion, and order, especially in the urban space. Proof of payment of the dog tax was required before a dog could be vaccinated; there was a nexus between economic and medical exigencies. When Akinpelu Obisesan, a diarist and member of the colonial intelligentsia in Ibadan, opined that "in a town where there was civilization there should be dog licence," he was pontificating a trope of colonial indoctrination, tying taxation to progress and modernity.[78] The sex of dogs in the dog-tax debate was of course important because of the procreative role of females. This is explicit in the minutes of a 1942 meeting of the Kano Township Advisory Board, which blamed bitches who "are prolific breeders and are in some cases continually adding to the already large number of unwanted dogs. These unwanted dogs eventually form themselves into packs and are directly responsible for the disturbance of the peace of residents in the Township which they invade in large numbers either in search of food or in the pursuit of bitches in heat."[79] Similarly, the idea that a dog tax would ensure that "every dog has a proper owner" reinforced the idea that the population of animals, like humans, can be properly enumerated for effective governance.[80] The extent to which consideration over revenue generation, on the one hand, outweighed public health, urban serenity, and modernity, on the other, was not static.

Regardless, the most difficult issue around dog taxation was not why it should be imposed; rather, it was how much to impose and when, who would collect it, and how contraventions of the law would be enforced.[81] The case of Shandam Division in Plateau Province can be used to further shed light on the difficulty of collecting the dog tax. Each household in this area kept from three to ten dogs in 1936. This meant that the government stood to realize significant revenue from a dog tax. However, settled communities in this division were not only far from the main center of colonial power; they were also composed largely of isolated hamlets and huts, covering several square miles. Similarly, the "pagan" communities on the outskirts of Kafanchan had a large canine population, with dogs "too numerous for our small Yan Doka force to control" were a new dog tax to be imposed, the assistant district officer of Jemaa worried.[82] The government thought that many would see the imposition of unequal dog license on communities across ethnicities and religions as unfair—a situation that could worsen the already deplorable relations between the colonial officers and the local community.[83]

Licensing dogs was a more popular policy in Lagos than in any other part of the country, not only because the city had a longer history of dog levies but also because taxes were generally easier to collect in the city than in the rural communities due to the numbers of police and town council officers. The regular outbreak of rabies in the city encouraged many to pay for dog licenses, which were a prerequisite for receiving a rabies vaccination. In 1936 the central government in Lagos attempted to provide a nationwide solution to the lack of enforcement of dog licensing. It recommended 15/- for female and 10/- for male dogs nationwide. The imposition of high taxes on female dogs recognized their higher economic value owing to reproduction.

This first major attempt to implement a dog tax across the country faced a myriad of challenges, partly because it was unpopular among the traditional elites whose support the government needed for smooth collection of the levy. Ideally any form of taxation that would swell the native authority's treasury should be welcomed by the chiefs. But public governance under colonial rule, as violent as it was, had to consider the impact that new legislation would have on the image of the traditional chiefs, who were closer to the people than were the district or resident officers. The *Ooni* (king) of Ile-Ife advised the government to reduce the cost of a dog license to 6d. for both sexes, arguing that a higher tax "would seem oppressive" to the class of people who kept dogs for security, religious sacrifice, sanitation, or hunting. His assertion that among his people a "dog is not kept as a pet" was informed by the established idea that Africans' dogs were kept for "practical" and "utilitarian," not aesthetic, values. Yet his caveat that government should increase dog taxes only if it "foresees any evil in not doing so" was political. It resembled one of the principles of indirect rule by which the traditional chiefs allowed the government to have its way in the interest of modernization and public order.[84] In this case, the "evil" of not enforcing the dog tax is clear, given that licensing was a means of requiring vaccination against rabies.

In 1937 Ibadan Division became the first area in the western provinces (outside Lagos) to commit to a new dog-tax regime. Instead of following the Lagos recommendation, it imposed a levy of 1s. and 7s. 6d. on Africans' and Europeans' dogs, respectively, regardless of sex.[85] Rural dogs used for hunting were excluded, partly because of the difficulty of collecting levies and the tensions it might cause. The "discrimination" in the taxes imposed on Europeans and Africans, the acting secretary of the southern provinces emphasized, "is justified on the ground that Europeans usually keep a dog as a pet whereas an African keeps a dog for hunting or other practical purposes."[86] Of course, Whites' dogs did help secure their masters' homes, but colonial officers and local chiefs treated them as "pets" with limited "practical" use. By the early 1940s most communities in the western provinces had dog taxes (ranging from 1s. to 2s.)—far from the 10s. to 15s. recommended by the central government in Lagos.

The idea that Africans should pay a lesser tax because their dogs were not pets contravened a core principle that taxation on hunting as well as breeding and selling of dogs was justified by authorities because these were economic transactions, on which taxes must be paid to the colonial state. The criticism of higher taxes for Whites' dogs was shaped by two closely related assumptions: that Europeans were better caregivers for their dogs and that dog taxes were high in Nigeria—higher even than in Britain, where residents paid 7s. 6d. The Ondo district officer's argument in critiquing higher taxes on Whites' dogs, that "it is not the European dogs which spread rabies," was incorrect—both African and European dogs were vectors of the disease.[87] The district officer of Ibadan's position that it is immaterial whether a dog was kept for "practical" purposes or as a pet established another dissenting voice against the idea of different taxes for Europeans and Africans.[88] Although it did not clearly say so, the government probably sought additional income from the European community because its expatriates, merchants, and representatives of foreign firms had good-paying jobs.

The transcript of the 1941 meeting of the residents of the northern provinces gives a vivid insight into the politics of licensing dogs in the region. Like in the western provinces, dog licensing had been in effect in the North since the first decade of the twentieth century, but the policy was rarely implemented. To administer dog licensing, an enumeration of household property would be required, according to colonial officers. Such a process would be difficult: treating dogs as items to be counted for imposing taxes would open another site of tension and increase the already difficult task of administrating "pagan" communities, which were mostly rural and far from urban centers and provincial capitals. The assertion by the resident of Adamawa Province that "it is difficult enough to count children in many places; it will be still more difficult to count dogs" points to one obvious problem of governance.

In the end, the resident officers imposed taxes of 15s. and 10s. on female and male dogs, respectively, in European areas; Africans in townships were to pay 7s. 6d. and 2s. 6d. on female and male dogs, respectively. Their counterparts in rural areas had to pay a tax of 1s. on bitches but none on male dogs. This tax regime was informed by race, social class, level of "enlightenment," and location.[89] The critique of the resident of Kano that dog licensing "is an imposition for which no return or service is made to the payers" would appear more valid in rural communities, with limited government infrastructure, than in townships, where residents enjoyed some benefits of taxation such as modern infrastructure.[90] This tax regime was maintained into the 1950s with some upward revision. A 1953 revision in Zaria imposed a fee of 15s. on male dogs and 20s. on bitches in the European neighborhood and 7s. 6d. and 10s. on males and females, respectively, in the African communities of Tundun and Sabo.[91]

The situation in the eastern provinces bore some resemblance to what obtained in the northern and western provinces.[92] Up to the outbreak of World War II, fewer people paid for dog licenses in the East. In Ogoja Province, for instance, only sixty-three dogs were licensed in 1937.[93] Unlike in the western and eastern provinces, race was not a factor in the imposition of the dog tax, but township and proximity to the district office were. In Onitsha Province, for instance, residents of the following towns, regardless of race, paid 10s. and 15s. for male and female dogs, respectively: Awgu, Awka, Nsukka, Nnewi, Udi, and Agbani.[94] Archival materials are silent over the response of the local chiefs to dog taxes. But the comment of the resident of Onitsha that no native authority in his province "is really fitted to administer" dog licenses suggests that he did not trust the chiefs to help collect an unpopular levy.[95] This is probably why dog licenses only covered territories within a radius of two miles from the district offices, to enhance effective compliance.[96]

Among the problems the post-1936 tax regime created was the failure to recognize the economic value of the animal, as determined by breed, size, and medical condition. In many rural communities in the 1930s, the local economic value of dogs ranged from 2s. to 7s. according to size and sex. A tax of 1s. would represent 50 percent of the animal's capital value. A yearly tax of 1s. and vaccination fee of 10s. would increase the cost of keeping a dog more than its real economic value within a year. The vaccination fee was administered irrespective of the diverse socioeconomic landscape of Nigeria and its inhabitants. The fusion of economic matters with concerns over public health in the designing of a dog tax and vaccination fee produced conflicting outcomes. Few people thought that their animals should be taxed; fewer believed the vaccine was effective against rabies. In the whole of northern Nigeria in 1953, only three thousand out of the ten thousand vaccines ordered by the government were expended, even after the cost of vaccines was reduced from 10s. to 5s. Vaccines were potent only if used within three months of production,[97] and most veterinary and medical offices lacked the facilities to store vaccines at the required average temperature of sixty degrees Fahrenheit. Northern Nigeria's acting civil secretary remarked that resistance to payment of the dog tax "means a loss of revenue to the native treasuries," emphasizing the economic impact of public disobedience to the law.[98] In 1953 veterinary officers in Enugu and Jos gave out (free of charge) their unused vaccines to avoid loss.[99]

The tying of dog licensing to control of rabies and the canine population was justified only when viewed entirely from the perspectives of the animals' lack of geographical mobility. The movement of animals across the Nigeria's physical geography was as fluid as that of humans. Thus, a rural dog today could be an urban one tomorrow, especially among the Yoruba, whose residential identity was never fixed but changed during different seasons of the year. Therefore, enforcing dog licensing and vaccinations in one area would reduce the risk only of dogs who never moved out of it. The statement by the assistant district officer of Jemaa that "nearly every pagan coming into Kafanchan is followed by his dog, a practice which it would be difficult to control," clearly highlighted the complication of protecting European neighborhoods from the allegedly rabid dogs from the outskirts of rural communities.[100]

Resistance to dog licensing was part of the general agitation against draconian colonial measures. It emphasized, as expressed in this chapter's first epigraph, the intimate relationship between humans and dogs to underscore mutual respect and indispensability. It was also a unique type of levy that did not have a direct economic benefit to the dog on which it was paid. Using a dog levy as a prerequisite for vaccination framed public health and social control as beneficial to individual animals. Its benefit to a dog consisted of not being destroyed if caught in the public by the town council during a rabies outbreak. In this way, a dog license essentially denoted the right of dogs to exist. Like in any form of taxation, an owner who obtained a dog license believed that it must entitle the animal to at least some rights, such as freedom of movement and freedom from molestation. For instance, in 1939 the rate of vehicular death of dogs on roads was so high that the government put a temporary ban on complaints against motor drivers in Ibadan. But dog owners would not accept this. A petition by a group who identified simply as "Dog Owners" associated a dog license with the animal's right to exist: "We know the benefit of our dogs, hence we licensed them so as to have them walk peacefully and freely in town," they emphasized. The group then went on to threaten that "if there is no chance for their freedom by licensing these poor animals, we better give up of getting them licensed."[101] Vehicular death of dogs at the hands of "reckless" drivers was about competition for space in a colonial society where urban infrastructure satisfied notions of urban modernity at the expense of nature and animals.

Conversely, rural dog owners worried less about vehicular death of their dogs; however, they agitated against the inconsistency over the geographical delimitation of the dog tax. In theory, most districts excluded rural dogs from taxation, but in reality tax officers knowingly and unknowingly attempted to enforce dog taxes in rural areas. This is obvious in the case of Mushin, a suburb of Lagos, around 1936, when locals kicked against the dog tax, arguing that their "dogs were replacing the police protection they so desperately needed."[102] In effect, their dogs were doing the job of the government.

The most ferocious resistance to dog taxes came from those most affected by them—breeders, hunters, and farmers who used dogs largely for economic activities. While it is easy to interpret the agitation of the hunters during World War II from the perspective of the hardship caused by the scarcity of gunpowder for their Dane guns, which thus intensified reliance of hunting dogs, the postwar fight to end the dog tax extended opposition to animal taxation beyond the discomforts of wartime.[103] Aside from writing petitions, hunters embarked on strikes to press home their demands. If the hunters' refusal to hunt and provide meat for the communities had a direct impact on food supplies, their abandonment of regular religious observances vital to the wellness of the community (as seen in the case of Ondo Province in December 1949) constituted "a state of emergency" for traditional institutions.[104] Aware of the need to integrate their agitation into mainstream nationalist agitation, local hunters began to publish petitions in the leading newspapers of the era. While maintaining some of the features of colonial language of opposition to injustice, such published petitions sought to educate the public about the real-life experience of hunting dogs and their human companions, with whom urbanites, constituting the largest readership of newspapers, were unfamiliar.[105]

The most instructive of newspaper petitions against dog licensing that I have seen was written by the Abomiti Farmers Association of Epe, published in the *Nigerian Daily Times* (NDT) on October 9, 1947. Instead of whipping up familiar rhetoric of the importance of hunting, the petition argued that imposing a tax of 2s. 6d. per dog, with a maximum projected revenue of £25, would be counterproductive for the government's scheme of increasing local food production. While honing the conventional notion that African farmers did not keep dogs as "pets" but rather to ward off animals that threatened to destroy their farms, the petition's emphasis that each farmer in the division provided "feed and upkeep" for five to ten dogs went contrary to the notion that Africans' dogs were scavengers that fended for themselves.[106]

The dog, humans' most intimate animal companion, is part of the picture of colonial Nigeria that has not been critically captured until now. The precolonial dog became a colonial and modern creature, not just because colonialism entailed modernity but also because the animals were expected to be modern. The vexed debate over dog taxation, for example, was shaped in part by the practical and symbolic role dogs played in human life as both pets and utility animals. In becoming modern dogs, the precolonial canines responded to new notions of urban planning and governance that forbade their public presence because of appearance, habit, and nutrition. When people protested the inordinate killing of dogs by urban vehicles, they were reinforcing one of the cardinal principles of taxation—protection of property by the government. The story of colonial dogs who accompanied their masters to the colonies asks scholars to look at imperialism from a nonhuman perspective. To underestimate how dogs aided colonialism is to miss something crucial about companionship. The next chapter continues the conversation of human-animal experience, placing artistic production at the center of colonial domination, modernity, nationalism, and nation building.

4 ↜ The Nigerian Political Zoo

Animal Art, Modernism, and the Visual Narrative of Nation Building

Anybody can say what he likes about feminine weakness. But I shall be the last to wait for a lioness.

> —Akinola Lasekan, "The Lioness of Lisabiland,"
> *West African Pilot*, February 22, 1949

Literature and Art are nothing but interpretational criticism of national mores and folkways. They tend, by visual education to attract attention to errors of omission and commission with a view to rectification.

> —Nnamdi Azikiwe, foreword to Akinola Lasekan's
> *Nigeria in Cartoons* (Lagos: Ijaiye, 1944)

ON DECEMBER 22, 1961, Justice Olujide Somolu of the Lagos High Court ordered the *West African Pilot* (WAP), one of Africa's most influential newspapers of the 1940s and 1950s, to pay £10,500 to three leaders of the Action Group (AG) political party (Obafemi Awolowo, Ladoke Akintola, and F. R. A. Williams) for defamation of character contained in a series of cartoons it published from 1951 to 1959 (see fig. 4.1).[1] The cartoons satirized the power struggle in the elections of the 1950s in western Nigeria, which the AG dominated, dramatizing the role of its leaders as dishonest politicians who criminally stole election victories from the National Council of Nigeria and the Cameroons (NCNC), led my Nnamdi Azikiwe (Zik), who was also the owner of the WAP. One of the cartoons in question, published on April 9, 1956, and titled "Beware of the Opportunist Rogue This Time," features a variety of animals who assume human identities to narrate political strife. A marauder hawk (the AG) can be seen stealing a fish (the

FIGURE 4.1. Cartoons by Akinola Lasekan. Left to right from top: "Beware of the Opportunist Rogue This Time," WAP, April 9, 1956; "Nigerian 'St. George' Returns from Historic Battle," WAP, November 26, 1958; "Another St. George Goes into Action," WAP, July 12, 1957; "The True Meaning of Democracy?," WAP, March 26, 1952.

fruit of NCNC labor) from a duck (the NCNC) as it paddles in the "sea of independence struggle."[2] The text of the cartoon "Memoir of 1951 General Election" enhances the visual protest by connecting the past to the present in the struggle for which political party would inherit the reins of Nigerian government after the anticipated demise of colonialism.

The WAP libel case of 1961 was a turning point in Nigeria's history of politics, law, print culture, and protest art in many ways. To begin with, it was the first major case of cartoon-specific libel in Nigeria. In his memoir, Somolu emphasized the importance of the case to Nigerian politics and print culture, describing it as "the first time that newspaper cartoons formed the subject matter of a libel action in any of our courts."[3] The monetary value of the libel award enhanced its unusual nature. Writing in 1968, revered journalist Increase H. E. Coker established that the libel settlement "was by far the highest of such damages ever awarded by a Nigerian court."[4] Second, by basing his judgment on the fact that the readers of the WAP knew whom the cartoonist was referring to, Somolu, himself a former journalist with WAP, gave a strong legal validation to the effectiveness of art in the struggle for power. He clearly affirmed that a visual narrative of political tension (sarcastic, metaphoric, symbolic, and humorous as it may appear) could in reality shape the tenor of politics. Third, it laid the foundation for newspaper libel jurisprudence that became a recurring element of political struggles in postcolonial Nigeria.

Pioneering Nigerian cartoonist Akinola Lasekan (1916–72) was the artist at the center of this controversy. His ordeal did not end with the 1961 saga. In June 1966 the military government of Aguiyi Ironsi arrested him for rekindling the political crisis that led to Nigeria's first military coup with a cartoon that continued the conversation of the supremacy of the NCNC over its rival party, the AG.[5] The cartoon in question features the rooster (symbol of the NCNC, the so-called promoter of national unity), standing gallantly on a fallen treelike object (intelligible to the public as a palm tree, the symbol of the AG), which Lasekan labels a divisive tribalist party.[6]

This chapter connects visual performance of nationalism with animal identities in the political cartoons of Lasekan, whose "biting humor," according to Coker, had "an exasperating effect on British administrative officers," in their portrayal of animals as both colonial subjects and modern nonhuman creatures.[7] It treats animal cartoons as both historical sources and polemical texts that complicate the meaning of human agency in the world inhabited by animals. A visual history is significant for amplifying the contributions of African modernist artists to nationalism and nation building. Indeed, the history of African nationalism transcends the mass textual narrative contained in the manifestos of political parties and ideas of leading political figures to include artistic expressions that compel audiences to rethink colonial subjectivities. Drawing on Lasekan's more than one thousand unique cartoons that used animal iconography to express the overlapping themes of modernity, colonial subjecthood, nationalism, ethnic and party politics, and the idea of nationhood, this chapter argues that the appropriation of the animal world in expressing human lived experience cannot be understood in isolation from the unstable perception of nature and from the oral and literary culture of the first half of the twentieth century. The intersections of oral and written text and of visual art in the discourse of party politics in 1940s and 1950s Nigeria have been grossly understudied.

If the WAP (with a certified average daily circulation of twenty thousand in the mid-1940s) was Nigeria's most popular newspaper up to the late 1960s, Lasekan's animal cartoons were the most consumed artistic work of the era. While Lasekan was not the first artist to place environment,

nature, and animals at the center of everyday life, conveying representations of animals as colonial subjects in cartoons through the modern
newspaper medium allowed him to pioneer a new creative genre that his
predecessors could only imagine. Arguably, Lasekan was Nigeria's most
visible visual artist of the mid-twentieth century partly because his animal
cartoons belonged to the "popular" art category—accessible to the public,
which is able to "perceive meanings with ease"—as opposed to the "high"
category, where art "became a challenge: a site of contemplation in which
forms morph at the blink of an eye and the viewer was forced to engage
in decoding or constructing meanings."[8] As I will demonstrate, although
Lasekan's animal cartoons were accessible (to varying degrees) to the public (regardless of literacy level), they also invite the audience to construct
new and unexpected meanings based on level of education, location, and
ethnoreligious identity. While literate Nigerians (predominantly urbanites,
the largest demographic of newspaper readership) who had an intimate experience of colonial power would easily decipher the title and dialogue of
the cartoons and topics related to city life that the animal characters propagated, rural dwellers who maintained daily interaction with livestock and
wildlife (and the cultural and religious sites through which they interface
with humans) would be able to read extended meanings—far from the
visualization of the urbanites and even of the artist himself.

This chapter is at the core of scholarship on nationalism, modernist art, and human-animal relations. Any discussion of nationalism and
party politics in Nigeria must commence with James Coleman's *Nigeria:
Background to Nationalism* and Richard Sklar's *Nigerian Political Parties*.[9]
These two works set the language and paradigms for understanding the
evolution of modern Nigerian politics by delving into the massive political,
economic, and social changes that gave birth to new expressions of self-
determination and nationhood espoused by leading African nationalists of
the 1940s and 1950s. Although scholars have expanded on these pioneering efforts, turning their searchlight on neglected communities, political
constituencies, and individuals and demographics, the approach (in terms
of sources and methodology) has remained largely the same.[10] With the
exception of a few new studies that use symbols such as postal stamps,
currencies, museums, and flags to engage the story of nationalism in other
former British African colonies, scholars have continued to depend on
written text from newspapers, memoirs, biographies, and parliamentary
debates, and oral data in making sense of the complex political actuality
occasioned by the collapse of the British Empire in Africa.[11] Few works
have placed art at the center of nationalism in a way that complicates the

changing dynamics of relations among Africans and between them and Europeans. Fewer have identified the intersection of animal symbolism and artistic expressions of nationalism. This chapter fills these voids by merging multiple historical sources to throw light on the narratives of nation building in 1940s and 1950s Nigeria. By turning political reality into thought-provoking visual stories and "action words" using animal identities, Lasekan empowered political processes in profound ways. Texts have stronger power when enhanced with visual tools.

African art historians have established the connection between modernism on the one hand and nationalism and the struggle against racism and colonial injustice on the other.[12] Pioneering modernists such as Aina Onabolu used their "art to dispel any racist assumption of the African intellectual inferiority."[13] From Onabolu, Lasekan, and Ben Enwonwu to Uche Okeke, Bruce Onobrakpeya, Dele Jegede, and Moyo Okediji, modernists and postmodernists were influenced by ideologies rooted in local, national, and transnational expressions of progress, pride, and honor for the emergence of a strong Nigerian state. Even the numerous works that would come under the rubric of "traditional" art (sculpture, painting, and woodcarving), deeply influenced by African religion, material culture, and orality, featured some degree of hybridity that responded to culture contact and social change under colonialism.[14]

This chapter broadens the scholarship on modernist art and nationalism by engaging Lasekan's cartoons as a sustained interface between humans and the animal world—a theme that is missing in existing works. Instead of focusing only on how Lasekan used cartoons to fight the idea of African racial inferiority, I extend the scope of analysis to interparty politics and the debate among leading Nigerian politicians over the best pathway to nation building. The visuality of nature is ubiquitous in art that tells human stories through animals. By appropriating and domesticating animal identities from their habitat to narrate a modern discourse of nationalism and party politics in the 1940s and 1950s, Lasekan disturbs the conventional meaning of nature. From the narratives of chaos to order in the natural world, the experience of animals as colonial subjects and of their divergent abilities renders an artistic window to viewing the colonial encounter.

CONTEXT AND BACKGROUND

Born in Owo in southwestern Nigeria in 1916, Lasekan started his career as a visual textile designer with the Compagnie Française de l'Afrique Occidentale in 1935. From 1936 to 1940 he worked with the Church Missionary Society (CMS) Bookshop, illustrating Bible stories and calendars while taking correspondence courses in cartooning, illustration, advanced drawing, commercial art, and fine art with the London-based Normal College of Art and the Washington School of Art in the United States. As we shall see later in this chapter, his stint with the CMS Bookshop would have a profound impact on his cartoons and pictorial naturalism. Lasekan came of full intellectual age in the mid-1940s as nationalism was taking a decisive turn. By this period, he had published his book *Nigeria in Cartoons*, using the image of such animals as the snake, horse, crocodile, sheep, wolf, lion, rat, and elephant, among others, to artistically reify and satirize the ordeal of colonialism, competition among political parties, and transnational processes.[15] A published review describing *Nigeria in Cartoons* as "an interesting study of all aspects of Nigerian life" definitely exaggerates in its evaluation, for the work mainly captures the overlapping themes of empire and subjectivity.[16] Yet a book telling Nigerian history through visuals was revolutionary for the literary culture of the era.

It was the WAP, not cartoon books, paintings, or art exhibitions that gave Lasekan the platform to channel his creative energy in a well-defined and consistent manner.[17] Although the story of newspapers in Nigeria dates to the 1850s, the founding of the WAP by Zik in 1937 represents a turning point in the history of print culture and nationalism in the country. Unlike most of its predecessors, which were mainly elitist, short-lived, and advertisement driven, the WAP (like other newspapers owned by Zik, such as the *Southern Nigeria Defender* and the *Eastern Nigeria Guardian*) championed a "populist" ideology and made the construction of an ideal independent Nigeria its main focus. Zik became Lasekan's main patron, just as leading elites (such as J. K. Randle, Mojola Agbebi, Herbert Macaulay, Akinwande Savage, and Ernest Ikoli) patronized the painter Onabolu. But beyond art patronage, Lasekan was, in all respects, a prodigy of Zik, not only because he used the WAP to express his ideas but also because his ideology was deeply influenced by the Nigerian nationalist. If Zik, the "Nigerian St. George" and conqueror who waged war against colonialism on horseback (fig. 4.1), had the text and oral language to express anticolonial sentiments and to demonstrate the superiority of his party over its rivals—the Nigerian Youth Movement (NYM) and the AG—Lasekan had the artistic ingenuity, economy of words, and poetic talent to codify massive textual information into engrossing animal caricatures for readers across social class and educational status.[18] Unlike the text of newspapers, which required time and some level of literacy to comprehend, cartoons are typically easier to interpret by a much wider group. Images featuring nonhuman characters could radically shape the tenor of political discourse, with more immediacy and, in some cases, effectiveness than text because they are strategically deployed to provoke reactions, generate debate, and secure the attention of government or rival parties.

Lasekan's cartoons, with their accompanying titles and dialogue, conceptually propagated two overlapping themes. First, colonialism, through its agents such as foreign merchant companies, is inherently exploitative and must be uprooted through a radical political consciousness that envisions a bright future for a decolonized Nigeria. This trend of creative endeavor took Lasekan to the core domains of colonial violence, excessive use of force by the army and police, skewed political representation, faulty constitutional amendments, and deplorable working condition for the labor force. He projected a liberal political inclination with thought-provoking discourse of a welfarism that could only be guaranteed by self-determination.

The second trend of Lasekan's artistic expression is inherently partisan. It focuses on party politics and ideological disagreement among the educated elites of the era concerning the best pathway for nation building. The expansion in African political participation after World War II intensified competition among political parties, which positioned themselves as credible managers of the ruins of the colony after independence. Zik, not someone else (Lasekan emphasizes in his art), was the ideal leader to pilot the country to independence, and his party, the NCNC, was the best vehicle for achieving this purpose. This second agenda entailed smearing the image of NCNC's rivals. The fact that Lasekan engaged in a "partisan nationalism" or a "politically biased nationalism," or a nationalist ideology promoting the supremacy of one political party over the others, affords scholars the opportunity to expand the intersections of art and nationalism in new ways. As I will demonstrate, the repertoire of animal symbolism in his art had a much-expanded interpretative meaning partly because he was engaging complex patterns of political affairs among Africans and between them and the British colonial establishment.

Nigeria in Lasekan's artistic imagination, which he translated into visual and literary metaphor, was a political zoo inhabited by animals who vied for power through unabated violence and intimidation.[19] If the Nigerian political zoo had a well-defined physical boundary (at least in Lasekan's conception), its inhabitants with their animalistic behavior did not have clear rules of engagement. At a very provocative level, British imperialism itself involved the domestication of the colonies into the "zoo" of the empire.[20] Hence, each colony in the empire was a "zoo." When Lasekan occasionally introduces humans into his animal world, he is not suggesting that humans are superior to animals. Rather, it was a matter of aesthetic priority, for he thinks that both the colonial state and the subjects are zoo and animals (real and fictional), respectively.[21] The real human could be a utopian figure—an ideal personality that actually did not exist in Nigeria in the 1940s and 1950s. One does not need to look far to connect Lasekan's lived experience with his preference for animal symbolism. His place of birth in Owo, where the animal world interfaced regularly with the human, definitely left an imprint in his imagination and provided some iconographic sources. What is more, Yoruba oral and written texts (proverbs, legends, folklore) are replete with animal fables and fantasies. By the time his career took an ascending turn in the mid-1940s, the newspapers had become a dense trove of literary expositions featuring animal-specific English-language idioms.[22] Nigerians literate in English, like Lasekan, had access to copious literary works of Euro-American origin that they used in their daily communication. The modern animal symbolism in Lasekan's work represents an amazing degree of creative individuality, yet it was the culture, tradition, and environment he encountered (directly and indirectly, literally and figuratively) that shaped his work.

It is not clear why Lasekan used animal symbolism in his cartoons. Beyond his highly ordered aesthetic preference, one plausible explanation is that many features of the animal world, its ecology and ecosystems, bear significant real and metaphoric resemblance to human lived experience. More than any other motifs, animal symbols are effective in translating human feelings of subversion, revenge, malice, fear, admiration, hegemony, anger, and indeed pathology into artistic idioms. Moreover, animal symbols gave Lasekan an expanded artistic flexibility that he could not achieve with human symbols alone. If humans generally think that animals do not have emotions and thus are incapable of feeling pain, Lasekan thought otherwise. In his creative hands, animals expressed their emotions about their unstable experience and spoke the language that members of their kingdom could understand.

The breadth and quality of Lasekan's animal codes firmly established his conviction that the colonial state's political structure involved "animalization"—a term he frequently used in his cartoons. According to him, animalization is the process by which humans degenerate into animals through irrational behavior. It includes political decisions that went against the grain of rationality.[23] The pace of animalization varied from one animal to another because of the inequality in the animal world—a product of unequal size, strength, and predatory ability.

Artistic commentary is not original to Lasekan—artists across location and time had historically used animal symbols (in their painting, sculpture, or woodcarving, among other genres of visual art) to tell human stories. Animal characters and figurines featured in performing arts (including those of masquerades) used to express political disaffection or rebuke leaders.[24] Animal representations are plentiful in all major types of pre-twentieth-century African sculpture—from village mud shrines to royal ancestral altar pieces. Their adumbration and the variety of contexts in which they are found are indicative of their importance in African thought, spirituality, and art.[25]

What is interesting in the case of Lasekan is the way he created a pan-Nigerian identity for animals by taking them from their ethnocultural enclaves. He achieved this by focusing on animals whose identity transcends ethnic or cultural boundaries or that would allow his art to speak to cross-cultural ideals of power and social relations. In this way, Lasekan turned animals into symbols of national discourse. The "Nigerianization or nationalization of animals" or the process of turning animals into colonial subjects or national bodies could not have been possible before the creation of the Nigerian state in 1914. It took place under imperialism and found significant expression in the work of an artist who knew that for his message to evoke the desired emotion and response, his audience across Nigerian ethnicities must be able to decode his animal art, even without description or caption. While the explanatory note empowered the imagery, the animal symbolism was itself the most important element of the art. This "detribalization" or "Nigerianization" or "nationalization" of the fauna was further made possible by the print idiom and capitalism that, according to Benedict Anderson, created "unified fields of exchange and communication," "gave a new fixity to language," and "created languages-of-power" different from everyday and administrative registers and vocabularies.[26]

THE LAMB, THE SHEPHERD, AND THE WOLF

Two arrays of representation shaped Lasekan's imagination of Nigerians, political parties, and the avarice of colonialism. He satirized the evolving Nigerian nation as a lamb/sheep (prey) and Zik and the NCNC as the protector (shepherd), on one hand, and the AG and colonial government, alternately, as the wolf (predator), on the other. At the heart of these framings is colonial victimhood. Other characterizations of the sheep—as hunger, unemployment, abused labor unions, financial insecurity, and pathologized bodies—directly speaks to Nigeria's experience of ruthless capitalism.[27] The danger that the sheep, among other domesticated animals, encountered goes beyond powerlessness to defend themselves against the predators. Rather, their vulnerability (a product of their lower intelligence), according to Lasekan, intensifies their lack of direction or their inability to resist being led down the wrong path by Zik's political rivals.

This artistic imprint draws from everyday life in rural communities where predators unleashed violence on domesticated animals on a regular basis. It is also influenced by transnationalism and culture contact. The image of a wolf and a shepherd, dressed in a free-flowing white robe, holding a long stick vertically, directly mirrors similar representations in Christian iconography. The man is definitely not the familiar image of an African herdsman or nomad. This religious theme must have appealed to the sentiment of educated Nigerians, the majority of whom were also Christians or professed Christianity. In "Leaving Us at the Mercy of the Big Wolf?" (fig. 4.2), Lasekan renders Zik as a shepherd who turns his back on leading Nigerians (sheep) as they ply the road to independence and are waylaid by the imperialist (wolf).[28] The cartoon implies that danger awaits Nigeria if Zik refuses to guide and guard the country through independence.

But the Nigerian masses did not always constitute a homogeneous, directionless flock of sheep. They were also goats or sheep of different ideological camps and ethnicities who fought one another over political power. In this instance, as in the previous, the position of the predatory lion or wolf is paramount as a threat to, or decider of, the sheep's future, their fate, and their very existence. In "The Problem Is, the Lion Must Live!" (fig. 4.2), Lasekan depicts the power tussle at the constitutional reform conference presided over by the lion (the colonial government), where Nigerians (goats) vied over whether they wanted regionalism or federalism as they debated the future of the country. This is another uncompromising critique of the politics of self-determination characterized by the failure of the nationalists to reconcile their ideological differences for the sake of national unity. If the goats disagree over the future of the colonial state, the lion does not. The lion's statement "Scheme for more food for the lion family" reemphasizes the superiority of the colonial government and its lack of genuine interest in the independence movement, which the constitutional reform conference sought to achieve.[29] When

FIGURE 4.2. Cartoons by Akinola Lasekan. *Left to right from top*: "Odudu-wa Pasture Land," WAP, April 4, 1957; "Leaving Us at the Mercy of the Big Wolf?," WAP, September 4, 1951; "The Problem Is, the Lion Must Live!," WAP, September 8, 1949; "The Lioness of Lisabiland," WAP, February 22, 1949; "Is Might Right?," WAP, March 15, 1949; "Nigeria and the Danger of the Big Wolf," WAP, September 12, 1952.

the Yoruba and Igbo (rams) fight each another over the supremacy of the flock while the vulture (imperialist) waits to consume their carcasses, we see unhealthy ethnic-centered competition for power capable of leading to self-destruction, which favors the colonialists.[30]

A similar line of thought can be found in the illustration of Yoruba, Hausa, and Igbo (sheep) having the following conversation: "Yoruba: 'You are dominating me.' Igbo: 'But how can a slave dominate his fellow slave?'"[31] By apportioning identical image and equal size to three sheep, each denoting the country's largest ethnic groups, Lasekan invites his audience to see modern politics beyond interethnic conflict. More importantly, the use of domesticated animals to represent ethnic bodies and their geographical space in a world moderated by real humans, as in several other cartoons, allows him to position the superior power of political leaders and their parties in directing the course of nation building. The NCNC's amazement at how the AG was able to push Yorubaland (sheep) into the prison of "narrow tribal nationalism" in another cartoon continues to paint Zik as a pan-Nigerian leader whose agenda transcends the parochial project of ethnic-centered nationalism promoted by Awolowo and the leaders of the NYM.[32]

One of the biggest political debates in the late 1940s was the role of labor unions in interparty politics and nationalism. Lasekan captures this contention in a series of cartoons, especially one titled "Misadventure," which features a lamb (the Trades Union Congress, or TUC) dying because the NCNC withdrew from its affairs.[33] The TUC was formed in 1942 "to demonstrate the strength of labor" in response to the colonial government's criminalization of strikes and lockouts by workers during World War II.[34] At its inception, all the parties and nationalists gave strong support to the TUC in order to gain political power. With time, the TUC would be affiliated with the NCNC alone. The cartoon was produced in early 1949 in the wake of the vote by a majority of the TUC members to withdraw from the NCNC.[35] By envisioning the likely demise of the TUC in the event of its leaving the NCNC, Lasekan reaffirms the partisanship of the union. The cartoon furthers the image of vulnerable colonial subjects (workers and trade unions) as a lamb that must be saved, not only from death but also from hunger, as seen in another cartoon titled "The Fateful Meal," which depicts the TUC (as a lamb) being lured away from the NCNC (as a shepherd) with "separatist propaganda food" by the Lagos intellectuals, a majority of whom were political enemies of Zik.[36] The decision of tribal unions (lamb) to remain with the NCNC (shepherd) in the cartoon titled "The Parting Member" while the TUC (another lamb) leaves it further predicts the danger of the TUC's withdrawal from Zik.[37] Perhaps the most humorous of the cartoons on the labor unions versus NCNC characterizes the revered labor unionist Michael Imoudu in a lion's skin mauling the TUC (goat).[38] Imoudu led other high-ranking members of the TUC to create the Nigerian National Labour Federation.

Zik and the NCNC are not always the savior shepherd—in some instances, Lasekan positions them as victims of the bitter politics of the colonial government and the AG. In "What Do You Hope to Gain from Zik's Imprisonment?," Lasekan illustrates young political followers as little calves being attacked by a bigger goat (the imperialists), while Zik (an imprisoned predator) watches from behind visible iron bars.[39] The cartoon gives the impression that the persecution of Zik would not solve the perennial disagreement between the colonial government and the electorate—or that both the colonial government and the AG need Zik (now imprisoned) to help them settle their disagreement. The posture of a tamed carnivore watching carefully as his enemies fight one another is contrasted with many other characterizations of carnivores as potential threats to goats and sheep. So also is the narration of Zik, the lion standing high and saying, "Fear not, pals, I will do you no harm" while his rivals (sheep/goats) take to their heels.[40] The same Zik, as lion or tiger king, can be seen intimidating the colonial government on behalf of the Nigerian workers at a labor dispute settlement in another cartoon.[41]

Put together, Lasekan manipulates bodily positions of animals in conflicting context to hone the visual metaphor of power. Thus, the carnivorous lion (the colonial government, the NYM, or the AG) contrasts with the savior lion king (Zik)—powerful yet benevolent.[42] Zik would not trade his "positive" lion persona with a rival political party. However, he would generously allow minority parties like the Northern Elements Progressive Union (NEPU), with whom he wanted to form a coalition, to take up the king-of-the-jungle identity. Against the colonialists' impression of northern Nigeria's minority parties and politicians as politically insignificant because of the slow pace of Western education in the region, Lasekan dedicates cartoons celebrating the true lionlike and assertive image of northerners.[43]

In addition, he allows Funmilayo Ransome-Kuti (the "Lioness of Lisabiland") to share the image of the benevolent king of the jungle with Zik (fig. 4.2). Ransome-Kuti's fervent protest against taxation of women (among other unsavory policies) by the colonial government and local chiefs culminated in the abdication of the *Alake* (king), Ademola II of Abeokuta, in 1949. A celebratory cartoon by Lasekan features Ransome-Kuti and her "Egba Women's Union" (actually named the Abeokuta Women's Union) mauling a goat (women's taxation) while the Egba native administration flees screaming a statement that contradicts the dominant perception of women: "Anybody can say what he likes about feminine weakness. But I shall be the last to wait for a lioness."[44] Artists usually tap into the animal world to express human lived experience partly because of the limitation of the human world. While nature is inexhaustible and superfluous, the human world has a limit or a set boundary. Hence, the metaphor of power relations in the animal kingdom gives an extended meaning to human stories. Lasekan wants his audience to see what animality actually constitutes in real terms by translating his mental impression into both human and animal bodies. The artistic feminization of the predator (lioness) mauling the prey (goat) is inevitable because colonialism, a thoroughly violent edifice, conceived of women and men as separate bodies—biologically and socially. In addition, Lasekan views Ransome-Kuti as a lioness in both the human and animal worlds because he was convinced that art could give complex meaning to everything, including language. Thus, the visual impression of the abdication of the Alake, especially the animal iconography, takes a historian a step closer to fully exhuming the unprecedented events of 1949. The predatory life in the animal kingdom is ambivalent—it can be benevolent and violence. Hence, there is honor in violence, depending on context and circumstances.

We see the influence of religion in the visual narrative of nationalism and party politics when Lasekan represents Zik as a lamb being roasted (persecuted) on the "regionalization altar" by the imperialists (fire) while holding in his mouth a message that reads, "One Nigeria, one God, one destiny." Zik as a sacrificial lamb is expected to evoke the feeling of selflessness toward a man who wanted to create a united country based on strong faith in God.[45] The religious sentiment of this cartoon gives the sheep a form of martyrdom, completely different from that of directionless prey found in most of Lasekan's cartoons. In this regard, the sheep is both an unfortunate victim of political violence and manipulation and a ritual hero who surrenders its life for the survival of the state. The nation as a sheep assumes another identity (a commodity on an auction block) in a visual story titled "Nigeria for Sale!" Uncle Tom (the colonial government) is seen armed with a "new butchery technique" as the NYM offers Nigeria for outright sale "to any foreigner instead of allowing her to be controlled by 'jungle' men and omolanke [cart] pullers." As in similar narratives, this cartoon paints rivals of the NCNC as unpatriotic Nigerians, who would prefer to allow foreign domination to continue than give the NCNC the opportunity to lead the country to independence.[46]

When Lasekan is not portraying Nigerians and the nation as helpless or directionless sheep, he is giving them other characteristics of subjectivity to evoke the emotions of his audience, which is experiencing political and economic marginalization. Unemployment, a high cost of living, limited political participation, aggressive capitalism, and hunger are also the metaphoric sheep and goats of the Nigerian political zoo, where the lion, fox, and wolf, among other predators, hold superior carnivorous power. The image of a fox (strong) killing a sheep (weak) while the lion (retribution) waits to consume the fox is an allegory of the hierarchy of violence in the colonial state, where the British (retribution) had the power to inflict supreme mayhem on the fox and everyone else (fig. 4.2). Lasekan uses this cartoon to speak to the danger of interparty violence.[47] Associating the hierarchy of power in the colonial society with a food chain gives an expanded political meaning to violence itself.

Colonial political structure that did not guarantee fair play and representation of Africans in the decision-making organs of the state also accounts for the skewed economic policies that intensified the exploitation of the labor force. Lasekan translates the NCNC's economic manifestos into a cartoon, rebuking the government for investing more in cash crops (which fetched more money for the colonial state) than in food crops (which were needed to feed the populace and reduce the cost of living). One cartoon in this genre features the mauling of "Nigerian food production" (sheep) by a predatory "exclusive cocoa farming and other get-rich-quick professions" (fig. 4.2).[48] More provocative is another image of high rent and cost of living (a predator) threatening the Gorsuch Commission (the sheep), formed in 1954–55 to investigate low wages of Nigerian civil servants, among other charges. The wolf's remark to the sheep—"Hello dear, so you've grown fatter, thank God!"—predicts the future of Nigerian workers, whose standard of living would remain deplorable (even with a wage increase) as along as the high cost of living went untamed.[49] The cartoon depicting hunger as a wolf being fenced out of the "safety garden for unemployed Nigerians" (flock of sheep) by the NCNC extends the conversation of promises of a better future for Nigerians under Zik's leadership.[50] The conversation about unequal distribution of political power continues with a cartoon titled "Nigerians Must Enjoy Universal Adult Suffrage, Says NCNC," which features the NCNC telling a fat colonial government officer (the imperialist), "I ask for a sheep [universal adult suffrage], not a wolf [electoral college system]."[51] The innuendo here was understandable to most followers of Nigerian politics during this period. The electoral college was not a true democratic system of representation, for it empowered a few people to appropriate enormous political power, even though they had fewer votes in popular elections conducted through adult suffrage.

The character of the Nigerian political zoo transcends its predatory habit. Lasekan also emphasizes the natural qualities of animals (size, color, height, strength) to artistically domesticate nature for political conversation. The image of a Nigerian wage earner (giraffe) stretching its long neck to reach the cost of rent, food, and imported goods (fruit) hanging high on a tree (cost of living), while the non-wage earner (a stunted sheep) wallows in poverty due to its short neck compels the audience to reflect over socioeconomic inequality within the colonial state (fig. 4.3). Although Nigerian wage earners were highly exploited by both the government and private firms, employment commissions set up to investigate their welfare did provide occasional bonuses, which nonsalaried workers did not get partly because they lacked the structure to articulate their demands. The printed remark of the sheep, "When you with such a long neck grumble about the height of the fruits, I wonder what you expect me to do," reproduces interpersonal relations among the colonial workforce, especially in the city, where the cost of living was highest.[52]

The narrative of socioeconomic inequality continues with a cartoon illustrating the elephant (foreign commercial combine) reaching high to pluck fruit (rich dividends) while Nigerian traders (goats) agonize about their underprivileged status. As in the previous cartoon, the spoken words of the elephant, "Don't blame me comrades, blame your diminutive stature," legitimize the exploitative habit of powerful economic interest in the unequal commercial relationship with Nigerians.[53] Hazing and intimidation in the Nigerian political zoo continues in a cartoon featuring a frog (Egbe Omo Oduduwa, the sociocultural arm of the AG) telling an elephant (NCNC), "I reckon I can be bigger than you when fully inflated" (fig. 4.3). In a blatant show of power, the elephant's response, "Provided you don't burst before then," foresees the apparent inability of the frog to achieve the extravagant status of the elephant and the deadly consequences of trying to do so.[54] Here, as in other cartoons of this type, Lasekan is preoccupied with showing that Zik's political supremacy is based on core natural features that his opposition cannot achieve—no matter how they try. The image of an elephant (NCNC) uprooting a tree (Nigerian political problems), while a dog (the NYM) barks validates the failure of the rival party that, due to its small status, could only criticize the massive work of Zik (the elephant), who is naturally endowed to tackle the big challenges of nation building (fig. 4.3).[55] The annoying bark of the dog contrasts with the useful trumpet of the elephant in a different cartoon. Here the elephant (NCNC) uses his trumpet to wake rivals (the NYM and the AG) from their sleep or political docility.[56] At least ten other cartoons reproduce Zik and the NCNC being disturbed by an opposition party—the barking dogs that could only complain while good deeds are being done.[57]

Lasekan seems convinced that interpreting political success as natural ability or gift, which are immutable traits, is more convincing than adducing it to acquired human qualities such as education, which Zik's main rivals also had. A mockery of legal degrees obtained from British colleges in three cartoons speaks effectively to the critique of legal knowledge in politics. Zik, who had degrees in anthropology and political science from American universities, and Lasekan, who took correspondence courses through British and American arts colleges, could be envious that the public respected lawyers, many of whom also went into politics.[58] One cartoon in this category features three Nigerian elites (as humans with goat and chicken heads) dressed in suits and en route to the United Kingdom to study law, while holding a printed document that reads, "We prefer animalization to regionalization." The additional text of the cartoon, "At least we should be able to produce something better than regionalization after completing our law studies," ridicules the legal profession for turning Nigerians into animals and/or miseducating the elite on the principles of good governance.[59] Taking this further, Lasekan speaks directly to Nigerians, advising them not to study law, with a cartoon of a youth making a wrong choice of catching an escaping fish (law), even though other fish (medicine, engineering, industrial technology) are floating and readily available to the hook.[60] This cartoon also articulates the big debate about the right education for placing Nigeria on the path of sustainable development after independence. While the humanities and law remained attractive to young Nigerians, many believed that industrial and scientific knowledge, which were in short supply, should be promoted.

Even when Lasekan generously portrays an opponent as a huge animal capable of achieving extraordinary goals, he is careful to contrast it with a calamity that requires a more powerful animal (Zik or the NCNC) to rescue it from danger. In "The 'Innocent' Devil," we see the NCNC (an elephant) pulling the NYM and AG (a whale) from the "Gulf of Confusion" while the imperialist (a tortoise—the con artist in many African folktales) offers sarcastic praise, "You can get the whole world ablaze and appear as innocent as the child. Thanks to the art of diplomacy."[61] In addition, representing a wolf as an animal "naturally opposed to sharing western Nigeria with anybody," the ass as "a natural beast of burden" that hates independence, and a peacock as one of "nature's masterpieces" that would not cooperate with "lower breeds" extends Lasekan's creative

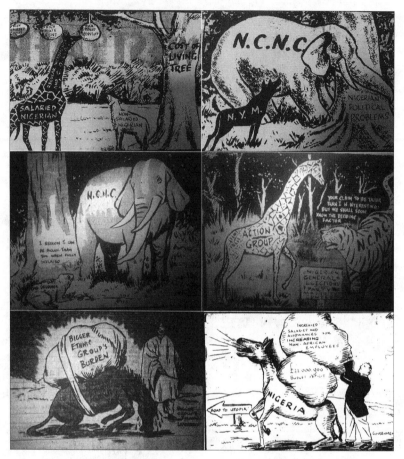

FIGURE 4.3. Cartoons by Akinola Lasekan. *Left to right from top:* "When You with Such a Long Neck Grumble about the Height of the Fruits, I Wonder What You Expect Me to Do," *WAP*, April 26, 1949; "Cousin, Can't You Get Something More Profitable to Do than Being Always on My Trail?," *WAP*, October 30, 1951; "Provided You Don't Burst before Then," *WAP*, February 12, 1953; "Poor Conceited Giraffe!," *WAP*, June 10, 1951; "Why the Creation of More States Is Imperative," *WAP*, June 19, 1957; "The Beast of Burden!," *WAP*, May 23, 1949.

imagination as he contrasts the qualities of the AG, the NCNC, and the NYM, respectively.[62]

Nigerian nationalist parties, regardless of their ideological differences, shared something in common—they were all led by educated African elites. This common feature, Lasekan is convinced, can be translated into the animal world. Both the giraffe and the zebra, on the one hand, and the tiger, on the other, have variegated skin patterns, Lasekan establishes.

And although the giraffe (AG) is taller than the tiger (NCNC), the former would not survive an encounter with the latter.[63] The utterance "You are striped and I'm striped, in what way then are you superior?" that Zik, the tiger, makes to the Nigerian Uncle Tom or the African loyalists of the colonial government (the zebra) is definitely deceptive in that it suggests equal ability between predator and prey.[64] Representing the AG as a giraffe appears factually correct, given that it was the ruling party in western Nigeria in the 1950s. However, as the cartoons in this category of Lasekan's visual politics explain, height does not matter in the contest between animals but strength, which aids the capacity to unleash maximum violence. The NCNC's predatory identity aligns with the spoken words of the tiger to the giraffe: "Your claim to be taller than I is interesting. But we shall soon know the deciding factor" (fig. 4.3).[65]

The last category in this section in the difficult task of schematizing Lasekan's work involves using animal images to speak to the burden and fallacies of colonialism. Here Lasekan positions humans as the problem animals face when they try to stretch their generosity as beasts of burden and companions beyond what they are naturally endowed to accommodate.[66] This is evident in the cartoon of a donkey (Nigeria) being harmed by loads (salary increase for European colonial staff and budget deficit) placed on it by the government, as it plies the road to Utopia, to which the British were supposedly leading Nigeria (fig. 4.3).[67] In clear terms, this visual narrative reproduces the image of the wastefulness of the colonial state, whose conception of a Nigerian future was unreal or bleak. Probably much more problematic is another cartoon featuring a camel (Nigeria) crumbling under the heavy weight of European expatriates and unemployed Nigerians while plodding down a million-mile road to independence. This cartoon foreshadows the increased agitation against the employment of high-paying European expatriates at a time when a lot of qualified Nigerians were without jobs.[68] Even the relationships among Nigerian ethnic groups could translate into the experience of the beast of burden. Here Lasekan presents a horse (small ethnic groups) collapsing under the weight of "bigger ethnic group's burden" to reproduce one of the most problematic questions of nation building, while calling for the creation of more states to cater to the needs of ethnic minorities (fig. 4.3).[69] The inequality in the Nigerian state, Akinola maintains, transcends relations between the colonial government and Nigerians—even Nigerians did inflict violence on other Nigerians, especially on the minorities. From the story of a reluctant horse (western Nigeria) being ridden by the AG (desperate rider) against the tide of high taxes and bad education policy on an arduous journey, to rendering literary expressions such as "a cat being let out of the bag," to visuals, Lasekan gives an expanded meaning to the discourse of decolonization and nation building using his artistic talent.[70]

"THE COCK NEVER FAILS"

The bird family of animals did not escape the creative gaze of Lasekan. The scope of his imagery here includes how he translates the popular idiom "To kill two birds with one stone" into an engrossing image in rebuking the Nigerian Uncle Toms, the so-called collaborators. It is public knowledge that the "collaborators" had problems maintaining their popularity among Nigerians without losing government privileges. This cartoon, which represents two labeled birds (Nigerians' adoration) and (government's favor), establishes the difficulty of serving two masters.[71] Tapping into the unique qualities of different species of birds, Lasekan uncovers relational and situational narratives of colonial Nigeria.[72] Another cartoon correlates the flying of birds from the "imperial poultry farm"—a metaphor for the British Empire—with freedom from imperialism. The transnational theme in this set of cartoons is clearly discernible. Lasekan thinks that the Gold Coast was moving faster in its fight to end colonialism in 1949 than Nigeria, which was held back by domestic troubles.[73] He would be proved right, as the Gold Coast became the first country (Ghana) in sub-Saharan Africa to receive independence, in 1957. In another cartoon published in 1957, he associates an eagle escaping from a cage as Nigeria outgrowing colonial entrapment (fig. 4.4).[74] At independence in 1960, the eagle became one of the symbols in the country's coat of arms.[75] Lasekan deploys its main characteristics (fearlessness, vision, vitality, leadership, and tenacity) to project what Nigeria would become after independence from Britain. Nigeria was expected to be as assertive as the eagle, which Lasekan believed is more than a flying animal. Yet the eagle holds transnational place in the conception of national glory. This explains why many countries inscribed it on their coat of arms.

Beyond the translation of popular literary ideas into visuals or the rendering of the colony as an "imperial farm," distinct qualities of birds are clear in Lasekan's political art. In many Nigerian cultures, the tweets of birds during certain periods of the day, season, or year signify danger, which Lasekan employs to warn his audience of the impending calamity either of allowing the AG to dominate Nigerian politics or of not acting aggressively to throw off the yoke of imperialism.[76] This is axiomatic in a 1954 cartoon titled "To Sing Again?," which emblematizes a bird (crises) displaying a message, highlighting the failure of the AG to fulfill its

FIGURE 4.4. Cartoons by Akinola Lasekan. *Left to right from top:* "The Eagle That Has Outgrown the Confines of a Cage!," WAP, May 25, 1957; "Talking Is Some Form of Action," WAP, January 1, 1955; "NEPU's Trouble Is Nigeria's Trouble," WAP, August 23, 1951; "The Frogs Once Demanded a More Dynamic King than the Log, and They Were Given the Stork!," WAP, October 8, 1952; "The Cock Triumphant," WAP, November 15, 1954; "Not Separatist Propitiation, but Sincere Patriotism Can Do It," WAP, June 14, 1951.

electoral promises of 1953, while warning the electorate not to vote for the party in upcoming elections.[77] In "Problem Bird in the Air Again!," he directs his critique at the colonial government being counseled by a bird (the Legislative Council) of the danger of insincere constitutional amendment planned for 1950. "Unless you heed to the voice of the people," the speaking bird warns, "the incidence of 1947 may happen again in 1950."[78] The Legislative Council, like many other political arrangements under colonial rule, gave limited power to Africans in political and legal matters. Nationalists called for an increase in African representation in lawmaking organs of the colonial state.

Politics in colonial Nigeria, as in other parts of post–World War II Africa, was often characterized by rhetoric and erudition. The manifesto of each party was both an exercise in self and collective pride and irreconcilable ideological posturing on nation building. A mainstream image of a typical Nigerian nationalist was that of a loquacious person. And no other animal is as verbose as the parrot, a bird that squawks a lot but is never taken seriously. Built around the Yoruba philosophical idea of *ai-yekoto* (the world detests the truth), Lasekan appropriates the personality of the parrot, as a bird that wastes effort by talking to deaf ears or not even understanding much of what it is being said, to graphically reproduce the wasted efforts of nationalists working for decolonization. Nigerians cannot be saved from their destructive path, Lasekan proverbializes through the parrot (fig. 4.4).[79] At another level of interpretation, Lasekan gives the parrot the image of a bird that can only complain without possessing the capacity to act and effect the desired change. Depending on the context, he gives the parrot's identity to either Zik or his opponents. On one hand, he allows Zik to assume the aiyekoto character to emphasize the failure of the electorate to vote for the NCNC despite being preached to about good governance; on the other, he uses it to explain the incapacity of rival parties to achieve their electoral promises, despite their loquaciousness.

Mammals like the lions and foxes are not the only animals who lead a predatory and scavenging existence. In a critique of ethnoregional politics, Lasekan depicts the scavenging vulture as representing the colonial government, reaffirming the animal's natural habit of consuming carrion. A cartoon in this vein pictures the NEPU, a minority party in northern Nigeria, represented as an agonized dying human tied up by antinationalist laws, while the colonial government (vulture) waits to feed on its carcass (fig. 4.4). The NCNC, in the image of a rescuer, wields a weapon to save the NEPU from its impeding death, while the AG walks out of the scene saying, "Thank God he [NEPU] is not of my region."[80] If the vulture is known for its scavenging behavior, the hawk's long-standing threat to chicks takes another important place in Lasekan's ideality of the undeservedly poor condition of the Nigerian workforce. His audience would easily decode the image of a chick (a Nigerian worker) surrounded by four hawks (a tax collector, a merchant, a food seller, and a landlord). The title of this cartoon, "Plans and Counter-Plans," artistically mirrors the plight

of Nigerian workers who constantly fought the government for wage increases, only to see their efforts at a better life jeopardized by the rising
cost of living.[81] While this cartoon would appeal to the universality of the
predatory habit of the hawk, another rooted in ancient Greek literature
that found its way into colonial Nigerian literary culture is fascinating.
In adapting to the Nigerian situation one of Aesop's fables, "The Frogs
Who Wished for a King," Lasekan renders an appraisal of the Macpherson
Constitution (1951), which replaced the Richards Constitution (1945).[82]
Nigerians (frogs) asked the British colonial government (Jupiter) for a constitution (king) that would guarantee social order and were sent a log (the
Richards Constitution). However, instead of enjoying the benevolence of
the log, the frogs demanded a better king. So Jupiter sent them a stork (the
Macpherson Constitution), a natural enemy of the frog, which instead
of improving their condition ended up being autocratic and annihilating
them (fig. 4.4).[83]

The most visible bird symbol in the narrative of nationalism and self-
determination in colonial Nigeria was, however, neither the hawk nor the
vulture. Rather, it was the rooster, the symbol of the NCNC. Historical
accounts of Nigerian nationalism are unclear on why or how the NCNC
picked the rooster as its symbol, but the connection between the attributes
of the bird and nation building is clear. A crowing rooster, as printed in
Lasekan's cartoons among other visual arts of the colonial era, signifies a
new beginning in the history of a people looking forward to all the gains
of self-rule. Like other represented animals, the rooster was also a speaking
bird, chanting such statements as "Arise, shine, for the dawn of thy glory
has come!," which speaks directly to humans' understanding of progress.
But there is more to this. Appropriating the quality of the rooster as a bird
that would not fail to crow in the morning positioned the NCNC as a
party that would not fail on its electoral promises and extends the frontiers
of human-animal relations in meaningful ways.[84] In addition, the rooster
has some domineering attributes, such as the ability to stand on objects to
carry out its usual morning habit. Lasekan's depiction of a rooster perch-
ing on a fallen palm tree (symbol of the AG) as it crows metaphorically
predicts the dominance of the NCNC over the rival party (fig. 4.4).[85] One
other quality of the rooster, not clearly espoused by Lasekan, is worth exploring. Lasekan brings gender, sex, and sexuality into the logic of char-
acterizing chickens as egg-laying females (promoting progress, a higher
standard of living, and the detribalization of Nigeria) that the rooster fertil-
izes or that are destroyed by the enemies of state, represented by the snake.

The male identity of the rooster intersects with the dominant masculine image of men as the savior of the state, while the hen's procreative ability corresponds with that of the state and the electorate as a bride or female who must be wooed or persuaded to acquire power.[86]

Although the rooster occupied a special place in party politics as the animal responsible for using his crowing talent to wake up Nigerians to the battle for self-determination, it also symbolized corruption, in the sense of unmerited access to the privileges of the colonial state.[87] Here Lasekan fuses prevailing religious practices with politics. In Nigeria, the chicken is the main animal for celebrating Christmas. Followers of traditional African religion also sacrifice it to the gods and goddesses. Cartoons denoting the promise of freedom of religion under the NCNC usually feature a turban-wearing male holding a massive book (the Quran), an Anglican priest with a Bible, and a seminude male holding a chicken being presented for spiritual offering.[88] In Awolowo's hand, in another cartoon (fig. 4.4), is a chicken (representing the AG), which he offers to a spirit medium (*orisha*), praying for a ministerial appointment at the federal level. This cartoon paints Awolowo as a selfish leader willing to sacrifice his party for personal aggrandizement.[89]

Zik's reflection over the WAP 1961 libel case is an appropriate way to bring this chapter to a close. In his 1970 autobiography, Zik puts the blame for the libel more on the "novelty" of preparing and publishing political cartoons "in this part of the world" than failure of his editor to prevent the printing of materials "which might carry innuendos of a highly libelous nature."[90] But anyone familiar with the visual narrative of nationalism and party politics in 1940s and 1950s Nigeria would disagree with Zik. The print media capitalized on the almost complete lack of regulation of political cartoons to increase readership (and by extension, sales and profits) and shape public perception toward colonialism and emergent Nigerian political parties and leaders. This chapter has examined the intersection of symbolic animal art and the visual narrative of nationalism and party politics in the Nigeria of that period. Lasekan deployed his talent vigorously, using animal symbols to sharpen public opinion toward both the government and the electorate. By inserting animals into Nigerian political debate through cartoons, Lasekan tapped into the unique qualities of a variety of animals, creating a visual language that expanded the meaning of self-determination beyond human lived experience.

PART 2

⤳

Pathology, Empathy, Anxiety

5 ⟿ "Beware of Dogs"

Rabies and the Elastic Geographies of Fear

> The position of Rabies in the Township is serious. Therefore, every dog caught by the Health Authorities, whether licensed or not, will not be returned to the owner but destroyed in a painless manner. If you have the slightest doubt as to whether your dog is rabid do not hesitate to send it for painless destruction, even if the dog has been licensed for 1945.
>
> —"Menace of Rabies," *Daily Service*, April 3, 1945

ON DECEMBER 13, 1948, Sport, a white female dog belonging to John, a teenage son of E. O. Daniel, the honorary general secretary of the Nigeria Royal Society for the Prevention of Cruelty to Animals (NRSPCA) who worked as a government public affairs officer, was seized by the dogcatchers of the Lagos Town Council (LTC). Describing the pet as "very well-looked after" and "a very good friend of John," Daniel, who was African, pleaded in his petition for Sport to be released from the government animal kennel, where she was held for mandatory observation for rabies. To further prove that Sport was a "pet" not a "stray" or "street" canine, Daniel included a photo of his son and the beloved companion with the petition.[1] The thin line between colonial construction of dogs as "pet" or "street" animals that shaped antirabies law and criminalization of the canine body came to light in this case. The petition to free a beloved parlor dog of an educated elite, who became a diseased body by virtue of being found in the street in contravention of rabies laws and was locked up with "feral" and "mangy" dogs, can reveal the ways the elites attempted to extend their privileges to their animal family member. Yet the LTC's decision not to release Sport sent an unusual message: the law is a respecter of no one, even a popular member of the animal compassion movement whose household owned five dogs and three cats in 1951.

This chapter delves into the story of rabies, a common zoonotic disease in colonial Nigeria, within the context of the ambiguous relationship between dogs and humans. Dogs served multiple roles as pets and utility animals within African and European populations (as outlined in chapter 3), but the regular outbreak of rabies placed their survival at the mercy of the colonial state, which treated them as dangerous subjects that must be controlled in the interest of human safety. How a beloved canine becomes a threat to the life of its owner and the broader community affirmed the thin line between culture and nature and between the tame and the wild. The story of rabies allows historians to capture how race, class, location, and power relations shaped encounter with the canine population.

To better understand the justification for violence against dogs throughout Nigeria's colonial era, one needs to look beyond the obvious scientific evidence that canines were the main purveyor of rabies to engage colonialism as an edifice of violence. The cruel manner in which dogs were treated, under the pretext of controlling rabies, should be considered an extension of the cruelty inflicted on humans. In colonial framing of power and authority, all colonial subjects, both humans and animals, must exist in accordance with the rigid ideals of civilization and modernity. Practices and conduct that negate colonial construction of decent, orderly, or ideal appearance and behavior were usually met with condemnation. Dogs, humans' most intimate animal companion, were expected to behave in a "civilized" manner. Yet their "ugly" appearance and filthy manner of socializing were a manifestation of their savagery, which needed to be curtailed with lethal force. If colonialism did not place a high premium on the sanctity of human life, one should not expect the valued possessions of communities, including their animals, artifacts, and monuments, to be spared.

THE HISTORICAL EPIDEMIOLOGY OF RABIES

Official colonial records established that rabies in a human being was first recorded in Nigeria in 1912, when an African woman and a European man were diagnosed with the virus in Eket and Bonny, respectively. Thirteen years later, the first laboratory confirmation of rabies in a dog through a demonstration of Negri bodies was made at the Yaba rabies laboratory in Lagos. In 1932, a Porto Novo woman in Lagos tested positive for the virus thirteen days after being bitten on the chin by a rabid dog. Four years later, in 1936, a schoolboy tested positive for rabies, forty days after being bitten on the foot by a mad dog.[2] The Dogs Ordinance, a gamut of legal, veterinary, and medical regulations aimed at controlling rabies, was on the books by 1915. Yet there is a probability that rabies existed in pre-twentieth-century Nigeria, given that rabies had local names among Nigerian ethnicities (e.g., among the Yoruba, *arun digbolugi*—disease of madness).[3] Indeed, to accept, without questioning, the validity of these twentieth-century discoveries is to validate the arrogance of imperial science (which always credited itself for major medical discoveries) and to deny the existence and credibility of indigenous veterinary medicine. Regardless of the unclear origins of rabies in Nigeria, what is certain is that its vector and etiology expanded with the creation of colonial cities, population increases, and massive movements of people across diverse climatic landscapes. It was thus a modern colonial disease because every element of its control aligned with a colonial philosophy of disease eradication, among both human and canine colonial subjects.

The identity of dogs as the principal purveyor of rabies in Nigeria did not contradict global experience. We know very little about rabies in jackals, foxes, and even domesticated animals like cattle and goats in colonial Nigeria. As table 5.1 shows, from 1928 to 1959, of the 2,749 animal brains received by Yaba Laboratory Service headquarters in Lagos for rabies testing, 2,470 were those of dogs. At the same laboratory during the same period, out of 1,100 laboratory confirmations of rabies, 1,046, representing 95.1 percent, came from dogs (see table 5.2).[4] In 1932 rabies was first microscopically confirmed in a horse (named James). The expansion of veterinary education after 1960 increased research on noncanid rabies, without altering the long-held understanding that dogs were the main culprit of hydrophobia.[5] The government probably decided to invest more in a dog antirabies campaign because it was cheaper and because of the intimate relationship between canines and humans.

TABLE 5.1. ANIMAL BRAINS RECEIVED FOR RABIES TESTING AT YABA LABORATORY SERVICE HEADQUARTERS, 1928–59

Animal	Brains	Animal	Brains	Animal	Brains
Dog	2,470	Squirrel	3	Baboon	1
Cat	208	Pig	3	Calf	1
Monkey	17	Antelope	2	Chevrotain	1
Horse	17	Bat	2	Donkey	1
Goat	8	Duiker	2	Leopard	1
Guinea pig	3	Mongoose	2	Parrot	1
Rabbit	3	Sheep	2	Rat	1

Source: L. R. Boulger and J. Hardy, "Rabies in Nigeria," *West African Medical Journal* 11, no. 6 (1960): 225.

Rabies was an urban phenomenon in colonial Nigeria. With a population of 230,356 inhabitants occupying an area of 27.22 square miles in 1950, Lagos, the epicenter of colonial modernity, suffered graver consequences of human and animal rabies than any other part of Nigeria (see fig. 5.1).[6] Yet this does not mean that rabies was actually greater in the quintessential African port city. Rather, it was an indication of awareness and access to modern laboratory facilities to track etiology. Villages and rural communities came under significant watch because of the firm belief that the "mangy" dogs that served as a reservoir of rabies were from there. The intersections of rural and urban settlement patterns aligned with the confidence in imperial science as the savior of African "primitivity" to give rabies an exalted place in this history of anxiety in Nigeria.

TABLE 5.2. LABORATORY-CONFIRMED CASES OF ANIMAL RABIES, YABA LABORATORY SERVICE HEADQUARTERS, 1928–59

Animal	Rabies cases	Percentage
Dog	1,046	95.1
Cat	48	4.4
Goat	4	0.3
Donkey	1	0.1
Pig	1	0.1
Total	1,100	100.0

Source: L. R. Boulger and J. Hardy, "Rabies in Nigeria," West African Medical Journal 11, no. 6 (1960): 226.

Aside from the medical data presented above, some of the earliest detailed political narratives about rabies emerged because it affected colonial officers, not Nigerians. Indeed, the common notion that only African dogs posed danger to Europeans was only valid for official colonial ordering and othering of the animal and human worlds; it did not reflect reality. On February 16, 1917, Resident Officer W. B. Thomson and District Officer H. D. Foulkes were bitten by a "mad" dog belonging to the latter in Maiduguri. "Unusual behavior," "change of attitude," or "madness" was, in the absence of definite laboratory evidence, the common means of identifying a rabid dog, as also in this case. Thomson's dog ran away for twenty-four hours after biting the two officers. "Judging from the appearance and behavior of the dog" when it returned, another colonial officer, J. H. C. Elder, "expressed the opinion" that the animal was mad. Physician H. L. Burgess thought the animal "appeared to be savage" and recommended its destruction, which was promptly carried out.[7] Frederick Lugard, Nigeria's pioneering head of government, did not waste time in approving the recommendation by Burgess for Thomson and Foulkes to proceed to the Pasteur Institute (in Dakar in modern Senegal), the most advanced medical facility for rabies treatment in West Africa, where they could start receiving their vaccinations before going home to Britain to complete the regimen.[8] Although medics thought that rabies virus took several weeks to incubate in humans, the erratic nature of global transportation and the occasional failure to accurately trace etiology necessitated a temporary stop in Dakar en route London.

TABLE 5.3. REGIONAL DISTRIBUTION OF CLINICAL HUMAN RABIES AND LABORATORY-CONFIRMED ANIMAL RABIES, 1928–59

Region	Humans	Dogs	Cats	Pigs	Goats
Lagos	9	331	12	1	—
Western	15	176	10	—	2
Eastern	25	227	4	—	2
Northern	12	236	15	1	—
Cameroons	17	72	6	—	—
Total	78	1042	47	2	4

Source: L. R. Boulger and J. Hardy, "Rabies in Nigeria," West African Medical Journal 11, no. 6 (1960): 227.

It would take another major dog-bite incident involving a European for the colonial government to begin rethinking the procedure for treating rabies. In April 1926 two assistant district officers, Capt. S. T. Harvey and Captain Cheeseman, were bitten in Opobo by a supposedly rabid dog belonging to Harvey.[9] British West Africa still did not have a dedicated rabies treatment facility, a situation that the secretary of state for the colonies, Leo Amery, described as "unfortunate." As a result, Harvey and Cheeseman, like previous European victims, had to be transported to the Pasteur Institute in Dakar.[10] The level of correspondence among the highest-ranked officers in the colonial service (the secretary of state for the colonies, the governor of Nigeria, the secretary administering the government of Nigeria, the director of medical and sanitary services [DMSS], and the chief veterinary officer) clearly revealed the seriousness with which the medical condition of Harvey and Cheeseman was taken.[11] In addition to this, Amery was probably worried about the cost of treating Harvey and Cheeseman in Dakar (which stood at around £172). He inquired about the possibility of establishing "a center for the treatment of persons bitten by rabid animals" in Lagos (Nigeria) and Accra (the Gold Coast).[12]

Avery's request paved the way for unveiling the historical epidemiology of rabies in Nigeria. According to DMSS Dr. Alexander, from 1913, when two persons (one European nonofficial and an African woman) died of rabies, to 1926, twelve cases were recorded, "but no definite details are available nor is it established that they were actually cases of rabies." Only one out of the twelve cases resulted in death. After presenting a short history of rabies in Nigeria, Dr. Alexander advised that the country was not ready for a special treatment center or for local production of antirabies vaccine. He believed that the incidence of rabies among the local populace and among Europeans was not high enough to warrant government investment, which would also include the training of bacteriologists. He reaffirmed the need to continue to depend on the Pasteur Institute, stating that the improvement of sea transportation meant that any officers bitten by a rabid dog could arrive in Dakar within fifteen to thirty days of the attack.[13]

The governor of Nigeria accepted the report of his medical officer without querying its obvious racial bias—its insistence that while foreign treatment for colonial officers was desirable, Africans should nevertheless continue to make use of the "inadequate" and "unsatisfactory" arrangement. Although the idea of local production of rabies vaccine was shelved in accordance with Alexander's recommendation, pathologists at the Yaba Laboratory Service headquarters in Lagos continued to experiment on extracting virus from laboratory animals. In 1928 and 1933 rabies virus was successfully extracted from rabbits and guinea pigs and from mice, respectively.[14] In 1956 bacteriologists at the same Yaba laboratory produced a Flury low egg passage vaccine for dogs for the first time, but they could not produce it in a large quantity for domestic use.[15] To the end of colonial rule, Nigeria continued to depend on a New York–based company (the Lederle Laboratories division of the American Cyanamid Company) for its rabies vaccine needs, spending in 1952 more than £10,000 for twenty thousand doses at 6s. each.[16]

However, aside from its overt racist bent, other medical sources across the country suggest that Alexander's report provided a misleading picture of rabies epidemiology in Nigeria to the Colonial Office, probably because he wanted the government to focus on other medical challenges confronting the colony instead of making another major investment. In the mid-1920s rabies in dogs in Nigeria was "definitely on the increase or at least an increasing number of cases" was being reported each year, another medical report indicated. During the outbreak of rabies in Jos in 1925, "several natives" reportedly died from hydrophobia.[17] Yet the term "several" in the report is vague. Evidence of the "high" incidence of rabies came from a June 1927 correspondence among the Crown agents for the colonies, an official trading firm of the government, and the medical establishment in London. When the Crown agents approached the Ministry of Health in London for a "large and routine supply" of rabies vaccine for Nigeria, the medics in the metropole advised the government that they did not keep a large supply. While the Ministry of Health simplified local production of vaccines with such encouraging words as "It is easily done" and "Any competent bacteriologist can readily acquire the necessary technical skill," colonial medics in Nigeria thought it would require enormous financial and human investment.[18]

The picture of the incidence of rabies from the 1930s became clearer as the colonial government increased its investment in public health, fearing the impact of epidemics on the breakdown of law and order. Massive population increase and movement across regional and international boundaries introduced epidemic diseases, including rabies, to places where they probably did not exist before. From 1933 to 1939 the number of people who went through prophylactic inoculation after contact with rabid dogs increased five times among the Europeans and nearly one hundred times among non-Europeans. The figures for positive diagnosis were 67 in 1933 among Europeans and 445 in 1935 among non-Europeans. It jumped to 159 and 1,060 in 1937 and 1939 in the European and African populations, respectively. These findings also indicate that the appearance of rabid dogs was "more readily reported than formerly."[19] Within ten weeks in early 1945, twenty-five cases of rabies were confirmed by doctors and veterinarians in Lagos.[20] Similarly, in 1941 the DMSS and director of veterinary service stated "conclusively" that the incidence of rabies "is steadily increasing" and that stricter control was necessary in the public interest. The last decade of colonial rule represented a turning point in rabies outbreaks across the country. Although government began free vaccination of dogs in Lagos in January 1959, this did not prevent a major outbreak the same year.[21] By 1959 forty-three cases of rabies in dogs and cats and three in humans were confirmed in an epidemic that lasted close to a year in Lagos. During the same period, about nine hundred dogs were vaccinated in what is among the most successful organized mass inoculations of canines in city history.[22] In summary, rabies, like other public health threats, provided the British colonial medical establishment with the opportunity to hone its relevance as an important arm of the civilizing mission in Nigeria.

THE MEDICALIZATION OF DOGS

The story of Sport, John, and Daniel is just one out of countless experiences of dogs and their owners who tried to navigate the Dogs Ordinance.[23] The duration of implementation was flexible, thus allowing local

authorities, including chiefs, to modify it to their specific situation. The ordinance was activated when a "mad" dog bit someone, died, or was killed
after demonstrating "abnormal" behavior or when a human victim died of
suspected hydrophobia. These observable signs were then followed by a
scientific laboratory proof. Thus, medical proof of rabies was not required
to place an entire community under rabies watch through the Dogs Ordinance. The owner of a suspected rabid dog was encouraged to send the
carcass's head to the veterinary office, which would conduct a microscopic
examination of the brain. The undamaged brain of a dog would yield the
best results if tested within twenty-four hours of the animal's death or longer if chemically preserved to prevent degenerative changes.

Not all veterinary offices had the facility to test dog brains for
rabies—in southern and northern Nigeria, only the veterinary offices in
Yaba (Lagos) and Vom, respectively, had the wherewithal to conduct such
a test, which would be positive if a Negri body were found. Depending
on the location of the incident, it could take up to four weeks for the lab
results to come back. Therefore, one case of rabies was enough for a local
authority to declare a rabies "epidemic," defining a community as a "diseased" area and initiating rabies anxiety through use of the ordinance.[24]
Popular diagnosis and scientific proof could happen at different times and
thus create conflicting antirabies campaigns, as we shall see. Much of the
anxiety over rabies was a result of the significant power that nonscientific,
or popular, observation—for example, automatically labeling any "mad"
dog as "rabid"—had in shaping legal and political processes.[25]

During a rabies outbreak, government officials would round up street
dogs found in public places, whether licensed and vaccinated or not. Unlicensed dogs were killed outright. The licensed would be observed for seven
days at the government kennel, which served as an animal detention center.
If a detained dog died within seven days, the government would invite its
owner (if known) for vaccination.[26] A component of the rabies law stating
that "the owner if known, will be prosecuted and will be liable to pay the expenses of seizure and detention" was rarely enforced.[27] Apparently, the killing of a stray dog was seen as punishment enough for keeping an unlicensed
animal. Yet even licensed dogs were killed outright, especially during major
outbreaks when the kennel could not handle the quantity of captured animals.[28] Application of the Dogs Ordinance could remain in effect for as long
as three months after the last recorded case of rabies.[29]

At times, dogs in private homes that were suspected of being rabid,
whose owners were accused of negligence, that were not on a leash, and

that were in contact with humans and animals—whether licensed or not—were also rounded up.[30] All licensed dogs were expected to wear their badge on their collar and be muzzled at all times. The lack of a license was itself an indication of the contravention of the Dogs Ordinance—as vaccination was a prerequisite for collecting a license.[31] Vaccination was only required for dogs above the age of five months, veterinarians having established that the vaccine was ineffective below this age. Dogs younger than three months old were not required to have a license. However, town councils and dog owners alike manipulated the records of dogs' ages either to enforce or to prevent seizures of animals. When this became a big problem during the outbreak of rabies in Jos Township in 1934, the government advised that all dogs as soon as they are able to walk should be licensed and vaccinated to avoid age controversy. In July 1959 Lagos extended the term of a dog license from three to six months to eliminate confusion over age and to bridge the gap between vaccination and licensing age.[32]

The physical geography of implementation of the Dogs Ordinance varied.[33] In most instances, the rabies ordinance was focused on the precise community where a rabid dog was found or where someone had died of hydrophobia.[34] However, the spatial distribution of population and the economic and political status of communities did shape the extent and, by extension, the cumulative effect of rabies control. For instance, the outbreak of rabies in Kano in 1942 brought an area of twenty miles radius with its focal point at the post office under watch for several months. Yet the entire city was declared a rabid city by the veterinary department in 1938.[35] After declaring Lagos Island rabies-free in March 1943, G. B. Williams, the president of the LTC, released an amendment to the Dogs Ordinance to empower its officers to capture all street dogs in Apapa, which was not included in the earlier ordinance.[36] In 1954 both the island and mainland areas of Lagos, with an estimated population of quarter of a million, came under a rabies watch.[37] In addition, neighborhood-based dog policing also took place. A case in point was the rounding up of dogs in the military areas of Yaba. Worried about an impending danger when the dog of a military officer, Sergeant Lovatt, died of rabies in April 1954, military authorities asked for imposition of the rabies law in the barracks, where an increasing number of stray dogs sought refuge.[38] The resultant raid produced seventy-two dogs, twenty-three of which were claimed by their owners after producing licenses. The fate of the remaining dogs is unknown. The government may have carried out the usual procedure of killing all unclaimed dogs.[39]

If the colonial medics and administrators initiated rabies hysteria, Nigeria's newspapers, controlled almost exclusively by African elites and nationalists, helped expand and consolidate it. The newspaper was the main media channel through which the government communicated concerning the Dogs Ordinance. By giving expanded coverage to rabies news, with headlines such as "Outbreak of Rabies in Afikpo," newspapers directly shaped public perception in the interest of the government.[40] Carefully written newspaper editorials with frightening headlines such as "Beware of Dogs" warned against hydrophobia, advising the public to respect rabies regulations issued by the very colonial establishment they were usually critical of.[41] The real and imagined geographies of rabies fear was always in a state of flux as Nigerians, especially urbanites, constantly worried about its epidemiology, seeking information about risk beyond the well-publicized warning to avoid dogs.

To worsen the situation, rabies law treated geographical delimitation for enforcement within a city as rigid space, disregarding the fluidity of human and animal movement across communities. Thus, the physical town planning maps used by medical and legal officers for declaring rabies within communities contradicted the actual patterns of human movement, which rarely acknowledge boundaries. Rumors spread in places with limited access to the official government gazette, newspapers, and informal means of communicating government decisions about which areas were under rabies watch. Even in places like Lagos, the center of media culture in Nigeria, confusion was regularly the result of the geographical enforcement of the Dogs Ordinance. A public notice titled "Dog Rules Explained" published in the *Nigerian Daily Times* (*NDT*) on November 27, 1946, clarified a rabies law published a week earlier, stating that "dogs may now be allowed to run free" on Lagos Island and in Ikoyi but that the law imposed restrictions on their counterparts in Apapa, Ebute Metta, Yaba, and Iddo. Aside from intensifying the hysteria over rabies, the unstable and confusing geography of imposition of the Dogs Ordinance intensified the criminalization of owners and the use of violence against dogs.

Propaganda found an important place in the campaign against rabies. One interesting feature of the Dogs Ordinance is how the government managed to combine the conventional threat of punishment for disobedience of law with advice and plea.[42] Rabies was among the few diseases in colonial Nigeria with this kind of ambivalent character. The admonition "If you love your dog, save it from being destroyed," found in a newspaper propaganda signed by medical officer of health (MOH) Dr. Isaac Ladipo

Oluwole, the pioneering physician of public health in Nigeria, sought to mobilize emotional sentiment for animals by associating disobedience of the Dogs Ordinance with lack of love for animals.[43] Another propaganda notice published in March 1945 in the *NDT* gives an interesting dimension to the intricate relationship between humans and animals:

> Are you satisfied that your dog is "securely confined" during your absence, that is, that it is tied up or led on a strong leash even within your premises?
> If not, why risk your life with a possibly rabid dog?
>
> Are you satisfied that your dog is not rabid?
> If not, why risk your life?
>
> In every case of doubt, be on the safe side and send your dog to the Health Office . . . to be destroyed in a painless, humane manner. "Beware of Dogs."[44]

This "friendly" notice is then followed by a verbatim reprint of the Dogs Ordinance (as contained in the law book) emphasizing the dual punishment of imprisonment and fines for defaulters. Radio broadcasts on rabies prevention, directed specifically at schoolchildren, conformed to the established practice of using minors to propagate practices such as cleanliness and hygiene. The school as a site through which "civilized" and modern practices were introduced and transmitted to the public had a place in the campaign against rabies because the government held that disobedience of the Dogs Ordinance owed largely to a "primitive mindset" (a product of lack of enlightenment). Thus, propaganda material titled "Rabies Epidemic: Information Bulletin No. 2" attributed the disease to "ignorance of the basic facts" and went on to provide a question-and-answer dialogue on symptoms and what to do if bitten by a dog.[45] From time to time, the government would revise the medium of propaganda by printing pamphlets in an indigenous language.[46] While this approach seemed to have worked in large monolingual communities, it was unsuitable for multiethnic ones with significant linguistic diversity. Even in big single-language communities, very few people could read the pamphlets circulated by the government. The use of town criers in smaller communities was also common.

Rabies law, like other colonial legislation, had many limitations. As previously mentioned, laboratory results of rabies tests did not have to arrive before an entire community could be declared rabid. Indeed, in many instances, colonial officers following the advice of their medical counterparts would impose the rabies ordinance, only to revoke it weeks after the test came back negative. However, many dogs were destroyed while the artificial scare was in place. For colonial and medical officers, the impact of a wrong judgment or negative test for rabies was not as important as the consequences of not taking action to place a community under a rabies watch. The general advice that people who were bitten by or came in contact with a "suspected" rabid dog were "automatically" infected led to the administering of rabies vaccines to uninfected persons. The unscientific assumption among both the colonial government and the public that any dog who bites is "mad" and "rabid" also contributed to anxiety over rabies. Killing of dogs that had bitten someone without any provocation was the usual practice in many communities.[47] Not only was it considered a way of preventing the spread of rabies; it served mostly as retaliation for the dogs' "unkind" attitude toward humans, regardless of the circumstances that led to the attack. The dog's bite could well have been provoked by a human's unkind action toward the animal.

Every outbreak of rabies came with a reiteration to the public of its epidemiology. Medical experts asked the public to look for "a pronounced change of conduct" in their dogs, which included unusual quietness, aimless running around, watering of the mouth, weakness (especially in the hindquarters), burrowing of nose under paws, overdemonstrativeness, and showing fierceness toward other dogs, such as a tendency to rush at and "savage" them without cause. The behavior of dogs before and after contracting rabies were opposing—"vicious dogs often become strangely quiet and even the good tempered sensible dogs may become ill tempered."[48] Other clinical symptoms included dropping of the lower jaw and a vacant expression on the animal's face. Paralysis of the lower jaw could then spread to other parts of the body. The dog would become unable to eat or drink. Photophobia, or a desire to hide in dark places, was another readily observable symptom of rabies. Colonial medics were convinced that the unhygienic behavior of dogs and humans and the disrespect for the Dogs Ordinance were inhibiting the campaign against rabies. "Theoretically, it should be a very simple matter to prevent rabies," Dr. Oluwole opined in a 1945 radio broadcast targeted specifically at schoolchildren; however, "control is very difficult," he concluded.[49] Dr. Oluwole and his fellow medics believed the virus would remain a recurrent problem, yet a challenge manageable through compulsory yearly vaccination of all dogs.

Nigerians had a mixed response to the Dogs Ordinance. On one hand, they feared hydrophobia, which medical officers constantly reminded the public was an incurable disease once a person was infected. On the other, they doubted colonial medicine. Rabies, like other diseases, placed indigenous African and European medicine in conflict. While both agreed that "madness" was a clinical symptom for rabies, they each adopted different methods for establishing the facts of a case. Among the Yoruba indigenous doctors, if a dog refused to eat pap (corn meal with a high water concentration), then it was considered to be rabid. Laboratory confirmation of rabies was conducted in a different way, using the brain tissue from the carcass of a suspected canine victim. Not all locals believed rabies was a zoonotic disease, as imperial science had established. In Ijesaland in 1942, for instance, High Chief Obanla claimed that his people "did not believe that rabies could be transferred from dogs to man."[50] But this irreconcilable understanding of the etiology of rabies mostly favored the European-trained doctors and veterinarians, who readily used the so-called ignorance of the people to further establish the superiority of colonial science wherever indigenous therapy failed. "This unnecessary waste of life could have been prevented," the MOH regretted, after the death of a twelve-year-old boy who was under the care of a traditional doctor after being bitten by a rabid dog in Zaria in November 1945.[51] The MOH then went to advise the public to seek European medical help immediately after being bitten by a rabid dog.

While indigenous therapy appeared to have failed in this case, the occasional failure of Western cures led to two complementary outcomes: it solidified the claim that local medicine was better than foreign medicine, while also heightening tension over the cure and spread of the disease. When a dog died after receiving rabies vaccine in Kaduna in 1935, the critics of colonial medicines seemed to have evidence to back up their belief that rabies vaccine, which cost an average of 10s. nationwide, was not as effective as indigenous medicine. To defuse the tension over the failure of the vaccine to prevent the dog's death, acting chief veterinary officer J. A. Griffiths issued a public notice stating that the dog had died twelve days and eighteen hours after vaccination and that the vaccine, which he defined as "merely prophylactic," required fourteen days to work.[52] Griffiths said that his circular was meant to counter the rumors of the inefficacy of rabies vaccines being circulated widely, "as the Kaduna news has been broadcasted over Nigeria by all and sundry persons."[53]

However, Griffiths's analysis of the difference between how humans and dogs are treated for rabies is interesting, for it demonstrates the unequal value placed on life in the colonial society. Humans bitten by rabid dogs received twenty-one or more doses of a vaccine over the course of several weeks. Although this treatment could also work for rabid dogs, Griffiths established, the probability that a diseased animal would infect another dog or human, he insisted, justified their outright destruction. The Kaduna case of 1935 was by no means an isolated instance. Cases of hind paralysis after vaccination happened even in Yaba and Vom, the two centers for veterinary laboratory in Nigeria. Instead of denying medical failure, the DMSS, W. B. Johnson, warned in a gazette article titled "Anti-Rabic Vaccination of Dogs" that "there is a slight risk of paralysis" after vaccination. The medics probably thought that publicly admitting the rare medical failure could help put to rest the rumor that such errors were widespread, which was injurious to the rabies eradication effort.[54] The effect of contradiction between Western and African medicine varied. Few dog owners would voluntarily give up their animal, even if they thought it was rabid. Rather, they would continue to administer indigenous therapy and medicine to their pets hoping they would recover. Others feared punishment for keeping an unlicensed dog.

But not all dog owners would wait for their dogs to be taken away from them or allow them to die at home. On September 30, 1949, an unnamed man in Lagos took his rabid dog to the Public Health Department and left a note for Dr. Oluwole. The dog died the following day. Fearing that the man's family may be infected, Dr. Oluwole placed a public notice in the newspaper advising him and his family to come out for testing and inoculation.[55] In its October 21 issue, the *Daily Service* reported that the man, his wife, and nine children later showed up for vaccination at the health department.[56] Another case involving a European simply identified as "Geddess" who worked with John Holt & Company, a European trading firm, in Kano revealed the extent to which some dog owners would go to avoid hydrophobia, even at their own discomfort. In September 1947, Geddess's dog was bitten in the neck by another dog, which disappeared. On October 24, his dog began to "act strangely and commenced salivating." Geddess "became worried" and shot the dog in the evening and took the corpse to the veterinary officer the following morning. However, the veterinary officer could not send the brain tissue to the regional veterinary office in Vom because it was badly damaged and decomposed.[57]

Rabies eradication definitely placed the colonial government and Nigerians in conflict with one another across location and class, but it also caused additional tension among Nigerians. Conflicts within communities, between neighbors, and within families were easily grafted onto the politics of eradicating rabies through a communal policing of the disease, promoted by the government and the newspapers, which advocated that "those who have no dogs can help by seeing to it that those who have comply with the request of the Health Authority."[58] An open petition titled "Wild Dogs in Sabongeri Kano," published in the *NDT* in 1947, placed an entire stranger community of a major northern Nigerian city under government watch. "In short these dangerous and carnivorous animals are doing more havoc in Sabongeri than one can describe," a resident of the community identified simply as "L. Y. N." (probably to conceal his or her identity and prevent a backlash) lamented.[59] When neighbors report their fellow residents or the entire community for keeping a "suspected" rabid dog, the town council would step in to take the animal for destruction, sometimes without screening for rabies. In some cases, owners might be charged in court if the health department and neighbors could prove the animal was rabid. Accusation and counteraccusation of disobedience of rabies laws in neighborhoods could last for weeks, snowballing into a much bigger communal conflict.[60]

In addition, the government's recommendation for dealing with suspected rabid dogs tended to promote violence against animals. People were expected to notify the town council if they found a stray dog in their compounds and were also allowed to kill the animal if it attacked them or their animals.[61] Few people would wait to ascertain if a stray dog that came to their dwelling or that attacked them was rabid or not before putting it to death. When a seven-year-old girl, Chinyere Iregbu of Ikeja, died of rabies in Lagos in July 1954, health officers used the occasion to warn that killing a suspected rabid dog or burying a dog that died of rabies without informing the government carried the same weight of punishment as not giving up a live rabid dog.[62]

ALL DOGS ARE NOT EQUAL BEFORE THE LAW

All animals, like humans, were not equal before the law. And this inequality manifested in the treatment of rabid dogs. How dogs were treated by medical and town council officers was influenced by the social class and race of their owners. Dogs of Europeans and educated upper-class Nigerians usually escaped large-scale roundups because of the assumption that their vaccinations were up to date. Europeans, especially those with significant political power, frequently disobeyed rabies laws in their constant quest to extend their privilege to their animal companions. Thus, when the dog of Sergeant Cartlidge of the Royal West African Frontier Force died of rabies in Jos on March 30, 1942, two days after leaving Kano, which was under a rabies watch, the local authority issued an additional notice emphasizing the importance of respecting the law.[63] It is unclear whether Sergeant Cartlidge was ever punished for violating the Dogs Ordinance. Such disobedience of rabies law by Europeans was common enough to compel the governor of Nigeria, Bernard Bourdillon, to issue a special order during the nationwide outbreak of rabies in 1940 insisting that the "non-African, including the European population, like the natives, must obey the regulation on the movement of dogs."[64] This notice did not stop Europeans from disobeying the Dogs Ordinance, however, nor did it change the official view that dogs in the poor and rural communities posed the biggest threat to public health because they lacked vaccinations. The affirmation of the DMSS that the "reservoir of infection for rabies is the large native-owned dog population" where rabies is "endemic" and his recommendation that the dog population of the "natives" be reduced to address the problem of rabies spoke effectively to the ordering of Nigerian population based on social class and race.[65]

Rabies control within the European expatriate community was also based on the notion that Whites had stronger emotional attachment to animals than did Africans. While Africans would certainly be sad that their dogs were destroyed under the pretext of rabies eradication, the Whites, the government thought, would be sadder. In some ways, colonial officers gave extended accommodation to Europeans (such as allowing them to take their dogs in and out of rabies-infested areas after receiving written authorization) because of the firm belief that the exotic thoroughbred dogs were more valuable and played a greater companionship role for Europeans than for Africans.[66] The following note by the assistant superintendent of police of northern Nigeria to the Jos Township authorities in February 1950 is among the clearest indication of the intersections of class, location, and race in the administration of the Dogs Ordinance: "I would therefore be very grateful if you could have a roundup, particularly in the olden part of this township, where there are a number of food hunting strays which look most unhealthy." His instruction on the roundup in the European section of the town contrasts with the "olden" one, where most locals lived: "A roundup in the GRA [Government Reservation Area] would have to be rather tactfully done—people are liable to lose their sense of proportion where dogs are concerned."[67]

The last portion of the senior police officer's instruction—"people are liable to lose their sense of proportion where dogs are concerned"—is by no means speculation. Cases in which Europeans fought town council officers who tried to "collect" their dogs are plenty. In the famous dog-bite case of 1954, Alexander Gregory refused to surrender his dog for rabies examination, despite police intervention. It would take days of pressure from high-ranking officers for him to release his dog for observation.[68] On January 21, 1955, Francis Gilmore, the European general manager of the West African Construction and Development Company, and his wife, Bernardina, were arraigned before the Yaba Magistrate Court for assaulting LTC dogcatchers and two police officers during a dog-collection effort in their neighborhood.[69] Europeans were also more likely to hire lawyers to fight the capturing of their dogs than were Africans. In September 1943 the Irving and Bonnar law firm, on behalf of J. G. Aldrich, petitioned the LTC on the "illegal" kidnapping of a twelve-month-old white mongrel belonging to Aldrich, asking the government to release the dog from the kennel, where it was being detained for rabies observation. According to the petition, the dog had broken loose from the deck chair to which it was chained and run out of the compound into the waiting hands of the LTC dogcatchers.[70] Instead of allowing the dogcatchers to take the dog away, Aldrich "took part in a tug-of-war holding on to the front legs while a dog catcher held onto the hind legs," the MOH said defending his staff.[71] Had Aldrich not engaged the dogcatchers in the "tug-of-war," the MOH might have allowed her dog to be released even before the seven days of observation ended. Europeans enjoyed the occasional privilege of having their captured dogs under examination let go before the full observation was complete. The usual justification for their plea for early release was that their animal might contract rabies in the unsanitary government kennel.

The documented violence of dogcatchers, who were invariably Africans, against Europeans' dogs can be seen as a form of resistance to colonial masters. For one thing, only in a few instances, such as during the rounding up of dogs, would dogcatchers, largely uneducated men, be able to inflict pain on Europeans or demonstrate their might. Like other agents of colonialism, such as tax collectors and police officers, dogcatchers were generally treated by the public with disdain. Added to this opprobrium was the unsavory and unsanitary aspect of their job—ending beloved animals' lives. European residential areas or homes, as sites of power, were constant reminders to Africans of their subjection. Being given a task to roam freely in search of stray dogs in European neighborhoods provided the dogcatcher a not insignificant power as an agent of the state. When T. A. Mumani, an LTC dogcatcher at Ikoyi in 1954, was reproached by

Europeans who criticized his method of catching their dog by "holding the dog by one hind leg and swinging it round above his head" before then dropping it into a cage, he allegedly said that "he could kill the dog if he wished."[72] Race and resistance alone are inadequate to explain the alleged improper behavior of dogcatchers in European neighborhoods. In 1938 the dog of Thomas Dustin, a produce buyer of the Compagnie Française de l'Afrique Occidentale in Jos, was captured "under his nose." In his official report on the matter, Dustin claimed that the dogcatchers appeared in his home without any form of identification and added that "as there is a high sale value locally for European dogs the implications are obvious." Dustin thus established the financial motivation for seizure of his dog.[73]

The popular notion that European dogs were rabies-free remained only in the documentation and imagination of colonial officers—it did not reflect reality. Even colonial officers, as seen in the case of Harvey and Cheeseman, were known to contract rabies from their own dogs. In June 1934 a dog described as "undoubtedly affected with rabies," belonging to Mr. Harley of the Bank of British West Africa, was destroyed by Jos Town Council officials. Two other dogs belonging to Europeans, Mr. Harries Jones of the Niger Company and Mr. Kettlewell of John Holt & Company, bitten by Mr. Harley's dog were held, pending instructions from the senior veterinary officer "as to their disposal."[74] The fate of these two dogs is unknown, but European dogs stood the chance of escaping outright destruction, even if bitten by a "suspected" rabid dog, because their owners were usually willing to pay the cost of having their dogs observed (which stood at 6 pence per day in Lagos in the mid-1940s) at the kennel until evidence of rabies could be ascertained.[75] This is particularly true in the case of a female dog belonging to Lieutenant Colonel Martin of Kano. On June 26, 1950, Martin's dog bit its owner and an African steward, but it did not show any sign of sickness and appeared to be eating and drinking fine. Martin did not destroy his dog as the government recommended. Two days after, on June 28, after showing some "slight change in character," the bitch was confined to the rabies kennel at the veterinary office. After the dog died on July 1, its brain later tested positive for rabies. Subsequently, seven dogs belonging to Europeans working in the veterinary, police, and district offices, and in private firms who had contact with Martin's dog were destroyed.[76] This may represent the most audacious destruction of European dogs in a single episode in 1950s Kano.

Regardless, rabies in European dogs was typically blamed on African dogs, which were stereotyped as purveyors of the virus. The expectation that well-bred foreign dogs would not leave the parlors or the immediate vicinity of the well-kept lawns of European neighborhoods and government stations where most Whites lived was not met. Like African dogs, foreign dogs, most of which were mixed breeds, went astray, socializing with African dogs to the disaffection of their owners. Obvious symptoms of rabies, such as absconding, were also commonly found among dogs of Europeans. After an Alsatian belonging to Lieutenant Burgess disappeared from home in George's Barracks, Kano, in July 1942, her three-month-old puppies all died of rabies in September. The Kano Veterinary Department was convinced that the mother of the puppies was definitely infected by rabies, causing her to "go mad" and run away.[77] Another dog of a European visiting Jos from the Gold Coast in May 1934 bit an African clerk. The dog was described as "normally not of the savage nature" type—a description meant to differentiate it from the teeming population of Africans' dogs. A public notice for the runaway dog described it as "an all-white smooth haired dog of the terrier class about one year old, short tailed, drooping ears, and wearing a collar."[78] It is not clear if this dog was ever seen again, but missing Europeans' dogs were normally easier to recover because of their unique breeds and distinctive appearances. On July 5, 1939, S. W. Ajediti of Idanre, in a letter to his district officer, "unexpectedly found a gray, hairy, robust and fine dog" roaming about the neighborhood and suspected it of belonging to a European "or a noble man" in the area.[79] After the district officer sent out a circular to the few Europeans in the area, J. C. Weddell of John Holt & Company came to claim the "fat" dog in question.

MANY WAYS OF DYING

As noted earlier, the rounding up of stray dogs during rabies outbreaks was the standard procedure of medical and town council officers for eradicating rabies. To worsen the situation, health officers rarely detained dogs for seven days as required by law before destroying them. "Mangy-looking" stray dogs captured in poor neighborhoods and unsanitary environments stood a more limited chance of being detained for seven days than those removed from European neighborhoods or the homes of upper- and middle-class educated Africans. The manner in which this was carried out was considered by many, including the nationalist newspapers, as being unfair to both the animals and their owners. Not only were they "baited, captured, and herded most cruelly into cages"; they were also brutally disposed (see fig. 5.1), according to the editorial of the *Daily Service*.[80] The story of rabid dogs was a dilemma—on one hand, the public, including

RABIES LAW

284 DOGS DESTROYED

One fatal bite

THE Health Authorities have destroyed 284 dogs in Lagos Island and Ikoyi since the anti-rabies by-law was brought in force in the last week of June.

One man has died following a dog-bite. Post-mortem examination revealed that cause of death was rabies.

The Public Health Authorities have warned over the week-end that Lagos is still a diseased area and that the public should observe the prohibition order against dogs straying within the Lagos township.

FIGURE 5.1. Newspaper report on a rabies outbreak (1954). *Source: Nigerian Daily Times,* August 30, 1954.

the press, wanted a disease-free society; on the other, the way in which the animals were captured and "wickedly disposed" of did not, animal advocates thought, treat the diseased dogs with dignity.[81] Animal advocacy by such groups as the NRSPCA called for compassion for dogs in the face of the threat that rabies posed to public health.[82]

In contesting the unjust killing of dogs, the NRSPCA and other critics of dog extermination attempted to draw a correlation between the ways diseases were policed among humans and animals. If humans are not extra-judicially killed because of their sicknesses, animals also should not be.[83] A succinct, yet problematic, correlation between human and animal sickness is expressed in an extract from a petition written by the Deji (king) of Akure to his senior district officer against the indiscriminate destruction of dogs in his town in 1948: "There are crasy [sic] people in nearly all towns, and villages all over the world." The Deji's claim is one that his district officer would likely agree with. His position, however, that "it will not be an admitted reason for anybody to say because a person is in-sane [sic] in a town or a village and therefore encourage the destruction of the whole town or village" attempts to establish a logic that the colonial officer would probably not accept.[84] The criticism of rabies control would probably have been successful if Nigerians spoke with one voice. However, many did feel that the safety of humans outweighed any consideration for the rights of dogs. "If you have the slightest doubt as to whether your dog is rabid," a front-page news item of the April 3, 1945, issue of the *Daily Service* advised, "do not hesitate to send it for painless destruction even if the dogs had been licensed for the following year." The title of the article "Menace of Rabies: Drastic Diseases Require Drastic Measures" conveyed approval of the government's policy and the extent to which Nigerians were willing to sacrifice dogs for their own wellness.[85]

In September 1950 the LTC, under increased pressure from the NRSPCA, pledged to detain all dogs for seven days as enshrined in rabies law—regardless of their ownership, appearance, or where they were captured. But this new development did not answer one of the biggest questions about animal seizing: Who would pay the cost of sheltering dogs during observation? The law stipulated that the owner of a seized dog would be responsible for the upkeep of the animal while it was in detention. However, because most of the animals captured were unlicensed, owners rarely claimed them to avoid prosecution or having to pay for the cost of upkeep. In addition, the veterinary office in Lagos, like those across the country, did not have the capacity to accommodate a large number of animals for a long time, and although most of the administrative towns had kennels for stray animals, the unhealthy condition of most such facilities facilitated the spread of disease among animals. Keeping a large number of individual animals in total isolation for long periods of time could only work if adequate facilities were available. Although veterinary officers and the government did advise that all dogs bitten by a rabid dog should be killed in their owners' "own interests and more of other people," the Dogs Ordinance did not approve the killing of suspected rabid dogs and their animal victims. Rather, they were to be taken into the custody of veterinarians for observation. However, the "conventional" practice across the country was to kill all stray dogs after they were captured. Being a stray, for the government, was synonymous with having rabies. The immediate destruction of suspected rabid dogs was a clear attempt by the government to avoid shouldering the responsibility of caring for dogs in custody. The anxiety of owners over the capturing of dogs owed largely to the unpredictable fate of the dogs, which might be impounded for seven days as stipulated in the law or killed outright.

The fate of captured dogs varied widely. One *NDT* article, "284 Dogs Destroyed: One Fatal Bite," reported on the final fate of dogs captured within two months of rabies enforcement in two areas of Lagos (the island

FIGURE 5.2. Death by hanging (1950s). *Source:* Cal Prof 3/1/1291, NAE.

and Ikoyi) in late August 1954 (see fig. 5.2).[86] In Ibadan in June 1939, of the 170 stray dogs captured, 51 were claimed, while 119 were destroyed.[87] From March 13 to 31, 1951, 522 dogs were captured in Maiduguri. A mere 10 were claimed by their owners; the remaining 512 were destroyed using a newly acquired cyanogas chamber.[88] During the outbreak of rabies from October to December 1950, 555 dogs were destroyed in the Lagos mainland area alone.[89] In Nguru town, a total of 324 dogs were destroyed in 1950.[90] The story of eastern Nigeria does not depart from that of other parts of the country. In Okigwi, for instance, 198 dogs were "reportedly killed" in what the *West African Pilot* (WAP) described as "a big campaign against rabies" in January 1957.[91]

The importance of the disparity between the figures of dogs claimed and destroyed goes beyond numbers—it allows us to see the intersections of class, race, and colonial violence. A 1945 case in Lagos can be used to buttress this assertion. Of the 317 dogs captured in January of that year, 136 were destroyed, 96 were released to their owners, 17 were sent to the pathologists for further diagnosis, and 5 more tested positive for rabies and were then killed. This leaves 63 animals unaccounted for. The 96 claimed dogs definitely had licenses and valid vaccinations—the only conditions for their release. They were dogs of both Europeans and Africans, including the pet of Dr. Maja, a prominent African elite. Indeed, both Nigerians and Europeans paid for dog licenses, not only because it was the prerequisite for vaccination but because it gave them a chance to reclaim their dog, if captured, from the town council. The 136 dogs killed in this episode in Lagos (as in other parts of Nigeria mentioned above) were unclaimed likely because their owners feared prosecution for lack of license. Even if the 17 dogs sent to the pathologists were all rabid and eventually killed, the total of 22 rabid dogs killed would stand at odds with the 136 rabid-free animals destroyed because they were unclaimed by their owners.[92] In policing rabies, the government set the boundaries of life and death for canines, using vaccination and licensing as the criteria to exist. While rabies created a formidable threat to human and animal lives alike, it helped the government to achieve its goal of reducing the African dog population under the pretext of fighting hydrophobia.[93]

The manner by which dogs were captured in Lagos and Akure, described as "wicked" by the NRSPCA and the Deji, would have appeared "humane" when compared to the practices in many parts of the country. In fact, only a few urban centers—Lagos, Calabar, Ibadan, and Port Harcourt—had trained dogcatchers, most of whom were also full-time staff of the town council working under the supervision of medical and sanitary officers. In rural communities in southern Nigeria, the government—as seen in the case of Ozara, near Ikene, in 1949—hired local hunters to shoot a local breed of hunting dogs (called *akataporo* by the Igbirra) during a major rabies panic. "The presence of these wild animals is causing great panic to the inhabitants," as the *Daily Service* reported the situation in the community.[94]

From the mid-1910s through the 1950s, shooting of stray dogs by the police, colonial officers, and magistrates was standard operating procedure for addressing the outbreak of rabies in many townships in northern Nigeria. In 1918, J. Aitken, a station magistrate, thought that shooting at stray dogs was part of his primary responsibility of keeping law and order in his jurisdiction.[95] Indeed, any European, regardless of hierarchical position or whether or not he or she were on the staff of the colonial administration, could kill stray dogs in the interest of public health. The big questions at stake were not the legality or ethicality of killing stray dogs but who would be responsible for ammunition and how to protect humans from being harmed by stray bullets or shot during the shooting. It was only in a few cases that dogs were captured by humans or caught in unmanned dog traps, which secretary of the Northern Provinces E. W. Thompstone reviewed as "inadequate" in dealing with stray dogs. His additional statement, in an April 4, 1941, correspondence to northern resident officers, that "the only way in which to reduce the nuisance is to shoot the dogs in suitable open space" gave further official sanction to an established practice.[96] Thompstone's subordinate, the resident of Kano, favored the mass shooting of all dogs in the suburbs and villages near Kano, where most of the stray dogs in the township allegedly came from. His specific comment on bitches exemplified the practice of turning opinion into law and the common stance that the procreative nature of female dogs constituted the biggest danger to public health: "Personally I should like to see all bitches destroyed for the next two years to come. This may be considered very high-handed but rabies are getting worse year by year and the only way to stamp it out is complete destruction of all stray dogs."[97] Similar calls for puppies to be destroyed at birth if born to unlicensed bitches surfaced in the midst of the heated debate on how to control rabies in particular and the dog population in general. The idea of allowing puppies to acquire the status of their mother sounded like one end of the spectrum of dog-control ideas discussed by the colonial officers, the majority of whom expressed limited positive emotions toward the dogs of Africans.

The individuals and groups responsible for shooting stray dogs varied widely. In Kaduna and Zaria, African police constables carried out the task using shotguns. In late 1941 in Kano, the government suggested the appointment of a "responsible European" to shoot stray dogs on a weekly basis, when the police force declined to take on the task after many incidents of stray bullets or shot harming innocent civilians.[98] Shooting of stray dogs was condemned by some Nigerians and Europeans who worked at private trading firms. However, this "objection," asserted E. C. Nottingham, the assistant inspector general of police of the Northern Provinces, was not matched by the willingness of the town council authority to employ paid staff and provide suitable equipment for rounding up stray dogs. The advocates of shooting emphasized that a lack of suitable equipment for dog catching put dogcatchers in danger of being bitten by rabid dogs. In northern Nigeria in the 1940s, to avoid harming humans, the government would issue public notices to communities announcing the time and date when stray dogs would be shot at. One such notice, issued specifically to the European neighborhood in Katsina on the eve of dog shooting on October 13, 1947, read thus:

> It is notified for your information that there will be a blitz on pi-dogs on Tuesday October 14th 1947, in the area of John Menguissoglou Limited and the new road to the Aerodrome (extension of Lagos Street). Shot-guns will be used and shooting will start approximately 5.30 pm.
>
> Householders are particularly requested to keep their dogs under strict control and also to warn their personal servants, night watch-men.
>
> You will be informed of the time and date of any subsequent shoots.[99]

Notices of this nature only apprised communities of the impending public execution of dogs; they did not totally prevent the danger of stray bullets or shot. In response to a gun accident involving a native authority policeman during a stray-dog shooting in October 1935 in Kano, R. F. P. Orme issued a directive on behalf of the secretary of the Northern Provinces to all resident officers in the region demanding that dogs must first be captured by a trap, tied to a "convenient tree," and then shot. "But the strictest precaution must be taken to avoid danger to the public," the directive stipulated. Another instruction by Orme that "the shooting should only be done under the direct supervision of a European" affirmed the prevailing perception of Africans being irresponsible with firearms. He then gave the following specification for constructing and managing a suitable dog trap: "A pit of five feet diameter and six feet deep is dug and a framework of light twigs or branches covered with grass is laid over it. A large piece of meat is then put in the centre as bait. The trap must be examined daily. . . . The public should be warned of the existence of the traps. Each trap should be surrounded with a rail 12 inches high, having an opening at one side."[100]

But Orme's directive did not answer the fundamental question: Who should be responsible for carrying out this task? Also, it was silent on whether or not dogcatchers would be used. The Kano Township Advisory Board gave a valid criticism of this plan—other, untargeted animals such as donkeys, cattle, sheep, and goats could be endangered by the trap. Similarly, the Kano Local Authority's plan to use the police to set the traps was met with stiff resistance when the commissioner of police insisted, "I cannot spare police to go from place to place" setting traps for stray dogs. But his objection went beyond the conventional unwillingness of the police authority to use its limited personnel: "It's hardly dignified for a uniformed policeman to hang about a trap hoping a dog will fall into it."[101] Yet if the police commissioner thought that using policemen to capture dogs was undignified, the order by the secretary of the Northern Provinces for public execution of captured dogs violated colonial laws forbidding the discharge of a gun in the township. But as was all too common, colonial laws applied only to colonial subjects, not to the colonial officers, who enjoyed immunity regarding their conduct involved with social control and public order. The idea of an unmanned trap did not always produce the anticipated result. Once, the meat of the experimental trap placed in the Bompai area of Kano was removed by "a human agent." And dogs were observed lying close to a trap placed near St. George's Church, trying to take the meat from outside the trap.[102]

The justification for shooting at dogs instead of capturing them alive received some scientific backing, even from the highest-ranked veterinary officers. A senior veterinary officer introduced animal psychology to a matter that had revolved mainly around medicine and public order. He thought that dogs who were accustomed to humans would only move close to a potential catcher and that most of the dogs responsible for spreading rabies were the class he described as the "wild and half-wild stray dog," which scavenge for food and look upon the humans "from whom it rarely receives anything but kicks and stones as an enemy to be given as wide a berth as possible." The dogcatchers, he wrote confidently, "cannot deal satisfactorily with this type."[103] The pedigreed hounds and parlor poodles belonging to Europeans and educated Africans, he inferred, were easier to catch because they socialized more with humans. Another northern officer, E. A. Chartres, noted that to catch a dog alive, the police would need a man "with the skill of a Texas Cowboy in throwing the noose and very persuasive power in inducing the dogs to come within his sphere of action."[104] These two scenarios may vary in their depth of description of how to catch a dog, but they are united in pointing out the role of persuasion and psychology in human-animal relations.

A "quick and absolutely painless" strike, to use the words of one MOH, was the most ideal method of destroying stray dogs.[105] Although electrocution of captured dogs, which Nottingham described as "quick and comparatively painless" compared to shooting, was carried out in Kaduna in early 1934, the difficulty and cost of capturing live stray dogs in large numbers hindered the institutionalization of this method.[106] In Kano in 1936 the local authority considered constructing a lethal chamber where captured dogs would be killed by exposure to carbon monoxide from a car exhaust pipe. In Maiduguri, rabid dogs were chloroformed. But a dog gas chamber, the method adopted in Lagos for disposing of captured dogs, appeared to be the most ideal and modern, even though the northern authorities claimed a lack of resources and manpower to conduct the exercise. When asked by northern authorities about the suitability of the Lagos dog gas chamber, the MOH gave the following description of the city's dog-killing facility for a "painless destruction" of animals:

> The [dog-catching] cart is divided into two portions, the partition being a box which is used for keeping the "noose stick" used in dog catching. Into each portion fits a portable expanded metal cage which is transferred (plus dog) direct into the lethal chamber; thus once caught the dog is not again handled until after death. . . . The dogs when caught are placed in the cages and the cages with the live dogs are then lifted from the cart and placed into the chamber one at a time. After filling up the water seal trough, the cover is put on, the vent pipe stopcock and "Cyanogas" pumped into the chamber. Allowing two or three minutes for death to take place the stopcock shown on the ventilating pipe is opened and fresh air pumped through the chamber. The cages are then removed from the chamber and the destroyed dogs disposed of.[107]

The criticism of shooting stray dogs was serious enough to compel the Jos Town Council to adopt a practice similar to that used in Lagos by employing dedicated dogcatchers, who were paid 6d. for every dog they caught. The city, with a sizable European populace, had four groups of dogcatchers of twelve members each. No sooner was this practice introduced that the government discovered that the dogcatchers were rounding up dogs under leash, with valid licenses, and kept on private property, in order to get the six pence per dog compensation.[108] Kano's experimentation with dog catching lasted only two months in 1939. In terms of opportunity cost, it amounted to a waste of money to spend on average of 8d. to 10d. on every captured dog—dogcatchers paid by the town council 3.10.d. captured fewer than ten dogs per month.[109] The dog-control method used in Lagos, which authorities in the provinces admired, even though they could not copy it directly, was informed by the status of the port city as the capital of Nigeria and the bastion of colonial modernity. Only Lagos, which spent an average of £60 per month on salaries of dogcatchers in 1948, Ibadan, and Port Harcourt had the human and medical resources to police dogs in "civilized" ways.[110] While criticism of brutal handling of stray dogs formed the basis of many editorials in nationalist newspapers, shooting at stray dogs in urban areas like Lagos and Ibadan (either at night or in broad daylight) would have been totally unacceptable.

The fact that Lagos and Ibadan had the "best" approach of capturing dogs (by the standards of the era) in colonial Nigeria did not mean that their dogcatchers were immune from the problems commonly faced across the country. Dogcatchers in other places were drawn into intracommunal politics as they "favored one side and disheartened others in no measured terms," to use the language of S. S. Oyetunde and his Ibadan copetitioners in 1942. The petitioners' affirmation that the conduct of the dogcatcher amounted to "dishonesty to their own masters [bosses]," aside from being strategically deployed to secure the proactive attention of the colonial administrators, fed into established colonial practice of highlighting behavior that contravened ideas of patriotic subservience to the British Crown.[111] Another petition, from Irede Village (near Mushin) on the outskirts of Lagos, connected financial gain, dietary habit, and ethnicity in protesting the activities of the "gang of dog-catchers sweeping our area of valuable dogs unjustly." Composed by Councilman J. B. Samuel on behalf of the "taxpayers," the petition alleged that the dogcatchers usually sold the animals to Igbo people, who eat dogs. To establish the veracity of his claim, Samuel alleged that owners of dogs "caught in great numbers" were unable to reclaim their animals at the government kennel because the LTC staff usually sold them en route to the government animal detention center. Like other petitions against indiscriminate dog catching,

Samuel emphasized the importance of dogs as guards against the "havoc the night marauders play nearly every night" due to the "shortage of policemen" on patrol. He pontificated that dogs helped the government in its primary function of securing communities, at which it was failing.[112]

Petitions against dogcatchers were usually glossed over by the government. In an unusual demonstration of apathy, the secretary of Western Provinces, J. A. Mackenzie, "sympathized" with Oyetunde and his co-petitioners but maintained that the capturing and killing of allegedly rabid dogs in the interest of public safety outweighed unsubstantiated allegations of corruption leveled against the dogcatchers.[113] For colonial officers, criticism of dogcatchers was essentially an act of resistance toward government policy, which itself was an offense. When the acting administrator of the colony, J. S. O. Ogunnaike, instructed dogcatchers to stop raiding Irede Village in response to Samuel's petition, he probably agreed with the petitioner that the staff of the LTC did not have any business rounding up dogs outside the Lagos city limits.[114] He was silent about the allegation that dogcatchers were selling "stolen" animals.

The road to humane treatment of stray dogs in northern Nigeria was finally closed in 1952 when a revised Dogs Ordinance emphasized that rabies control was a regional matter and empowered township authorities with the "right to destroy or shoot at sight by any lawful means dogs wandering, not under control" during an outbreak of rabies.[115] The emphasis that rabies control was a regional matter "under the present constitution" sought to centralize the procedure—by legally validating the shooting of stray dogs over capturing them in order to achieve a consistent outcome across the region. It was cheaper, the government held, to kill all stray dogs than to capture them alive and have to keep and care for them in kennels. It relaxed township laws that forbade the discharge of firearms, so long as the target was a dog.[116] The implementation of this new Dogs Ordinance varied from place to place. In Kano, the police continued to shoot at stray dogs, up to the last years of colonial rule. Town council workers in Kaduna would smash a massive iron rod on captured dogs at the site of capture before disposing them in a prepared pit outside the township. With its sizable White population, Jos did not implement the 1952 order within the European residential areas (only in the African communities) to avoid conflict with both colonial officers and foreign expatriates who owned "valuable" and "thoroughly bred" dogs.[117]

The paradox of colonial subjecthood with specific focus on the dog was the central theme of this chapter. In securing humans' health, colonialism was willing to ignore all the services of dog. The thin line between companionship and danger in human-dog relations was constantly threatened by the outbreak of rabies, a zoonotic disease that imperiled human and nonhuman colonial subjects. From public health and urban planning and governance to resistance to colonialism, rabies sat at the intersections of race and class, providing another dimension to understanding colonial contradictions. Like humans, all dogs were not equal before the law. The class and racial prejudice in the implementation of rabies law should be seen as incorporated into the mechanism of imperial domination, with its barrage of inequities.

6 ⤳ The Lion King in the Cage

Nature, Wildlife Conservation, and the Modern Zoo

> This is to inform you that there are elephants in the Rubu bush in the
> Districts of Tsaskiya and Ruma. They are confined to the region and do
> no harm to men. This has been their resort from time immemorial where
> they have found refuge from man's persecution. Nowadays, they do not
> exceed twenty all told. They do not cause any annoyance to the men of
> Tsaskiya and do no damage. For this reason, it is our wish that we should
> put a stop to molesting them and that they should be left in peace. If we
> hear that they have caused damage, then we will inform you they may
> be killed. This is my wish if you approve but I request that immediate
> measure be taken for protection of the Elephants and I wish that a like
> protection be extended to Giraffes.
>
> —Muhammad Dikko dan Gidado, Emir of Katsina, to the district
> officer of Katsina, May 4, 1929[1]

A CRITICAL understanding of how colonialists perceived wildlife conservation is needed to grasp the nuances of this chapter's epigraph. In
mainstream discourse of wildlife conservation in colonial Nigeria, which
blamed Africans for heartless destruction of the gifts of nature while overlooking the wanton killing of the same creatures by European trophy hunters, it was inconceivable to the government that a local chief would lead
an attempt to protect elephants in his domain. The request by Muhammad Dikko dan Gidado, widely recognized as the most progressive northern traditional ruler of the era, prompted by a killing not by an African
but by a European "scientist" who mauled a small elephant, represents an
unusual dimension to colonial resistance that scholars have ignored. The
Emir was making an important point about humans' obligation to nature.
His belief that elephants could be "molested" went against the grain of
the dominant Eurocentric narrative, which saw Africans as lacking any

emotional attachment to animals and thus unable to perceive their suffering. His plea to the imperial authority was answered when a five-year ban was placed on the killing of elephants and giraffes in his region.[2]

Gidado's request also found a meaningful expression in the transcultural conception of the elephant's image as a gentle giant. The animal was not only the largest land creature at the time but also one of the most hunted species, killed for its ivory—a highly lucrative item of international trade. Unlike the roving leopards or unruly hyenas, the elephant displayed serenity, enhanced by its majestic bodily movement in herds—a useful addition to the tableau of natural wonders that local and metropolitan authorities admired and sought to preserve by balancing, albeit in an often contradictory manner, modern principles of animal preservation with human exploitation of nature. In mainstream and popular discourse of animal ethology, elephants would only "misbehave" if disturbed by humans who fired a gun at them or converted their habitat to farms or settlements. But the consequences of their "disorderly" behavior were unparalleled. They could force an entire community to vacate its homes and cause unimaginable damage to farm crops.

Like human subjects of colonialism, wildlife was ordered, sorted, and indexed to meet the colonialists' narrow conceptions of materiality, nature conservation, and even principles of power. Wildlife conservation policies were esoteric and, in many instances, based on the colonial government's notions of rarity, unusual appearance, degree of "wildness," "traffickability," and the economics of the international trade in animal trophies. Indeed, any animal, aside from the popular domesticated ones, was a "protected" animal occupying different hierarchical places on the ladder of vulnerability to "extinction." Ironically, all these factors did not take into consideration the geographical distribution or demographics of wild animals in relation to ecosystems.[3] A species verging on "extinction" in one part of the country might be overpopulated in another, posing enormous danger to human and nonhuman creatures alike. From ostrich feathers to ivory, from live lions to python eggs, Nigerian wildlife occupied an ambivalent status in imperial aesthetics of nature and global capitalism.

The narratives in this chapter oscillate between culture and the wild. Essentially, they focus on the idea that the natural environment and wild animals can be effectively governed in both their interest and the interest of humans who exploit them. In the process, new perspectives about how Africans should exploit nature expanded the instrumentality of colonial domination. Wild animals in Nigeria became experimental bodies of imperial science anchored by European "naturalists" and "conservators" who were fascinated by their biophysiological traits, among other exotic attributes.[4] Their stories would find a racialized place in nature journals and autobiographical writings consumed by Westerners. Some Europeans desired to encounter Nigerian wildlife beyond the text—in real life. They often joined the colonial service, kept leopards and lions as pets, and even served as "consultants" and "experts" on African fauna and flora to zoos and botanical gardens across Europe. The wild creatures of Nigeria became part of the global diaspora of animals from colonial realms. Confined in the cages of metropolitan zoos, their lives provided entertainment and an alternative means of encountering nature for Europeans who could only wonder about lands beyond their physical reach. The imperial zoo, both in the metropole and in the colonies in the twentieth century, turned wild creatures into modern colonial subjects as well as performers and legitimizers of modernity—while also exemplifying the skewed notion that animals can best be protected from poachers by being placed in captivity.

NATURE AND DANGER

Colonialism did not introduce nature conservation to Africa. Centuries before the imposition of foreign rule, an ethos of wild animal conservation existed in real and imaginative impressions found both in religious practices and in the rituality of power and authority.[5] Precolonial societies conserved wildlife, in part by restricting hunting of animal trophies to the elites. Even the ivory trade, over centuries of global commerce, was coordinated by the elites, who manipulated supply to enhance their economic power. The makers of precolonial African civilizations viewed humans as superior to wild animals because of their ability to reason. However, they regularly returned to the wild themselves to appropriate untamed, natural elements to mend their own weakness or amplify their ability or both. In stationing animal symbols and trophies at courts and palaces, indigenous authorities sought extra help instilling fear in and securing loyalty from their subjects, thus broadening the terrain of their power (see fig. 6.1). In the allegory of violence, the king was a carnivore, capable of mauling a nonroyal subject. Symbolically, the dominion of the king extended to the wild—where he presides over all creatures, the human and nonhuman.

With colonialism came liberalization of gun possession, making firearms accessible for economic activities such as commercial hunting and trade in animal trophies, and an increase in "collecting" for "educational" and "scientific" purposes. Europeans and Africans circumvented

FIGURE 6.1. Oba Olateru Olagbegi II, the *Olowo* of Owo (1959). *Source:* Eliot Elisofon Photographic Archives, National Museum of African Art, Smithsonian Institution.

indigenous customs by trapping animals and selling their trophies to multinational corporations. More than that, as towns gave way to cities and villages transformed into larger polities, the natural habitat of animals shrank at the expense of humans' need for a built environment. All this took place as largely uninhabited forest was opened up for cash crop plantations, especially cocoa in southwestern Nigeria and oil palm in the Southeast. Colonial agricultural policies, driven largely by capitalism, did not take account of the negative impacts of cash crop production on the nonhuman creatures of Nigeria.[6] Similarly, the commercial logging in forest reserves, another natural home of large-game animals, had major, often unintended, consequences for the ecosystem.[7] Deprived of habitat and threatened by the incessant sounds of guns and logging activities, wildlife were regularly forced to interact with human settlements in search of food and a safe abode.

Petitions and characterizations by native authorities, newspapers, and private citizens of roving and rogue wild animals had the effect of turning nonhuman creatures into active criminals or outlawed bodies whose excesses must be tamed in the interest of human safety and colonial progress.[8] They resembled similar petitions about armed bandits and unrepentant criminals. These petitions also inserted humans into the animal kingdom and the lawlessness it represented, both metaphorically and practically.[9] Humans were reminded of the limits of their own power, accentuated by the physical might of wild animals and colonial laws that protected them against "indiscriminate" killing. The story of elephants invading and temporarily occupying farmsteads gained front-page coverage in Lagos newspapers like the *West African Pilot* (WAP) and the *Daily Service* that sympathized with the people's agony.[10] One story detailed how a herd of twenty to sixty elephants caused "incalculable losses," destroying thousands of heaps of crops and forcing villagers to leave their homes.[11] Another story decried the "alarming" destruction caused by elephants in Auchi and urged authorities to take action to help "poor peasants."[12] In one of the goriest stories of an elephant atrocity, one animal killed four people in Iseyin in 1952 before returning to the forest. Its victims included a pregnant woman on her way to fetch water from a stream.[13] In attempting to avoid legal responsibility for the "misdemeanor" of the animals or having to compensate farmers for their loss, the government argued that "it may cause further demands which could not be checked"; its inaction increased the tensions between locals and authorities.[14]

Aquatic wildlife also shared the blame of human insecurity and by extension loss of economic capital and livelihood. Humans have shared the West African waterways with massive water creatures, like the hippopotamus and crocodile, for centuries. But the creation of the Nigerian state and expansion of commercial activity and mobility increased movement across the natural homes of these species. The advancement in water transportation technology, which saw the building of massive vessels and ferries, disturbed the animals in ways hitherto unknown. Modern vessels, unlike their premodern counterparts, could venture into uncharted waters, where most of the hippopotamuses sought refuge. Wildlife ethology recorded in colonial archives explicitly blames heavy vessels for the animals' increased aggressiveness and the subsequent loss of life when vessels capsized. The economic implications of the hippopotamus threat are legion. In Katsina-Ala, vessels carrying economic goods and passengers were compelled to dock for several days until water passage was deemed safe from hippopotamuses. Perhaps no other aquatic wild animal occupied as contradictory a position in the lexicon of West African conservation as the manatee.[15] While some fishermen despised them for capsizing their boats and damaging their fishing nets, others who specialized in killing them for their livelihood frowned at the protective status given to the "sea cows."[16]

The killing of animals in self-defense is not sufficient to explain why Nigerian wildlife was depleted during the colonial era. Rather, and as hitherto mentioned, the commercialization of animal parts, such as hides and tusks, as well as the unchecked activities of European trophy hunters, carried more weight. By the 1930s local traders, including the Nigerian Ivory Trading Company, had established a lucrative business of collecting elephant tusks predominantly for the international market.[17] In 1907 the Royal Niger Company was bartering guns or gunpowder, or both, for tusks that weighed over twenty-two pounds in some areas in northern Nigeria.[18] In 1952 two thousand pounds of ivory was worth about £1,000 in Lagos.[19] In January 1951 a Japanese firm, Tokyo Sales Inc., contracted with a Nigerian trading company, Bright Way Stores, to supply it with two thousand pounds of ivory—a quantity that government officers described as "large" and that was the most they had ever approved.[20] An average elephant tusk from Nigeria weighed forty to forty-five pounds; therefore, the fulfillment of the request by Tokyo Sales would claim around twenty-five elephants. While much of Nigerian ivory was trafficked abroad, there was also a local market for other elephant parts, some of which were used for traditional medicine. One Mallam Alli of Ibadan, in a March 1951 correspondence to the government, valued an elephant tooth, used for native medicine, at £100.[21]

FIGURE 6.2. Advertisement for Hercules bicycles (1955). *Source: Nigeria Magazine,* no. 47 (1955).

Amid all these apparent crises over nature and governance, the growth in consumer culture intensified public anxiety, all in a bid to promote international commerce. Advertising for brands of bicycles, such as Raleigh, manufactured in England, specifically targeted rural areas, praising the product for its capacity to help its rider escape from a possible lion or crocodile attack through its reliable high speed (see fig. 6.2).[22] The steel of another brand of bicycle—the Hercules, alias "Strongest of All"—was touted as being so strong that an elephant could ride on it.[23] Moreover, two elephants could not dismember it, if pulled from two ends, so the ad claimed.[24] In other instances, the wild received some positive commentary that further exploited its identity for global capitalism. According to one ad, humans could be sure to have the talent of the elephant for remembering things if they bought Platignum pens.[25] In another, a human could lift an entire elephant with one hand after a drink of Bovril blood tonic.[26] The toughness of a lion was used to promote a brand of shoe by the famous Bata trading firm.[27] And consumers could expect their homes not to crumble if a hippopotamus stood on top, provided they were built with Burham portland cement.[28]

THE WILD ANIMALS PRESERVATION ORDINANCE

Newspaper accounts and government documents on rural insecurity and destruction of farms caused by wild animals tended to imply that Nigerians lacked the capacity to control the animal world. But this was not the case. In fact, most communities had expert wildlife hunters. Nigerians' response to the perpetual conflict between humans and wild animals was made difficult by colonial wildlife conservation laws.[29] From the early 1900s the government responded to the unprecedented killing of elephants, among other wild animals, through passage of the Wild Animals Preservation Ordinance (WAPO) and creation of forest reserves where hunting was prohibited.[30] The following are the core elements of the ordinance: Before a wild animal can be killed, a district officer must visit the community under threat and assess the level of danger. The community then organized hunters, who had to obtain a permit, which normally would expire within thirty days; share the animal meat with the entire community; and, if the animal was an elephant, deposit its tusks with the district officer, whose responsibility it was to send them to the central government treasury in Lagos for public auction.[31] Proceeds went to the government.

The British imposed a deliberately high, one-time permit of £10 to discourage people from hunting elephants. Other hunting rules included the hunter must not chase the elephants into the wilderness or government reserve; the killing must take place within the farmland being allegedly destroyed. Only adult bulls could be killed; it was an offense to kill females and young animals, regardless of the circumstances involved. Hunters, even those who were licensed, could be prosecuted if each tusk weighed less than twenty-two lbs. Hunters were required to inform their district officer of the killing of an elephant within three to seven days.

However, the killing of one or two elephants, out of a herd that ranged from ten to thirty, did not end the menace of the creatures. Rather, it only pushed them to new areas, as they sought refuge from human violence. Shooting an entire herd would appear to be the solution to the elephant menace. However, not only was this impossible under the hunting culture of the era; it also would contravene the ideology of colonial conservation in its entirety.

Game laws had the effect of turning Nigerians into poachers, even in their own communities.[32] Colonists from Britain could not be poachers, by definition; rather, they were deemed to be naturalists, conservators, or adventurers engaging in recreational shooting to relieve the stress of colonial service carried out in the "selfless" interest of advancing the backward race of Africans.[33] Or they were considered to be helping communities to get rid of dangerous beasts with their highly efficient rifles, which only they could own. Even when they captured young animals for metropolitan zoos while killing the adults, their action was still treated as beneficial in that it involved removing animals from a dangerous landscape plagued by "poachers" to a "safe" location in the colonial metropolis where their survival was "guaranteed." The language of colonial paternalism thus extended to the practice of animal "conservation." The fauna and flora of the empire were the exclusive preserve of Europeans, who controlled each colonial site, guarding it from other nationalities. Thus, the action of one Edward Weber, an Austrian who was "living on the products of his gun" by slaughtering wild animals, including hippopotamuses, and selling the meat to "natives" in the market, was treated as a violation of international treaties of colonial possession, even though Weber was himself a European.[34] In 1912 Weber was accused of living "like a native." A year after his presence caught the attention of colonial officers, he became a penniless beggar, beseeching British officers for money and ammo for his gun.[35]

Nothing is known about Weber after 1913, when efforts were made to repatriate him. But this episode did not end recreational and commercial wildlife shooting by European (and American) nonofficials. As colonial infrastructure and commercial power intensified, so also did the population of expatriates, representative of multinational corporations, and missionaries increase. This group, like the officials of the colonial state, also thought they were entitled to the African fauna. In September 1955 R. Forrest Webb, the sales manager of SCOA Motors in Kano, applied for a permit to kill an elephant. "Before I leave, I should like to fulfil an ambition, that of shooting an African elephant." Webb's request was unusual among his European contemporaries, especially those from Britain, who would not even seek permission before shooting.[36] Not only was his application granted within two weeks, but the conditions under which Africans were allowed to kill elephants (destruction of crops or threat to human safety) were also deemed to not apply to him.[37]

This form of racial privilege did not go unchallenged by Africans. Some petitions, like the one by Shaki and the District Hunters Association to the Nigerian Council of Ministers in January 1953, placed wildlife conservation in racial perspective, as it questioned the granting to Europeans of access to plunder wildlife.[38] This petition sought to integrate the politics of wildlife conservation into the discourse of nationalism and decolonization. Although the government did occasionally grant free licenses to hunt elephants, communities far from government offices killed elephants without government approval. Yet the felling of an elephant would rarely go unnoticed by the government because, by custom, the entire community would feast on it. The news of the killing of wild animals tended to travel fast and far. What is more, the rules for killing an elephant were hard to follow. Hunter-farmers were unwilling to pay £10 for the right to kill elephants, which they considered an inalienable privilege to exploit their community's natural endowment. Few hunters would wait for the animal to arrive on their farm and cause damage before shooting at it. Seasonal movements of animals in response to weather changes inhibited successful hunting by people who had game licenses. In March 1948 the *Orimolusi* (king) of Ijebu Igbo pleaded with his district officer to extend the game permit granted to his community to kill one bull elephant because hunters "reported that the elephants have left for a swampy area outside my jurisdiction during this dry season, and that they are likely to return to my area during the forthcoming rainy season."[39]

One of the flaws of government animal-conservation regulations was their overwhelming emphasis on the economic value of wild game hunting—"largely a commercial business," in the words of the conservator of forests in 1933.[40] In fact, to local communities, the cultural, medicinal, symbolic, and aesthetic value of animals was as important as their economic value. Chiefs directly and indirectly supported the contravening of the WAPO because the law disregarded the existing customary laws on big-game hunting.[41] According to most local customs, the tusks, bones, and hides of wild animals, among other parts, embodied cultural symbolism tied to social class, gender, and power relations.[42] In Ibadan, the king was entitled to one of the tusks of any elephant killed in his territory because "in ancient times it was a sign of good luck to any head of a town in whose reign an elephant was killed." After a lot of political rumbling about the tusks of an elephant killed in the area in 1946, the district officer allowed the monarch to keep one for "ornamentation" of his palace.[43]

In other instances, the conflict over the rights to possess an animal trophy was not between the colonial officers and local chiefs but between traditional authorities and their subjects. In early 1953 the *Alaafin* (king) of Oyo, Adeyemi II, petitioned his district officer against one Ogunosun, who had a license to kill one elephant. "He is going to finish up all the elephants in this Division," the king said, forecasting the outcome of Ogunosun's action, the alleged killing of seven elephants in the area.[44] While the king's query sounds like a legitimate interest in conservation, it can also be interpreted in terms of conflict over ownership of the ivory—that is, his exclusive entitlement, according to tradition. The fact that Ogunosun was allegedly selling the meat of the elephant in the public market instead of allowing the entire community to feast on it, as enshrined in indigenous custom, was taken as evidence of the purely economic self-interest of the hunter.[45]

What is correct about the elephant is true of other classes of animals as well. It was common to hear of the "lack" or "excess" of leopards or lions—a complex ecological matter simply defined as an imbalance of the ecosystem—a by-product of strict, or lax, game regulation in certain parts of the country. In some places, the population of baboons and wild pigs (a common pest of farm produce) increased because of a decline in the population of leopards, their natural predator, due to hunting. Yet leopards were also viewed as "occasionally troublesome" animals in places where they were "plentiful." "It is interesting to note," said the senior resident of Benue Province, giving his impression on the regional disparity of leopard populations, "that those that have leopard in any number are anxious to destroy them."[46] The intensity of game law enforcement—determined by the administrative dexterity of colonial officers and the size of their area of jurisdiction—also shaped the movements of big-game hunters. Perhaps the most provocative method of wildlife control was adopted in Bauchi Province in 1951 where forest conservators used sodium arsenite to poison baboons accused of destroying farms.[47] The baboon population in this area had increased, as in Kabba, Igala, and Igbirra Divisions, because of a reduced leopard population.[48]

Hunting as an ancient practice expanded under colonial rule not only because of access to firearms but also because of the opportunity to hunt in places hunters would not have been permitted before the Pax Britannica was imposed on Nigeria. Indigenous regulations on hunting gave way to imperial laws, which provided all colonial subjects, regardless of origin, an expanded but "controlled" access to nature, including wildlife. The new legal regime intensified commercial hunting of large game, a unique type of animal materiality geared toward exploiting animals as commodities, essentially for cash. Colonial-era capitalist hunting stood in contrast with precolonial hunting, which, aside from providing subsistence access to protein, was also integral to the religious ritualization of nature. The outcome of this change included intensification of inter- and intraethnic conflict over land and hunting rights.[49] In 1909 the people of South Kaiama in the villages near the southern borders complained that the inhabitants of Kishi, Saki, and other northern Yoruba towns were crossing the "border" during the dry season and building temporary huts where they settled to hunt elephants in large numbers. "Before the present regime, these Yorubas would not have dared to leave their country and hunt in the Kaiama bush," reported a resident officer, "but now, owing to the present security throughout the country they do this with impunity"; in this way the community's hunting rights were transformed by colonialism.[50] In Lafia Division in 1939 "stranger" hunters were identified as Tiv from the South and Eggon and Ankwe from the north of the area.[51] Wildlife hunting by a "band of strangers" was unacceptable to many communities because the interlopers did not have "hereditary hunting rights" in the region and showed "no interest in allowing certain areas to recuperate" after being depleted of game. The chiefs and colonial administrators believed that locals were more mindful of their natural resources than outside hunters. By the early 1950s the WAPO required "strangers" to apply for a special permit, a "Resident Non-Native Licence," and pay a high levy of £25 to hunt away from home. This law still did not end "stranger hunting," partly because it gave the colonial government, not the local chiefs, the power to use residency status as condition for hunting.[52]

In addition, group, mass, or communal hunting took on a different dimension under colonialism. In precolonial times, it served as a means of regulating animal populations, as occasions of socialization of boys, and as expressions of spiritual veneration of the earth gods and goddesses believed to be responsible for maintaining the cosmos in favor of humans. However, under imperial rule, collective hunting took on a purely capitalistic dimension, devoid of any relationship to indigenous nature-conservation practice. Such hunting took place irrespective of communal affiliation or residency status and was disrespectful of customary practices that enhanced regeneration after hunting. The indigenous culture of balancing the ecosystem meant nothing to capitalist hunters of the colonial era, who sought "to kill and sell as much game as possible."[53] The size of group or capitalist hunting differed. Representatives of the Minerals Research Syndicate in Kafanchan observed two groups of thirty boys and men carrying out what they termed a "game drive" over the course of several days in March 1936.[54]

Instead of waiting for the colonial government to determine the illegality of hunting by strangers, local chiefs began dispensing laws in contravention of colonial statues. In early 1952 the Emir of Nasarawa sentenced one Amadu, a Ganagana from Koton Karfi, to six months in prison for abusing the "hospitality of his host" when he killed a small elephant whose tusks weighed just three pounds each. Amadu's argument that he had killed the young animal in self-defense was not persuasive because he shot it with a long poisoned harpoon, which is not used for smaller game.[55] However, the district officer of Nasarawa claimed the Emir did not have the power to administer game laws.[56] This case was just one of many examples. In February 1960 the Lowland Native Authority of Plateau Province passed a local law preventing communal hunting, except in the form recognized by indigenous custom, restricted "small scale hunting" only to indigenous people in the area, and imposed an annual fee of £5 on strangers who sought to hunt. The council defined "communal/group hunting" as hunting by more than ten persons and "small scale hunting" as by fewer than ten people.[57] In Minna "professionalization" of the hunter guilds was the community's own way of defending its prerogatives from outside hunters.[58]

As previously noted, the commercialization of live animals and trophies was driven, in part, by the high economic value of these items on the international market. However, some loopholes in export regulations intensified such commercialization. For example, people could export live animals if they claimed to be donating them for "scientific" purposes. Among the foreign institutions that claimed to be collecting wild animals for scientific purposes were independent nongovernmental organization like the US-based National Foundation for Infantile Paralysis, which sought twelve chimpanzees and fifty monkeys in 1944; the Barcelona Zoological Garden, which came for lions, leopards, cheetahs, giraffes, hippopotamuses, antelopes, zebras, elephants, and wild birds; and the University of Bergen in Norway, which wanted Marabout storks.[59] The connections between scientific imperialism and wildlife destruction was an important discussion in the empire. While concerns were raised about the growing commercialization of trophies among Europeans, little to nothing was done to stop it. Commercial firms (African, European, and multinational) exporting live animals were expected to have obtained the items "lawfully"—that is, from sellers who had the permission to kill or capture live animals. However, if they did not have the required documentation, the firms could file an affidavit, a "Free Disposal Permit," claiming they could not locate the sellers.[60]

At different times, administrators would blame themselves for lack of foresight in projecting another implication of the WAPO—for example, not acknowledging wildlife as mobile creatures. Natural factors generally determined the habitat of wildlife, causing inevitable seasonal movements in response to population pressure, environmental degradation, or human threat. Consequently, a human community could encounter an "elephant problem" suddenly and thus be unprepared to address it.[61] Unlike forest regulations, game law was not enforced by a dedicated government department. Nigeria did not have a "game ranger" or any officers specifically responsible for ensuring compliance. Rather, political officers (district and provincial administrators) carried out the role of game conservator and naturalist, even though most who did so lacked training. This problem was further compounded by the lack of geographical delimitation of game licenses. It was possible for someone to acquire a game license in Lagos and use it to kill animals as far away as Bornu. Game law would have been best administered by foresters and conservationists of the Forestry Department; however, it was treated as a political and economic matter reserved for district and provincial administrators. The Forestry Department was equally unwilling to include game conservation in the list of its obligations without a significant expansion in its workforce.

One of the rarely acknowledged facts about colonialism is that dissent by colonial officers occurred on many matters, even those at the core of imperial philosophy. Historians have limited access to these voices, not only because they were rarely acknowledged publicly and officially but also because they tended to be undocumented. Even when documented, unpopular political statements by colonial officers rarely received any serious attention that might have served as a basis for transformation in colonial practice. It is surprising that a top colonial officer, the secretary of the Northern Provinces, in an elaborate official correspondence would disagree with the punishment of Africans for killing "without restriction such ugly, dangerous and destructive beasts as the rhinoceros, hippopotami and gorillas which ought long ago to have passed away with the dinosaurs and other pre-historic animals." He criticized the prejudiced origins of wildlife conservation as mistakenly focused solely on "provid[ing] big game hunting for Europeans" in order "to amuse naturalists" while overlooking the fact that "the native of Africa" possessed the "primary right to what he can kill for his food and for the protection of his crops." He then made a cultural comparison that would have angered most of his colleagues—saying that to ask Africans to stop killing wild animals that destroyed their crops is like asking the British to outlaw their pastimes of cricket, soccer, and horse racing. His assumption that his views would be considered "eccentric" was followed by yet another provocative statement that challenged the science of wildlife conservation and environmental imperialism: humans should not worry about game regeneration, for the forces of nature shaping the diverse landscapes would naturally replenish the flora and fauna.[62] This critique was matched by another equally provocative statement by the resident of Ilorin Province that described European field naturalists "whose delight is to observe wild animals in their natural state" as "the killer (unfortunately not unknown) who seems obsessed with the lust of slaughter." Neither of these dissenters changed prevailing colonial attitudes toward nature or the activities of their compatriots.[63]

NIGERIA'S FIRST NATIONAL PARK

The idea of a game reserve, a natural physical enclave where wild animals could be shielded from hunting to prevent their "extinction" while serving naturalist ideals and recreational game hunting for Europeans, was as old as the history of the WAPO and the Forestry Department.[64]

Although forest reserves were established chiefly for commercial exploitation of timber, they were also de facto sanctuaries for large game, since it was illegal for anyone to exploit any natural resource in them. In 1933 the Society for the Preservation of the Wild Fauna of the Empire led a push to establish a game reserve in northern Nigeria.[65] But this idea could not come to fruition, plausibly because the government thought that a game reserve, unlike a forest reserve, had limited financial prospects to add to the colonial treasury. However, from the early 1950s foresters, naturalists, and conservators, among other classes of administrators, would constitute themselves into the Northern Regional Game Preservation Committee to deliberate on the creation of a "national park" that would serve as a game and breeding sanctuary—a "multiplication" center, where conscious attempts would be made to breed small game for food like trade cattle. Revenues to run the park would come from game licenses. The national park would also serve "educational" and "zoological" ends, according to the committee's projections in its inaugural meeting of September 28, 1953.[66] After this meeting, district officers swung into action, collating animal species in their domains to determine where the proposed national park would be sited.[67]

As expected, some high-ranking officers in the conservation field such as D. R. Rosevear, the inspector general of forests, thought that Nigeria was not ripe for a national park. He highlighted obvious constraints—money and human resources—to running it effectively. "I personally feel that in a country where it is difficult enough to secure an adequate forest estate it is asking a lot to set aside yet other areas for game alone," Rosevear said, expressing his reservations. Since much of the drive for a national park in Nigeria was influenced by a similar trend in eastern and southern Africa, he educated his colleagues about regional disparities in fauna and flora, climatic conditions, racial composition of the regions, and aspects of global large-game hunting culture unique to each region:

> Because something is successful in A it must be equally applicable to B is a commonly held thesis. Because National Parks attract many visitors in East Africa and provide a good revenue they must also do the same for Northern Nigeria is the theme of Section 7 (of the convention). Nothing could be further from the truth. In South and East Africa there are large resident European populations which provide the majority of visitors to the National Parks. It must be assumed that a large number of Africans are going to visit the parks or that tourists are going to flock to West

Africa just as they do to the pleasant highlands of the East. But what are all these visitors going to see? Tall grasses—for at least nine months of the year.[68]

Rosevear insisted that eastern and southern Africa had more game than Nigeria and that the country would never be able to run a national park profitably. Rosevear's critique and that of the inspector general of Animal Health Services, who opined that "99% of the population of Nigeria think we are slightly mad" when they hear about the plan to create a game reserve, could not silence the idea of a national park.[69] In early 1957 the Yankari Game Reserve came into existence as Nigeria's first national park, in Bauchi. It was a cheap endeavor in terms of financial outlay: £650 was expended in demarcating 130 out of the 720 square miles of territory, and another £100 went toward creating road access.[70] More than a dozen prominent European naturalists and conservationists were employed as "honorary game wardens" to patrol the reserve and enforce the WAPO.[71]

The game reserve satisfied the imagination of naturalists for a safari-like culture in West Africa. It was only open from December to May; visitors were required to apply a month ahead of their visit and encouraged to stay for at least one night to see a "representative selection" of animals, which included lions, elephants, hippopotamuses, giraffes, and leopards, among other wild beasts. In keeping with the income-generation agenda of its supporters, the reserve charged about 25s. for adults and gave free entry to visitors under sixteen (see fig. 6.3).

Like any regulated public space, the reserve had a code of conduct designed to anticipate subversion of rules regarding treatment of game. Not only were the use of firearms and camping outside designated places prohibited; visitors were also warned against harassing or startling the animals. The last rule, a sober warning and disclaimer, was equally the most important for understanding the limitations of humans' centuries-long attempts to tame nature for their amusement: "Visitors entering the Game Reserve do so entirely at their own risk and the Government of Northern Nigeria cannot be held liable for any damage, injury or loss, either to the visitors themselves or their property."[72]

From the outset, the Yankari Game Reserve was integrated into Nigeria's mainstream culture of public education through the school system, even though most of its visitors were projected to be foreigners. Newspaper articles and promotional materials justifying wildlife conservation as the solution to the extinction of beautiful and interesting animals, defining excess hunting, and emphasizing the responsibility of humans as custodians

FIGURE 6.3. Promotional postcard for the Yankari Game Reserve (1970s).
Source: GEN/TEC/6/S vol. 3, National Archives, Kaduna.

of nature were printed in large quantities for schoolchildren.[73] One should not be surprised that schoolchildren were the main target of these "propaganda" materials. Like the campaign against cruelty to animals, wildlife conservation was constituted as a modernist project that schoolchildren could help propagate.[74] To give the agenda a truly national identity, even though much of the resources and political will that created it came from the Northern Region in the era of decolonization, an "All-Nigeria Wildlife Preservation Committee" convention was held at Enugu in February 1958.[75]

THE MODERN ZOO AND ANIMAL EXHIBITION

African wildlife should be considered part of a diasporic network of bodies, ideas, and practices within and outside Africa. For centuries, the diffusion and spread of animals have changed the ecosystems of societies, allowing humans to exploit a natural endowment that did not originally thrive in their immediate locality. The formation of the Zoological Society of London and the London Zoo in the first half of the nineteenth century represented a turning point in the history of human dominance over the natural world and of the British Empire's mastery over remote territories across the world. For one thing, it made the collection of exotic captive wild animals for educational and scientific purposes a public good conceived by a few empire builders and aristocrats but sustained through a metropolitan ideal that resonated across the empire. While the establishment of the London Zoo did not end the proliferation of private menageries that carried out zoological exhibitions for economic gain, it nevertheless made stocking and restocking of public zoos in Europe a patriotic obligation of the colonies, which must respond to the zoological proclivities and crowd-pleasing sensibilities of both the European aristocrats and the public.

It is within this context that one should understand the 1905 gift of two lion cubs to King Edward VII of the United Kingdom by the *Shehu* (king) of Bornu in northern Nigeria. The gift, a token of the Shehu's allegiance to the British Crown, subsequently became a collection in the London Zoo. Throughout the twentieth century, Nigerian wildlife would find their way to European private and public zoos in large numbers as part of the exploitation of the colonies, made possible by the influx of colonial officers and expatriates and representatives of trading companies who constituted themselves as "naturalists" and "conservators," writing books to enlighten the world about the wonders of Africa's natural environment, collecting trophies as insignias of social status, and directly justifying wildlife imperialism. A 1946 Lagos newspaper report, authored by one P. E. N. Malafa on the depletion of the London Zoo due to World War II, claimed that this group constituted the largest donors of animals to the imperial project.[76]

One should expect the lives of Nigerian wildlife to be transformed in their new homes, where they were displayed in heavily secured cages for the amusement of metropolitan citizens who probably cared less about the global inequality that enabled their encounter with "Africa" thousands of miles away in London. Film footage of the arrival from Lokoja, Nigeria, of two lion cubs named Mary and Loja, which had been presented to the Prince of Wales during his visit to the colony, at the London Zoo in 1925 featured children who were fascinated to see an uncommon creature.[77] The Nigerian wildlife in metropolitan zoos were fed special meals quite unlike what they would taste while living free, exposed to a new routine of life, given new names, and used as subjects for medical and scientific research. The physical presence of African wildlife in Europe thus expanded the scientific understanding of African fauna in ways that could only be imagined during the pre-twentieth-century encounter.

One of the paradoxes of modern zookeeping was the way it transformed how even Africans encounter the wild creatures of their own land. Some Africans visiting the United Kingdom were then given privileged access to metropolitan zoos to "reunite" with animals from their communities but now packaged as a benefit of modernity in the metropole. Newspaper coverage of the visit by Emir Muhammad Dikko dan Gidado to the London Zoo in 1921 provide a racialized imprint of the reactions of a Senegambian lion to the African visitor: "A curious incident occurred here. The Senegambian lion, usually bored to tears with the ordinary visitor, was dozing when the Emir entered. But when the Nigerian came to his cage he stood up, fixed them with his eyes, raised his head in the air, and sniffed." This remark was not intended as complimentary at all. In colonial framing of otherness, Africans had a closer affinity with animals because they shared similar traits of primitivity, which could be addressed through domestication and colonization. The remaining portion of the racist report noted that the lion "'has smelled the old food of his tribe' someone said. At any rate, the lion had evidently recognized an old familiar scent, and he stood at the center of his cage and continued to sniff as the party passed on."[78] Ibrahima, the *Atta* (king) of the Igbirra, had a similar experience when he visited the London Zoo in 1929. The report of the visit, titled "Ibrahima, Atta of the Igbirra, Visits London Where He Has a Surprise Encounter," mirrors similar metropolitan unfamiliarity displayed by African elites. "The feeding of the various animals was watched with interest by the Atta and his party, and the antics of the chimps cause much amusement," the report stated. However, the "real enthusiasm and excitement" for the Atta was sighting one of the lions taken from his domain earlier in the year.[79] If it was a privilege for African chiefs to visit London, it was equally a privilege for their animals to be kept in a metropolitan zoo for the amusement of the metropolitan world.

Yet the keeping of captive wild animals was not a colonial invention. In precolonial times, caging of wild animals was practiced as part of the religious and spiritual life of communities that viewed nonhuman creatures as part of their cosmology. Animals helped "Nigerians" in the precolonial period to unlock the mystery of life or gain access to narratives and ideas beyond the reach of the "ordinary" eye.[80] Precolonial culture of wildlife domestication fitted into indigenous conceptions of nature conservation and of family, community, and lineage histories. To understand animal behavior (ethology) is to unmask why humans act in certain ways. The secularization of wildlife domestication in Nigeria started with the consolidation of Islam and Christianity, two foreign religions that condemned indigenous spiritual practices. It also found expression in the obsession by European and American residents (many of whom were members of the Nigerian Field Society) with keeping private menageries. They kept an assortment of wild animals—from lions and leopards to ostriches and palm squirrels—as pets. In the 1930s the *Nigerian Field* published accounts of pets and their owners, which clearly revealed the incredible obsession with African fauna.[81] Dorothy H. Bostock even kept a Bosman's potto named Tunde and her newborn baby. The animal was given to her by a filmmaker who had already used the primate in a picture. Tunde's scene showed her lying in a tree where she was to be "attacked" by a snake. Tunde, who was usually shy, ate papayas, oranges, and pineapples and arrived in her new home "with a Garboesque detachment," Bostock wrote in her 1937 article in the *Nigerian Field*. Bostock then made some speculations, while emphasizing the amusement of having a pet potto: "Whether they will ever be as tame as a 'Tree Bear' is said to be; whether the baby will follow me all round the compound as a Cerval Kitten used to, I have grave doubt. Nevertheless, since they are taken captive, anyhow, I am glad they found their way to our care for they are quaint little pets."[82]

Bostock lived with a friendly wild animal—Tunde's attempt to snap ended in a lick "when she discover[ed] whose hands are playing with her."[83] However, many Europeans' wildlife pets were ferocious animals. From the 1900s or earlier, Lagos newspapers carried stories of how pet leopards of Europeans escaped from their captivity to attack "law-abiding" people.[84] Janus, the popular columnist of the *Lagos Standard*, condemned the proliferation of private menageries in his June 11, 1912, article, posing the question "To what extent is a man allowed to indulge in an inclination for keeping vicious and outlandish animals as pets?" He believed his question deserved an answer in the interest of peace and safety for disadvantaged citizens like elderly women and for the public in general.[85]

This outcry failed to transform official attitudes toward private ownership of wild animals and the danger to the public. In January 1959 Morris Solomon, an expatriate, was arraigned in a Lagos court for "not taking necessary precaution against any probable danger" that his monkey posed to the public. Solomon's monkey had escaped from its cage to bite two young children named Bolaji Sule and Grace Chuku.[86]

The news of Nigerians' encounters with wild animals in the metropolitan zoo circulated across the country. From newspaper articles to travel narratives, Nigerians and Europeans alike who visited the zoo wondered about the wisdom of reproducing the animal kingdom in the human world. Their opportunity for a similar experience in Nigeria was limited. Few private menageries, whether owned by Africans or by Europeans, were open to the public. Most of them had just one species of animal, mostly leopards, crocodiles, or monkeys. Many were in family compounds in the hinterlands where they enjoyed restricted access, but the spectacle of traveling menageries featuring hyenas and snakes was common in the big cities.[87] The "inauthenticity" of the power of snake and hyena charmers to tame animals and then command them to do their bidding for public amusement was revealed when, occasionally, the animals attacked and killed their handlers (see fig. 6.4).[88]

FIGURE 6.4. Snake charmer in front of the US consulate in Lagos (1959). *Source:* Eliot Elisofon Photographic Archives, National Museum of African Art, Smithsonian Institution.

While Nigerians continued to have secular and nonsecular access to wildlife through itinerant and permanent menageries throughout the period covered in this book, a transformation in animal spectacle came about from the 1920s or earlier with the proliferation of botanical and zoological gardens privately owned by self-styled naturalists, both European and African, affiliated with the Nigeria Royal Society for the Prevention of Cruelty to Animals (NRSPCA) and the Nigerian Field Society. Modeled along the lines of similar projects in Europe, botanical and zoological gardens, in all their dressed-up artificiality, were marketed to Europeans and elite Africans as sites for the appreciation of the wonders of nature, a place to relax and enjoy a scientific and educational exchange. They became a center of attraction and scenic fascination for urbanites who craved natural scenery, as the built environment and population growth consumed green spaces within cities. Two of these sites, owned respectively by White businessman A. F. Hooper and Black businessman W. H. Biney, were popular in 1940s Lagos. Occupying about two acres of land, Hooper's zoo and botanical gardens exhibited pigeons, a giant tortoise capable of carrying an adult human, and pigs five feet long. All the animals were described as "healthy" and "well-fed and free from disease" by an inspection team of the NRSPCA in 1947.[89]

Biney, a boxing promoter from the Gold Coast (present-day Ghana) who made Nigeria his home, founded what appears to be the first modern zoo in Lagos. Biney's collection in 1946 included a leopard and rhinoceroses, in addition to porcupines, hawks, antelopes, guinea pigs, and civets. By the late 1950s the zoo boasted of tigers, gorillas, and crocodiles. The biggest gorilla, named John, was reported to smoke cigarettes and drink alcohol—behavior that fascinated zoo visitors. In early 1956 the WAP celebrated the arrival at Biney's zoo, from northern Nigeria, of a six-foot-tall lion, estimated to be worth £1,000.[90] Projected to be the "king" of all the animals in the zoo, the lion was described by promoters, in an attempt to allay the fears of zoo-goers, as "hav[ing] been tamed"; they assured potential visitors that a special iron cage was being constructed for it. By 1960 Biney's zoo was the biggest in the country, exhibiting up to a hundred animal species, including a six-year-old chimpanzee also named John.[91] Biney's animals became "modern" colonial subjects as well as performers and legitimizers of modernity. Special themed exhibitions tapped into nature to present animals' affinity with humans. The language of animal spectacle mirrored that of colonialism itself: the domestication of nature was said to expand the frontier of human advancement. So, impressed by

Biney's zoo, one M. O. Okigie wrote a poem published in the *Nigerian Daily Times* (NDT) on May 13, 1946:

> Inside white square walled fence like block heaps upon ground
> Is the Biney's zoo that holds in thrall the caged bird:
> And the porcupine, heavy shelled tortoise, and hound,
> And horned antelope, ostrich with neck like the guard;
> And the smart guinea-pig, the bush cat, and bush-pig,
> And the anthropoid ape that is old as is big.
>
> While above the head under the canopied heaven
> Are bunch ripe fruits of mango tree with green foliage,
> Spreading like the Chief's large umbrella, uneven.
> And protecting the flowers in the row as of lineage,
> That forth blossom sweet multiple colours with odour,
> Or illuminate the paths as of many a corridor.
>
> For here we trace the likeness of Garden of Eden,
> Where did congregate various and tall beauteous trees;
> And the shrubs, and the plants, and the flowers with the pollen
> And all the kinds of beasts, and of birds and of bees;
> And the parents Eve, Adam, who made love of creation
> They admired, and for which they both gave approbation.[92]

Biney's and Hooper's zoos were not the only menageries in colonial Nigeria. When the University College Ibadan opened its Department of Zoology in 1948 for undergraduate education, it established a zoological garden as an experimentation station for teaching and research. Sensing the commercial viability of animal exhibits, the school opened the zoo to the public in the early 1950s. The success of the Ibadan Zoo, which in 1957 attracted as many as seventy thousand visitors (mostly children), who paid an entrance fee of 3d., was directly linked to a public-school curriculum (promoted also through the print media and special television programs on animals) that included both real and fictionalized narratives about animals' lives and behaviors.[93] Animals had a place in indigenous African folktales transmitted orally from generation to generation. However, the expansion of Western education, print technology, radio, and television brought these stories to a larger audience. Adult columnists such as Miss Silva and Uncle Kebby, as well as zookeepers, combined local and cosmopolitan narratives to expand children's imaginations about their "animal friends."[94] Moral teaching about kindness toward animals and concerning their behavior, reproduction, ecology, and history of migration were common topics in public schools. Animals' lives were creatively inserted into the gamut of narratives, even of comic book heroes: animals, like humans, can rescue the world from impending catastrophe! After reading and listening to stories about animals, schoolchildren wanted to encounter the wild in a safe space. Zoo excursions, in addition to expanded school curriculum, also shaped childhood experience. Without the zoo, rural children would probably not have had reason to visit the city and witness such creatures, even though they may have seen them in the wild or their carcasses. For their urban counterparts, visiting a zoo was perhaps the only way to experience wildlife and temporarily escape the bustling city life.

Children even received lessons against believing in the power of animal charmers, such as one Professor Benson (alias "Wizard of Day and Night"), whose fame as the "friend and playmate" of cobras fascinated the public in Lagos in the 1950s. What was problematic about Professor Benson, whom Uncle Kebby described as a charlatan, was not just his professed power to tame cobras but also his selling of a "black wonder soap" capable of helping students to pass exams.[95] A photo journalism piece titled "Charmer or Charlatan?," featuring snake charmer Mallam Mohamodu, whose former assistant was reportedly bitten to death by a snake, explicitly warned children to "keep off this man." Media skeptics doubted he had the power to truly charm the four cobras he was exhibiting and said that if his power was real, he should seek gainful employment with the University College Ibadan Zoo instead of deceiving spectators.[96] Apparently, the problem with animal charming was not only its seemingly unsafe milieu but also the "illicit" activities, such as the sale of charms, that took place unconnected with the animal exhibition itself.[97] Besides the scientific and educational missions of the modern zoo, commercial motivations also were involved. Unlike the London Zoo, which received animals as gifts from naturalists from around the world, the Ibadan and Biney zoos had acquired their animals by direct purchase from private collectors, who captured and sold the animals for cash. Only business-spirited individuals like Biney would pay as much as £1,000 for a live lion in the 1950s. Biney did not conceive the zoo as a public project, involving the investment of patrons who believed in its "altruistic" or "scientific" purpose. Although the NRSPCA praised Biney's zoo "as an ideal one," adding that it was striking "that such a humanitarian work could be undertaken by a single man," it was an all-purpose business venture. The zoo was Biney's private investment, run from proceeds from animal exhibitions and his other ventures, especially hotel and boxing promotion. Ibadan Zoo was by contrast a government establishment that was open to the public, for both economic and educational purposes.

Having caged and chained the animals, humans had to feed them with an assortment of natural meals, which had to be purchased. The leopard in Biney's zoo, for example, consumed 4s. 6d. worth of meat per day in the mid-1940s. In 1960 it cost an average of £100 per month to run the zoo, which also had a dedicated veterinary officer and an animal ambulance, the only one in Lagos.[98] To maintain public interest, zoos had to continue to grow their collections, often in the face of rapid declines, such as in the wake of a disease outbreak. What humans possessed in unlimited quantity was the power to capture and cage exotic animals, but the wildlife science necessary for keeping them healthy and alive was underdeveloped, even at the University College Ibadan Zoo. Veterinary science could not be of any significant help to the colonial zoos because it was developed to cater to cattle capitalism.

The ideology shaping wild animal collection for zoos was meant to stand in contrast to the violence the animals generally encountered at the hands of humans or as targets of predators in the wild. Indeed, modern zookeepers argued they were saving the fauna by preserving animals in captivity, providing them a sanctuary where they could breed to prevent extinction. An announcement of the 1925 arrival of Mary and Loja read, "Baby lion cubs—newly arrived from Nigeria—thoroughly enjoy their freedom in the sunshine. London zoo."[99] However, the reverse was often the case. Wild animal collecting for zoos and scientific establishments in Europe and Africa intensified the depletion of wildlife—the killing and capturing of wild animals went in tandem. "The usual and almost the only way of collecting Chimpanzee," wrote the senior resident of Benue Province in mid-1956, "is by shooting Mothers."[100]

The contradictions inherent in wildlife exploitation did not help matters. Private individuals working on behalf of zoological gardens required a license to capture or kill a wild animal; however, they did not need a license to buy or sell animals. In response to this "mad rush" for Nigerian animals, administrators used their discretion to disapprove game-collecting requests, citing many reasons that were unacceptable to the applicants. When C. L. Bowen applied to capture gorillas, monkeys, chimpanzees, and ostriches in Benue for the Royal Zoological Society of Ireland in 1956, he received an official response that such animals did not exist in that area.[101] This kind of disapproval often proved counterproductive as it indirectly fueled wildlife trafficking.

Colonialists believed in their capacity to save all colonial subjects, both human and nonhuman, from imperilment. In devising wildlife conservation regulations, little thought was given to the diversity of the zoological zones within Nigeria's geography, and the liberalization of gun laws and of rules governing animal trophy collecting directly fueled the wanton destruction of wildlife. Thus, the conflict between humans and wildlife over the dominance of nature needs to be understood from multiple perspectives, including environmental degradation. It was also about animal agency. In responding to humans' encroachment on their habitat, wild animals acted in ways that led to a chain of economic and political policies. The contradictions of scientific conservation also are obvious in the history of the modern zoo, which claimed to protect animals from the danger of the wild. In exhibiting animals for humans' amusement, promoters of the modern zoo turned animals into performers and legitimizers of modernity, often to the animals' detriment.

7 ∽ "Let Us Be Kind to Our Dumb Friends"

Animal Cruelty in the Discourse of Colonial Modernity

> It will be admitted that the worst crime that any human being can com-
> mit to his conscience is to ill-treat and be cruel to dumb and innocent
> creatures, which glaringly, have not the means to retaliate. . . . The days
> are no more when any one can just get hold of a creature and put it to
> death for no just cause whatsoever. We now live in the days when dumb
> creatures have as much protection at the hands of the law as any human
> being has.
>
> —"Cruelty to Animals," *West African Pilot*, December 10, 1942

SUSUANA PHILLIPS and Safuratu Lawani were neighbors on Bamgbose
Street in Lagos. On August 10, 1938, Phillips, who had a small dog named
Tatters, gave her pet a small bone to chew on. However, Peju, Lawani's
maid, allegedly snatched the bone from Tatters. The provoked Tatters
sprang onto Peju and bit her. Phillips, having previously warned Peju to
desist from seizing Tatters's bone, treated the wound inflicted on her by
the angry dog. Relations between Lawani and Phillips became sore. In retaliation for biting Peju, Lawani was alleged to have bitten Tatters, inflicting wounds on her. On August 17 and 18, Phillips claimed she saw Lawani
remove a hot rod from a fire and strike Tatters with it. The injured Tatters
had to be taken to physician Dr. Kofoworola Abayomi, who treated her
for a wound about two and a half inches long. This conflict between two
neighbors and a dog became a criminal issue when Lawani was charged
for cruelty to a dog and arraigned at St. Anna Magistrate Court on September 9, 1938. During court proceedings, Dr. Abayomi testified that the
wound on Tatters's back must have been caused by a "sharp instrument."
Not only did Lawani deny striking Tatters with any rod; she testified that

Phillips had told her that the wound on Tatters's back "was the result of a fight between their dog and another." She also denied knowing about the Peju, Tatters, and Phillips confrontation. In his judgment, Magistrate A. Desalu considered the "lengthy and touching appeal" of Phillips's counsel, S. H. A. Baptist, and found Lawani guilty of cruelty to an animal. The magistrate sentenced her to fourteen days in prison or a fine of 21s. She was also ordered to pay a guinea to Phillips as compensation.[1]

In another case, also in Lagos, a man named Agari was awakened at four o'clock on the morning of August 17, 1938, by the "cry of his chicken." Upon getting to his backyard, he found a cat "enjoying the meat" of his poultry. In anger, Agari hit the cat on the head with a stick. The cat escaped to the bush behind his house. The following evening, Agari's neighbor Lawrence Mensah, arrived at his door with police and holding his dead cat in his hands. Agari was arraigned in court on charges of cruelty to an animal. During the court hearing, he did not deny hitting Mensah's cat with a stick in retaliation for killing his chicken but said that he thought the cat was a "wild one"—claiming he did not know it belonged to his neighbor. Magistrate A. Desalu, the same judge who presided over Phillips and Lawani's case, did not find Agari guilty of cruelty to an animal as charged by the police. He subsequently "discharged him with a caution."[2]

It is unclear why Desalu let Agari off the hook. It appears that he felt Mensah's cat, unlike Tatters, was not a "household" pet and that its "wild" behavior of killing another animal resembled the invasion of dreaded beasts, like the leopard, that threatened domesticated animals and humans. In Nigeria, as in many parts of the world, the cat assumed an ambivalent image—both "tame" and "wild"—an animal that sought to live independently from humans despite centuries of domestication. He probably believed that a "good" pet must stay within the premises of its owner in a colonial society, which deployed the concept of "stray" in policing the animal body and punishing it for being in a "wrongful" place. In a similar way, no one questioned the killing of a "wild bush cat" that, according to the West African Pilot (WAP), "strayed" into a house in Surulere in Lagos in early 1956 and bit twelve-month-old Babatunde Oluwagbohun in his cot.[3] The act of neighbors who "chased and killed" the "invader" after hearing the "unusual cry" of the infant, who was later hospitalized, was viewed as equivalent to the benevolence of intrepid hunters risking their lives to confront a dangerous beast. Apparently, to the public there were two types of cats—namely, "household" and "wild/bush," a fluid category based on the threat to humans or other animals.

The dichotomy between tame and untame animals was not the only basis for determining cruelty in the colonial court, nor was the infliction of physical pain on animals or their unlawful public presence. A domesticated animal did not have to threaten humans and other animals, or behave in a disorderly conduct, to deserve protection. In June 1958 Kadiri Ishola, also of Lagos, was sentenced to one month in prison or a fine of £10 for leaving Lucky, his pet monkey, in the rain for three days.[4] The judgment fused moral responsibility and religious sentiment in favor of a tamed brute: "It is a sin to allow rain to beat down on a monkey. If you have an animal as a pet, you must look after it well." The judgment went on to say that "doctors still find difficulty in distinguishing between the blood of a man and that of a monkey," a statement that dovetailed with the rhetoric of animal compassion emphasizing the evolutionary similarity between humans and animals.[5]

All these cases have something in common — the colonial court recognized domesticated animals as colonial subjects and modern creatures that can feel pain and possess the right not to be cruelly treated.[6] While cruelty to animals was not an entirely permissible act under indigenous law and custom, colonialism imposed new ideals by using the language of civilization to justify the protection of certain classes of animals and establishing the context in which humans could be punished for cruel behavior toward them.

But there is more. Colonialism sought to transform both humans and some animals into modern creatures, drawing from the notion that how humans treat animals cannot be divorced from broader social behavior and law and order. Colonial officers and some educated elite Nigerians combined racial ordering and class in positioning a new regime for human-animal relations. Positive sentiment toward other sentient beings became a marker of a superior class identity that some educated Nigerians wanted the "illiterates" to cultivate. Coercive power imposed on animals was interpreted as a product of underdeveloped or thwarted intelligence — one of the hallmarks of racial ordering. This explains why the most diverse cases of cruelty to animals took place in Lagos — the center of British judicial power and a bastion of modernity in Nigeria. In proscribing good relations between people and animals, the colonial government and educated Nigerians Africanized a problem that transcended location and racial boundaries.

LEGAL AND IDEOLOGICAL CONTEXT

Cruelty to animals was a sociopolitically, historically, and legally constructed criminal act in colonial Nigeria. While the legal definition contained in the criminal code is immutable or fixed, the popular and social construction continued to be revised and reinterpreted in accordance with the perspective, power, hierarchical position, and racial identity of particular individuals and groups. It is this personal agency in the interpretation of the law and circumstances that shaped Magistrate Desalu's decision not to punish Agari for killing Mensah's cat. Like most behavior conceived as peculiar with lower class, it was constructed as addictive, practically impossible to resist, with far-ranging consequences for public life and social control. A 1950 official government document titled "Prevention of Cruelty to Animals" summed up over four decades of the evolution of legal and social thought on compassion for animals in Nigeria. It defined animals as captive and tamed creatures (including birds, fish, and reptiles) that served human material or symbolic needs. Cruelty, this document emphasized, includes "acts of being unkind, unmerciful, inhumane, brutal or barbaric" to these animals. Cruelty could also take the form of "over-riding, over-loading, infuriating or terrifying an animal." Harming domestic animals for destroying crops or household items, abandoning and depriving them of food, water, and basic care, or adopting a slaughtering method that delayed death and prolonged suffering all were deemed forms of cruelty. However, putting an animal to death because of infirmity, old age, or incurable sickness in a "painless" manner was a "merciful act"—it was benevolence to end the life of a hopeless creature, thus terminating a sorrowful and painful existence.[7]

Colonialists thought that wild animals deserved to be protected through conservation and game laws aimed at preserving pristine nature. Dogs, cats, and goats, among other household animals, deserved humane treatment for a different reason: having lost their beastly power through centuries of domestication, they relied on humans for protection. A colonial ethic of kindness did not hold that wild animals, including predators like lions, which threatened humans, could be treated cruelly probably because they can defend themselves. Of course, some domestic animals could defend themselves from ill-treatment, but their capacity to do so was limited compared to the untamed beasts, which humans also could subdue by outright killing with guns, among other lethal weapons. Thus, the idea of limiting the definition of cruelty to captive and domesticated animals was informed by the degree of power that humans had over the nonhuman creatures. Hence, the "best" animals were the docile and industrious ones like the donkey and horse that served humans; thus, they required protection. The "worst" included the wild beasts like leopards, who challenged human supremacy while also refusing to be servile. Such animals, provided they remained in their natural abode, should be protected through game laws but should be exterminated if they ventured into settled human communities. Thus, violence and gentility coexisted in the carefully modulated hierarchy of power between the human and animal kingdoms.

Two categories of animal advocates within the racialized colonial society emerged at various times during the first half of the twentieth century. The first was colonial administrative and legal officers who experienced, on a daily basis, the unkind manner in which some Nigerians treated their animals and sought to change their minds through propaganda—colonial parlance for education and sensitization aimed at shaping public opinion in favor of the government—and legal actions. In administering justice to punish alleged lack of compassion toward animals, colonial officers and judges were influenced not only by the provisions of the law but also by their own "friendly" disposition toward animals. Yet to interpret protection of animals as an altruistic gesture on the part of colonial officers is to miss a cardinal component of colonialism—law and order. Colonialism involved maximum control of virtually all spheres of humans' engagement with the state and the natural order. Laws pertaining to cruelty to animals, which were directly imported from Europe, served an intended purpose of expanding the boundary of social control and by extension the domain of colonial violence.

The second category was Nigerian educated elites—such as newspaper editors, medical doctors, religious leaders, and public servants—the majority of whom had imbibed Western culture and thought that Nigerians should be educated on how properly to treat their animals. Not only did they write comprehensive articles and editorials in the newspapers and make radio broadcasts decrying cruelty to animals; they also played a crucial role, as we shall later see, in the formation of the Nigeria branch of the Royal Society for the Prevention of Cruelty to Animals (RSPCA). They derived their vocabulary from epistolary advice literature and cautionary tales and poems about animals published in North America and Europe and circulated across the British Empire. The Christianization of relations of power that humans possessed over animals by this group was inevitable, given that most of them were Christians or professed Christianity. From special church services for animals to newspaper and radio propaganda, educated elites gave an expanded meaning to sin by viewing inhumane treatment of animals as an act that God frowned upon. The involvement of Africans in animal protection campaigns revealed that the ordering of

Africans' intellectual capacity was not monopolized by Europeans. Indeed, educated Africans played a crucial part in extolling Eurocentric ideals of African primitivity with a focus on human-animal relations. They expanded the framing of modern animals and how humane treatment of nonhuman creatures should reflect in the lives of colonial subjects. Like debates over marriage, political representation, public infrastructure, and education, discussions over how to measure compassion toward animals had a modernist frame.

Both European and African animal rights advocates fought for the protection of their nonhuman friends in four complementary ways: (1) attributing cruelty to ignorance and thoughtlessness, (2) humanizing animals—that is, advising people to connect emotionally with animals or to care for them, (3) highlighting the indispensable material and symbolic importance of animals to humans, and (4) contrasting the ways animals were treated in Nigeria to how they were treated in Britain, the mother country.[8] Let us elaborate on all this. Animal advocates attributed cruelty more to "ignorance" than to "inconsideration," "brutal lack of thought," or "complete absence of a sense of wrong doing."[9] The assistant director of veterinary services for the eastern provinces included "lack of imagination" in his long list of reasons why Nigerians treat animals badly.[10] When the resident officer of Niger Province remarked that "in so far as the process of inculcating new ideas into a population resembles that of sending a child to school," he was emphasizing colonial paternalism—the prevailing ideology that civilization involved socializing a child (i.e., any colonial subject, regardless of age, status, or sex) into a "proper," "modern," and law-abiding subject through Western education and transformation of backward attitudes unique to a premature psychological and physiological developmental stage of humans.

In this way, framing animal cruelty as a behavior shared by a majority of Nigerians validated the authority and responsibility by their social superiors (colonial government and educated African elites) to protect the defenseless brutes. Taken together, whether depicted as a superior species within an animal kingdom where other lower species who suffered cruelty also lived or as a completely different species (taxonomically, intellectually, and otherwise) above the animal world, animal rights advocates viewed cruelty to animals as a deviant but correctable behavior. And the metropole provided living proof of this correctability. If the British people could leave their brutish ways of treating animals by abandoning blood sports (such as dogfighting, cockfighting, and animal baiting), animal advocates believed that Nigerians, too, could be civilized to show compassion toward the lower creatures.[11]

Colonial paternalism within the context of animal rights went beyond the rhetoric of power and imperial privilege. It also played out in the notion that Africans must be reintroduced or resocialized into the "animal ways" to mend the harmonious relationships that were present at the beginning of time but had deteriorated due to humans' complete dominance over nature. In advice manuals and propaganda documents against cruelty, animal rights advocates expressed the belief that it was easier to raise children to be friends of animals than to change adults' opinions. Thus, didactic literature, including columns dedicated to children's affairs in the WAP and the *Nigerian Daily Times* (*NDT*), was specifically developed for schoolchildren, with instructions on keeping pets in order to learn the habits of animals so that the children would grow up to have sympathetic concern for animals.[12] In this way, pet keeping was framed as more than an eccentric personal indulgence, raised to an emotional behavior with a significant dose of moral uplift. Although children are born with natural emotions of kindness, they require socialization to extend those feelings to nonhuman creatures. Connecting a love for animals to human physio-psychological development clearly exonerates animals from the blame of cruelty, focusing only on the human as the real wicked brute. Moral lessons about kindness toward animals were an essential element of literary and childhood education. In some children's literature, animals assumed human identities in part to emphasize the significance of humane treatment. In many ways, animals and children were considered as sharing similar traits, such as innocence and vulnerability, that adults must protect through kindness.[13]

Evolution, as a means of explaining the origins of humans, was not popular in colonial Nigeria, where both indigenous and foreign religions upheld the sanctity of creationism. However, in their bid to humanize animals, animal rights advocates were willing to disturb the conventional wisdom by considering humans and animals as being of the same stock during the early stage of evolution. The evolutionary affinity between humans and animals, according to them, was responsible for many common traits that humans and the lower animals exhibit—they all "eat, live, feel, and die." The main difference between humans and animals, one Jay Gee established in his April 1938 article in the WAP, "Man's Inhumanity to Animals," is "reasoning faculty possessed by man and lacked by the lower animals, and hence the superiority and dominance of the former over the latter."[14]

The idea that animals were created or "ordained" to serve the material and symbolic needs of humans (as food, pets, beasts of burden, companions) and that cruelty amounted to abuse of nature's privilege emphasized animals' role as indispensable in the maintenance of natural harmony.

But not all animals belonged to the same stock in the representation of their affinity to humans. "No other animal enters so intimately into our daily lives, none is so entirely friendly, so unselfish, so sympathetic, so faithful or so wise" as the dog, said G. L Adebesin, the general secretary of the Kaduna Nigeria Royal Society for the Prevention of Cruelty to Animals (NRSPCA), who stated the attributes of dogs in a radio campaign against animal cruelty. He went on to advise people to communicate with their dogs and guaranteed the animal would understand them and respond through the "eloquent language" of his or her eyes, tail, and ears. Other notable qualities of a dog such as its "sense of justice," retentive memory, power to perceive scent, and "general tractability," Adebesin continued, "raised the dog high above all other animals," giving it a clear distinction as a human's "firmest friend." People cannot, according to Adebesin, fully comprehend the dog's inestimable intelligence. But a dose of "fairness and justice," honesty, and kindness, in addition to attending to its bodily and mental needs, would be enough.[15] In another vein, animals, like humans, are capable of suffering mental anguish—they are not "inanimate objects like wood or steel," a WAP editorial argued. Thus, their response to pain is not that different from the ways humans feel when in anguish.[16] Noticeable aspects of appearance provided apparent evidence that an animal was in pain—for example, the straining and redness of a cow's eye sockets when its horns are connected to a winch and it is raised from the ground by force, its huge body dangling in midair, for loading onto ships.[17] When animals refused to enter a location or reacted strangely to a person, another anticruelty pamphlet established, it was because they were recalling past ill-treatment, which stayed with them.[18]

As animal advocates emphasized a reconfiguration of attitudes toward their animal friends, they were equally aware of a backlash. When J. H. W. Vincent opened his broadcast with the statement "If in the talks which I have already given I appear to have been rather profuse in my praise of the English man's good points, I beg you to think twice before condemning me," he was preempting the reaction of people who might accuse him of being a puppet of European civilization. The second portion of Vincent's opening line—"because I have always gone out of my way to find out their finer qualities, in the hopes that we in West Africa might adapt these points to make our lives better and brighter"—would certainly appeal to most educated Nigerians.[19] For Vincent, although Europeans subscribed to the common practice of "minding your own business"—that is, not interfering with other people's affairs—they would not overlook cruelty to animals at the hand of another person. They were willing to speak up for the "dumb creatures," even to their own detriment. This self-imposed obligation of protecting animals functioned because British society, unlike Nigeria's, was amenable to a love of animals. That society was also informed, according to him, by the well-entrenched ideology that protection of animals was a civic responsibility that could not be left to the police and the RSPCA alone. Vincent stated that Africans had "never really learned to love animals" as Englishmen did; the latter would mobilize the police, fire department, and civilians to save a dog or cat in danger and even exercise caution to ensure the rescue operation did not inflict additional pain on the animal victim. Moreover, an Englishman would pull over after hitting an animal with his car, not just because he feared the RSPCA inspectors who might "appear in unexpected place" but because he would not want to leave the animal in pain. These characterizations fed into the established norm of comparing European modernity with African protomodernity.

Vincent then went on to emphasize that there are a myriad of ways of getting animals to follow human commands without inflicting pain on them: a dog who stole a piece of meat would only stop if the owner fed it well and kept the food where the animal would not see or smell it. Instead of beating a neighbor's dog for stealing meat, Vincent advised Nigerians to ask the owner to pay for it. Punitive measures inflicted on animals after such a transgression would not bring the stolen item back. The cruel job of the "illiterate cow-boys" who beat cattle on their way to the slaughterhouse could be replaced, Vincent advised, with a trained dog that shepherded livestock, such as in the Scottish Highlands.[20] Vincent thought that carrying fowl upside down by their legs demonstrated "only laziness," for with a little effort they could be carried in a more humane manner. He ended his elaborate broadcast with the story of a collie in Britain that for three years had carried a penny in his mouth every morning to help his mistress buy a newspaper. One day the vendor discovered that the dog had not brought any money. Everyone thought something bad must have happened. So they took the animal to the veterinary hospital, where an X-ray revealed he had swallowed the penny. Surgery was immediately performed to remove the penny from the dog's stomach. As we shall see later, these various provocative ideas about animal compassion did not go unchallenged by Nigerians.

Anticruelty laws appeared on the books early in the period of colonial rule, as animal advocacy in Nigeria also dates to this era. Colonial and legal officers combined their administration of animal-cruelty law with nonpunitive advocacy for the "dumb creatures." However, animal compassion advocates believed that the law alone was inadequate in protecting animals—propaganda was also required. It does not appear that any animal advocacy group existed in Nigeria before 1930. In October of that year, the RSPCA in London sought the "sympathetic consideration" of the governor of Nigeria in establishing a local branch of the society in Nigeria, citing abuse of animals such as overloading of cattle in wagons and poultry in crates.[21] The benefit of a Nigerian branch of the RSPCA, the correspondence anticipated, included the establishment of veterinary clinics for sick and wounded animals.

This idea did not sit well with colonial officers. The administrator of the Lagos Colony believed that "the time [was] not ripe" for Nigeria to have a branch of the RSPCA. "I feel that if established even in Lagos," he projected, "it might do as much harm as good when started and would very rapidly become comatose."[22] A careful reading of correspondence suggests that colonial officers thought that the body was trying to arrogate power in the administration of animal-cruelty laws. The governor of Nigeria, Graeme Thomson, was concerned that the RSPCA could become another imperial watchdog of the activities of the men on the ground, forcing their own perspective on a colony they knew little to nothing about. He probably did not want the RSPCA to transfer their controversial identity to Nigeria.[23] Colonial officers seemed to abhor the RSPCA's "militant" approach to the question of cruelty to animals and believe that "at the present stage of development" of Nigeria, propaganda, not prosecution, would solve the problem. To prove that his government was policing animal cruelty, Governor Thomson included a copy of the 1927 pamphlet *Extracts from Hadiths and Muslim Text Books on the Subject of Treatment of Animals*, developed by native authorities in northern Nigeria.[24] The RSPCA's statement that officials in Nigeria, not a foreign body, are "naturally in the best position to know what shall be done" about animal cruelty recognized a potential conflict of interest or clash of roles among the so-called agents of civilization.[25]

The RSPCA seemed not to have been discouraged by the initial rebuff from Nigerian authorities. Its London officers tried to shape public opinion toward the care of animals by awarding Meritorious Service Medals to Nigerian chiefs and elites who had "taken a real personal interest" in protecting animals against cruelty.[26] The award also benefited the RSPCA by enabling it to show its gratitude to deserving individuals for helping to achieve its mission and to encourage other chiefs to take a keen interest in animal protection. First instituted in Nigeria 1937, the RSPCA Meritorious Service Medals came in bronze and silver, with a certificate. Potential awardees had to be recommended by their district or resident officers. The award was officially presented during important ceremonies such as Empire Day, changes of political leadership, and visits of important colonial officers, which gave it some public visibility and integrated it into the fabric of colonial power. While colonial officers agreed to present the RSPCA medals to local chiefs, they declined another offer to allow police officers and firefighters to wear the medal on their regular uniforms, except for "local occasion."[27]

The Meritorious Service Medal was more than an ordinary medal—it became another means through which individuals and groups highlighted their relevance to their community. Colonial medals, regardless of their purpose, conferred power and social capital on both the Africans who received them and the Europeans who commended them. When the resident of Niger Province was asked to nominate deserving elites for the award in June 1937, however, he simply replied, "I do not consider that any chiefs in this province have taken a real personal interest in this cause or have achieved personal result." He was optimistic, though, that the award would "serve as a stimulus to personal interest in the future."[28] His Plateau Province counterpart, L. R. Delves-Broughton, also thought that no chief in his area of jurisdiction deserved the medal.[29] Probably discouraged that Nigerian officers were not forthcoming in recommending deserving local chiefs, the RSPCA went ahead to issue medals to the Emirs of Katsina, Sokoto, Gwandu, Argungu, Daura, Zaria, and Kano, as well as the Sultan of Sokoto, thereby bypassing the official bottleneck.[30] As it turned out, these local chiefs received the medals not for what they had done on behalf of animals and the RSPCA but for what they should be doing.

Discontented that colonial officers did not allow the establishing of a branch in the country, the RSPCA sponsored a propaganda effort aimed at smearing the image of the colonial administration. On May 7, 1938, the British tabloid *Weekly Illustrated* published a photo of a featherless live chicken, a mouse trapped in a cage, a ten-year-old girl carrying a goat bound by its legs on her head, and a flock of sheep shepherded by a naked boy holding a stick, with which he "drives his noisy charges" (see fig. 7.1).[31]

Of these four images, that of the featherless chicken caught the most attention of government and animal advocates. The feathers, according to the photo caption, were removed because customers "want their fowls plucked, and the meat keep[s] better alive." The article further described the practice as a "custom," "revolting and grotesque"—even though "it seems natural" to Nigerians. Anyone familiar with the image of Africa in Western media from the nineteenth century would not be surprised by these photos. Colonialism was sustained in part by demonstrating the legitimacy of Western civilization through textual and visual narratives depicting Africans as primitive people in need of Westernization. But how the animal body was inserted into the politics of imagery is a fascinating story. For colonial officers, humans were extending the frontiers of their savage nudity to the animal world. Animals (unlike humans) came with their natural clothes—removing their fur or feathers for economic purposes was a barbaric act and an undue interference with nature.[32] In his reaction to the featherless-chicken-sales-presentation scandal, a practice described by the district officer of Ogoja as a "labor saving device," British academic Dr. Eric Sutherland took Nigerian administrators to task wondering if "an enlightened civilization can help to end ignorant practices which must inflict needless suffering on dumb animals."[33]

However, the *Weekly Illustrated* misrepresented the identity of the featherless chicken. Its frame of reference and interpretation aligned with the mind-set of precolonial visitors and travelers who painted graphic images of Africa out of historical and cultural context. The investigation ordered by the Colonial Office produced an unanticipated outcome—it unmasked the unique story of the chicken in question. The senior resident of Onitsha, A. E. F. Murray, in whose jurisdiction the featherless chicken had been found, visited the home of its owner, Abudu Salami, where he also found the featherless fowl "foraging with others in a yam patch" and ready to lay an egg. The chicken's "condition, apart from the hideousness of its appearance, was good and it did not appear to be suffering any discomfort. The animal is well-known in Onitsha as an extraordinary freak," Murray reported. He concluded, contrary to the *Weekly Illustrated*, that the chicken had not been offered for sale and that "no Ibo would dream of eating such a monstrosity."[34] As it turned out, the Onitsha fowl was naturally featherless. It suffered from a rare genetic mutation.

In 1936 Nigeria's first known animal protection organization, the Nigerian Animal Aid Society (NAAS), was established by Bernard Bourdillon, one of the longest-serving governors of British Nigeria, who also

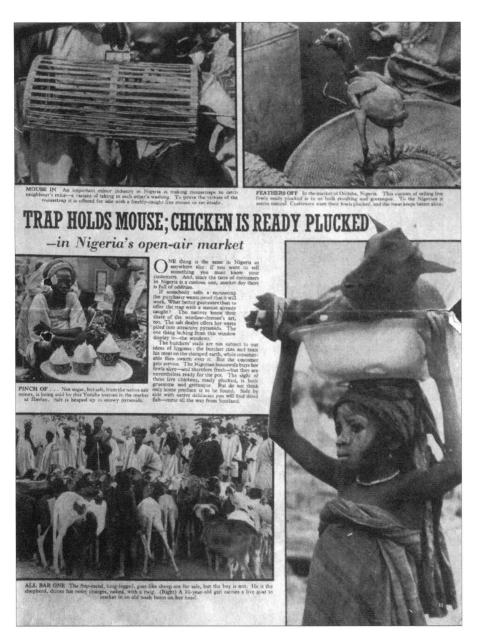

FIGURE 7.1. Article in the *Weekly Illustrated* (May 7, 1938) that includes anti-animal-cruelty propaganda. *Source:* Commissioner of the Colony Office, Lagos (ComCol) 1136, National Archives, Ibadan.

served as the organization's founding president. A promotional article in the *NDT* commemorated its founding "hope that all lovers of animals will become members."[35] The newspaper then presented the justification for establishing the NAAS, deploying the familiar colonial paternalistic language: "For a long time there has been existing a general impression that something should be done to educate the peoples of Nigeria towards a better understanding of their responsibility towards domestic and other animals."[36] Although established by the head of the British government in Nigeria, the NAAS was a nongovernmental organization run largely by European officials and nonofficials. The few African committee members included Dr. J. C. Vaughn, a founding member of the Lagos (later Nigerian) Youth Movement, and Dr. I. Ladipo Oluwole and Dr. Akinwande Savage, two leading African medical doctors.[37] Bourdillon's love for animals was known to the public. When he made an unscheduled visit to the Apapa wharf in early 1938 to monitor the loading of cattle onto ships, a newspaper article praised him for going to a "lowly working place" to study the fate of "brute creation, even at the expense of bodily pain to himself." The article thought his humanitarian spirit must have spoken to him, to echo the words of sixteenth-century English poet Sir Philip Sydney, "Thy need, O, my comrade, is greater than mine."[38]

The NAAS was a personal project of Bourdillon's, and its activities were restricted to Lagos. It appeared that, like his predecessors, Bourdillon did not want his group to develop into or have the power of the RSPCA. There is no record that the NAAS facilitated the prosecution of any animal offenders or had uniformed inspectors who supervised markets and horse stables like the RSPCA did in search of violations of anticruelty laws. The NAAS died when Bourdillon's tenure as the governor of Nigeria ended in 1943. A number of animal protection groups run by private individuals and groups, including churches, but not officially recognized by the colonial establishment existed even before the 1930s. One was the Animal Defenders, coordinated by Rev. S. Ade Oduwale, who later served as pastor of King's Church in Lagos. Records are unclear on how Oduwale first established contact with the RSPCA. What is obvious is that after months of correspondence with the group, Oduwale transformed Animal Defenders into the Nigerian branch of the RSPCA. The inaugural service of the NRSPCA was conducted by Rev. R. Armstrong, the acting warden of students of St. Andrew's College, in Oyo, on October 12, 1946.[39] Of the fourteen inaugural members, eight carried the title of reverend. None of its founding members (as gleaned from surnames) was European or non-Yoruba. Oduwale then enrolled members of the Boy Scouts and Girl Guides as well as Sunday school teachers as leaders and advisers of his new association.[40]

It is difficult to tell why Oduwale went behind colonial officers to establish the NRSPCA. The RSPCA may have lured locals like Oduwale into its fold, having failed to convince the government of the value of having a branch in Nigeria. The tension between Oduwale and the Lagos authorities was clear from the correspondence they exchanged after the church inauguration of the NRSPCA in Oyo. Secretary to the Government A. W. Moss and Commissioner of the Colony E. A. Carr were dissatisfied that Oduwale did not inform them before establishing contact with the RSPCA and formally creating the NRSPCA.[41] Carr stated that he declined Oduwale's request to serve as the patron of the group because it did not have any European member based in Lagos, and it is clear that he disassociated from the group because it was not "legitimate" in his eyes, having not been formally approved by the Council of the Society, the body that granted permission for operation of associations in Nigeria.[42] It took an official acknowledgment of the RSPCA of the existence of the NRSPCA, another inauguration ceremony at the Glover Memorial Hall in Lagos on June 10, 1947, approval by the Council of the Society, and enrollment of 145 African and European members based in Lagos and other parts of western Nigeria for the NRSPCA to achieve formal recognition by the government of Nigeria.[43]

Why did Nigeria finally accept a local branch of the RSPCA in 1947, after having declined it seventeen years earlier? The scandal of cruelty to horses and donkeys and the international outcry against horse trafficking in eastern Nigeria justified the ratification of the NRSPCA. The government had come to accept its inability to fully police cruelty to animals, and it sought a fairly inexpensive way to do so through the aid of nonstate actors. The aims of the NRSPCA were threefold, as explicitly stated in its inaugural and invitational pamphlet: (1) "to work to improve the lot of animals, particularly domestic animals as a whole throughout the country," (2) "to educate the people in the proper care and treatment of animals. Contact with the schools and such movements as the Boy Scouts is already established," and (3) "to provide clinics where people can bring their animals for attention." Much of the work of the NRSPCA was performed by Nigerians who were given the role of "inspectors." The NRSPCA's Animal Welfare Week, aside from its regular pamphlet, newspaper propaganda, and radio broadcast, gave visibility to the activities of the society in the big cities.[44] In its 1948–49 annual report, the NRSPCA praised its inspectors for their excellent work of giving first aid to sick and injured animals, supervising the transportation of animals and their treatment in the marketplace, patrolling streets and harbors looking for endangered animals, inspecting fairs and menageries, humanely killing injured animals, and providing "friendly advice" to the public on animal humaneness.[45] The opening of the NRSPCA headquarters in Lagos in March 1951 represented a turning point in the institutionalization of the animal welfare campaign and its full acceptance as part of colonial modernity. Like its counterpart in Britain, the NRSPCA headquarters had facilities for a veterinary clinic, meeting space, and offices for its inspectors. By serving as an animal detention center and a place to lodge animal-cruelty complaints, the NRSPCA office appropriated some of the powers of the veterinary office and the police—a development that, as we shall see later, led to palaver within the colonial establishment.[46]

The formation of the NRSPCA excited the parent body in Britain. In its 1948 annual report, the RSPCA gave the following wishful commendation for what is regarded as its first "oversea branch": "great things will result from this seemingly small beginning." "A little band of workers in Nigeria," the report stated, "are full of enthusiasm, and they look anxiously to the mother society in England for guidance in the planning of their campaign against the ignorance and cruelty that abound there, as here."[47] The RSPCA intensified investment in the Nigerian branch by sponsoring members' trips to Britain for training on animal welfare issues. One such trip by Honorary General Secretary E. O. Daniel in 1951 lasted six months. A published account of it in the popular West Africa magazine described him as a "lover of animals by inclination" and a government public relations officer by profession. Daniel, a proud owner of five dogs and three cats, the profile states, committed his after-hours time to serving as the mouthpiece of Lagos pets, advising people on "how to look after their animals."[48] Up to the end of British colonial rule in Nigeria, the relationship between the NRSPCA and its parent body remained cordial.[49] A reception in honor of W. A. Sibly, member of the executive council of the RSPCA, in January 1956, attracted the creme de la creme of Lagosian society, including the Oba (king), Adeniji Adele II, who served as the council chairman.[50]

The role of schoolchildren in the NRSPCA was well defined from its inception.[51] Working with the Boy Scouts and Girl Guides, the NRSPCA was convinced that it was easier to change attitudes toward animals from childhood. The scout law that stated, "A scout is a friend to animals. He should save them as far as possible from pain, and should not kill any animal unnecessarily, even if it is only a fly—for it is one of God's creatures," provided a convincing template for a mutual relationship with the NRSPCA.[52] The practice of using essay competitions to promote modernist ideas also resonated with the activities of the NRSPCA. The 1947 NRSPCA essay competition, titled "My Duty towards the Lower Animals," had more than one hundred entries from elementary schoolchildren. From the story of a boy who was rewarded by an elephant he had previously helped to that of a girl who freed an antelope captured by a hunter's trap (as narrated by Harold Cooper, the vice patron of the NRSPCA, during the presentation of prizes to the winners of the 1947 contest), the rhetoric of reciprocal kindness was central to the work of the body, which also enlisted pupils into its Animal Defender Corps.

Like the colonial government, the NRSPCA derived its strength from ordering Nigeria's population to hone its relevance. By popularizing narratives of wickedness toward animals, the group "blackmailed" specific communities and challenged colonial officers to redouble their civilizing efforts. Northerners, for instance, were blacklisted by the NRSPCA as "principal offenders" of animal rights in Nigeria.[53] "As someone who has travelled extensively in many parts of Northern Nigeria," S. B. Hogan (probably a colonial officer) wrote in an article published in the *Daily Comet* newspaper, laying down his qualifications for understanding the diverse Nigerian geographical terrain, "I can say with authority that the treatments given to beasts of burden and their death rate particularly during the rainy season, are most appalling." His next statement categorically dismissed the attitude of northerners toward their animals: "Those who know what I mean, can bear witness that so far as kindness to animals is concerned, Northerners are quite devoid of this quality." He characterized the treatment of animals by northerners as "a breach of human kindness to less fortunate and dumb creatures."[54] After seeing a pregnant donkey being overloaded and unable to move while also being tortured in Kano in 1951, T. N. Douglas Okebugbu, an NRSPCA member and former president of the Ngwa Clan Union who called himself "a natural friend of animals," claimed to have moved "nearer to speak for this beast."[55] Like Hogan's, Okebugbu's depiction of the pains of northern Nigerian animals was a call for action:

> Have you ever travelled to the North before? Perhaps not, but there is much to be done in order to prevent cruelty to animals; there is no human being here who has not lamented at the ill and

cruel treatment being meted to animals in this part of the country, especially the beasts of burden. They are being tortured to a point far beyond what words can tell. Their cries have gone from man to heaven, this time not for vengeance, but for mere intervention. The situation is horrible. Animals are being used from morning till night, often without food. Their masters do not even allow them to graze; they flog and curse them mercilessly should any one of them stop to pick a bit of food from the ground, even without any cause whatsoever. All day these beasts have their mouths tightly tied up with a basket-like material (muzzle) in order to prevent them from eating or drinking. You may not believe this, but it does happen here in Kano.[56]

The cultural landscape of each location shaped how the NRSPCA mobilized to protect animals. In Lagos, for instance, the government did not worry about any potential breakdown of law and order arising from the work of the NRSPCA. However, in Kano, administrators were unwilling to risk public disorder that might emerge in the aftermath of the unpopular position on animal welfare in the ancient city. The senior resident of Kano advised the NRSPCA to exercise caution in how it promoted its work among northerners, noting that an "appeal to Moslems will not be the same as to the Christians and problems arising from this difference will require some thought." He advised the NRSPCA to liaise with "prominent members" of the Kano community.[57] This caution was important, given the public outcry following a fifteen-minute radio broadcast in Kaduna in September 1949 by NRSPCA representative G. L. Adebesin, titled "Let Us Be Kind to Our Dumb Friends." The demands of the district officer of Kano, D. A. Pott, were more specific. Not only did he ask the NRSPCA officers to work with local chiefs, whose approval was necessary before the "Animal Cruelty Message" was broadcast; he also said they should not promote humane killing, supervise the loading of animals into trucks, or confiscate ill-treated animals. Rather, they should report transgressions of the animal-cruelty laws to the police.[58] In all, he warned against creating the impression that the NRSPCA was just another idea conceived by the Christian South to impose on the Muslim North. The ethnic origins of the founding members of the Kano NRSPCA did not help the public relations efforts. Out of the twelve founding members, ten were Yoruba; the ethnicity of the remaining two members is not clear. For local chief Wakilin Waje, this was problematic: the language barrier and ethnic difference, he anticipated, would hinder the activities of the group among a predominantly Hausa population. Not only did he think that broadcasting anticruelty laws would not work; he also argued that the NRSPCA's mission to build an animal clinic and provide first aid to suffering animals in Kano would duplicate the work of the veterinary department.[59]

KILLING WITH MERCY

The oxymoronic title of this section best explains the campaign to end "unmerciful slaughtering" of animals for food. Animal-cruelty laws criminalized the popular manner of slaughtering animals (by severing the throat with a knife), which many people came to consider unkind because it prolonged the animal's pain and death. To make matters worse, the knives used for slaughtering animals were often blunt or jagged-edged, thus incapable of severing the throat cleanly. Moreover, because animal blood was also used as food, the slaughterer delayed cutting the main vertebrae to ensure that the maximum amount of blood was collected, the NRSPCA alleged. This inhumane act of violence reached its height during Christmas and Eid-al-Kabir when religious beliefs or "superstitious propensities," according to a *WAP* editorial, required the "mass" slaughtering of "innocent goats, sheep, fowls et cetera." This critic worried about the "gory" sight of animal blood dotting the landscape of many homes and communities during the festivals and the "uncivilized" way animals were put to death.[60] A particularly horrendous instance of slaughtering practice took place in Nsukka, according to an assistant district officer, where after dragging a horse to an open space,

> the slaughterer then tried to sharpen a small piece of metal, 9 inches long and 1 1/2 inches broad. . . . The slaughterer then knelt on the neck and attempted to saw through the throat. The horse screamed and struggled violently and threw him off without his having cut the skin. The horse was again secured and a second attempt made — this also failed. After a certain amount of argument, a third attempt was made and after prolonged sawing with the knife the slaughterer was strong enough to succeed in severing the main artery of the neck. Two minutes later the horse was dead.[61]

The officer described the final death of the horse as a "merciful release to suffering" that started with torture "in a most brutal and revolting manner" and that lasted for about twelve minutes.[62] The humiliation of the horse and the performance of cruelty continued after death—the draining of the animal's blood was equally an ugly sight: "The moment artery was severed, the blood was driven to the animal's neck by jumping amongst the young boys. With each jump the blood came quicker."[63]

The unsanitary condition of slaughterhouses also added to the spectacle of violence inflicted on the "unfortunate brutes." Animal welfare advocates thought that animals should not witness the killing of fellow animals, especially in government slaughterhouses, which lacked facilities to handle the number of livestock required for daily public consumption. For instance, the Kano government slaughter slab was initially constructed to accommodate just seventy cattle, which were slaughtered simultaneously. However, by the early 1930s, about one hundred cattle were being slaughtered—the remaining thirty animals thus witnessed the brutal process. On March 1, 1933, the NDT published an article by a self-identified "Animal Lover" about the inhumane spectacle of slaughtering animals on the Kano slab.[64] This critique, which corroborated a photograph of the same slaughter slab that had appeared on February 18, 1933, brought readers a step closer to the final minutes of animals' lives at the location.[65] The writer echoed the prejudice of critics of Islam that the religion "does not make much provision for the comfort and well-being of animals" and went on to quote a section of Ruxton's Maliki Law, which states that "it is blamable to kill one's animal in view of another," to establish that the problem in Kano was not Islam itself but the refusal of the Muslims of northern Nigeria to follow the tenets of their religion.[66] As anticipated, an NDT editorial titled "Cruelty to Animals," the article by "Animal Lover," and the published photo of the slab attracted the attention of Kano authorities.[67] In his reaction to the article and photo, the resident of Kano did not deny the deplorable conditions at the slaughtering facility but assured the public that the government was planning to extend the slab so that all livestock could be slaughtered at once. A partition wall would be constructed to separate animals being slaughtered from those awaiting their death. Ideally, he pointed out, the best process would be for each head of cattle to be kept in its own stall, but the expense to do so "would be heavy."[68]

It is against this backdrop that the animal welfare movement popularized methods of humane killing that would guarantee "death as quick and painless as possible" or stop the "unnecessary and prolonged suffering."[69] Humane killing could involve stunning by hitting the skull with a poleax or a club or by delivering an electric shock to the brain with an instrument designed for the purpose. Essentially, any instrument capable of abruptly ending the functioning of the brain and heart could help accelerate death and reduce its agony. Thus, the technology that came to be called "humane killer"—a captive-bolt pistol loaded with a blank cartridge—was introduced to Nigeria in the 1940s and 1950s. When fired to the head of the animal, "it does not kill but only makes the animal senseless and impervious to pain," according to a newspaper promotional article on the implement that quoted officers of the RSPCA.[70]

The challenges faced by the popularity of this method were cultural and religious, as well as logistic. In the first place, some Muslims thought the humane killer "deadened" or killed the animals before the use of a knife to sever the throat as stipulated in Islamic doctrine. In Lagos in late 1949 a section of the Muslim community was distributing anti–humane killer posters that read: "The meat of the animal slaughtered with Humane Killer is Islamically speaking unlawful for the Muslims."[71] As with many a new technology or practice, the antipathy toward the humane killer was based primarily on misinformation and rumor about how the tool actually worked and concern for the transformative effect it would have on "normal" ways of slaughtering animals. Many people believed the slitting of an animal's throat would become unnecessary after firing the gun to its head because the bolt would kill it. Others thought that the humane killer actually fired poisonous bullets and that meat of the animals killed with it could harm humans. To worsen the matter, the Muslim community feared that the government would impose compulsory use of the humane killer across their territory. To dispel these rumors, the acting medical officer of health (MOH) in Lagos invited the chief imam of the central mosque and the leaders of the Ahmadiyya community to a meeting in December 1949. At the meeting, the officer assured the Muslim leader that his brethren "need not worry about this matter (humane killing adoption)."[72] Institutionalizing the humane killer thus involved changing deep-rooted religious practices, not only in the predominantly Muslim North but also in the South, where many butchers were Muslims.

Advocates of the humane killer introduced ethnoreligious politics into the debate. They argued that antipathy toward the method was sponsored by the "less enlightened" Muslims, whom they viewed as old, conservative, and willing to uphold a savage practice in the face of obvious advantages of civilization.[73] When a group of Lagos "Muslim young men" decided to stage a public debate on the humane killer in 1950, a WAP editorial voicing the perspective of the predominantly Christian educated elites emphasized that the "progressive" Muslims, "young and educated,"

FIGURE 7.2. Anti-cruelty material (1950s). *Source:* ComCol 1136, National Archives, Ibadan.

understood the advantages of "civilized" treatment of animals better than their "illiterate" and "conservative" coreligionists.[74] The press could not hold back its criticism of Islam. Its professed intention not to "disrespect the religious susceptibilities" of Muslims was countered by the admonition that they must accept the humane killer to "dispel any impression that the Muslims have less regard for progressive measures than other sections of the community."[75]

When the news spread to Nigeria that the humane killer was "popular" among Muslims in the Gold Coast, the press featured a story that portrayed Nigerian Muslims as lagging behind their counterparts in other countries in accepting a progressive practice.[76] The title of the story, "Gold Coast Shows Nigeria How 'Humane Killer' Is Applied," was strategically aimed to appeal to the moral sensibilities of colonial officers and Nigerians. Newspapers took the politics of comparative modernity to another level when they published correspondence between the NRSPCA and Gold Coast authorities on the popularity of the humane killer in the Gold Coast.[77] Interestingly, Islamic practices, like "traditional" African ones, came under attack by the educated elites who held a contradictory posture toward "modernity."

Aside from the resistance from the Muslim community, the humane killer failed to gain in popularity because the government did not have the resources to institutionalize it. Like modern medical and veterinary science, it was beyond the financial reach of most Nigerians. Veterinary clinics, sites where humane killers were in common use, were located mostly in the big cities and commercial centers. Few butchers were willing to wait for days to have an assistant veterinary officer kill their livestock with the humane killer. The captive-bolt pistols, like shotguns and rifles, were classified as "arms of precision," which only Europeans and a select group of educated Nigerians were allowed to use. When George Cockerill, the honorary secretary of the League for the Protection of Horses, lamented the "grave shortage of the right type of Africans" to use the humane killer, he was probably thinking about the condition that only bearers of arms of precision were permitted to use it. He could also have been echoing the established sentiment among European administrators that Africans did not have the intellectual capacity to handle any arms of precision.[78] The acuteness of the shortage of humane killer users varied across the country. In Rivers Province, only one person, a sanitary inspector, was qualified to use the tool. He was only available at the government slaughter slab one out of every nine weeks.[79] When the humane killer was first adopted by native authorities in northern Nigeria in 1941, the government could only afford twenty-six for the entire region.[80]

THE NRSPCA AND THE POLITICS OF PUBLIC ORDER

The activities of the NRSPCA raised concerns about the role of nonstate actors in policing animal cruelty. Although the police had historically arrested people for cruelty to animals, officers did not have any specialized training in animal welfare. When Lagos police superintendent A. T. G. Trumble asserted that the rank and file of the Nigeria Police Force (NPF) were not qualified to deal with ill-treatment of horses by "unskilled and ignorant riders," he was problematizing cruelty in such common practices as the army's galloping of horses on hard roads, which contravened the law. The NPF was established to police humans, not animals, Trumble probably thought.[81] This void in the administration of justice for animals was filled when the NRSPCA began to train its inspectors on standards of animal welfare. The elite African and European communities generally agreed on the importance of policing cruelty to animals; they differed over how much power that NRSPCA inspectors should wield in "arresting" and even filing cases of abuse, while "policing" markets and train stations. The plea by the NRSPCA that citizens should report cases of cruelty of animals, with the caveat that the identity of the complainant would be protected, mirrored conventional policing by the NPF.[82] The fear by administrators that the NRSPCA would take over the work of police and veterinary officers thus came to pass. Not even the insistence by NRSPCA acting general secretary R. A. Jaiyeola in a radio broadcast that his establishment was not arrogating the work of the police could change the public perception toward its growing notoriety.[83]

One example at the Ilorin railway station in 1955 can be used to explore the conflict between the NRSPCA inspectors and veterinary officers over who would take the lead in animal protection. NRSPCA inspectors filed a complaint about overloading of cattle, which were subjected to "rigorous torture" as they trampled on and gored one another during transit, causing blindness and even death.[84] The veterinary development officer, in an exercise in the show of power and hierarchy within the colonial society, responded by insisting that the loading of animals at the railway station be supervised by "trained staff of the veterinary department, and invariably by a European." The explicit identification of the loading supervisor as "European" was meant to assert racial superiority, informed by advanced knowledge. The veterinary development officer also argued that the "powers that be," who he felt knew more about possible cruelty than did the NRSPCA inspectors, made the regulation limiting the number of cattle in each train car to twenty-five; in doing so, they redefined the unstable concept of overloading. He explained that it was necessary to reduce the space between the animals because jostling caused accidents.[85] Similarly, when the chairman of the Ibadan NRSPCA, Lt. Col. G. W. P. Thorn, complained about the dragging of animals around the city with ropes on the hind and fore legs, the district officer asked him to contact the police, citing the existing animal-cruelty law that punished violators with a £25 fine or five months in prison. The tone of the district officer's letter plainly suggested that the NRSPCA had no legal or executive power to police animal cruelty.[86]

The Ilorin and Ibadan cases were not by any means isolated. No other part of Nigeria witnessed the conflict between the NRSPCA and veterinary officers and police like Lagos. Not only were the activities of the NRSPCA more pronounced in the colonial capital, but the city also had a long history of corruption among governmental and nongovernmental institutions and officials, many of whom attempted to manipulate the law for personal gain. Accusations and counteraccusations were inevitable, either out of ignorance of the law or to uphold self-interest. In March 1950 the Public Health Department accused Jaiyeola of entering the municipal abattoir without a government permit, only Lagos Town Council workers, veterinary officers, and the police being allowed there. But another accusation—that Jaiyeola was using his position as the NRSPCA general secretary to obtain meat at cheaper prices—added corruption to the charges against him.[87]

In addition, NRSPCA promoters were stereotyped as individuals who would rather fight on behalf of animals than for their fellow humans. Perhaps no other critic placed animal advocacy at the center of colonial resistance better than Jubril Raji, whose satirical fiction used a neighbor of an NRSPCA officer to present the idea of animal protection, what kinds of animal would be protected, and the ambiguity of the colonial setting, where the insanitary conditions of Lagos and its major public health challenges were not dealt with. Raji was likely a pseudonym because his petition, published by the WAP, contained neither his physical address nor the name of the NRSPCA officer in question. In addition, an "authentic" petition would normally include some language of allegiance to the British Crown. It is worth reprinting an extract here:

> A next-door neighbor of mine is an officer of the Royal Society for the Prevention of Cruelty to Animals. The very house in which he lives is affected by the Slum Clearance Scheme but at present he is still there. I think the rats in his house are over 200. He seems to love them and feed them by leaving crumbs of food about. May I know from the authorities if they [NRSPCA inspectors] are interested in rats and if the laws of RSPCA are favourable to rats as well? If RSPCA member must not kill rats, let all of them go to Iddo and live there and while they go let them go along with their rats.[88]

The above criticism of the NRSPCA was informed by the power they should not have in policing cruelty and fraud—it does not argue against the role of nonstate actors in the animal compassion movement. Rather, it centered on rivalry among multiple forms of regulatory agencies. Another array of petitions and criticism, from Nigeria and Britain, focused on the alleged Eurocentrism of the NRSPCA and its inability to achieve the main purpose for which it was created. A *Manchester Guardian* correspondent who accompanied Queen Elizabeth II on her royal visit to Nigeria in early 1956 criticized the NRSPCA for existing "more in name than in fact in a country where animals and birds have not much importance save as food and pet keeping"; the writer also criticized the society because its representatives were not in attendance at the reception of Lagos voluntary organizations held for the queen.[89] The NRSPCA expressed embarrassment over this negative impression of its work. In his rebuttal, NRSPCA president A. Omololu described the newspaper report as "stupid and baseless ridicule" and the author as a "ghostwriter," while insisting that he had attended the reception and met the queen. Regardless, the *Manchester Guardian* report did not have a negative impact on relations between the NRSPCA and its parent body in London.[90] In late 1956 top-ranked officers of the RSPCA visited Nigeria and expressed satisfaction with the work of their counterparts.[91] A positive appraisal by the RSPCA was important because the NRSPCA depended on its benefactor to exist.

Compassion for animals was one index for measuring the level of enlightenment of a people—so insisted the colonialists and some educated Nigerians. Animals require humane treatment not only because they share some affinity with humans but also because they serve humans in many ways. Violence against animals was therefore abuse of nature. In making cruelty toward animals a sign of primitivity, modernist notions of humane treatment created a new regime of human-animal relations that precolonial Nigeria had not experienced. Animals became a subject of criminal prosecution in court as judges, combining their personal beliefs with the law, made judgments that punished humans for cruelty toward "dumb creatures." The politics over the establishment of the NRSPCA, its activities, and criticisms of the society all point to one fact: colonial Nigerians' and their British overlords' perspectives on agency and protection of animals evolved over time. Yet it was the idea that civilized people must be concerned with animals' welfare that led to the normalization of the NRSPCA in the southern cities of Ibadan and Lagos. The animal welfare movement could not succeed in the North because its ideology was arrogantly embedded in a Christian ethos, which Muslims generally condemned.

8 ⮌ "A Great Evil Ritual Murder"

The Save-the-Nigerian-Horse-and-Donkey Campaign

> The known facts are as follows: The Mohammedans of Northern Nigeria
> are horsemen and, while they are not generally humanitarians by any
> means, they do understand horses and have been associated with them
> for centuries. The Ibos in the South, on the other hand, are pagans who
> do not understand horses, are afraid of them, hate them, and are as cruel
> to them as they are to all other animals.
>
> —Dr. A. H. B. Kirkman, "Horses in Nigeria," *The Field*,
> February 2, 1952

THE EPIGRAPH above is taken from an article on cruelty to horses published in a British magazine of sport hunting and country life and authored by an academic who held leadership positions in the Royal Society
for the Prevention of Cruelty to Animals (RSPCA) and the University of
London Animal Welfare Society.[1] Dr. A. H. B. Kirkman worried about the
illegal trafficking in an estimated five thousand worn-out horses per year,
who trekked more than four hundred miles from northern to southeastern
Nigeria, where they were slaughtered for traditional ceremonies in a manner he likened to "a great evil ritual murder."[2] He quoted an eyewitness
account of the arduous journey of the horses, so weary that they appeared
"often nothing more than walking skeletons and lame at that."[3] Kirkman
was not convinced of the effectiveness of propaganda, which colonial officers claimed they were using to stop the "terrible" and "callous" cultural
practice. In another correspondence on the matter, Kirkman described
the Igbo and Nigerians in general as "a people surely *not quite* prepared
by 'education' for self-government" during the era of decolonization. It
would take outright criminalization, he asserted, not just education or propaganda, to end the "excruciating cruelty."[4]

"Owing to the publicity in the press, public opinion has certainly been aroused," one L. R. Buxton affirmed the impact of Kirkman's article.[5] *The Field* and newspapers including the London *Times* published additional articles under such headlines as "Help the Horses" and "Cruelty to Horses: Ritual Slaughter in Nigeria" by British residents who questioned the inability of their government to protect horses abroad from being "literally beaten to death" "in the most revolting manner."[6] There was even accusation that horses' tails were severed before the animals were burned alive and that the government of Nigeria was reluctant to intervene in order to prevent the people from returning to *human* sacrifice, a much more barbaric practice that the British civilizing mission had helped to end.[7] RSPCA officials started a campaign to raise £3,000 for humane killer captive-bolt pistols for the horses in Nigeria, thinking that if they were unable to get administrators to end the traffic, they could at least help the "unfortunate victims" of a brutal anachronistic tradition experience a "merciful dispatch."[8] From October 1952 to May 1953 the body, according to its vice president, Winifred Portland, raised £1,900 to purchase "substantial shipments" of humane killers for Nigeria.[9]

The "save-the-Nigerian-horse campaign" did not end on the pages of London's newspapers and with RSPCA fund-raising efforts. Concerned citizens who typically identified themselves as "animal lovers" wrote letters to their representatives in Parliament pleading that they use their position to outlaw the practice. L. Rutledge, who also contributed money toward the RSPCA-led campaign, echoed the commonly accepted imperial responsibility in his letter to British prime minister Winston Churchill: "It fills one with horror to think that such a thing can happen particularly in a British possession."[10] Another writer, Faith Parsons, worried in her letter to MP John Profumo why "such cruelties should be allowed in a civilized world."[11] The practice was "almost as great a disgrace to the British protectorate," another petitioner regretted.[12] MP J. A. L. Duncan, after receiving similar protest letter from one of his anxious constituents, raised the matter in Parliament demanding the secretary of state for the colonies, Oliver Littleton, provide an explanation for the "hideous cruelty."[13]

As intense as the outrage generated by Kirkman's article was, it was not the first time that a Eurocentric conception of cruelty originating from the metropole would be a subject of the animal welfare movement. The previously mentioned 1938 photo of a live chicken whose feathers had allegedly been plucked to facilitate sale in a market in southeastern Nigeria had led to a diplomatic uproar between metropolitan critics of abuse of animals and the colonial officers in the country.[14] However, the Kirkman episode is unique for a number of reasons. First, it was by far the most vociferous debate about animal welfare with specific focus on the horse during the last decade of British rule in Nigeria. Second, the RSPCA and other metropolitan critics of the colonial government in Nigeria were convinced that this most "noble" and "aristocratic" animal of all, which complemented humans' conception of pride and honor, should not experience such a "wicked" fate. A sick or lame horse needed to have a "painless" ending through use of a humane killer carefully administered by a "responsible" person in a government-approved knackery—not marched hundreds of miles and sacrificed to some primitive gods in a "disgusting," "abominable," and "shocking" manner. Third, it further emphasizes an uncommon paradigm in the colonial conception of justice: that animals, like humans, were also subject to being trafficked and that the movement of animals, even within fixed colonial boundaries, could be treated as a moral issue and indeed criminalized. The horse was the only domestic animal to be labeled trafficable in colonial Nigeria.

The horse was designated as a trafficked animal not because it was a protected species or because it was illegal to trade in horses or because horses were transported via illegal routes. Rather, it was because they were classified as "sorry specimens" by colonial officers and metropolitan critics and were being used for "uncivilized" purposes. Understanding this unusual definition of animal trafficking is fundamental for coming to terms with how animal welfare ideologies defined cruelty in accordance with species, the circumstances under which animals were transported, and the material and symbolic utility they represented for humans. What is more, the horses being sold in eastern Nigerian markets in 1940, at an average of £1, could not be healthy animals, according to critics, given that a full-grown and healthy horse would cost as much as £50 or more in northern Nigeria. Here, the economic value of the animal shaped the moralization around its movement and body. By arguing in his 1940 report that the proceeds of trafficking went mainly to northern Nigeria, colonial officer A. Milne invoked an "intra-colonial economic separatism" that the very creation of the Nigerian state in 1914 had been expected to end.[15]

Moreover, it recognized animals as imperial subjects whose safety and welfare transcended rigid boundaries. Nigerian horses, like their counterparts in Europe, critics felt, must be protected from all forms of cruelty. This view placed animal welfare and civilization in conversation with each other. Kirkman's reference to "education" as a condition for self-determination and other writers' emphasis on the failure of their government abroad ginned up the conventional rhetoric that colonialism was supposed to create modern civilized subjects. Why the treatment of animals became a yardstick for measuring the success of colonialism cannot be separated from the notion that an unkind attitude toward animals was itself a sign of human primitivity. Yet this animal-centered explanation of savagery on the part of colonial subjects was not homogeneous countrywide or across ethnic groups, as Kirkman and other critics claimed.

This chapter investigates why Nigerians, colonial officers, and watchdogs of colonialism in Britain believed that the horse—which aided imperial conquest, brought thousands of people together at races and polo games, enhanced the performance of imperial and local powers at durbars, and complemented humans' conception of respectability—should not be treated inhumanely. Further, in reviewing the circumstances under which the donkey, which traveled hundreds of miles helping to transport human and material resources that sustained imperial capitalism, was framed as an animal that needed to be protected from abuse, I turn my searchlight on the unstable meaning of civilization and the place of animals in it. Whether the subject is the bits used in riding horses, the overworking of donkeys in northern Nigeria, the doping of racehorses in Lagos, or the practice of horse sacrifice in the Southeast, what made these animals important also was ironically responsible for the ill-treatment they received from humans who sought to maximize their economic, cultural, and symbolic value in everyday life. In explaining the connection between religious practices and shifting conceptions of cruelty, this chapter further affirms the central argument of this book that colonialism turned animals into modern and colonial subjects through the imposition of ideals that mirrored understandings of the place of animals in colonial civilization.

IN THE INTEREST OF CLEAN RACING

From debates over the inappropriateness of holding race meets during World War II, betting, and other illicit activities at the races to the exorbitant prices of racehorses sold to other West African locations, lack of safety on the courses, and handicapping and doping of animals, observers of horse racing criticized the exploitation, commodification, and objectification of the animals for their entertainment value. Accidents leading to death or severe injuries of jockeys were inseparable from the critique of the health and temperament of the racehorses, which was shaped in large part by the care given to them by their owners, trainers, jockeys, and grooms.[16]

The moral economy of horse racing during the two world wars tested its degree of indispensability. Racing was suspended during World War I because British authorities viewed the gathering of many people as a public threat to the empire at war. However, horse racing was not prohibited during World War II, leading some critics to argue that "indulgence in this form of sport fits badly into the picture of general suffering and sacrifice presented by the empire as a whole."[17] The decision not to ban horse racing during the war was influenced by the significant transformation of the event from 1914 to 1939. In all of Nigeria in 1914, only Lagos had a well-organized racing meet, which occurred about three times a year. The interwar years, characterized by the consolidation of colonialism, saw a major expansion in racing across the country. By 1939 all the first-class townships, which also doubled as provincial capitals, had regular meets (as often as four times a year). To suspend racing was to terminate an event that had both symbolic and practical value to an empire on the verge of collapse. Critics of racing during wartime paid less attention to its political and economic functions; rather, they focused on the leisure component.

The response of the Lagos Race Club to the charge of the "inappropriateness" of racing during World War II boosted the popularity of the sport in a country that was "becoming more and more Turf-minded," as evidenced by the "large and enthusiastic crowds" that it attracted. While the question of public safety at races sounded legitimate, that of "illegitimate gaiety" and insensitivity to the "suffering" of the empire did not. Throughout the war, social gatherings, dancing, and shows specifically organized to raise funds for the war effort were on the rise. As for the Lagos Race Club (LRC), its donation of £3,000 to the Win-the-War fund from July 1940 to November 1941 could "hardly be beaten, or even equaled by any other source of its class." Supporters of wartime racing labeled racing critics as "strangers" who "only see half of the picture."[18] The LRC then publicized its donation of £700 to the Red Cross and other welfare groups involved in the war effort and its loan of £400 to the imperial government "free of interest for the duration of the war" from the profits it made at the December 1942 and January 1943 race meets.[19]

Instead of canceling races, race clubs across the country utilized the wartime donation mantra to popularize their activities, appending such statements as "In Aid of War Charities" to encourage people to attend.[20] When the government canceled the April 1942 race meet in Ibadan because of a lack of railway cars to transport horses from the North, letters to the editor of newspapers like the *Nigerian Daily Times* (*NDT*) emphasized the importance of donations from race clubs to the Win-the-War fund.[21] Ibadan, like other cities in southern Nigeria, could not keep horses in large numbers because of the threat of the tsetse fly. The practice of using racing to exploit the wartime charity culture did not end after the cessation of hostilities. In 1946 and 1947 race clubs in Ibadan, Lagos, and Kano held Victory Day races and publicly advertised that they would donate proceeds of the event to charity.[22] "A noteworthy feature of the meeting," the *NDT* reported after the 1946 Lagos Victory Cup race, "was the decision of the Committee to devote the whole of the proceeds of this meeting to charity."[23] The well-covered donation of race clubs to the National Ex-Servicemen's Welfare Association was part of the postwar politics of reintegration of former soldiers into civilian life—a project that many critics of colonialism thought was unsuccessful.[24]

The handicapping rules of race clubs in Nigeria were too severe for the animals, some critics insisted. Handicapping involves requiring horses to carry weights (based on their previous performance) to ensure that all horses started a race with a more or less equal chance of winning. The handicap could be as much as fifteen pounds. An *NDT* editorial written on behalf of race enthusiasts expressed the worry that such weights exposed horses to "grave risks of physical injury likely to become permanent."[25] The negative consequence of excess weight, according to this critical editorial, was responsible for the "continuous exodus" of the best horses from Nigeria to the Gold Coast, where race organizers were mindful of the weight carried by handicapped horses.[26] The editorial provided some evidence for this claim. In less than twelve months, Lagos had lost to the Gold Coast the high-performance horses Gaman-Katar, Zouzou, Panama, and Victory.[27] Another critic, who self-identified as "Turfist," claimed he had observed how "excellent horses are sometimes ruined within a short time" because of heavy weights.[28] This criticism did not go away. As late as 1958, critics continued to complain about the impact of heavy weights on the health and performance of their favorite horses.[29]

As in the matter of holding races during World War II, the LRC defended its actions. Adeyemo Alakija, the Nigerian nationalist who became the chairman of the LRC in 1946, felt that Lagos horse owners were selling their horses abroad not because of alleged cruel handicapping regulations but because of high prices offered in the Gold Coast. To illustrate what he called "insatiable greed" by horse owners, he provided the original purchase and sale prices for the following top-class Nigerian horses sold to the Gold Coast: Gaman-Katar (£75/£600), Zozzou (£120/£400), and Panama

(£53/£500).[30] Victory, whose story he said "would make unpleasant reading," was bought for £200 and sold to the sister colony at £700. In some cases, such as that of Zozzou, horses were sold without the consent of their co-owner. For Alakija, the LRC was "the most generous" race club in Nigeria in terms of handicapping rules. He disagreed that a seven-pound weight carried by a horse over a mile-and-a-quarter race could be injurious to the animal.[31] Interestingly, criticism of cruel handicapping was also shaped by outcomes of betting on racehorses. The extent to which concerns over the quality of horse racing, which guaranteed a successful betting enterprise and greater spectatorship, outweighed genuine care about cruelty to animals, and vice versa, probably depended on the particular individual's or group's perspective.[32]

Another criticism of horse racing centered on the medical condition of the racehorses themselves. Government regulations forbade keeping a private stable in the South, in order to check for negligence and prevent an outbreak of animal disease. In Lagos, Ibadan, and Enugu, racehorses were stabled at government-approved locations in Obalende, Agodi, and the Government Station, respectively. But disease outbreaks in government-approved stables were actually common. To improve the situation, a new regulation backed by the Lagos Town Council government that came into effect in 1944 made mandatory the registration by the veterinary office of all horses coming into Lagos. It also empowered a veterinary officer to make unannounced visits to the stables, inspect horses, and force horse owners to pay for medical expenses. No horse could be used in any event until it was certified medically fit to do so. To make sure that retired horses were cared for instead of sold for food or ceremonial sacrifice, no horse could leave Lagos without the approval of a veterinary officer. Violation of this rule brought a fine of £50 or twelve months' imprisonment. Regulations also required that a registration book detailing the life history of every horse, the name of its owners, the number of races it took part in, and its medical and physiological condition be kept by all horse owners and their grooms.

The practice of transporting horses from the South to the North during the rainy season helped improve the health of horses, but it did not eliminate danger. Owing to the scarcity of railway cars for horses, the LRC experimented with transporting racehorses by road for the March 1946 meet. This action was not totally successful. The NDT ran a panic story titled "Reported Arrival of Sick Horses in Lagos" to beam a bright light on the medical condition of these horses (two of which were believed to have died after passing through the tsetse-infested zones of Minna and Jebba).[33] The LRC secretary responded that none of the horses transported by road was entered for the event, in an attempt to satisfy the "humanitarian feeling which prompts one to prevent apparently unhealthy horses from participating in a race where public money is involved."[34] This case, like that of handicap weights, reveals that the public was sensitive to animal cruelty, despite the wealth and amusement that horses generated.

What happened to racehorses after retirement? It was common, as late as 1955, to see "thin and scraggy-looking" retired racehorses constituting "a nuisance and a [public health] danger to the members of the public," according to the Lagos medical officer of health (MOH).[35] The regular practice after a racehorse was injured and unable to do well on the turf was to sell it for meat. In Lagos, they were also used to pull carriages in the expanding but grossly underregulated tourism industry. Their appearance "evoked greatest pity for those poor creatures," which were popularly called "taxi horses,"[36] In 1944 one Salami of Lagos was caught hiring out two "unsound" horses, one very lame and the other with a sore back, to sailors and was forced to return the fee.

Betting was about money as much as about the horses that made it possible. Indeed, it was a major economic reason for the popularization of horse racing. People who lost money often expressed their dissatisfaction about the poor performance of their favorite horses, allegedly caused by unfavorable racing rules and deplorable condition of the turf. They felt that their horses deserved to win. However, illegal gambling and betting by both Africans and Europeans was common, which tended to foster disorderly conduct around the racecourse. "I remember seeing three or four of the most prominent men on the mine field seated at a huge green table with piles of bank notes in front of them," wrote colonial officer Rex Niven, recalling a familiar scene of illegal gambling at a race meet in Jos around 1926.[37] According to a report on the 1947 Eid-al-Kabir racing in Kano, "the meeting which might have proved very successful in view of the large attendance was unfortunately marred by the presence of [a] huge crowd of gamblers who instead of patronizing the race converted the whole area around the course into a gambling place, the presence of the police notwithstanding."[38]

The moral economy of racing intersected with religious ideology. Critics of betting thought it was unethical to exploit animals for economic purposes. Betting on animal labor, R. A. Denton of the Methodist Church opined, can be likened to slavery. The horse, he argued in a 1931 letter to the commissioner of the colony, was treated like a chattel who did not have power to resist any form of economic transaction made on its behalf. The following year, all the 273-member congregation of the Wesleyan Church in Olowogbowo signed a petition asking the government to end betting on horses. The church was not the only group that opposed betting on horse racing; secular doubts as to the ethicality of betting were common.[39] Newspaper petitions like the one written by A. Ade Adedokun and published in the June 29, 1950, edition of the *West African Pilot* (WAP) argued that, aside from exploiting horses, betting led to laziness on the part of people who gamble. "Which lazy lout will see the picture of a 'lucky' race-goer carrying his bag of £150 won with a two shillings' ticket and will not be moved to attend the next races to try his own 'lucky stars'?" Adedokun queried.[40]

Drugging racehorses to enhance their performance was one of the consequences of betting. By 1952 the increasing incidence of doping was becoming intolerable to many. "If this had started long ago, I would have sold my colts," reported one newspaper, quoting a racehorse owner while the saliva of a horse suspected of doping was being collected by veterinary officers for testing ahead of an event in mid-1958.[41] The punishment for doping included fining horse owners and/or temporarily or permanently banning their horses from racing. However, owners refused to take responsibility for a positive doping test because so many people (trainers, jockeys, veterinary officers, grooms, and even fans) had access to the animal and could have doped it for their own gain. Accusations even blamed veterinary officers for declaring a fake doping result to ostracize a high-performing horse. There was no clear consensus over the source of doping, which ranged from synthetic drugs to natural plant-based substances. In 1960 the federal veterinary service described as "quite untenable" the "belief among certain people" that normal grasses and cereal were responsible for some positive results obtained in doping tests.[42] The following scenarios in a newspaper article opposing animal cruelty titled "Campaign against Doping at Lagos Race" sought to expose the apparently flawed system for testing suspected doping cases and the mutual distrust and suspicion within the racing industry: "I) The saliva may be replaced with another which actually contains dope or which does not by interested persons; II) It may be destroyed; III) It may be stolen." The author, simply identified as "Sportsman," then recommended that no officer of the race club "shall have anything to do" with the saliva sample after it was taken until the results were out. The saliva may be deposited in a police station until laboratory testing, Sportsman advised. After the result was out, the race club was not to make an immediate pronouncement or punish the horse and its owner "to avoid miscarriage of justice," for the owner may not even be aware of doping. Rather, an extensive investigation should be conducted to identify the main culprit.[43]

"LUCKILY A DUMB ANIMAL"

Colonial officer C. T. Lawrence captioned one of his 1902–3 photos of the conquest of northern Nigeria featuring a donkey carrying cases of rifles as "luckily a dumb animal."[44] One does not need any extensive knowledge of military warfare or human-animal relations to come to terms with the conditions under which the donkey in question was working to aid the subjugation of a major theocratic society in West Africa. Aside from providing visual evidence of the role of the donkey in warfare, the photo equally establishes that humans got away with inflicting pain on the donkey because it is a "dumb" animal—incapable of speaking up for itself.

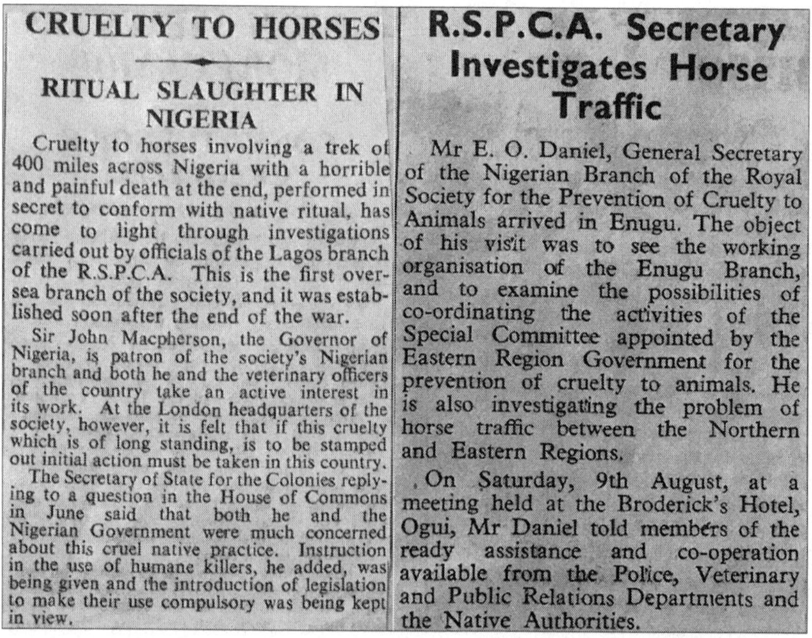

CRUELTY TO HORSES

RITUAL SLAUGHTER IN NIGERIA

Cruelty to horses involving a trek of 400 miles across Nigeria with a horrible and painful death at the end, performed in secret to conform with native ritual, has come to light through investigations carried out by officials of the Lagos branch of the R.S.P.C.A. This is the first oversea branch of the society, and it was established soon after the end of the war.

Sir John Macpherson, the Governor of Nigeria, is patron of the society's Nigerian branch and both he and the veterinary officers of the country take an active interest in its work. At the London headquarters of the society, however, it is felt that if this cruelty which is of long standing, is to be stamped out initial action must be taken in this country.

The Secretary of State for the Colonies replying to a question in the House of Commons in June said that both he and the Nigerian Government were much concerned about this cruel native practice. Instruction in the use of humane killers, he added, was being given and the introduction of legislation to make their use compulsory was being kept in view.

R.S.P.C.A. Secretary Investigates Horse Traffic

Mr E. O. Daniel, General Secretary of the Nigerian Branch of the Royal Society for the Prevention of Cruelty to Animals arrived in Enugu. The object of his visit was to see the working organisation of the Enugu Branch, and to examine the possibilities of co-ordinating the activities of the Special Committee appointed by the Eastern Region Government for the prevention of cruelty to animals. He is also investigating the problem of horse traffic between the Northern and Eastern Regions.

On Saturday, 9th August, at a meeting held at the Broderick's Hotel, Ogui, Mr Daniel told members of the ready assistance and co-operation available from the Police, Veterinary and Public Relations Departments and the Native Authorities.

FIGURE 8.1. *From left:* "Cruelty to Horses: Ritual Slaughter in Nigeria," *Times,* October 14, 1952; "RSPCA Secretary Investigates Horse Traffic," *Eastern Outlook,* August 14, 1952.

As chapter 2 explicates, with the establishment of colonial rule, the donkey took on a new status. The beast became the "official" pack animal of the colonial state, thereby helping multinational corporations, merchant companies, and their Nigerian agents to transport solid minerals and cash crops such as cotton and groundnuts from the mines and farms to trading and railway stations. While it was common for the animal to be heavily overloaded during the era of conquest, the narratives of "modernity" and "civilization" after the firm establishment of colonialism turned the beast into a modern creature whose weight-carrying capacity needed to be regulated. The critics of "unmerciful" weight imposed on the donkey included colonial officers who worried that the animals were not properly fed while being expected to carry as much as 250 pounds of goods. They argued against the ruthlessness that sought to improve profit margins at the expense of the animal. Drivers of pack donkeys frequently allowed dogs to bite the animals to speed them up and for their own amusement.

By the second decade of the twentieth century, colonial officers had established an overlapping distinction between "domestic" and "commercial" donkeys. While this distinction may have existed in an indigenous construction of social and economic roles of the donkey before the twentieth century, it was under British imperialism that these roles were used to account for the degree of violence imposed on the animal. On the one hand, domestic donkeys were deemed as those used by their direct owners, who rode them and used them to transport goods for home or household needs. They were essentially "pets" that maintained some emotional connection with their owners and members of the household. Commercial donkeys, on the other hand, were used purely as a factor in production to transport economic goods. They were highly susceptible to cruelty because they were often overworked by managers who had limited interest in their welfare. Colonial officers, though not immune to cruelty, generally took better care of their domestic donkeys than their commercial counterparts. Yet domestic donkeys could also be hired out to perform largely commercial roles—just as commercial donkeys, after many years of serving multiple owners and nearing the end of their productive lives, typically were retired to a less arduous, purely domestic role.[45] It was generally accepted that the domestic donkey received better care because its owner would suffer if the animal fell ill and died.[46] Moreover, the commercial donkey, unlike the domestic one, could easily be replaced because they were bred in large numbers. Hence there was little motivation to act sympathetically toward them.

After taking a long, bloodstained stick from a boy who had been beating a donkey that would later die from the wound sustained, the senior resident officer of Zaria, E. H. B. Laing, wrote a comprehensive report in early 1926 to "enlist the sympathy" of the British Cotton Growing Association (BCGA) and major cotton merchants operating in northern Nigeria (e.g., the Niger Company, G. B. Ollivant, the African Grown Cotton Company, and W. Redfearn & Sons) toward transport donkeys. He recommended that the trading companies blacklist agents caught maltreating donkeys and advised that animal fitness should be considered when making financial transactions. According to Laing, a pack donkey should not, in line with global standards, carry more than 120 pounds of merchandise. This number could be increased but not above 140 to 145 pounds, equally distributed into two sacks.[47] Laing's suggestion received some medical backing from the chief veterinary officer (CVO) of northern Nigeria, who believed "an average sized animal in good health and condition" should be able to carry 120 pounds comfortably.[48]

Laing's recommendation was well received among his colleagues in the residents' offices across northern Nigeria, but it did not go over well with the trading companies for a number of reasons. The economics of production and distribution of cotton was beyond the power of the resident officer; export prices were fixed by the BCGA (the largest cotton buyer) based on the global market. Since profits for cotton agents, who were predominantly Nigerians, were based on the margin between the price fixed by the BCGA and that set by local producers, the more cotton they allowed their donkeys to carry per trip, the higher their income. For Redfearn & Sons, each donkey had to carry a minimum of 160 pounds of cotton for their African traders to accrue a profit. Thus, thirteen donkeys would be required to move a total of a ton per trip. If the donkeys moved less than 160 pounds apiece, more animals would be required to transport each ton, a situation that would close the profit margin for donkey operators and African traders. European trading firms, like Redfearn & Sons, could not impose any weight limits on African traders.[49]

The idea of weight limits for pack donkeys raised four fundamental questions. First, who had the power to determine if a donkey was "fit" or in "good condition" (however those terms were defined)? Unlike motor vehicles, which had to pass a road-worthiness test based on clearly defined parameters, there was no institutionalized means of determining if a donkey was healthy. The domestic quarantine project of the veterinary department focused only on trade cattle, which had to be certified disease free for public consumption, but animals such as the donkey received less attention. Although esoteric, the term "fitness" in the thought of colonial officers meant the ability of the animal to work without showing "any evidence of fatigue or exhaustion." Second, the idea of minimum weight did not consider the physical data of the donkey, such as its age and weight. Thus, goods weighing 120 pounds would have a different impact on donkeys of different sizes and ages.[50] Third, the routine of each donkey varied. A weight of 120 pounds would have more impact on a donkey reloaded with a new consignment, immediately upon returning from a twenty-mile trip, compared to another starting the same journey after two days of rest. Fourth, pack donkeys covered varying distances. This is probably why CVO W. W. Henderson recommended that animals plying a shorter distance could carry "greater weight than an animal carrying a load in long continuous journey."[51] His statement that he would consider the loading of a "weakly and emaciated" donkey with 120 pounds as a worse form of cruelty than allowing a strong donkey to lift 180 pounds further complicated the unstable relationship between weight and condition of the animal.[52]

The ways that Islam shaped political realities in northern Nigeria have attracted the attention of scholars. Religion also featured in the politics of animal cruelty. The colonial government realized that the native authorities and the emirates, which served as the central point through which Islam derived its legitimacy, could tackle the problem of cruelty to pack animals better than colonial laws, which most residents distrusted for their roots in Western civilization. In January 1927, less than a year after Laing, whom a contemporary described as a "great lover of animals," reopened the matter of cruelty to animals, the native authorities of northern Nigeria completed an important task of compiling sections of the Quran, hadiths, and important Islamic texts authored by prominent clerics, including the famous Usman dan Fodio, the founder of the Sokoto Caliphate. The central colonial office in northern Nigeria printed a thousand copies of a twelve-page pamphlet, written in English and Arabic, that was expected to serve as an advice manual to native authorities and colonial officers. The circulation list for *Extracts from Hadiths and Muslim Text Books on Subject of Treatment of Animals* was extensive—from mosques and organizations in Africa to foreign university libraries and research institutes such as the Anthropological Institute, Royal Geographical Society, and British Museum (see fig. 8.2). One thing clear from its distribution list is that educating the public through formal institutions and powerful people was significant in debunking the claim that Islam condones cruelty to animals. The document read in part:

> From the "Fatuhat ul Wahabiyat" by Ibrahim ul-Shabrakhiti on the 40th commentary of Nuwiyat on the 17th Hadith of Shadad bin Awis, p. 190: "Allah has enjoined kindness to all things. Thus [the] animal should not be kept hungry or thirsty or beaten unnecessarily, or put to a task too heavy."
>
> From the "Fasidat ul Ajamiyat fi hakuk ul dawab" by Sheikh Othman di Fodoye, written in Fulfulde. "Stalled animals cannot get out to graze and so must be fed by hand. Pack animals must only be loaded within their strength for they have no free choice."
>
> From the "Madahalu" the book of Dan Hajji in the Chapter on Travel. He says the traveler should rest his animals, dismount and allow them (rest) in the morning, in the evening and when ascending or descending steep and difficult hills.
>
> Extract from the Writings of the Shekh al Tabarani and the Shekh Al Hakim with a Quotation from Ahmad Ibn Hanbal to Abu Ya'ati of Mousul. "Ride ye on the beasts kindly and without cruelty." "Do not sit on them as if they were chairs for your conversation whether on the roads or in the markets." "For there are beasts ridden which are better than their riders in the sight of God."[53]

This pamphlet proved an important point, which critics of Islam rarely acknowledged: some of the British ideals on humane treatment of animals actually agreed with Islamic law and practice. In fact, Islamic civilization was ahead of the British civilizing mission in the protection of animal subjects of colonial Nigeria. But this was not the first time that Islamic aristocrats would use the Quran and other texts to highlight the humane treatment of animals. At the peak of the Sokoto Caliphate in the nineteenth century, the jihadists consistently viewed the "pagans" as "uncivilized" for their inhumane treatment of animals. Indeed, during this period, Islamic civilization did just what the British did in the twentieth century—that is, explain cruelty to animals as a product of "primitivity."[54] To Muslims in the nineteenth century, the primitive and pagan were those who resisted Islam, whereas to the British colonialists in the twentieth century, all colonial subjects, including Muslims, were considered to be "primitive." Only a few educated Nigerians escaped this labeling. It is interesting how religion, time, and political power shaped what constitutes civilization within the context of animal welfare.

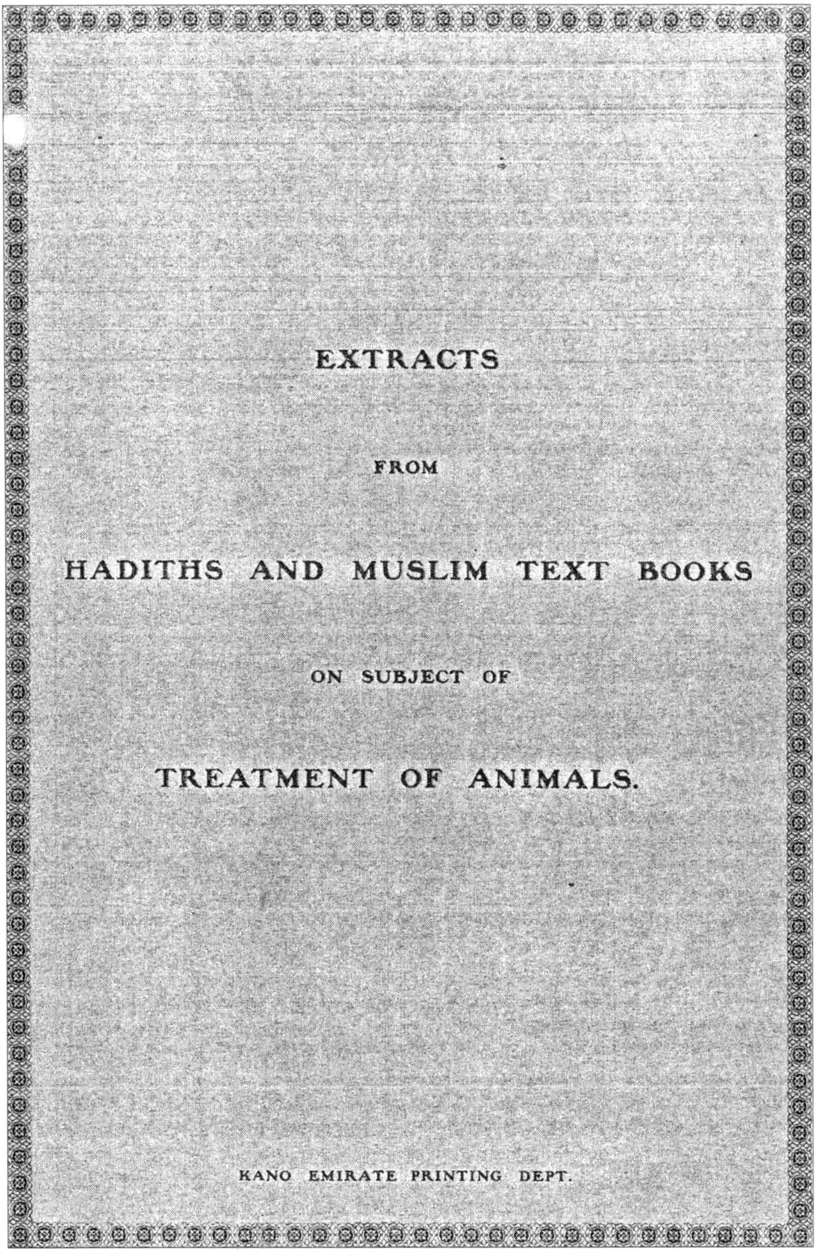

EXTRACTS

FROM

HADITHS AND MUSLIM TEXT BOOKS

ON SUBJECT OF

TREATMENT OF ANIMALS.

KANO EMIRATE PRINTING DEPT.

FIGURE 8.2. Anti-animal-cruelty propaganda material (1927). *Source:* ComCol 1136, National Archives, Ibadan.

The nineteenth-century notion that the "pagans" who resisted Islam were the main culprits of animal cruelty was carried into the colonial era.[55] "The unnecessary infliction of pain on animals is recognized as an offence by local Moslem courts, but it is not so by native custom," wrote the resident of Ilorin Province, making a comparison that fit into the prevailing British practice of viewing African indigenous culture as inferior to Islam.[56] Two years later, he singled out the Yoruba of Ilorin as the main culprits of cruelty to animals: "The Yoruba is notoriously lacking in animal sense, so that his disregard of humane treatment is due rather to insensitivity and ignorance than to intentional cruelty." Although Ilorin had a large Muslim Yoruba population, there was a constant attempt to dress the Hausa-Fulani's Islam as a superior version of the religion. The colonial government in Ilorin, as in other parts of northern Nigeria, favored the Hausa-Fulani population over the Yoruba group in social and political matters.

In other words, what constituted civilization and its role in the humane treatment of animals was determined by the religious affiliation of the critic, the power he occupied in the colonial hierarchy, and his sphere of political authority. Neither the law nor an appeal to religious sentiment would end cruelty to the donkey. In July 1931 the Emir of Kano, Abdullahi Bayero, released the following order: people must not draw blood from their donkeys, ride them without a saddle, or allow them to carry loads "beyond their capacity."[57] From January to September 1932, 114 prosecutions for cruelty toward animals were carried out in the native court in Kano. This was an important move for an Emir embarrassed that his emirate was consistently rated by the government and animal welfare advocates as the poorest in terms of animal welfare.[58]

CRUEL BITS AND DISHONORABLE HORSEMANSHIP

The process through which the donkey became an animal to be protected against human cruelty was like that which attended the horse. Many of the horses used for the conquest of northern Nigeria by the colonial force were seized from local belligerents. These horses used local bits, which early military officers praised for their effectiveness. But by the second decade of the twentieth century, the colonial government began to criticize the use of local bits for being harmful. The pulling of the reins caused the bits (especially the long-tongued, spiked, or serrated kind) to abrade the roof of the mouth, while the narrowness of the mouthpiece chafed the sides, causing irritation and bleeding.

If the government determined the local bits were cruel, the locals believed otherwise. The debate over the use of local bits mainly centered on specific aspects of horse-riding culture, which varied across societies. The local bits aided in the execution of the jahi salute, widely recognized across northern Nigeria as the peak of a horse's display of power. It involved forcefully rearing the horse—the head yanked back, the hind legs splayed, throwing the entire weight of the rider onto its hind quarters.[59] The maneuver was easier to pull off with the locally made bits, which animal compassion groups advocated against. The irritation caused by the local bits gave the rider a greater degree of control over the horse, forcing the animal to hold up its head, be a "high-stepper," and ride alongside other horses. The pain and sores caused by local bits, animal advocates argued, exposed the animal to disease and prevented it from feeding well, leading to ulcers and emaciation.[60] Another instance of inhumane treatment of the horse included scoring the animal's back to make sitting on it, with or without a saddle, more comfortable for the rider. Scoring caused the flesh to swell, thus forming a sort of cushion or saddle.[61] During his inspection tour of Dimmuck and Shendam, the resident officer of Plateau Province claimed that out of the eighty-seven horses he saw, fifty-eight had saddles of one kind or another, while twenty-nine did not have any. Four horses were suffering from back sores.[62] His counterparts in Ilorin Province noted that of the more than 120 horses he saw while on tour, only 10 had "decent" saddles. Most of the horse riders, according to him, used pads, which would not qualify as saddles capable of cushioning the friction of human bodily contact on the horse's back.

Two options presented themselves to the colonial government and the native authorities as potential solutions to cruelty to the horse. One was to enforce animal-cruelty laws already on the books, which were rarely implemented in northern Nigeria because of the fear of public disorder and the pressure on the understaffed native and magistrate courts. "The Government must deal tactfully with the scoring of ponies in the pagan areas," the secretary of the Northern Provinces cautioned his colleagues. "His Honour [the governor of Nigeria] does not want to see a whole series of prosecutions being launched," he added, echoing the sentiment of the head of the colonial government.[63] The other option was to intensify propaganda, not only among the so-called uncivilized natives but also among schoolchildren, a majority of whom were wards of the elite members of native authorities. As the resident of Adamawa Province projected, these children "will probably own horses when they grow up and some will hold responsible positions in the Native Administration or in the Government service."[64] The public sensitization effort, as propaganda was euphemistically called, was aimed at reducing the workload of the criminal justice system. When the Crown counsel opined that "no cruelty law can be successful without a transformation in public opinion," he was emphasizing the transformative power of propaganda.[65]

Propaganda also involved changing the public's negative attitude toward European-made bits, which animal welfare advocates considered humane. European bits were more expensive (about 12s. in the 1930s) than the local version, which cost under 1s.; however, they could, as colonial officers held, be produced locally by blacksmiths in large quantities and then sold in local markets at the "affordable" price of 3s. If native authority members (all of whom had horses) used the local adaptation of the European bits, the larger population would follow suit, colonial officers argued. But popularizing European bits could have a potential negative impact on the jahi salute and alter long-standing traditions of indigenous horse riding.[66] Local horse riders thought that it would take a longer time to train a horse using European bits.[67] Similarly, the publicity endorsing European bits was anchored on the assumption that all horses, regardless of their owners and the environment in which they are raised, could easily adjust to any horse-riding equipment, if properly handled by their custodians. When the Emir of Gombe galloped with his large stallion and did the jahi salute with his spear in hand using the European bit during the 1934 Eid-al-Fitr festival, the district officer expressed pleasure and congratulated him "on the example he has set to his people in this matter."[68] However, this isolated demonstration of the merit of the European bit had little positive effect on public opinion.

THE RITUAL HORSE OF EASTERN NIGERIA

The diplomatic rift that horse sacrifice caused between the metropole and the colony, as highlighted earlier in this chapter, only explains a Eurocentric conception of cruelty to animals; it does not engage the indigenous perspective. If horses were used predominantly for racing and performance of imperial power across Nigeria, they would, in addition to racing, play an important role in the southeastern part of the country, where cultural conceptions of honor and respectability shaped their ritualization.[69] To demonstrate their political power and affluence, some Igbo groups of Nsukka Division would sacrifice horses, which were not only rare in the community but also the most expensive of domestic animals. The horse, as a sacrificial being, was held in high esteem in this area—just as it was in many others, where the sacrifice of a living animal enhanced the social prestige of influential people. Horse sacrifice was required for taking the highly coveted chieftaincy title of *Amusi* in the area. Like many social hierarchies, higher titles, such as *Ogbu-zulu* (killed and satisfied), were reserved for the Amusi who has killed more than one horse. The killing of horses for a remembrance ceremony was largely to demonstrate opulence, not only of the departed but also of the living relatives.[70]

What appeared to many as an honorable way to celebrate success and immortalize loved ones, however, was interpreted as cruelty by the colonial government, which saw a moral problem in it. Consumption of meat from "unhealthy" horses, after the sacrifice, was as deplorable as the sight of horses dropping dead on their way to the local markets after enduring a treacherous journey from northern Nigeria. A 1938 commission of inquiry instituted by the acting secretary of the Southern Provinces in September shed some light on the stories about horses. In Afikpo in early 1939, according to the district officer, about ten horses were brought from the North every month during the dry season (fewer during the wet season) and sold in the Uburu market. In comparing the condition of horses transported within Nigeria with those sent from Europe to Africa, he placed the blame for animal trafficking on economic factors like opportunity cost in the use of animals for divergent purposes: "The Northerner only sends to the South his useless and old animals in the same way the custom for England to export her old race horses to the continent." "Most of the horses," he noted affirmatively, "appear to be in a very poor condition on arrival."[71] In Abakaliki Division, out of 210 horses that passed through four markets, 18 were sold for horse titles and burial ceremonies. Acting resident F. A. Goodliffe of Bamenda Province described the horses passing through the Mamfe-Ikom Road as "sorry nags."[72] A report from Obudu Division with a specific reference to a particular case brings us closer to the experience of Nigerian animals. In November 1938 Isa Damagudu was found riding an "almost blind and very poor" horse that he claimed he bought for £2. After examining the horse, the district officer of Obudu submitted that it could not have been bought for more than 30s. Its estimated value locally would be around 3s., according to him. The horse in question did not have any open sores but was deemed "useless for work," yet the animal was not "sufficiently ill-conditioned" enough for the district officer to prosecute Damagudu for animal cruelty. But to ensure that he did not profit from the sale of a dilapidated horse, the district officer compelled Damagudu to slaughter the animal in his presence.[73] Many of the 3,829 horses slaughtered in Onitsha Province on a yearly basis were used for title-taking in Nsukka. The figure was definitely lower than the actual number of horses because it was derived from a census of slaughtering in private residences and shrines, not in the government-approved abattoirs.

In addition, it was difficult to legislate against horse "trafficking" from northern to southern Nigeria because animal-cruelty laws did not differentiate between "fit" and "worn-out" animals within the context of transportation. Neither did they criminalize animal sacrifice. Animal-cruelty laws can only be enforced if handlers were seen physically maltreating the animal. The government deliberated on many ways to ameliorate the problem. While some colonial officers thought of building government slaughterhouses specifically for horses, allowing only government-trained and licensed slaughterers to kill the animals in a humane manner, others called for imposing an extra tax on horses used for burial or title-taking sacrifice.[74] But all this would be difficult to achieve because the native authorities, according to the prediction of Chief Commissioner F. B. Carr of the eastern provinces, would be "reactionary," "conservative," and "unhelpful" in legislating against a practice that legitimized their status.[75] Even religious authorities, or the so-called juju men, who "demand this revolting practice" were important members of the native courts and the communities that wielded influential power.[76] Building a government-approved slaughterhouse for horses would only work in cities, where veterinary and sanitary assistants monitor abattoirs because of public health concerns. Many of the cultural practices associated with horse sacrifice took place in rural communities that were not served with a modern slaughterhouse.[77] In addition, the few educated Igbos whom the government relied on to enlighten their people were equally horse-title holders in a society where the indigenous conception of respectability complemented other such signs as the acquisition of Western education.

If legislation against horse slaughter were passed, the resident of Ogoja Province predicted that "a few people might be unable to take the Horse Title, and that would matter not at all in the view of the usual disgusting cruelty to the horses."[78] His statement that government must be ready "to face any outcry" that may arise from criminalizing horse sacrifice dovetailed with the use of violent force to establish colonial ideals.[79] The outcome of another proposal to stop the horse trade between the North and the South was easy to predict: it would intensify the trafficking of horses via unofficial routes and create a black-market economy. It would also drive the slaughtering of animals into secrecy and prevent the government from acting against violators. Moreover, legislating against horse trafficking would be difficult without jeopardizing the highly lucrative cattle trade. In addition to being sold for sacrificial purposes, horses were also used to transport essential commodities to the eastern provinces from the North.[80] The central government in Lagos seemed to appreciate the economic value of interregional horse trading, when the acting principal veterinary officer of the eastern provinces commented, "The powers that be will not consider total prohibition of the trade."[81]

What seemed practicable, then, was not abolishing cultural practices or promoting humane killing of horses but monitoring the condition under which they were transported from the northern to the eastern provinces, even though the Control of Trade Cattle Regulation, which regulated the work of veterinary officers, only applied to trade cattle. Attempts by veterinary officers to extend this regulation to other animals met with limited success. If the word "cattle" were to be replaced with "animal" in the framing of existing laws, the director of veterinary services thought, his colleagues would have the legal power to monitor other animals such as horses, mules, donkeys, and even dogs used for sacrificial purposes and consumption.[82] He predicted the outcome of such a legislative change: "The suggested amendment is an attempt in the first place to stamp out or at least limit the traffic in horses whilst in the second place it attempts to nip in the bud the possibility that other animals would be used for sacrifice, should the horse trade became nil or negligible."[83]

Horse sacrifice and ritual slaughter continued in eastern Nigeria despite all legal and political interventions. In 1956, four years before the end of the British imperial presence in Nigeria, George Cockerill, the honorary secretary of the International League for the Protection of Horses, asserted in correspondence with the *Manchester Guardian* that "everything is being done in Nigeria to put an end to the ritual slaughter of horses." In September of the same year, the conference of the Animal Welfare Society announced that it had made a representation to the government of Nigeria to stop horse trafficking.[84]

In drawing down the curtain on the campaign to save the horses and donkeys of Nigeria, this chapter will return to where it started—an international scandal over the treatment of a horse. That instance of cruelty to the horse can serve as the basis for demonstrating how, in terms of metropolitan politics, critics of imperialism viewed the animals of the empire. For them colonialism could not be a success until the colonial subjects came to treat animals with compassion. Metropolitan critics saw the horse and donkey as vital living machines of imperialism, which they wanted to preserve. What is more, the agitation to protect the horse and the donkey was also informed by these animals' unique symbolic and material value. They did not deserve to be treated with cruelty, critics thought, because of their aristocratic as well as economic importance.

Conclusion

IN BRINGING this book to a close, I would like to return to where it started—the 1956 royal visit of Queen Elizabeth II to Nigeria. Africanist scholarship, I argue, has excluded animals from the politics of curating the British Empire. In all manners, the visit established that the fast-subliming dominion of the queen extended beyond the human to include the nonhuman inhabitants and the natural environment in general. This accounts for how animals featured, often on contradictory planes, during the state visit.

In conceptualizing animals as colonial subjects, I have been drawn to the core features of human imperial subjecthood, which are informed by obligations, exploitation, and paternalism, to mention but a few. Colonialism was preoccupied with maximizing the resources of the colonies. In doing so, the lives of the colonial subjects, both human and nonhuman, were reconstituted to fit imperial ideals of law and order and of capitalist expropriation. The symbolic materiality of animals as food, wealth generators, athletes, companions, and indices of modernity and progress were easily upturned by the outbreak of zoonotic diseases like rabies. In colonial framing of normality and safety, the most indispensable element could easily become a dispensable one. The best species could become the worst, and a good specimen of a human or animal could quickly degenerate into nothingness and savagery. This contradictory existence, shaped by unstable value, materiality, and utility, is one of the hallmarks of colonial human subjecthood.

Yet the primary agenda of this book goes beyond establishing a parallel between human and nonhuman colonial subjecthood or arguing for the inclusion of animals in the framing of imperial subjecthood. It also extends to accounting for the place of animals in Nigeria and, by extension, in African history. This is thus the first multispecies study of animals in twentieth-century colonial Africa. The choice of animals whose experiences were detailed here for the first time was informed by the nature of sources—a reflection of how both Nigerians and the British viewed the place of animals in their world. How beef became the primary meat of colonial Nigeria went beyond taste. Changes in nutrition could not have happened without a carefully organized cattle trade that derived its strength from veterinary medicine. It took place because of population explosion, urbanization, and superfluous built environment—all of which destroyed the natural home of game animals and made reliance on livestock like the cattle indispensable. It was not by accident that the raising of beef cattle was one of colonial Nigeria's most important types of agriculture.

This materiality-centered story of how cattle became the most important food animal in Nigeria stands in contrast with the multiple symbolism of the dog. In the preceding pages, I have attempted to unveil how the precolonial dog became a colonial canine within the context of the changes in the relationship between humans and their canines. The Nigerian dog population under colonialism increased for three principal reasons. First, the end of internecine wars in many parts of the country paved the way for economic or commercial game hunting that relied on dogs. Second, the use of dogs as watch animals increased as criminal activities soared. Third, dogs, like colonial officers, were also colonial agents. Very few colonial officers, expatriates, and nonofficial Europeans and North Americans came to Nigeria without a dog. But beyond this, two other factors made the inroad of foreign dogs important for Nigeria's colonial encounter. First is the diversification of the local dog population through active crossbreeding with foreign dogs. The second is how dogs became part of the dressing of colonial authority and an agent in policing racial boundaries. From official state photos to memoirs, the representation of dogs in the material culture of colonialism found strong expression in the indispensability of canines in colonial adventures. What made European segregated communities unique was not just their beautiful layout, concrete environment, and home architecture; it was also the presence of exotic dogs that had been trained to loathe Africans.

When scholars write about colonial modernity and Westernization, they focus on how Africans acquired Western education, dressed like

Europeans, and adopted Western culture—all in the name of benefiting from the gains of non-African modes of existence. But how city dwellers began to keep dogs as pets to copy Europeans is another aspect of modernization that has not received worthy attention. Exotic dogs became common members of educated, nuclear African families from the 1950s. Like Europeans' pet dogs or Europeans themselves, African pet canines also enjoyed all the privileges of living in modern cities. They ate foreign food, shared private spaces, and even accompanied their owners to public spaces like the cinema, as seen in the case of Oye Shobo and his dog. But by making them a taxable being, in addition to being a pet or utility creature, the colonial state turned them into an economic asset. The controversy over dog taxes was informed by a neoliberal colonial ideology that every economic activity, such as hunting, that had significant economic multiplication should be taxed. But this principle only applied to people who kept hunting dogs. For some owners of pet dogs, such as European officers, dog taxes were an unnecessary taxation. Yet the unstated motives of dog taxation in some communities—to reduce the African dog population in order to control rabies and noise pollution—dovetails with the colonialists' practice of modulating nature for its own selfish gain.

The preceding analysis on the making of the colonial dog is similar to the transformation of the equine under British imperialism. The experience of the horse and donkey that took active part in pre-twentieth century Nigeria changed. These animals would distinguish themselves as living tools of imperialism, not just because they aided the conquest of Nigeria but also because they were one of the primary means of transportation needed for daily running of the colonial state. Motorized transportation only came after the horse and donkey had helped bring vast territories under British dominion. Europeans did not introduce horse racing, polo, and durbars to Nigeria, but equine sports and rituality of power became another tool of extolling imperial might. It is easy to position the horse as an indispensable tool of imperialism when we realize that racing, polo, and durbars, which aimed imperial framing of power, could not have been popular without it.

In sum, this book considered the transformation of the interface between the human and nonhuman creatures of Nigeria under colonial rule. It recounted how colonialism laid new rules between humans and animals: how Africans should treat their animals and when and how they should be slaughtered for food, hides, religious observances, and trophies—and which animals deserve state protection and under what circumstances.

This way, animals came under state paternalism as subjects to be protected from humans and from fellow animals. But it was in the anticruelty laws that animal-centered colonial paternalism became obvious. The contradiction here is clear. The British who could not guarantee rights for human colonial subjects thought that animal subjects deserved protection. Still, this contradiction is not surprising—in its totality, colonialism sought to pitch one subject against another for maximum control. Hence, animal protection legislation was another site of colonial control, not a genuine desire to care for the nonhuman creatures. We saw this in the correlations drawn between "civilization" and animal compassion. Africans' cruelty to animals was explained as a manifestation of "primitivity." From churches to schools, the animal compassion movement, which included some educated upper-class Nigerians, believed they could raise a new generation of "animal lovers" who would treat animals with kindness because of biological and anatomical affinities to humans.

THE POSTCOLONIAL ANIMAL

On June 25, 2019, the federal government of Nigeria announced its plan to establish the Rural Grazing Area (RUGA) settlement program, a master plan to address decades of criminality and ethnoreligious crisis emanating from the failure of successive postindependence administrations to design a comprehensive modern animal husbandry infrastructure. While conflict between farmers and herders dates to the precolonial era, it was under postcolonial dispensations that it became a major threat to national security and a manifestation of the breakdown of institutions of quality governance. Under colonial rule, the British, with the aid of superior firepower, succeeded in reducing inter- and intraethnic violence while exploiting the population economically and developing a trade cattle–centered veterinary program. The main provisions of RUGA speak to the heart of the fundamental question of most societies—land. The project required that each state create a grazing zone that would develop into a comprehensive animal husbandry center, with infrastructure like roads, homes, schools, and electricity. According to the government planners, a gamut of agriculture-centered economic activities will emerge around RUGA, which also promises to attract foreign investment.[1]

If administrators thought that RUGA would improve the security situation in the country, critics saw it as an attempt by the pro-Fulani government to secure free land for the nomadic people. Ethnic and economic concerns fueled the resurgence in the public memory of the nineteenth-century Hausa-Fulani conquest of many ethnicities that led to the creation of the Sokoto Caliphate, the largest Islamic state in West Africa in the early twentieth century. To worsen the situation, the involvement of herders in kidnapping and banditry, especially in southwestern Nigeria, pushed the debate over RUGA off the rails, as local militias and vigilante groups intensified their participation in community watch groups in the wake of the failure of the state to protect the citizenry. In short, a majority of Nigerians failed to accept the vision that RUGA would accelerate economic growth and promotion of interethnic harmony.[2] The strength of their criticism compelled the government to shelve the plan.

RUGA and the debate it engendered would not have taken place without cattle. In the postcolonial period, the flesh-and-blood cattle, along with cattle used as a symbol, have occupied an important echelon in the discourse of national progress or retrogression while maintaining their practical material value as food. The stereotype of Fulani herders as people who love cattle more than their fellow human beings and are willing to exterminate an entire community in order to eliminate cattle rustlers is about economic self-interest as well as the prime place that animals hold in the imageries of socioeconomic power. It is easy to understand why the violence stemming from controversy over cattle grazing would be central to the question of nation building in 2019, as it had been in previous decades. Agriculture was the mainstay of the colonial and immediate postindependence economy up to the late 1960s. By the early 1970s crude oil had overtaken agriculture as the primary source of Nigeria's wealth. One implication of this change was the abandonment of all projects aimed at modernizing animal husbandry that had been developed by the colonial government and then nurtured by the nationalists up until the first military coup in 1966. Cattle trails, which reduced conflict between farmers and herders, disappeared, and ranching projects and animal experimental stations of the regional government ceased as the country became dependent on easy wealth from oil exports.

No one can say exactly how many cattle are slaughtered in Nigerian abattoirs or what the cattle population of the country is. Such estimates were possible during colonial rule because cattle were taxable livestock and because the public abattoir system was government controlled. After independence, not only were cattle no longer taxable, but the government also lost control over abattoirs as institutions of governance. The veterinary and public health departments went comatose. Despite the absence of reliable data on beef consumption, it is safe to say that beef is the number one protein food in twenty-first-century Nigeria. At various times "ordinary" and "powerful" Nigerians have called for a boycott of beef to punish the Fulani herders. But the question at stake goes beyond social and economic sabotage to a structural crisis that prevented Nigeria from diversifying its protein supply. Postindependence governments neglected to build up commercial fish farming, which had attracted significant attention as part of colonial development schemes in the late 1950s. Rather, they left animal husbandry to the private sector and thus undermined the capacity of the veterinary department to expand its reach. Coupled with the growing population, a new ethos of socialization that increased demand for meat fueled the intensification of cattle herding and all its attendant impacts on humans and their environment, interethnic relations, and security. While the population of meat eaters has increased, the model adopted for rearing cattle has remained the same since the precolonial era.

The number of zoos expanded tremendously after the 1960s in response to the proliferation of departments of zoology in postcolonial Nigerian universities. Their philosophy has continued to align with similar ones across the world: wildlife is exhibited for purposes of scientific research, public education, and leisure. Aside from university zoos, some cities, like Kano in 1971, established a municipal zoo.[3] One of the clear outcomes of the proliferation of zoos in postcolonial Nigeria is the deepening of knowledge about Nigerian fauna on the part of Nigerians across all educational levels—from elementary schoolchildren to college professors. Nigerians know more about animals in captivity than did their forebearers. Zoo-going continues to be child-centered and aided by a public-school curriculum that conceives witnessing the exhibition of captive animals as part of childhood socialization. Animals had a place in indigenous African folktales told to children orally, but with the expansion of Western education, print technology, radio, and television, these stories could reach a wider audience. After reading and listening to stories and seeing television depictions of them, schoolchildren craved to encounter wildlife in a safe space. The dexterity with which animal exhibition was maximized for economic gain was a response in part to children's new cultural standing. Postcolonial zoos hosted school parties in designed play areas, as pupils enjoyed the unique ambience of the menagerie. In this way, the zoo further integrated humans into the curated animal world. About 250,000 people (mostly children) visited Ibadan Zoological Garden in 1979, "more than any other public attraction of any kind in Nigeria," according to the zoo's first curator, Bob Golding.[4]

A look at the biographies of some postcolonial wild animals can take us a step closer to understanding how animals in general shaped human experience. From 1964 to 2009 generation after generation of schoolchildren in southwestern Nigeria encountered nature through Aruna and Imade, two western lowland gorillas, whose fame traveled far and wide.[5] These animals exemplified what evolutionists have insisted for a long time—that there is a developmental affinity between humans and apes. Yet it was their performance of human traits, more than problematic evolutionary theories, that amazed everyone who met them. At the peak of their productivity, Aruna and Imade obeyed commands in Yoruba and English, swam, and expressed contrasting emotions that challenged humans to rethink their alleged superiority to animals. But Aruna and Imade's lives did not begin in captivity. In December 1964 they were captured in a Cameroonian forest by foreign animal traffickers of "Asian appearance" and offered for sale at the University of Ibadan Zoological Garden. The animals were "small, miserable and frightened-looking," showing signs of maltreatment, according to Niels Bolwing, the head of the university's Department of Zoology.[6] Instead of buying the animals, Golding called the police on their captors and built a massive cage and water-moat enclosure for them (see fig. C.1).[7] Aruna died in 1995, Imade fourteen years later.[8] Today the embalmed bodies of the apes, on permanent exhibition at the zoo, remind people of the animals who left an indelible mark on their childhood.

FIGURE C.1. Aruna and Imade entertaining zoo visitors (1970). Courtesy of Bob Golding.

From one national park in 1957, Nigeria now has eight, with dedicated park rangers armed with guns to secure animals from poachers. This represents a major advance from the colonial past, when the first game rangers were European volunteers appointed after the establishment of the Yankari Game Park. And the idea of who constitutes a "poacher" has changed in the postindependence era; it now includes hunters and anybody exploiting the resources of the national park, whether wood or pasture.

But if the government of Nigeria is unable to protect humans, one cannot expect it to effectively safeguard its nonhuman subjects. In 2019 the National Park Service, the government agency responsible for managing the national parks, stated that it has lost twenty rangers to poachers since 1991 when the first batch of park police were deployed. He decried that his rangers were "underequipped, underpaid and under-honoured."[9] Corruption among park rangers and in law enforcement in general has also fueled the continued trafficking of live animals and trophies across and within the country.[10] The Yankari Game Reserve claimed in its 2017 annual report that one Ilu Bello, a notorious poacher "responsible for killing a ranger in 2012 and numerous elephants[,] was released from custody on bail and has since resumed poaching."[11] The common sight of leopard skins, among other wildlife trophies, in indigenous-medicine markets probably suggest that most locals and hunters are either ignorant of wildlife conservation regulations or are just lawbreakers.

While Western naturalists and conservationists had a monopoly on understandings of the fauna of Nigeria in the precolonial era, the increasing number of universities of agriculture, departments of wildlife, and veterinary schools in postcolonial Nigeria have increased the involvement of Nigerian academics in wildlife research. Much of the study of Nigerian wildlife is carried out for academic purposes. Despite constant efforts by the Nigerian Field Society to foster nature and wildlife appreciation and to make it part of the public education curriculum, progress is not advancing at the speed desired by promoters.[12] Aside from university-centered research activities, international wildlife protection groups (such as the Elephant Crisis Fund and the Wildlife Conservation Society) have been instrumental in providing resources and equipment for Nigeria's national parks (see fig. C.2). Regardless, nature conservation since independence shared the philosophy of the colonial incarnation—wildlife must be protected in the interest of the animals and their habitats. Humans, conservationists insist, have an obligation to secure wildlife from total "extinction" by fighting what threatens them—enemy number one being poachers.

FIGURE C.2. Bob Golding (*center*) and students of the University of Ibadan on an expedition to the Borgu Game Reserve (1974). Courtesy of Bob Golding.

Humans' exploitative claims to the gifts of nature cannot supersede the rights of wildlife to exist without fear, so conservationists continue to argue, even as pressure on land and other natural resources challenges the rationale behind preservation.

Fewer postcolonial Nigerians, especially in the South, know about horses, unlike their colonial counterparts. This is largely attributable to the demise of horse racing. Horse racing lost its state sponsorship as a sport after independence when the Europeans whose social and economic power held the sport together left the country in large numbers. The sport came to be viewed as an anachronism in an era of nationalist pride. Consequently, the racecourse was renamed Tafawa Balewa Square in the 1970s for Abubakar Tafawa Balewa, the first indigenous ruler of independent Nigeria, as soccer took over as the national sport. Horse racing and polo remain part of elite culture in race and polo clubs, however, and while there are constant attempts to market the sports, the public has proved unwilling to jettison their love for local and international soccer.[13]

The durbar is one reason that horse keeping has not died out in the North. It is the only aspect of colonial equine culture not affected by the postcolonial transformation. Today typical northern elites, including Emirs and district heads, have stables of carefully groomed horses they ride only during a durbar, which has remained a spectacle for celebrating the might of indigenous rulers, as well as democratically elected politicians, and for paying homage to important visitors. Thus, the durbar has accommodated new forms of political structure (such as institutions of democracy) and been transformed to meet new realities. Sallah, an important Muslim festival, has retained its importance among Muslims. As the durbar celebrated the might of colonial power during British rule, it was used to espouse the beauty of self-rule and Pan-Africanism during the Second World Black and African Festival of Arts and Culture, which was held in Nigeria in 1977. The politicization of the durbar—as represented by the directive of the governor of Kano, Abdullahi Ganduje, that district heads should not participate in the 2019 Sallah durbar of the Emir of Kano, Sanusi Lamido Sanusi, because of a rift between the two men—can be seen as an example of the enduring power of the horse to enhance human honor.[14] Similarly, the practice of dressing durbar horses in beautiful costumes derives inspiration from the past as well as from the contemporary politics of self-fashioning. Current trends include the use of motifs of political parties to reify interpersonal politics.

Donkeys have not disappeared completely from the economic landscape of northern Nigeria, despite the popularity of mechanized transportation. Just like their ancestors, donkeys in the twenty-first century can be found in northern Nigerian cities and villages helping humans to carry heavy loads. Their continued relevance is necessary in a society that cherishes its ancient infrastructure while also adapting to the gains of twenty-first-century globalization. Donkeys especially help to transport essential daily supplies to communities and homes inaccessible to cars. And within the villages, they also transport people and agricultural produce. While political debates about the overloading of donkeys were frequent in colonial Nigeria, today most people seem not to worry about the daily experience of the beast, who remains visible yet taken for granted. In November 2018 the Nigerian National Assembly held a public hearing on a bill, sponsored by Garba Datti Mohammad of Kaduna State, to prohibit the killing of donkeys and the export of donkey meat and hides. According to Mohammad and his supporters, the increase in foreign demand for donkey meat (chiefly from China) had increased the local value of donkeys from $50 to $370 a head. He believed that foreign exportation was depriving local communities of access to donkeys for transport labor. However, some veterinarians from the National Animal Production Research Institute, as well as the Donkey Skin Processors, Marketers, and Exporters Association of Nigeria, among other groups, disagreed with Mohammad and his constituency.[15] For them, donkey products have the capacity to attract as much as $2 billion yearly in foreign exchange and to generate domestic employment, especially for Nigerian youth.[16] A close reading of this debate revolves around how best to exploit the donkey. While one group wants it to remain a beast of burden, the other seeks a more expansive role as a meat-producing animal for the international market, an option that did not exist under colonial rule.[17]

After many years of inaction, the NRSPCA, now the Nigerian Society for the Prevention of Cruelty to Animals, is reorganizing its efforts to protect animals. The society's current priorities include revising existing animal-cruelty laws bequeathed by the colonial government that are seen as anachronistic in the twenty-first century.[18]

WHERE DO WE GO FROM HERE?

The African history of human-animal relations has a bright future. Upcoming studies promise to focus on neglected eras and themes while offering fresh conceptual and theoretical frameworks for the colonial era, which has received more attention (in part) because of the availability of declassified documents. But a lot remains unknown about this period, not because of paucity of data but because scholars are not looking in certain directions. For instance, a comprehensive history of colonial veterinary science would complement existing scholarship. As we saw in chapter 1, zoonotic diseases were about animals as much as about humans. The field of African medical history has largely ignored animal medicine.

Similarly, historical scholarship on the precolonial and postcolonial animals are scarce. Writing about the precolonial animal would entail excavating surviving oral traditions and placing the dense narrative about animals in anthropological works produced by Europeans during the colonial era in historical context. Creative writings of African novelists from the colonial period are also useful sources, for they are inspired by oral traditions and folklore and are far more conscious of the inseparability of the human and the animal worlds than most sources. Animals have historically been part of archaeological discoveries. Material culture, including potsherd pavements and figurines, tell the histories of human-animal relations in shifting context.[19] Our knowledge of origins, domestication, and extinction of animals can only be improved by archaeological scholarship that is conscious of social, political, economic, and cultural history.[20]

The expansion of university education in postcolonial Africa complements early investment in colonial veterinary medicine, forestry, and governmental and international animal-conservation foundations like Pandrillus in Cross River State.[21] Colonial and postcolonial veterinary medicine and game conservation share similar ideologies and purposes: to save nature from humans' destruction and to protect endangered animals from going into extinction. New scholarship on postcolonial African animals would benefit from the works of veterinary schools, game reserves, and zoos. Although official documents of most postcolonial African governments have not been declassified, pamphlets, promotional materials, and scientific reports (in such journals as the *Tropical Animal Health and Production, Transactions of the Royal Society of Tropical Medicine and Hygiene,* and the *West African Medical Journal*) can be placed in historical context. Collaborations between historians and animal science scholars could produce multidisciplinary scholarship capable of expanding our knowledge of human-animal interface in new directions.

New works on the postcolonial animal may build on the discourse of the interrelatedness of animals and nation building. Detailed scholarship on how African nationalists of the 1950s and 1960s used animal identities, images, and modern animal husbandry to articulate a new era in Africa's development is required. For instance, in the case of Nigeria, the oil boom of the 1970s led to the abandonment of agriculture, which was the main source of national wealth up to the late 1960s. It was in this context that cattle herding lost institutional control of the colonial era, leading to widespread violence between nomadic and sedentary farmers. The new drive to return to animal husbandry connects the past with the present and offers a new perspective for viewing human-animal relations.

This book is a multispecies study of human-animal relations; future works on single species of animals hold prospects in terms of depth. In disaggregating each animal species for detailed study, they promise to chart new theoretical lines that escaped the purview of this book. Single-species study would benefit from the scholarship of postcolonial veterinary medicine. Unlike the colonial veterinary medicine, which focused mostly on cattle trade, postcolonial animal science is far more expansive in its detailed study of a wide variety of animals. For instance, from the late 1950s the British government sent expatriates nicknamed the "Fishery Mission" to the colonies as part of the colonial development schemes. The agendas of missions such as this one changed under independence in response to the politics of nationalization of waterways, the home of aquatic animals, which scholars of African animal studies have largely excluded.[22] It would be interesting to see how politics decolonization and the constant redrawing of African maps affect humans' encounter with water and its animal creatures.

In looking at the intersections of animal lives and art, this work only focused on political cartoons. It excluded the representation of animals in painting and sculpture, among other aspects of African expressive and visual culture. Across many communities in Africa, there are surviving animal arts (sculptures and paintings) produced from the precolonial era that can be used to engage themes such as religion and spirituality, class, and self-representation.[23] The expansion of media technology in postcolonial Nigeria has increased artistic flexibility, allowing artists to express their ideas in ways their predecessors could only imagine.

Notes

INTRODUCTION

1. Rex Niven, *Nigerian Kaleidoscope: Memoirs of a Colonial Servant* (London: C. Hurst, 1982), 259.
2. Video clips of the visit are available at "Queen's 1956 Tour of Nigeria," accessed on January 20, 2018, https://www.britishpathe.com/workspaces/2e6592077f92958a84d91602b25fa58d/Queen-s-1956-Tour-of-Nigeria.
3. See all the issues of major Nigerian newspapers of the time (*West African Pilot, Daily Service,* and *Nigerian Daily Times*) from late January to the third of February 1956 for photographs and stories of the queen's visit.
4. "Milk for Her Majesty," *West African Pilot* (hereafter cited as WAP), February 6, 1956.
5. "Bird That Welcomes the Queen," WAP, February 3, 1956.
6. Joan Sharwood-Smith, *Diary of a Colonial Wife: An African Experience* (London. I. B. Tauris, 1992), 138; "Report on the Royal Durbar," March 1, 1956, VN 10/7D, National Archives of Nigeria, Kaduna (hereafter cited as NAK).
7. "Examination of Horses for the Queen's Visit," February 1, 1956, VN 10/7D, NAK.
8. Ahmadu Bello, *My Life* (Cambridge: Cambridge University Press, 1962), 179.
9. Sandra Swart, "Writing Animals into African History," *Critical African Studies* 8, no. 2 (2016): 98.
10. Swart, 97.
11. Robin Law, *The Horse in West African History: The Role of the Horse in the Societies of Pre-colonial West Africa* (Oxford: Oxford University Press, 1980); Nancy Jacobs, *Birders of Africa: History of a Network* (New Haven, CT: Yale University Press, 2016).
12. Edward L. Steinhart, *Black Poachers, White Hunters: A Social History of Hunting in Colonial Kenya* (Athens: Ohio University Press, 2006); William Beinart, *The Rise of Conservation in South Africa* (Cambridge: Cambridge University Press, 2003); Jane Carruthers, *The Kruger National Park: A Social and Political History* (Pietermaritzburg, SA: UKZN, 1995); Jane Carruthers, *Wildlife and Warfare: The Life of James Steven-Hamilton* (Pietermaritzburg, SA: University of Natal Press, 2001); William Beinart

and Lotte Hughes, *Environment and Empire* (Oxford: Oxford University Press, 2007); Alan Mikhail, *The Animal in Ottoman Egypt* (Oxford: Oxford University Press, 2013); Karen Brown, "Political Entomology: The Insectile Challenge to Agricultural Development in the Cape Colony, 1895 to 1910," *Journal of Southern African Studies* 29, no. 2 (2003): 529–49; Clapperton Chakanetsa Mavhunga, "Mobility and the Making of Animal Meaning: The Kinetics of 'Vermin' and 'Wildlife' in Southern Africa," in *Making Animal Meaning*, ed. Georgina Montgomery and Linda Kalof (East Lansing: Michigan State University Press, 2011), 17–43; Jacob S. T. Dlamini, *Safari Nation: A Social History of the Kruger National Park* (Athens: Ohio University Press, 2020).

13. Lance Van Sittert and Sandra Swart, eds., *Canis Africanis: A Dog History of Southern Africa* (Leiden: Brill, 2008); Sandra Swart, *Riding High: Horses, Humans, and History in South Africa* (Johannesburg: Wits University Press, 2010); Karen Brown, *Mad Dogs and Meerkats: A History of Resurgent Rabies in Southern Africa* (Athens: Ohio University Press, 2011); Jacobs, *Birders of Africa*.

14. Mahmood Mamdani, *Citizen and Subject: Contemporary Africa and the Legacy of Late Colonialism* (Princeton, NJ: Princeton University Press, 1996), description on dustjacket.

15. A. E. Afigbo, *The Warrant Chiefs: Indirect Rule in Southeastern Nigeria, 1891–1929* (London: Longman, 1972).

16. Bill Freund, *Capital and Labour in the Nigerian Tin Mines* (London: Longman, 1981).

17. Rina Okonkwo, *Protest Movements in Lagos, 1908–1930* (Lewiston, NY: E. Mellen, 1995).

18. Saheed Aderinto, *When Sex Threatened the State: Illicit Sexuality, Nationalism, and Politics in Colonial Nigeria, 1900–1958* (Urbana: University of Illinois Press, 2015).

19. "Agricultural Show in Birnin Kebbi," *Nigeria Magazine*, no. 59 (1958): 329–40.

20. Olufemi Taiwo, *How Colonialism Preempted Modernity in Africa* (Bloomington: Indiana University Press, 2010); Oluwatoyin Oduntan, *Power, Culture, and Modernity in Nigeria: Beyond the Colony* (New York: Routledge, 2018).

21. Frederick L. Brown, *The City Is More than Human: An Animal History of Seattle* (Seattle: University of Washington Press, 2016), 9.

22. "Wild Bird Shooting at Ikoyi: An Appeal," *Nigerian Daily Times* (hereafter cited as *NDT*), May 11, 1950; H. C. Ketley, "Bird Life of Okene Reservoir," *Nigerian Field* 7, no. 3 (1938): 124–25.

23. "Chief Secretary to the Government to the Commissioner of the Colony," August 28, 1950, Commissioner of the Colony Office, Lagos, 1136, National Archives of Nigeria, Ibadan (hereafter cited as NAI).

24. Sir Bernard Bourdillon, "Terns on Lagos Beach, Nigeria," *Nigerian Field* 11 (1943): 20–22.

25. Richard Lander, *Records of Captain Clapperton's Last Expedition to Africa*. 2 vols. (London: Henry Colburn and Richard Bentley, 1830); Henry Barth, *Travels and Discoveries in North and Central Africa*. 3 vols. (New York: Drallop, 1890); Dixon Denham and Hugh Clapperton, *Narrative of Travels and Discoveries in Northern and Central Africa* (London: John Murray, 1826).

26. Olaudah Equiano, *The Interesting Narrative of the Life of Olaudah Equiano or Gustavus Vassa the African, Written by Himself*, ed. Shelly Eversley (1789; repr., New York: Modern Library, 2004).

27. J. Ki-Zerbo, ed., *General History of Africa*, vol. 1, *Methodology and African Prehistory* (Paris: UNESCO, 1981).

28. G. Mokhtar, ed., *General History of Africa*, vol. 2, *Ancient Civilizations of Africa* (Paris: UNESCO, 1981).

29. Susan Feldmann, ed., *African Myths and Tales* (New York: Dell, 1963); *Keita: The Heritage of the Griot* (San Francisco: California Newsreel, 1994).

30. D. O. Fagunwa, *Ogbójú Ode Nínú Igbó Irúnmalè* (1938; repr., Edinburgh: Thomas Nelson, 1983).

31. Adeleke Adeeko and Akin Adesokan, eds., *Celebrating D.O. Fágúnwà: Aspects of African and World Literary History* (Ibadan: Bookcraft, 2017).

32. Amos Tutuola, *My Life in the Bush of Ghosts* (London: Faber & Faber, 1954).

33. William Beinart, "African History and Environmental History," *African Affairs* 99, no. 395 (2000): 269–302; Vimbai Kwashirai, "Environmental Change, Control, and Management in Africa," *Global Environment* 6, no. 2 (2013): 166–96.

34. Kwashirai, "Environmental Change," 166–96.

35. The Editor, "The Nigerian Field Society: A Talk—Broadcast from the Lagos Studio on 16th August 1938," *Nigerian Field* 8, no. 1 (1939): 33–37.

36. "The Nigerian Field Society's Natural History Survey," *Nigerian Field* 13, no. 2 (1948): 40–42.

37. "Queen's 1956 Tour of Nigeria"; "Family History of Francis and Betty Humphreys," accessed August 5, 2019, http://www.mueller-humphreys.de/Humphreys/DicksonElizabeth/selbst/Nigeria/NigeriaFrankFoiE.html; "The Nigerian Nostalgia 1960–1980 Project," https://www.facebook.com/groups/nigeriannostalgiaproject/.

38. Nnamdi Azikiwe, *My Odyssey: An Autobiography* (New York: Praeger, 1970); Bello, *My Life*; Obafemi Awolowo, *Awo: The Autobiography of Chief Obafemi Awolowo* (Cambridge: Cambridge University Press, 1960).

39. Azikiwe, *My Odyssey*, 15–16.

40. "Three Strokes of the Cane and £120 Fine or 12 Months Jail for Pottery Officer Gregory," *WAP*, June 30, 1954.

41. Mason Begho, *The Dog-Bite Magistrate: His Struggles* (Lagos: Daily Times, 1988).

42. W. R. Crocker, *Nigeria: A Critique of British Colonial Administration* (London: George Allen & Unwin, 1936); Constance Larymore, A

Resident's Wife in Nigeria (London: George Routledge, 1908); Langa Langa (H. B. Hermon-Hodge), *Up against It in Nigeria* (London: George Allen & Unwin, 1922); Joan Sharwood-Smith, *Diary of a Colonial Wife: An African Experience* (London. I. B. Tauris, 1992); Lassie Fitz-Henry, *African Dust* (London: Macmillan, 1959); A. J. N. Tremearne, *The Tailed Head-Hunters of Nigeria* (J. B. Lippincott, 1912); Martin Kisch, *Letters and Sketches from Northern Nigeria* (London: Chatto & Windus, 1910).

43. Frederick Lugard, *The Diaries of Lord Lugard*, ed. Margery Perham and Mary Bull, 4 vols. (Evanston, IL: Northwestern University Press, 1959).

CHAPTER 1: A MEATY COLONY

1. G. G. Briggs, "Eastern Region Trade Cattle Toll Bill, 1952," MJ 141, National Archives of Nigeria, Enugu (hereafter cited as NAE).
2. "Acting Secretary of Southern Provinces to the Superintendent of Agriculture," September 18, 1935, OW 2511, NAE.
3. Alfred W. Crosby, *Ecological Imperialism: The Biological Expansion of Europe, 900–1900* (Cambridge: Cambridge University Press, 1986).
4. "Wonders of Veterinary Science," WAP, June 30, 1954.
5. "Cattle Industry in Nigeria," 1926–1932, 2 vols., CSO 14827, National Archives of Nigeria, Ibadan (hereafter cited as NAI).
6. "Value of Agricultural Shows," NDT, August 26, 1946; "Animal Show in Hadeijia," *Daily Service*, February 11, 1949.
7. "Her Majesty and a Prize-Winning Cow," WAP, July 24, 1957.
8. "Shortage of Beef in Lagos," NDT, January 15, 1947; "Meat Control," NDT, February 25, 1947; "Cattle Raising," NDT, June 27, 1947; "Beef Shortage Hits Lagos," *Daily Service*, September 30, 1950; "Lagos Butchers Promise to Co-operate with the MOH," *Daily Service*, February 20, 1951.
9. "1,000 Ibadan Butchers on Strike: Fishermen Do Good Businesses," WAP, May 22, 1958.
10. "Butcher's Strike: Report on May 29, 1958," MLG (W) 1–10, 163337/5, NAI.
11. "Butcher's Strike Still On," WAP, May 23, 1958.
12. "Control of Poultry Prices by Weight" and "Control of Poultry Prices," NDT, July 28, 1944.
13. "Cattle Dealers Make Protest against Increase in Rentage," WAP, March 28, 1951; "Cattle Dealers Appeal to LRC Over Increased Rates," WAP, April 6, 1951; "Ojikutu Says Scarcity of Meat Is Due to the Cattle Men's Unreasonable Reaction," WAP, April 20, 1951; "One Cattle Dealer Saves Lagos Temporarily from Meat Crisis," WAP, April 21, 1951; "Spokesman of Dealers in Cattle Explains the Meat Situation," WAP, April 24, 1951; "Policemen Manage to Prevent Trouble in the Cattle Lairage," WAP, May 5, 1951.
14. "Meat, Meat, Meat," WAP, August 30, 1958; "Ram Dealers Send Protest to Railways for Quick Service," WAP, September 3, 1951; "Rubber and Livestock Boards Are Mooted," WAP, May 7, 1952.

15. "Dried Meat (Biltong) Industry," 1934, BP 937, NAI.
16. "Hausa Grazing Cattle," WAP, January 19, 1957.
17. J. H. D. Stapleton, "In Their End Is Their Beginning: A Fulani Crisis," *Nigerian Field* 13, no. 2 (1948): 53–59.
18. *Advice on Tsetse Surveys and Clearings* (Kaduna: Government Printer, 1934), 1.
19. "The Integration of Cattle into the Agrarian Picture of the Northern Region of Nigeria," 1952, MAHFR 185, NAI; Howell Davies, *Tsetse Flies in Nigeria: A Handbook for Junior Control Staff* (Ibadan: Oxford University Press, 1977).
20. "Bye Laws for the Control of Cattle," 1942–51, Cal ProF 3/1/2687, NAE; "Cattlemen Convicted," WAP, January 24, 1956.
21. "Exportation of Cattle to Fernando Po," 1954–55, Cal ProF 7/1/1008, NAE; "Application to Export Livestock," 1947, OW 4188/1, NAE.
22. "Chief Veterinary Officer of Northern Nigerian Provinces to the Secretary of Northern Provinces," February 13, 1931, SNP 17 K8440, National Archives of Nigeria, Kaduna (hereafter cited as NAK).
23. "Acting Secretary of Northern Provinces to the Chief Secretary," August 30, 1934, ABADIST 14/1/341, NAE.
24. "Balogun Opens Parley on Animal Disease Today," WAP, January 7, 1957; "Veterinary Experts to Meet in North," WAP, August 14, 1958.
25. "Ghana Lifts Ban on Cattle," WAP, June 10, 1957; "Seminar on Cattle Meets in Congo Next Month," WAP, May 12, 1958.
26. "Beiram Festival Is Celebrated in Lagos with Usual Pageantry," WAP, August 22, 1953.
27. *The Utilization of Animal By-products in the Colonial Empire* (Lagos: Government Printer, 1938), 8–9.
28. "2075 Cattle for Lagos Last Month," WAP, December 13, 1952.
29. Federal Department of Veterinary Research, *Annual Report for the Year 1959/1960* (Lagos: Government Printer, 1960), 55.
30. "50,422 Livestock Eaten in East for 9 Months," WAP, December 14, 1957.
31. "Slaughtered Livestock," WAP, October 28, 1955.
32. "Disease of livestock, 1952," CSO 26/1980, NAI.
33. "Disease of livestock, 1952."
34. "Farming in Northern Nigeria: Northerners Learn to Farm with Bullocks," WAP, January 18, 1957; "Grazing Cattle," WAP, January 19, 1957; "Piggery," WAP, December 21, 1957; "Piggery," WAP, December 25, 1958.
35. "Photo: Eastern Region Minister of Agriculture, Hon. P. O. Nwoga, Inspecting a Horse," WAP, April 20, 1957.
36. "A Ram for Dr. Azikiwe," WAP, November 5, 1959; "The Onitsha Inland Branch of the NCNC Presents Zik with a Cock," WAP, December 16, 1959; "Presentation of Cow," WAP, March 8, 1958; "Battling Ram for Zik," WAP, December 1, 1955.
37. "Zik Presented with a Fat Bull," WAP, December 15, 1959; "Presentation of Cow," WAP, August 21, 1959.

38. "East Makes 1st Export of 21 Cattle to Fernando Po," *WAP*, January 31, 1959; "East Collects £3,466 from Cattle Tax," *WAP*, December 21, 1959; "Photo of Agricultural Show," *WAP*, January 5, 1960; "Teaching of Poultry Farming in East Urged," *WAP*, May 27, 1960.

39. "Agric Shows in the North," *WAP*, February 6, 1960.

40. "Meat Shortage May Be Tabled Today," *WAP*, August 4, 1953.

41. "Northern Chiefs Debate Cattle Improvement and Good Roads," *WAP*, February 17, 1953; "Cattle-Ranching Scheme for Ogoja and Sack Manufacturing Being Planned in the East," *Daily Service*, August 5, 1950.

42. "Beef Production Scheme Account," 1940–45, CSO 36170/S.3, NAI.

43. "Cattle Fattening Scheme: Agege Accounts II and Agege Dairy," 1945–52, Commissioner of the Colony Office, Lagos (hereafter cited as ComCol), 36170/S.15, NAI.

44. "More Cattle Fattening Stations," *Daily Service*, August 1, 1944.

45. "The Farming Industry," *NDT*, November 1, 1944; "Facts about Cattle Fattening Farm," *Daily Service*, August 1, 1944.

46. W. Burke, "Umuahia Cattle Control Post," June 13, 1940, OW 2511, NAE; "Going the Stockfish Way," *WAP*, June 22, 1955.

47. "Cattle Trade in Oyo Province," 1935–36, Oyo ProF 1576, 2 vols., NAI.

48. "Animal Husbandry," *NDT*, July 10, 1944.

49. "The Cattle Industry," *NDT*, July 18, 1944.

50. "Obudu Cattle Ranch," *Nigeria Magazine*, no. 60 (1959): 22–29. "Secretary of Eastern Provinces to the Resident of Ogoja Province: Obudu Cattle Range," *WAP*, July 27, 1950; "Obudu Cattle Ranch Gets Manager," *WAP*, July 9, 1957.

51. "Nigerian Beef: The Story of a Stock-Rearing Experiment," *Nigeria Magazine*, no. 40 (1954): 314–27.

52. "Control of Movement of Pigs," *NDT*, October 16, 1945.

53. A. Mpama, "Home of Pigs," *WAP*, August 24, 1957.

54. "Complaint about Wandering Pigs at the West Mole Camp Tarquah Bay Village," 1941, ComCol 3/23, 19, NAI.

55. See the collection of documents titled "Impounding of Animal-Rules and Orders Made by Native Authorities," MLG 16758, NAI.

56. "Re-Keeping of Pigs in Aparaki Village," letter to the editor, *Ijebu Review*, January 3, 1947, Ijebu ProF 1, 19/11/45, NAI.

57. "Upcoming of Pig in Idanre Village," November 25, 1945, Ijebu ProF 1, 19/11/45, NAI.

58. "Secretary of the Northern Province to the Chief Secretary to the Government," July 28, 1944, WP 16759, NAI.

59. "Goats and Sheep," *NDT*, November 4, 1944.

60. F. G. G., "The Goats of Yaba," *NDT*, March 26, 1941.

61. H. Millicent Douglas, "The Goats of Yaba," *NDT*, March 24, 1941.

62. "Lagos Town Council: Beiram Festival-Keeping of Sheep," *Daily Service*, September 25, 1946.

63. "Keeping of Animals," *NDT*, April 3, 1945.
64. "Animal Keeping," *NDT*, August 7, 1945; J. M. Johnson (Sgt.), "Keeping of Animals," *NDT*, April 16, 1945; "Keeping of Sheep and Goats in Lagos," *NDT*, September 21, 1945; "Keeping of Sheep in Lagos," *NDT*, September 26, 1946; "Restrictions on Keeping Rams," *NDT*, November 11, 1946.
65. "That Sheep and Goats Bye-Law," *Daily Service*, August 7, 1945.
66. "Scrap the Undemocratic Bye Law," *Daily Service*, September 22, 1945.
67. For an example of a pro-Muslim letter, see "Goats and Sheep Bye-Law in Lagos," *Daily Service*, September 22, 1945.
68. "Sheep and Goats in Lagos by Ajao: A Sanitary Inspector," *Daily Service*, July 28, 1945; "Significance of Animal Sacrifice," *WAP*, June 27, 1958.
69. "Sir Adeyemo Alakija Opens Big Mass Meeting with Soul-Stirring Address," *Daily Service*, September 20, 1945; "Control of Ram Prices," *NDT*, November 14, 1944.
70. "Nigerian Railway: Public Notice," *NDT*, October 15, 1945.
71. "Control of Rams," *Daily Service*, November 11, 1944.
72. "An Appeal to the Public: In Aid of £20,000 Education Fund," *NDT*, November 24, 1944.
73. "That Sheep and Goats Bye-Law," *Daily Service*, August 7, 1945.
74. "Goats and Sheep," *Daily Service*, February 1, 1946.
75. "Restrictions on Keeping Rams: Town Council Discusses Relative Regulations," *NDT*, November 11, 1946.
76. "Veterinary Officer to Director of Veterinary Services," August 7, 1956, SNP 17 K8440, NAK.
77. Pauline Von Hellermann, *Things Fall Apart? The Political Ecology of Forest Governance in Southern Nigeria* (New York: Berghahn, 2013), 14.
78. "Chief Conservator, Forestry and the Use of Grass in Forest Reservation," 1942, MAHFR 185, NAI.
79. "Chief Conservator, Forestry."
80. "Director of Veterinary Services to the Chief Conservator of Forests," January 2, 1951, MAHFR 14449/S.I, NAK.
81. "Acting Conservator of Forests of Northern Nigeria to the Secretary of the Northern Provinces," April 29, 1942, MAHFR 185, NAK.
82. Conservator of Forests, "Grazing," 1950, MAHFR 185, NAK.
83. "Grazing," MAHFR 615, vol. 2, 1959–60, NAK.
84. M. P. Ford, "Native Authority Ranch," September 13, 1956, MAHFR 185, NAK.
85. "Fined £10," *Nigerian Citizen*, July 4, 1956; "Chief Conservator of Forests of Northern Region to the Conservator of Forests for Plateau," July 4, 1956, SNP 17 K8440, NAK; "Permanent Secretary of the Ministry of Natural Resources to the Chief Conservator of Forests," September 10, 1956, MAHFR 14449/S.I, NAK.
86. "Restriction of the Import of Animals and Livestock into Nigeria, 1928–1932," vol. 1, CSO 14251/S.3, NAI.

87. Federal Department of Veterinary Research, *Annual Report 6.*
88. "Veterinary Committee Meets," *WAP,* July 29, 1957.
89. "Animal Resources of Nigeria," *NDT,* March 22, 1941.
90. "Grazing Cattle," *WAP,* January 19, 1957.
91. "Twenty-Seven Students Pass Veterinary Assistant Exam," *WAP,* July 13, 1954.
92. Federal Department of Veterinary Research, *Annual Report 6.*
93. H. I. Field, "The Development of Veterinary Education in Nigeria," *Veterinary History* 2, no. 3 (1982): 112–14.
94. R. Brewster, "NBS Broadcast on Careers: Veterinary Science," *WAP,* November 23, 1953.
95. "Government and Veterinary Assistants," *WAP,* April 24, 1951.
96. James Oko, "The Case of Veterinary Assistants," *WAP,* June 17, 1952.
97. "Government and Veterinary Assistants," *WAP,* April 24, 1951; "Veterinary School Chief to Retire," *WAP,* June 28, 1956.
98. "Veterinary Assistants," *WAP,* July 29, 1952; "Veterinary Officer Back from UK," *WAP,* August 24, 1957.
99. "Future of Veterinary Assistants," *WAP,* July 12, 1958.
100. "Animal Health Committee," 1948–50, MAHFR 374, NAK.
101. "Rinderpest Kills Gwara Cattle," *WAP,* November 14, 1958.
102. "Outbreak of Animal Diseases," 1946–50, RP 6280, NAE.
103. "Diseases of Livestock," 1937–53, ComCol 1958, NAI.
104. "The Diseases of Animals Ordinance, 1917," CSO 14251, vol. 1, NAI.
105. "An Ordinance to Amend the Diseases of Animal Ordinance," March 21, 1941, CSO 14251, vol. 2, NAI.
106. "Trade Cattle Inoculated," *WAP,* September 25, 1956.
107. "Cattle Control Point Moved," *WAP,* December 13, 1955.
108. "Provincial Veterinary Officer of Adamawa to the Director of Veterinary Medicine," April 23, 1956, VN 13/11, vol. 5, NAK.
109. "Provincial Veterinary Officer."
110. "Veterinary Officer of Jos to the Director of Veterinary Services of the Northern Region," May 25, 1957, VN 13/11, vol. 5, NAK.
111. "Director of Veterinary Services of Northern Nigeria to the Director of Veterinary Research," June 10, 1957, VN 13/11, vol. 5, NAK.
112. "Quarantine Stations for Animals," 1929–1934, ComCol 835, NAI.
113. "Acting Secretary of Eastern Nigeria to Director of Veterinary Services," May 13, 1947, CSE 10431/2, NAE.
114. "A Law to Enable a Toll to Be Levied upon Cattle Entering the Eastern Region," 1952, MJ 141, NAE; "Veterinary Dept. to Survey Cattle Trails," *WAP,* February 16, 1958.
115. "Cattle Law in East Operates on Friday," *WAP,* March 30, 1955.
116. "Another Case of Animal Slaughtering without Permit: Old Man Fined £5 by Magistrate," *NDT,* November 25, 1942.
117. "Private Slaughter of Animals," *Daily Service,* February 13, 1943.
118. "Private Slaughter of Animals," *NDT,* February 26, 1943.

119. "Market and Slaughtering Bye-Laws," *NDT*, February 24, 1941.
120. "Lagos Town Council: Public Health Ordinance, Chapter 56: Lagos Abattoir," 1943, ComCol, 867, NAI.
121. "President of the Lagos Town Council to the Chief Secretary to the Government," December 9, 1933, ComCol, 867, NAI.
122. J. H. Best, "Cattle Trade and Trade Cattle at Umuahia," January 1940, OW 2511, NAE.
123. "Director of Veterinary Services to the Commissioner of the Colony," November 12, 1943, ComCol, 867, NAI.
124. "Director of Veterinary Services."
125. "Director of Veterinary Services."
126. "Veterinary Officer to the Medical Officer of Health," June 10, 1944, ComCol, 867, NAI.
127. "Director of Veterinary Services to the Commissioner of the Colony," September 12, 1944, ComCol, 867, NAI.
128. M. A. Shokunbi, "Slaughter House," WAP, November 28, 1955.
129. "Medical Officer of Health Issues an Invitation: Reply to Allegation Regarding Sale of 'Rotten Meat,'" *NDT*, July 29, 1946.
130. "Meat Poisoning Again?," WAP, August 10, 1953.
131. "Sale of Rotten Meat in Markets," *NDT*, July 25, 1946.
132. "Meat," *NDT*, March 24, 1943.
133. "Protect the Butchers," *NDT*, September 28, 1950.
134. "Minna Butchers Go on Strike Again," WAP, December 17, 1954.
135. "Protection of Butchers by E. A. Carr, President of the Lagos Town Council," *NDT*, October 2, 1950.
136. "Prime Agege Beef," *NDT*, March 31, 1944.
137. "Advert: Local Produce Is Vital for the War Effort," *Daily Service*, July 1, 1944.
138. "Port Lamy Fresh Meat," WAP, November 20, 1954; "Klim: Fresh Tasting Milk," *Daily Service*, March 22, 1946.

CHAPTER 2: THE LIVING MACHINES OF IMPERIALISM

1. "Mutual Admiration: Sir Adeyemo Alakija K.B.E. and His Favourite Horse 'Jubilee' Which Won the Victory Cup Race on Saturday June 22," *NDT*, June 24, 1946.
2. "Sir Adeyemo Alakija and Jubilee II," *Daily Service*, June 24, 1946.
3. "Dark Horse of the Elections," WAP, October 13, 1951; "We Suspect a Dark Horse," WAP, May 15, 1950; "The Cart before the Horse," WAP, January 8, 1955; Arnold Meme, "Backing the Wrong Horse," WAP, June 5, 1956; "Jaded Horse?," WAP, December 24, 1956; Akinola Lasekan, "Who Will Be at the Rein?," WAP, August 31, 1954; "Trojan Horse," WAP, August 16, 1957.
4. References to cavalry warfare in precolonial Nigeria can be found in the following works, among others: Robin Law, *The Horse in West African*

History: The Role of the Horse in the Societies of Pre-colonial West Africa (Oxford: Oxford University Press, 1980); Robin Law, "Horses, Firearms, and Political Power in Pre-colonial West Africa," *Past and Present* 72 (1976): 112–32; and Robin Law, "A West African Cavalry State: The Kingdom of Oyo," *Journal of African History* 16, no. 1 (1975): 1–15.

5. Wendy Griswold and Muhammed Bhadmus, "The Kano Durbar: Political Aesthetics in the Bowel of the Elephant," *American Journal of Cultural Sociology* 1, no. 1 (2013): 129.

6. "Lagos Polo Club," 1936–57, Commissioner of the Colony Office, Lagos 1812, National Archives of Nigeria, Ibadan (hereafter cited as NAI).

7. Ahmadu Bello, *My Life* (Cambridge: Cambridge University Press, 1962), 30.

8. "Christmas Day: Race in South Bornu," ca. 1903, CO 1069/66, part 2, National Archives of the United Kingdom.

9. Anthony Kirk-Greene, "Breath-Taking Durbars," in *Advancing in Good Order: Northern Nigeria Attains Independence* (Zaria: Gaskiya Corp., 1959), 16.

10. For more on the precolonial horse, see Law, *Horse in West African History*.

11. "F. D. Lugard to the Under Secretary of State for the Colonies," March 6, 1889, SNP 15, ACC no. 5, National Archives of Nigeria, Kaduna (hereafter cited as NAK).

12. A. J. N. Tremearne, *The Tailed Head-Hunters of Nigeria* (Philadelphia: J. B. Lippincott, 1912), 308.

13. Herbert C. (Johnny) Hall, *Barrack and Bush in Northern Nigeria* (London: George Allen & Unwin, 1923), 52–54.

14. Hall, 52–54.

15. Hall, 55.

16. Hall, 55–60.

17. Constance Larymore, *A Resident's Wife in Nigeria* (London: George Routledge, 1908), 268.

18. Hall, *Barrack and Bush*, 74.

19. Hall, 80.

20. Gabriel Ogundeji Ogunremi, *Counting the Camels: The Economics of Transportation in Pre-industrial Nigeria* (New York: NOK, 1982), 111.

21. Ogunremi, 111.

22. Ogunremi, 111.

23. Anthony Kirk-Greene, *Hausa Ba Dabo Ba Ne: A Collection of 500 Proverbs* (Ibadan: Oxford University Press, 1966), 8.

24. "Oh! For a Hercules, the Finest Bicycle Built To-day," WAP, January 8, 1955.

25. J. D. Falconer, *On Horseback through Nigeria* (London: T. Fisher Unwin, 1911), 8.

26. Rex Niven, *Nigerian Kaleidoscope: Memoirs of a Colonial Servant* (London: C. Hurst, 1982), 94.

27. Hall, *Barrack and Bush in Northern Nigeria*, 118.

28. Kenneth J. Bryant, "30 Years On," in *Advancing in Good Order: Northern Nigeria Attains Independence* (Zaria: Gaskiya Corp., 1959), 22.

29. Bryant, 22–23.
30. Kirk-Greene, "Breath-Taking Durbars," 119.
31. Larymore, *Resident's Wife in Nigeria*, 257.
32. "The Annual Athletic Sports of the European Cricket and Recreation Club," *Lagos Weekly Record* (hereafter cited as *LWR*), December 30, 1898.
33. "Lagosians on Dits," *Lagos Standard*, November 11, 1903; "Lagosians on Dits," *Lagos Standard*, November 13, 1907.
34. For a photo of polo on a military base, see Larymore, *Resident's Wife in Nigeria*, 8; Langa Langa (H. B. Hermon-Hodge), *Up against It in Nigeria* (London: George Allen & Unwin, 1922), 118b.
35. Langa, *Up against It in Nigeria*, 117–18.
36. Langa, 117.
37. Martin Kisch, *Letters and Sketches from Northern Nigeria* (London: Chatto & Windus, 1910), 49, 95, 96, 128, 169.
38. Anthony Kirk-Greene, *Symbol of Authority: The British District Officer in Africa* (London: I. B. Tauris, 2006), 38.
39. Hall, *Barrack and Bush*, 54.
40. Kisch, *Letters and Sketches*, 100.
41. Kisch, 65, 69, 78, 102, 104, 108, 110, 114–15, 125, 128, 134, 138, 169.
42. Hall, *Barrack and Bush*, 57.
43. Hall, 59.
44. Hall, 59.
45. Hall, 74.
46. Hall, 75.
47. Hall, 75.
48. E. C. Adams (Adamu), *Lyra Nigeriae* (London: T. Fisher Unwin, 1911), 42–44.
49. Kirk-Greene, *Symbol of Authority*, 171.
50. Kirk-Greene, 171.
51. Kirk-Greene, 171.
52. Sani Abubakar Lugga, *Dikko Dynasty: 100 Years of the Sallubawa Ruling House of Katsina, 1906–2006* (Kaduna: Lugga, 2006), 120–43.
53. Lugga, 142.
54. "The Annual Races," *LWR*, November 9, 1901.
55. "Administrator of the Colony to the Chief Secretary to the Government," March 2, 1932, CSO/26, 03634, vol. 1, NAI.
56. "The Lagos Race Club," *NDT*, April 6, 1945.
57. "Kaduna Race Club," *NDT*, December 27, 1944; "First Race Meeting at Barakin Ladi," *NDT*, November 2, 1943; "Plateau Turf Club: Spring Race Meeting," *NDT*, April 10, 1946; "Zaria Race Club's Easter Meeting," *NDT*, April 29, 1946.
58. "The Nigerian Race-Horse: A Suggestion," *NDT*, March 7, 1946.
59. "Transporting Horses or Cattle by Air," *NDT*, June 1, 1946.
60. "Brilliant Performances at Kano Race Meeting," *NDT*, October 31, 1947.
61. "The Lagos Race Club," *NDT*, April 6, 1945.

62. "Forthcoming August Meeting of the Lagos Race Club," *NDT*, August 1, 1947.
63. "Weekly Notes and Comments," *LWR*, July 19, 1919.
64. "Eastern Meeting of Lagos Race Club," *NDT*, March 31, 1941.
65. "The Lagos Races," *LWR*, October 27, 1894; "Opening of Christmas Meeting of Lagos Race Club," *NDT*, December 28, 1942. Adeyemo's stable was called Akuro. The newspaper described racing as his "hobby" and as the "Sport of Kings."
66. "Lagos Race Club Elects New Officers," *NDT*, July 20, 1946.
67. "The Lagos Race Club," *NDT*, April 6, 1945; "Opening of Christmas Meeting of Lagos Race Club," *NDT*, December 28, 1942.
68. "Lagos Race Club's October Meeting—First Day: Juno Makes Successful Debut Winning Her First Two Races," *NDT*, October 6, 1941; "Lady Alakija's Rosemary Wins Mile Race," *NDT*, December 27, 1945.
69. "Weekly Notes and Comments," *LWR*, July 19, 1919.
70. "Commissioner of the Colony to the Chief Secretary to the Government," December 17, 1931, CSO/26, 03634, vol. 1, NAI.
71. "Secretary of the LRC to the Chief Secretary to the Government of Nigeria," March 2, 1932, CSO/26: 03634, vol. 1, NAI.
72. "Horse Racing Should Pay More," *WAP*, February 16, 1952.
73. "Opening Day of Christmas Meeting: Mrs. G. Winterbottom Springs Surprise," *NDT*, December 24, 1945.
74. Helen Callaway, *Gender, Culture, and Empire: European Women in Colonial Nigeria* (Urbana: University of Illinois Press, 1987), 3–29.
75. "Second Day of Easter Race Meeting," *NDT*, April 24, 1946; "Lagos Race Club Critic Blunders," *NDT*, December 19, 1947.
76. "Opening Day of Christmas Meeting."
77. "Racing Notes and News," *Daily Service*, December 16, 1947.
78. For more on gender and sports in colonial Nigeria, see Saheed Aderinto, "Modernizing Love: Gender, Romantic Passion, and Youth Literary Culture in Colonial Nigeria," *Africa: The Journal of the International African Institute* 85, no. 3 (2015): 478–500, and Saheed Aderinto, "Empire Day in Africa: Patriotic Colonial Childhood, Imperial Spectacle, and Nationalism in Nigeria, 1905–1960," *Journal of Imperial and Commonwealth History* 46, no. 4 (2018): 731–57.
79. John Smith, *Colonial Cadet in Nigeria* (Durham, NC: Duke University Press, 1968), 47.
80. "Lagos Race Meeting Today," *NDT*, August 1, 1942.
81. "Photo of C. M. Booth and Spitfire," *NDT*, April 1, 1941; "August Meeting of Lagos Race Club: Record Number of Entries: Brilliant Racing Foreshadowed," *NDT*, August 2, 1943; "Photo of Dakota," January 15, 1947.
82. "Record Crowds Watch Zouzou Carry Off Open Miles Purse," *NDT*, August 2, 1943; Interested Onlooker, "Polo in Lagos," *NDT*, November 20, 1943; "Golden Miller Creates Sensation in Maiden Four Furlongs Race,"

NDT, April 3, 1944; "Polo Club Meeting at Race Club," *NDT*, May 24, 1944; "Mrs Alakija's Rosemary Wins Open Mile Race," *NDT*, July 31, 1944; "Trumpet Wins Open Mile Race," *NDT*, March 28, 1945; "Poker Wins Race for Chairman's Prize," *NDT*, April 9, 1945.

83. "August Meeting of Lagos Race Club," *NDT*, August 2, 1943.

84. "End of Christmas Meeting of Lagos Race Club," *NDT*, January 11, 1943.

85. "New Horses Create Excitement among Punters," *WAP*, August 6, 1946.

86. See Hasta, "1936 Racing in Northern Nigeria," *Nigerian Field* 6, no. 2 (1937): 85–87.

87. "Lagos Race Club: Classification of Horses," *NDT*, September 5, 1947; "From the Editor's Bag: Racing Rules by A Turf-Enthusiast," *NDT*, November 22, 1947.

88. "Questionable Performance at Races by Race-Goer," *NDT*, August 7, 1947.

89. F. de F. Daniel, "The Horse in Native Hands," *Nigerian Field* 5, no. 2 (1936): 54.

90. "Meeting of Race Horse Owners," *NDT*, November 24, 1944.

91. F. R. C. Darcher, "The Nigerian Race-Horse: A Suggestion," *NDT*, March 7, 1946.

92. "Crack Horse Bought for £800," *NDT*, May 12, 1947.

93. Hall, *Barrack and Bush*, 75.

94. Obafemi Awolowo, *Awo: The Autobiography of Chief Obafemi Awolowo* (Cambridge: Cambridge University Press, 1960), 84.

95. "Nigerian St. George Now to Face the New Dragon," *NDT*, August 10, 1951; "The Desperate Rider," *NDT*, March 16, 1954.

96. Lasekan, "Who Will Be at the Rein?"

97. "New Kano Air Terminal," *WAP*, May 6, 1957.

98. Hall, *Barrack and Bush*, 76.

99. Larymore, *Resident's Wife in Nigeria*, 27.

100. "Adunni Oluwole on Horse," *WAP*, January 30, 1956.

101. "Miss Adunni Oluwole on Horse Back," *WAP*, August 12, 1954.

102. G. O. Olusanya, "Olaniwun Adunni Oluwole," in *Nigerian Women in Historical Perspective*, ed. Bolanle Awe (Ibadan: Bookcraft, 1992), 122–31.

103. Larymore, *Resident's Wife in Nigeria*, 80.

104. Kirk-Greene, "Breath-Taking Durbars," 16.

105. Andrew Apter, *The Pan-African Nation: Oil and the Spectacle of Culture in Nigeria* (Chicago: University of Chicago Press, 2005), 167–99.

106. Apter, 167–99.

107. Callaway, *Gender, Culture, and Empire*, 57–59.

108. Apter, *Pan-African Nation*, chap. 5.

109. "Royal Visit: Horses Arriving in Kaduna," December 1955 to February 1956, VN 10/7D, NAK.

110. "92 Horses Bound for Kaduna," *WAP*, January 10, 1956; "Over 50,000 to Watch Durbar at Kaduna," *WAP*, January 26, 1956; "Queen's 1956 Tour of Nigeria," accessed on May 21, 2018, https://www.britishpathe.com

/workspaces/2e6592077f92958a84d91602b25fa58d/Queen-s-1956-Tour-of
-Nigeria.

111. Kirk-Greene, "Breath-Taking Durbars," 15.

112. "Preparing for the Durbar: The Great Trek Begins in North," *Nigerian Citizen*, January 14, 1956.

113. "Report on the Royal Durbar," March 1, 1956, VN 10/7D, NAK.

114. "Report on the Royal Durbar."

115. "Preparing for the Durbar."

116. "Preparing for the Durbar."

117. "Director of Veterinary Service to the Veterinary Officer," February 26, 1956, VN 10/7, NAK.

118. Bello, *My Life*, 175.

119. Niven, *Nigerian Kaleidoscope*, 260.

120. "Examination of Horses for the Queen's Visit," February 1, 1956, VN 10/7D, NAK.

121. Bello, *My Life*, 81; Sharwood-Smith, *Diary of a Colonial Wife*, 138; Kirk-Greene, "Breath-Taking Durbars," 20.

122. Bello, *My Life*, 81.

123. Andrew Apter, "On Imperial Spectacle: The Dialectics of Seeing in Colonial Nigeria," *Comparative Studies in Society and History* 44, no. 3 (2002): 564–96.

124. Kirk-Greene, "Breath-Taking Durbars," 20.

125. Kirk-Greene, 16.

126. Niven, *Nigerian Kaleidoscope*, 265.

CHAPTER 3: "DOGS ARE THE MOST USEFUL ANIMALS"

1. "S. S. Oyetunde and Three Others to the Chief Commissioner, Senior Resident, Medical Officer of Health, Senior District Officer, and Olubadan in Council," January 28, 1942, MLG 16770/7, National Archives of Nigeria, Ibadan (hereafter cited as NAI).

2. Ulli Beier, "Yoruba Attitude to Dogs," *Odu* 7 (1959): 31–37.

3. Beier, 31–32.

4. Ulli Beier, *The Hunter Thinks the Monkey Is Not Wise . . . The Monkey Is Wise, but He Has His Own Logic: A Selection of Essays*, ed. Wale Ogundele, African Studies, no. 59 (Bayreuth, Germany: Bayreuth University, 2001), 77.

5. Beier, 77–80.

6. Dixon Denham and Hugh Clapperton, *Narrative of Travels and Discoveries in Northern and Central Africa*, vol. 1. (London: John Murray, 1826), 198.

7. Constance Larymore, *A Resident's Wife in Nigeria* (London: George Routledge, 1908), 210.

8. O. Temple, *Tribes, Provinces, Emirates and States of the Northern Provinces of Nigeria* (Cape Town: Argus, 1919), 19, 32, 44, 46, 65, 81, 110, 191, 262, 275, 276, 277.

9. C. K. Meek, *Law and Authority in a Nigerian Tribe* (Oxford: Oxford University Press, 1937), 27, 100.

10. Meek, 103–4.

11. Beier, "Yoruba Attitude to Dogs," 31–37; J. Olowo Ojoade, "Nigerian Cultural Attitudes to the Dog," in *Signifying Animals: Human Meaning in the Natural World*, ed. Roy Willis (London: Routledge, 1994), 215–21.

12. Beier, "Yoruba Attitude to Dogs," 31.

13. "Leopards at Abeokuta," *Nigerian Pioneer*, May 19, 1916.

14. "Deji of Akure to the Senior District Officer of Ondo Division," February 18, 1948, Ondo Div 482, NAI.

15. A. J. N. Tremearne, *The Tailed Head-Hunters of Nigeria* (Philadelphia: J. B. Lippincott, 1912), 136.

16. Tremearne, 241.

17. G. T. Basden, *Among the Ibos of Nigeria* (London: Seeley, Service, 1921), 56.

18. C. K. Meek, *A Sudanese Kingdom: An Ethnographical Study of the Jukun-Speaking Peoples of Nigeria* (London: Kegan Paul, 1931), 148, 223; Meek, *Law and Authority in a Nigerian Tribe*, 55, 153, 154, 218, 305; Arthur Leonard, *The Lower Niger and Its Tribes* (London: Macmillan, 1906), 454; Amaury P. Talbot, *Life in Southern Nigeria: The Magic, Beliefs and Customs of the Ibibio Tribe* (London: Macmillan, 1923), xvii; O. Temple, *Tribes, Provinces, Emirates and States of the Northern Provinces of Nigeria* (Cape Town: Argus, 1919), 20, 48, 58, 61, 105, 106, 137, 147, 175.

19. Sandra T. Barnes, ed., *Africa's Ogun: Old World and New* (Bloomington: Indiana University Press, 1989).

20. Beier, "Yoruba Attitude to Dogs," 31–37.

21. Beier, 37; Ojoade, "Nigerian Cultural Attitudes to the Dog," 215–21.

22. "Motor Drivers Mark Anniversary with Killing of Dogs," *Daily Service*, January 11, 1952.

23. Janheinz Jahn, *Through African Doors: Experiences and Encounters in West Africa*, trans. Oliver Coburn (New York: Grove, 1960), 59–60.

24. Beier, *The Hunter Thinks the Monkey Is Not Wise*, 77–80.

25. Meek, *Sudanese Kingdom*, 291.

26. Mason Begho, *The Dog-Bite Magistrate: His Struggles* (Lagos: Daily Times), 1988.

27. Lance Van Sittert and Sandra Swart, eds., *Canis Africanis: A Dog History of Southern Africa* (Leiden: Brill, 2008), 34.

28. Frederick Lugard, *The Diaries of Lord Lugard*, 4 vols., ed. Margery Perham and Mary Bull (Evanston, IL: Northwestern University Press, 1959), 67; Langa Langa (H. B. Hermon-Hodge), *Up against It in Nigeria* (London: George Allen & Unwin, 1922), 15; Larymore, *Resident's Wife in Nigeria*, 221–26.

29. Lassie Fitz-Henry, *African Dust* (London: Macmillan, 1959), 15–17.

30. Joan Sharwood-Smith, *Diary of a Colonial Wife: An African Experience* (London: I. B. Tauris, 1992), 81.

31. Fitz-Henry, *African Dust*, 15.
32. Facebook communication with Derek Miles Greening, March 2, 2019.
33. Larymore, *Resident's Wife in Nigeria*, 221.
34. Larymore, 221.
35. *Annual Report of the Department of Veterinary Research of the Federation of Nigeria, 1954–1955* (Lagos: Government Printer, 1957), 14.
36. Larymore, *Resident's Wife in Nigeria*, 222.
37. "C. T. Lawrence and His Dog," CO 1069/66, pt. 3, National Archives of the United Kingdom (hereafter cited as NAUK).
38. "Walter Egerton, Colonial Officers, and Dogs," ca. 1904, CO 1069/59, NAUK.
39. "Family History of Francis and Betty Humphreys," accessed August 4, 2019, http://www.mueller-humphreys.de/Humphreys/DicksonElizabeth/selbst/Nigeria/NigeriaFrankFoiE.html.
40. Tremearne, *Tailed Head-Hunters of Nigeria*, 32.
41. Martin Kisch, *Letters and Sketches from Northern Nigeria* (London: Chatto & Windus, 1910), 10.
42. Langa, *Up against It in Nigeria*, 123.
43. *Annual Report of the Department of Veterinary Research*, 11, 24.
44. Larymore, *Resident's Wife in Nigeria*, 221.
45. Lugard, *Dairies of Lord Lugard*, 61.
46. W. R. Crocker, *Nigeria: A Critique of British Colonial Administration* (London: George Allen & Unwin, 1936), 50–51.
47. Langa, *Up against It in Nigeria*, 123–24.
48. Crocker, *Nigeria*, 51.
49. Larymore, *Resident's Wife in Nigeria*, 134.
50. Larymore, 134–35.
51. "Walter Egerton, Colonial Officers, and Dogs."
52. "Three Strokes of the Cane and £120 Fine or 12 Months Jail for Pottery Officer Gregory," *West African Pilot* (hereafter cited as WAP), June 30, 1954.
53. Langa, *Up against It in Nigeria*, 92.
54. Langa, 123–24.
55. "Three Strokes of the Cane."
56. Begho, *Dog-Bite Magistrate*, 60.
57. Begho, 60.
58. Begho, 60.
59. "Dog Which Bit Hausa Trader Was Flown from UK with £100," WAP, June 28, 1954.
60. "British Official (Corporal Punishment)," accessed on May 30, 2018, https://hansard.parliament.uk/Commons/1954-07-07/debates/eoca8013-e61b-4b6d-8932-cb82ac67e4a6/BritishOfficial(CorporalPunishment); "Britain Told Matchets and Knives," *Daily Service*, July 10, 1954; "Questions and Answers," WAP, August 21, 1954.

61. "The Defence Was a Tissue of Lies," *Daily Service*, August 1, 1954.
62. "Britain Told Matchets and Knives."
63. "Dog-Bite Judgement," WAP, July 13, 1954.
64. Basden, *Among the Ibos of Nigeria*, 56; Tremearne, *Tailed Head-Hunters of Nigeria*, 229.
65. Langa, *Up against It in Nigeria*, 28.
66. Langa, 124.
67. Crocker, *Nigeria*, 51.
68. Sharwood-Smith, *Diary of a Colonial Wife*, 81.
69. Fitz-Henry, *African Dust*, 15.
70. For more on rabies, see chapter 5.
71. Carolyn Johnson, ed., *Harmattan, a Wind of Change: Life and Letters from Northern Nigeria at the End of Empire* (London: Radcliffe, 2010), 42.
72. "Dog Show Held in Aid of the Blind," *Daily Service*, July 8, 1953.
73. "Chief Secretary to the Government of Nigeria to L. F. Crossland and Co.," August 29, 1946, CSO 47543, NAI.
74. "Matobs Stores to the Chief Secretary to the Government," February 26, 1948, CSO 47543, NAI.
75. "Dog in Complete 'Suit' for Festival," *Daily Service*, July 28, 1949.
76. Oye Shobo, "Emotional Dog!," *Daily Service*, July 17, 1954.
77. "Man Earns Fine for Dog Licence Default," WAP, July 27, 1955.
78. "Extract from Minutes of Ibadan Native Administration Divisional Council Meeting Held at Map Native Court No. 3 on 8th April 1942," Oyo ProF 1482, NAI.
79. "Extract from the Minutes of the Township Advisory Board," May 5, 1942, Kano ProF 749, National Archives of Nigeria, Kaduna (hereafter cited as NAK).
80. "Acting District Officer of Ife-Ilesha Division to the Senior Resident of Oyo Province," March 22, 1937, Ife Div 425, vol. 1, NAI.
81. "Dog License in Abeokuta Province," February 18, 1954, Abe ProF 252, NAI.
82. "ADO of Jemaa Division to the Resident of Plateau Province," April 14, 1941, Jos ProF 1795.
83. "Dog Badges in Niger Province, December 1, 1940," Niger ProF 615, NAK.
84. "The Oni of Ife to the District Officer of Ife Division," January 17, 1941, Ife Div 425, vol. 1, NAI.
85. "Secretary of Southern Provinces to the Chief Secretary to the Government," May 1, 1937, Ife Div 425, vol. 1, NAI.
86. "Acting Resident of Southern Provinces to the Resident of Ondo Province," March 21, 1939, Ondo Div OD 482, NAI.
87. "District Officer of Ondo to the Resident of Ondo," April 10, 1941, Ondo Div OD 482, NAI.
88. "District Officer of Ibadan to Resident of Oyo Province," April 9, 1942, Ibadan Div 1668, NAI.

89. Dogs Ordinance in Northern Nigeria, 1941, Zaria ProF 2307, vol. 2, NAK.
90. "Resident of Kano to the Kano Township Advisory Board," June 1, 1940, Kano ProF 749, NAK.
91. Dogs (Prevention of Rabies) Law, 1953, Zaria ProF 2307, vol. 2, NAK.
92. "Acting Resident of Calabar Province to the Secretary of the Eastern Provinces," February 24, 1942, CSE 12/1/352, National Archives of Nigeria, Enugu (hereafter cited as NAE).
93. "Resident of Ogoja Province to the Secretary of the Southern Provinces," June 5, 1937, OG ProF 131, NAK.
94. "Resident of Onitsha Province to the District Officers," February 3, 1942, ONDIST 12/1/774, NAE.
95. "Resident of Onitsha Province to the District Officer," January 22, 1942, ONDIST 12/1/774, NAE.
96. Dogs Ordinance: Eastern Provinces, June 4, 1940, MINJUST 2/1/3, NAE.
97. "Chief Secretary to the Government to the Crown Agents for the Colonies," February 28, 1928, CSO 26/21279, vol. 1, NAI.
98. "Acting Civil Secretary of the Northern Region to the Residents of Northern Provinces," November 5, 1953, Zaria ProF 2307, vol. 2, NAK.
99. "Resident of Plateau Province to the Civil Secretary of Northern Region," November 12, 1953, VN 31/2/193, NAK.
100. "ADO of Jemaa Division to the Resident of Plateau Province," April 14, 1941, Jos ProF 1795, NAK.
101. "The Dog Owners to the District Officers," June 28, 1939, Iba Div 1668, NAI.
102. Sandra T. Barnes, *Patrons and Power: Creating a Political Community in Metropolitan Lagos* (Bloomington: Indiana University Press, 1986), 40.
103. "Oluwo of Iwo to the District Officer of Ibadan Division," May 4, 1942, Ibadan Div 1668, NAI.
104. "Night Guards in Ondo," December 2, 1949, Ondo ProF 3271, NAI.
105. "Hunters in Ijebu Province," *Daily Service*, February 1, 1952.
106. "Dog Licence and Farmers," *NDT*, October 9, 1947.

CHAPTER 4: THE NIGERIAN POLITICAL ZOO

1. Increase H. E. Coker, *Landmarks of the Nigerian Press: An Outline of the Origins and Development of the Newspaper Press in Nigeria, 1859 to 1965* (Lagos: Daily Times, 1968), 44.
2. "Beware of the Opportunist Rogue This Time," WAP, April 9, 1956.
3. Olujide Somolu, *Olumo: The Mystique of an Alluring Symbol; The Memoirs of the Honourable Justice Olujide Somolu, Chief Justice of the Western State, 1967–1971*, ed. Kayode Somolu, Femi Somolu, and Seke Somolu (Lagos: Florence & Lambard, 2011), 130.
4. Coker, *Landmarks of the Nigerian Press*, 44.
5. "Dawn of a New Era," WAP, June 3, 1966.
6. "Lasekan Detained," WAP, June 6, 1966.
7. Coker, *Landmarks of the Nigerian Press*, 44.

8. Dele Jegede, "Art in Contemporary Africa," in *Africa*, vol. 5: *Contemporary Africa*, ed. Toyin Falola (Durham, NC: Carolina Academic, 2003), 706.

9. James S. Coleman, *Nigeria: Background to Nationalism* (Berkeley: University of California Press, 1958); Richard L. Sklar, *Nigerian Political Parties: Power in an Emergent African Nation* (Princeton, NJ: Princeton University Press, 1963).

10. Nina Emma Mba, *Nigerian Women Mobilized: Women's Political Activity in Southern Nigeria, 1900–1965* (Berkeley: University of California Press, 1982); Cheryl Johnson-Odim and Nina Emma Mba, *For Women and the Nation: Funmilayo Ransome-Kuti of Nigeria* (Urbana: University of Illinois Press, 1997).

11. Harcourt Fuller, *Building the Ghanaian Nation-State: Kwame Nkrumah's Symbolic Nationalism* (New York: Palgrave Macmillan, 2014).

12. Olu Oguibe, "Appropriation as Nationalism in Modern African Art," *Third Text* 16, no. 3 (2002): 243–59; Moyo Okediji, *Western Frontiers of African Art* (Rochester, NY: University of Rochester Press, 2011); Chika Okeke-Agulu, *Postcolonial Modernism: Art and Decolonization in Twentieth-Century Nigeria* (Durham, NC: Duke University Press, 2015); Sylvester Ogbechie, *Ben Enwonwu: The Making of an African Modernist* (Rochester, NY: University of Rochester Press, 2008); Tejumola Olaniyan, "Cartooning Nigerian Anticolonial Nationalism," in *Images and Empires: Visuality in Colonial and Postcolonial Africa*, ed. Paul Stuart Landau (Berkeley: University of California Press, 2002), 124–40; O. A. Gbadegesin, "The Intersection of Modern Art, Anthropology, and International Politics in Colonial Nigeria, 1910–1914" (master's thesis, Emory University, 2007); Abayomi Ola, *Satires of Power in Yoruba Visual Culture* (Durham, NC: Carolina Academic, 2013).

13. Okeke-Agulu, *Postcolonial Modernism*, 64.

14. Henry John Drewal, *African Artistry: Techniques and Aesthetics in Yoruba Sculpture* (Atlanta: High Museum of Art, 1980); Rowland Abiodun, *Yoruba Art and Language: Seeking the African in African Art* (Cambridge: Cambridge University Press, 2014); Babatunde Lawal, *The Gelede Spectacle: Art, Gelede and Social Harmony in an African Culture* (Seattle: University of Washington Press, 1996); Aderonke Adesanya, *Carving Wood, Making History: The Fakeye Family, Modernity, and Yoruba Woodcarving* (Trenton, NJ: Africa World, 2012).

15. Lasekan, *Nigeria in Cartoons*.

16. "Akinola Lasekan Publishes 50 Cartoons Showing All Aspects of Nigerian Life," WAP, June 14, 1944.

17. "Lasekan to Exhibit at Enugu," WAP, April 9, 1956.

18. "Nigerian 'St. George' Returns from Historic Battle," November 26, 1958; "Nigerian St. George Now to Face the New Dragon," WAP, August 10, 1951; "Another St. George Goes into Action," WAP, July 12, 1957.

19. "The Battle Royal Ahead," WAP, June 5, 1952.
20. "Gold Coast Is Ready!," WAP, October 29, 1949; "Banquets to Britain This Time," WAP, May 7, 1953.
21. "Exposing the Real Wolf," WAP, December 28, 1954; "Truth Will Out," WAP, January 7, 1949.
22. For examples of idiomatic expressions in the WAP that also shaped visual narratives of nationalism, see "A Wild Goose Chase to Africa," September 22, 1950; "Dark House of the Elections," October 13, 1951; "Hunting for a Scape Goat," January 11, 1951; "We Suspect a Dark House," May 15, 1950; "Birds of the Same Feather!," September 14, 1950; and "The Cat Is Out of the Bag!," April 14, 1951.
23. "Everybody Is Doing It," WAP, September 2, 1949.
24. Ola, Satires of Power.
25. Paula Ben-Amos, "Men and Animals in Benin Art," Man 11, no. 2 (1976): 234.
26. Benedict Anderson, Imagined Communities: Reflections on the Origin and Spread of Nationalism (London: Verso, 1983), 44–45.
27. "The Fateful Meal," WAP, May 17, 1949; "The Parting Member," WAP, February 28, 1949; "Nigeria for Sale!," WAP, March 12, 1949; "The Order of the Day," WAP, March 19, 1949.
28. "Leaving Us at the Mercy of the Big Wolf?," WAP, September 4, 1951.
29. "The Problem Is, the Lion Must Live!," WAP, September 8, 1949.
30. "Thank You, Good Old Friend, Goad Them to Fight to Death, So I Can Feed Fat on Their Carcasses," WAP, October 22, 1949.
31. "Domination?," WAP, December 20, 1952.
32. "Yorubaland at the Mercy of the Action Group," WAP, October 1, 1952. A couple of cartoons also depict the AG's violence against political communities dominated by the NCNC within the Western Region: "I Hear All You Say about Your Innocence, but the Question Is, What Must I Eat?," WAP, June 13, 1955; "New Head-Ache for Selfish People," WAP, November 11, 1955.
33. "Misadventure!," WAP, March 23, 1949.
34. Coleman, Nigeria, 356.
35. Sklar, Nigerian Political Parties, 76.
36. "Fateful Meal."
37. "The Parting Member," WAP, February 28, 1949.
38. "Order of the Day."
39. "What Do We Hope to Gain from Zik's Imprisonment?," WAP, November 6, 1951.
40. "The Great Sequel!," WAP, May 10, 1954.
41. "Gracious! I Asked You to Bring Peace-Makers and Not War-Mongers!," WAP, September 29, 1949. A similar cartoon depicts the colonial government fleeing after being threatened by the All Northern People's Conference. "Northern Nigerian Lion Awakes," WAP, August 23, 1949.

42. "Great Sequel!"
43. "Northern Nigerian Lion Awakes"; "A Pleasant Surprise," WAP, October 23, 1953.
44. "The Lioness of Lisabiland," WAP, February 22, 1949.
45. "Him They Want to Sacrifice as Oblation for Them," WAP, March 3, 1952.
46. "Nigeria for Sale!"
47. "Is Might Right?," WAP, March 15, 1949.
48. "Nigeria and the Danger of the Big Wolf," WAP, September 12, 1952.
49. "Hello Dear, So You've Grown Fatter, Thank God," WAP, September 21, 1955.
50. "Unemployed Nigerians Must Be Helped and Protected," WAP, March 20, 1953.
51. "Nigerians Must Enjoy Universal Adult Suffrage, Says NCNC," WAP, September 2, 1953. An additional cartoon in this category is "Nigerian Teachers' Problem," WAP, July 30, 1949.
52. "When You with Such a Long Neck Grumble about the Height of the Fruits, I Wonder What You Expect Me to Do," WAP, April 26, 1949.
53. "Don't Blame Me Comrades, Blame Your Diminutive Stature," WAP, October 30, 1952; "Comrades It Would Be Our Greatest Achievement So Far, If We Could Surround and Crush Him," WAP, October 6, 1949; "Making a Mountain Out of a Molehill," WAP, March 11, 1949.
54. "Provided You Don't Burst before Then," WAP, February 12, 1953.
55. "Cousin, Can't You Get Something More Profitable to Do, than Being Always on My Trail?," WAP, October 30, 1951.
56. "Thanks to the NCNC," WAP, February 16, 1949.
57. "I Have Learnt That It Takes More Than Chronic Barking to Get Things Done," WAP, March 23, 1951; "Barking to Death Is Some Action Anyway," WAP, June 19, 1951.
58. "Everybody Is Doing It"; "Reason for Becoming a Race of Lawyers?," WAP, September 12, 1949.
59. "Everybody Is Doing It."
60. "Reason for Becoming a Race of Lawyers?"
61. "The 'Innocent' Devil," WAP, February 2, 1949.
62. "Portrait of a Nigerian Reactionary Politician," WAP, October 11, 1951.
63. "The Pity Is No Zebra Ever Survives an Encounter with the Tiger!," WAP, May 11, 1953.
64. "Pity Is No Zebra Ever Survives."
65. "Poor Conceited Giraffe!," WAP, June 10, 1951.
66. "Why the Creation of More States Is Imperative," WAP, June 19, 1957.
67. "The Beast of Burden!," WAP, May 23, 1949.
68. "Imperialist's 'Grand March' to Freedom Land with Colonial Nigeria!," WAP, December 31, 1951.
69. "Why the Creation of More States."

70. "The Desperate Rider," WAP, March 31, 1954; "Who Will Be at the Rein?," WAP, October 6, 1954; "Talking of the New Constitution," WAP, March 24, 1952; "The Cat Is Out of the Bag!!!," WAP, February 23, 1953; "But the People Can See the Inner Stuff," WAP, February 27, 1953.

71. "The Problem of Killing Two Birds with One Stone," WAP, February 9, 1949.

72. "It All Depends on How Our Leaders Interpret This," WAP, January 15, 1957.

73. "Gold Coast Is Ready!"

74. "The Eagle That Has Outgrown the Confines of a Cage!," WAP, May 25, 1957.

75. "Powerful Wings for the Great Flight," WAP, May 24, 1958.

76. "To Sing Again?," WAP, April 29, 1955. Another presentation of birds in Lasekan's work is "The Best Way to Dispose of You Little Rascal Is to Knock You Cold against This Rock," WAP, August 23, 1955.

77. "To Sing Again?"

78. "The Problem Bird in the Air Again!," WAP, March 29, 1949.

79. "Talking Is Some Form of Action," WAP, January 1, 1955.

80. "NEPU's Trouble Is Nigeria's Trouble," WAP, August 23, 1951; "A Prayer Answered," WAP, October 10, 1950.

81. "Plans and Counter-Plans," WAP, July 12, 1955.

82. For the fable, see "Aesop for Children," Library of Congress, http://read .gov/aesop/o48.html.

83. "The Frogs Once Demanded a More Dynamic King than the Log and They Were Given the Stork!," WAP, October 8, 1952.

84. "The Cock Never Fails—Vote for Him Always," WAP, September 27, 1954.

85. "The Cock Triumphant," WAP, November 15, 1954.

86. "Kill the Serpent," WAP, April 23, 1951.

87. "Not Separatist Propitiation, but Sincere Patriotism Can Do It," WAP, June 14, 1951.

88. "NCNC's Guarantee of Religious Freedom," WAP, April 11, 1953.

89. "Not Separatist Propitiation."

90. Nnamdi Azikiwe, My Odyssey: An Autobiography (New York: Praeger, 1970), 352.

CHAPTER 5: "BEWARE OF DOGS"

1. Petition by E. O. Daniel, Esq., General Secretary of the Nigeria SPCA, December 17, 1948, Commissioner of the Colony Office, Lagos (hereafter cited as ComCol) 2667/S.I, vol. 1, National Archives of Nigeria, Ibadan (hereafter cited as NAI).

2. L. R. Boulger and J. Hardy, "Rabies in Nigeria," West African Medical Journal 11, no. 6 (1960): 224.

3. "Some Hints about Rabid Dogs by Mr. M. A. A. Odujukan, General Secretary of the Medical and Health Association," Daily Service, April 4, 1945.

4. Boulger and Hardy, "Rabies in Nigeria," 225–26.
5. Jarlath Umoh and E. D. Belino, "Rabies in Nigeria: A Historical Review," *International Journal of Zoonoses* 6 (1979): 41–48; M. O. Ojo and A. Adeoye, "Rabies in a Nigerian Dwarf Goat," *Bulletin of Epizootic Diseases of Africa* 15 (1967): 409–10; L. R. Boulger and J. S. Porterfield, "Isolation of a Virus from Nigerian Fruit Bats," *Transactions of the Royal Society of Tropical Medicine and Hygiene* 52, no. 5 (1958): 421–24.
6. Akin L. Mabogunje, *Urbanization in Nigeria* (London: University of London Press, 1968), 257.
7. "Notes in Connexion with the Cases of Mr. W. B. Thomson and Lieutenant-Colonel H. D. Foulkes, Who Were Bitten by a Mad Dog at Maiduguri on Friday, February 16, 1917," N.650/1917, NAI.
8. "Frederick Lugard to the Secretary of State for the Colonies," March 9, 1917, N.650/1917, NAI.
9. "Director of Medical and Sanitary Services to the Chief Secretary to the Government of Nigeria," April 20, 1926, CSO 26/15842, NAI.
10. "Chief Secretary to the Government of Nigeria to the Secretary of Southern Provinces," May 20, 1926, CSO 26/15842, NAI.
11. See "Anti-Rabic Treatment for Individual Cases, 1926–1930," CSO 26/15842, NAI.
12. "Secretary of State for the Colonies to the Governor of Nigeria," September 11, 1926, CSO 26/15842, NAI.
13. "Director of Medical and Sanitary Services to the Chief Secretary to the Government of Nigeria," October 3, 1926, CSO 26/15842, NAI.
14. Boulger and Hardy, "Rabies in Nigeria," 225.
15. "Inspector-General of Police to the Chief Secretary to the Government," July 28, 1952, VN 31/2, vol. 1, National Archives of Nigeria, Kaduna (hereafter cited as NAK).
16. "Acting Director of Veterinary Services to the Civil Secretary of Northern Nigeria," April 8, 1952, VN 31/2, vol. 1, NAK.
17. "Resident of Bauchi to the Station Magistrate of Jos," February 9, 1925, Jos ProF 887, NAK.
18. "The Ministry of Health to the Crown Agents for the Colonies," June 2, 1927, CSO 26/15842, NAI.
19. "Acting Chief Secretary to the Government to the Secretary of Western Provinces," March 13, 1941, B.P. 1033, NAI.
20. "Beware of Dogs," *Daily Service*, March 26, 1945.
21. "Notice: Free Vaccination of Dogs against Rabies," *WAP*, January 24, 1959.
22. "Dog Owners Warned," *WAP*, July 21, 1959.
23. "Lagos Town Council: Rabies," *NDT*, January 5, 1945.
24. "Medical Officer of Health to the Senior District Officer of Maiduguri," March 24, 1945, Kano ProF 4211, NAK.
25. "The Danger and Prevention of Rabies: A Broadcast Talk to Schools by Dr. I. Ladipo Oluwole, Medical Officer of Health," *NDT*, March 17, 1945.

26. "Medical Officer of Health to Mr. Egem Okonkwo," October 30, 1948, ComCol 2667/S.I, vol. 1, NAI.
27. "Rules Made under the Dogs Ordinance (No. 15 of 1942)," ComCol 2667/S.I, vol. 1, NAI.
28. "Notice: Rabies in Dogs in Lagos," *NDT*, February 26, 1945.
29. "Rules Made under the Dogs Ordinance (No. 15 of 1942)," *Daily Service*, September 9, 1946.
30. "Rabies in Calabar," *WAP*, January 29, 1958.
31. "Dogs Ordinance, Chapter 56," *WAP*, September 19, 1958.
32. "Dog Owners Warned," *WAP*, July 21, 1959.
33. "Menace of Rabies: Drastic Disease Requires Drastic Remedies," *Daily Service*, April 3, 1945.
34. "Control of Dogs Rules and Orders Made by Native Authorities: Colony," MLG (W) 1, 16770/8, NAI.
35. "Order Made under the Dogs Ordinance (Chapter 56)," *Daily Service*, March 9, 1951.
36. "Notice," *Daily Service*, April 16, 1943.
37. "Rabies and Control in Lagos, May 1954," ComCol 2667/S.I, vol. 3, NAI.
38. "Lieutenant Colonel to the Administrator to the Colony," April 20, 1954, ComCol 2667/S.I, vol. 3, NAI.
39. "Medical Officer of Health to the Lieutenant Colonel, April 29, 1954," ComCol 2667/S.I, vol. 3, NAI.
40. "Outbreak of Rabies in Afikpo," *Daily Service*, January 9, 1950; "Beware of Dogs."
41. "Beware of Dogs."
42. "Rabies in Lagos Township," *NDT*, September 18, 1945.
43. "Rabies in Lagos Township," *NDT*, September 11, 1946.
44. "Rabies," *NDT*, March 31, 1945.
45. "Rabies Epidemic: Information Bulletin No. 2," *WAP*, December 8, 1958.
46. "Rabies: Arun Kogbogun" [meaning "Rabies: An Incurable Disease"], May 1947, MLG (W) 1, 16770/8, NAI.
47. "Assistant District Officer of Lafia to the Medical Officer of Makurdi," July 1, 1949, Lafia Div 255, NAK.
48. "Outbreak of Rabies: New Instruction, May 1, 1940," ComCol 2667/S.I, vol. 3, NAI.
49. "Danger and Prevention of Rabies."
50. "Extract from Minutes of Ilesha Executive Committee Held on March 3, 1942," Oyo ProF 1482, NAI.
51. "Medical Officer of Health to the District Officer of Zaria," November 6, 1945, Zaria Div, NAI.
52. "J. A. Griffiths, Acting Chief Veterinary Officer to the Secretary of the Northern Provinces," July 26, 1935, Jos ProF 887, NAK.
53. "J. A. Griffiths, Acting Chief Veterinary Officer."
54. "Gazette Notice No. 572: Medical: Anti-Rabic Vaccination of Dogs, 1936," CSO 30945, NAI.

55. "Man Leaves Infected Dog for MOH," *Daily Service*, October 13, 1949.

56. "Owner of Infected Dog Sees MOH," *Daily Service*, October 21, 1949.

57. "Veterinary Officer to the Senior Medical Officer," October 29, 1947, Katsina ProF OFF/18, NAK.

58. "Beware of Dogs."

59. "Wild Dogs in Sabongeri, Kano," *NDT*, September 1, 1947.

60. "Medical Officer of Health to the President of the Lagos Town Council," July 14, 1954, ComCol 2667/S.I, vol. 3, NAI.

61. "Rabies in Calabar," October 31, 1946, Cal ProF 3/1/1291, National Archives of Nigeria, Enugu.

62. "Port Health Officer to the Health Superintendent," July 14, 1954, ComCol 2667/S.I, vol. 3, NAI.

63. "Notice by Local Authority Office, Kano," April 7, 1942, Kano ProF 749, NAK.

64. "Governor of Nigeria to District and Resident Officers," September 2, 1940, CSO 26/15842, NAI.

65. "Medical Officer of Health to the District and Resident Officers," September 2, 1940, CSO 26/15842, NAI.

66. "E. V. R. Hackett to the Medical Officer of Health," July 22, 1954, ComCol 2667/S.I, vol. 3, NAI.

67. "Assistant Superintendent of Police of Northern Nigeria to the President of Jos Town Council," February 17, 1950, Jos ProF 887, NAK.

68. Mason Begho, *The Dog-Bite Magistrate: His Struggles* (Lagos: Daily Times, 1988), 21.

69. "Man and Wife on Assault Charge," *NDT*, January 22, 1955.

70. "Irving and Bonnar to the Administrator of the Colony," September 13, 1954, ComCol 2667/S.I, vol. 3, NAI.

71. "Medical Officer of Health to Irving and Bonnar," September 18, 1954, ComCol 2667/S.I, vol. 3, NAI.

72. "Architect of PWD to the Medical Officer of Health," May 13, 1954, ComCol 2667/S.I, vol. 3, NAI.

73. "Thomas Dustin to Jos Township Authority," June 14, 1938, Jos ProF 887, NAK.

74. "Commissioner of Police of Plateau Province to the Senior Medical Officer," June 3, 1934, Jos ProF 887, NAK.

75. "Notice: Rabies in Dogs in Lagos," *NDT*, March 26, 1945.

76. "Senior Veterinary Officer to the Resident of Kano Province," July 6, 1950, VN 31/2, vol. 1, NAK.

77. "Notice by Local Authority, Kano," September 15, 1942, Kano ProF 749, NAK.

78. "Commissioner of Police of Plateau Province to the District Officer of Jos," May 29, 1934, Jos ProF 887, NAK.

79. "S. W. Ajediti to the District Officer of Ondo Division," July 20, 1939, Ondo Div OD482, NAI.

80. "Cruelty to Animals" (editorial), *Daily Service*, January 27, 1951.

81. "Cruelty to Animals."
82. "Cruelty to Animals."
83. R. A. Jaiyeola, "Stop Cruelty to Rabid Dogs," *WAP*, January 27, 1951.
84. "Deji of Akure to the Senior District Officer of Ondo Division," February 18, 1948, Ondo Div 482, NAI.
85. "Menace of Rabies."
86. "284 Dogs Destroyed: One Fatal Bite," *NDT*, August 30, 1954.
87. "Medical Officer of Health to the District Officer," July 10, 1939, Ibadan Div 1668, NAI.
88. "Medical Officer of Health to the Resident of Bornu Province," August 15, 1951, Kano ProF 4211, NAI.
89. Jaiyeola, "Stop Cruelty to Rabid Dogs."
90. "Divisional Officer to the Medical Officer," January 15, 1951, MAI ProF 4210, NAK.
91. "Anti-Rabies Campaign in Okigwi," *WAP*, January 18, 1957.
92. "Positive Cases of Rabies, 1945: Lagos Township," ComCol 2667/S.I, vol. 1, NAI.
93. "Warning to Dog Owners," *WAP*, May 13, 1959.
94. "Wild Dogs Cause Panic in Ozara," *Daily Service*, January 7, 1949.
95. "Extract from Kano Township Report for the Period 1st January to 31st August 1918," CSO 26/11516, vol. 1, NAI.
96. "Secretary of the Northern Provinces to Resident Officers," April 4, 1941, Kano ProF 749, NAK.
97. "Resident of Kano Province to the Secretary of the Northern Provinces," April 10, 1941, Kano ProF 749, NAK.
98. "Senior Assistant Superintendent of Police, Kano, to the Local Authority," February 1942, Kano ProF 749, NAK.
99. "Circular, Dated October 13, 1947," Katsina ProF OFF/18, NAK.
100. "Secretary of the Northern Provinces to the Residents of Provinces: Shooting of Dogs," October 25, 1935, Kano ProF 73/1028, NAK.
101. "Commissioner of Police to the Kano Local Authority," March 17, 1936, Kano ProF 73/1028, NAK.
102. "Extract from the Minutes of the Meetings Held on April 24, 1936," Kano ProF 73/1028, NAK.
103. "Senior Veterinary Officer to the Local Authority, Kano," July 17, 1940, Kano ProF 73/1028, NAK.
104. "Extract from Kano Township Report for the Period 1st January to 31st August 1918," CSO 26/11516, vol. 1, NAI.
105. "Kano Local Authority to the Resident of Kano," January 6, 1936, Kano ProF 73/1028, NAK.
106. "Assistant Inspector General of Police (Northern Provinces) E. C. Nottingham to the Commissioner of Police, Jos," October 19, 1934, Jos ProF 887, NAK.
107. "Medical Officer of Health, Lagos Dog Gas Chamber," January 11, 1936, Kano ProF 73/1028, NAK.

108. "Dog-Catcher in Jos," March 1940, Jos ProF 887, NAK.
109. "Veterinary Officer to the Local Authority," March 20, 1939, Kano ProF 73/1028, NAK.
110. "President of the Lagos Town Council to the Medical Officer of Health," December 17, 1948, ComCol 2667/S.I, vol. 1, NAI.
111. "S. S. Oyetunde and Three Others to the Chief Commissioner, Senior Resident, Medical Officer of Health, Senior District Officer, and Olubadan in Council," January 28, 1942, MLG 16770/7, NAI.
112. J. B. Samuel to the District Officer of Ikeja, May 19, 1954, ComCol 2667/S.I, vol. 3, NAI.
113. "Handwritten Memo by J. A. Mackenzie," February 6, 1942, MLG 16770/7, NAI; "Resident of Oyo Province to the Secretary of the Western Provinces," March 7, 1942, MLG 16770/7, NAI.
114. J. S. O. Ogunnaike to the Medical Officer of Health, July 2, 1954, ComCol 2667/S.I, vol. 3, NAI.
115. "Section 6 (Prevention of Rabies) Law of 1952," *Northern Region Gazette*, no. 31, October 23, 1953.
116. "Circular: From the Civil Secretary, Northern Region, to the Residents of the Provinces," August 30, 1952, Jos ProF 887, NAK.
117. "Re: Circular: From the Civil Secretary, Northern Region, to the Residents of the Provinces," April 29, 1953, Jos ProF 887, NAK.

CHAPTER 6: THE LION KING IN THE CAGE

1. "Emir of Katsina, Muhammad Dikko dan Gidado, to the District Officer of Katsina," May 4, 1929, Kat ProF 500, National Archives of Nigeria, Kaduna (hereafter cited as NAK).
2. "Resident of Sokoto to the Secretary of the Northern Provinces," June 4, 1932, Kat ProF 500, NAK.
3. P. A. Allison, "Elephant in the Ondo Province," *Nigerian Field* 11 (1943): 180–84.
4. R. J. Newberry, "Some Games and Pastimes of Southern Nigeria," *Nigerian Field* 7, no. 3 (1938): 131–32.
5. See animal trophies in religious dance: "Egbukere Dance," *Nigeria Magazine*, no. 56 (1958): 52–64.
6. D. R. Rosevear, "Nigerian Animals That Don't Exist," *Nigerian Field*, 13, no. 1 (1948): 6–14.
7. "Hunting in Forest Reserves," 1955–58, MAHFR 771, NAK.
8. "Chiefs of Abini to the District Officer," June 26, 1952, Cal ProF 7/1/2370, National Archives of Nigeria, Enugu (hereafter cited as NAE).
9. Saheed Aderinto, *Guns and Society in Colonial Nigeria: Firearms, Culture, and Public Order* (Bloomington: Indiana University Press), chap. 2.
10. "'Troops' of Wild Elephants Ravage Farms in Ogbomoso Districts," *Daily Service*, August 24, 1951; "Stray Elephant Tramples Four People to Death in Oyo Area," February 19, 1952; "Elephant Menace on Crops Is Increasing," WAP, August 8, 1953.

11. "'Troops' of Wild Elephants Ravage Farms."

12. "Wild Elephants Put Up Hectic Chase of Man, Wife and Child," *WAP*, May 13, 1949.

13. "Stray Elephant Tramples Four People."

14. "J. R. Patterson to the Resident of Zaria Province," February 26, 1936, MNR 9749, vol. 1, NAK.

15. "Senior Resident Officer of Calabar Province to the Secretary of the Southern Province," May 29, 1933, Cal ProF 3/1/1087, NAE.

16. "Conservator of Forests to the Resident of Calabar Province," October 3, 1934, Cal ProF 3/1/1087, NAE; "The Manatee as a Food Animal," *Nigerian Field* 8, no. 3 (1939): 124–26.

17. "Nigerian Ivory Trading Company to the Commissioner of the Colony," February 17, 1943, Commissioner of the Colony Office, Lagos (hereafter cited as ComCol) 1094, vol. 1, National Archives of Nigeria, Ibadan (hereafter cited as NAI).

18. "Resident of Muri Province to the Secretary to the Administration," July 25, 1907, Muri ProF 2557/1907, NAK.

19. "Mohamed Nagaraba to the Administrator of the Colony," May 6, 1952, ComCol 1094, vol. 1, NAI.

20. "R. W. Ayres to the Commissioner of the Colony," September 10, 1951, ComCol 1094, vol. 1, NAI.

21. "Malam Alli to the Commissioner of the Colony," March 28, 1951, ComCol 1094, vol. 1, NAI.

22. "Raleigh: The All-Steel Bicycle," *WAP*, July 17, 1951.

23. "Hurrah for Hercules," *WAP*, December 13, 1953.

24. "Strongest of All," *WAP*, October 8, 1952.

25. "Never Forget," *WAP*, October 20, 1951.

26. "Bovril for Strength," *WAP*, August 2, 1955.

27. "Lion Brand," *WAP*, June 23, 1952.

28. "For Stronger Building Use Burham Portland Cement," *WAP*, March 7, 1956.

29. A couple of sentences in this section of this chapter have appeared previously in Saheed Aderinto, *Guns and Society in Colonial Nigeria: Firearms, Culture, and Public Order* (Bloomington: Indiana University Press, 2018), 65–72.

30. "Wild Animals Preservation Ordinance," in *Annual Volume of the Laws of Nigeria Containing All Legislation Enacted during the Year 1936* (Lagos: Government Printer, 1937).

31. "Wild Animals Preservation Ordinance."

32. "Elephant-Hunter Fined for Killing without Permit," *Daily Service*, December 28, 1946. For the story of Kenya, see Edward L. Steinhart, *Black Poachers, White Hunters: A Social History of Hunting in Colonial Kenya* (Athens: Ohio University Press, 2006).

33. "A Local Leave in Northern Game Country," *Nigerian Field* 7, no. 1 (1938): 21–27.

34. Resident of Jebba Province to the Resident of Niger Province, November 7, 1912, SNP 159/1912, NAK.

35. "Resident of Jebba Province to the Resident of Niger Province," May 25, 1913, SNP 159/1912, NAK.

36. "R. Forrest Webb to the Resident of Zaria Province," September 12, 1955, Zaria ProF FOR 27, NAK.

37. "Resident of Zaria Province to R. Forrest Webb," September 26, 1955, Zaria ProF FOR 27, NAK.

38. "Shaki and District Hunters Company to the President and Members of the Nigerian Council of Ministers," January 8, 1953, Oyo ProF 1/3492, NAI.

39. "Orimolusi of Ijebu Igbo to the District Officer," March 8, 1948, Ije ProF 1129, NAI.

40. "The Conservator of Forests to the Director of Forests," October 19, 1933, Kano ProF 2184, NAK.

41. For the impact of colonial forest reserve policies on the politics of land ownership, see Pauline von Hellermann, *Things Fall Apart? The Political Ecology of Forest Governance in Southern Nigeria* (New York: Berghahn, 2013).

42. Amaury Talbot, *The Peoples of Southern Nigeria*, vol. 4 (London: Frank Cass, 1969), 914; O. Temple, *Tribes, Provinces, Emirates and States of the Northern Provinces of Nigeria* (Cape Town: Argus, 1919), 142; "Hunter Kills Leopard," *Daily Service*, March 27, 1954.

43. "Extract from the Minutes of the Ibadan Native Authority Inner Council Meeting Held on April 15, 1946," Ibadan Div 1/1 1057, NAI.

44. "Hadji Adeyemi II, Alafin of Oyo, to the District Officer of Oyo," February 10, 1953, Oyo ProF 1, 3492, NAI.

45. "Hadji Adeyemi II, Alafin of Oyo, to the District Officer of Oyo," February 10, 1953, Oyo ProF 1, 3492, NAI.

46. "Senior Resident of Benue Province to the Permanent Secretary, Ministry of Natural Resources," November 13, 1957, FOR 12, NAK.

47. "Baboons: Method of Destruction of," November 7, 1951, MAHFR 54/1927, vol. 1, NAK.

48. "Secretary of the Northern Provinces to the Residents of Igala, Igbirra, Kabba Division," October 3, 1950, Idah Div 21, NAK.

49. "Divisional Officer of Lafia to the Resident of Benue Province," April 12, 1939, Lafia Div 213, NAK.

50. "Extract from Resident Kontagora's Report No. 46 for the Quarter Ending 30th September, 1909," SNP 6, 5400/1909, NAK.

51. "Divisional Officer of Lafia to the Resident of Benue Province," April 12, 1939, Lafia Div 213, NAK.

52. "Senior Agricultural Assistant to the Senior District Officer of Ibadan," June 5, 1952, Ibadan Div 1/1 1057, NAI.

53. "Senior Agricultural Assistant."

54. "Messrs. D. R. Pengilly and N. de B. Priestly to the Provincial Office of Zaria," March 6, 1936, Zaria ProF FOR 27, NAK.

55. "Assistant District Officer of Nasarawa Division to the Resident of Benue Province," March 1, 1952, Mak ProF 64/SI, NAK.
56. "District Officer of Nasarawa Division to the Resident of Benue Province," September 24, 1952, Mak ProF 64/SI, NAK.
57. "Resident of Plateau Province to the Permanent Secretary of the Ministry of Animal Health and Forestry," February 5, 1960, Jos ProF RUL/50, NAK.
58. "Hunters Association," 1953, Minna ProF 7691, NAK.
59. "Edward A. Kelly to Commissioner of the Colony," December 9, 1944, ComCol 1976, NAI; "Mario Fumagalli to the District Officer," July 28, 1946, ComCol 1976, NAI.
60. "Hassan and Company Limited," September 10, 1928, ComCol 1976, NAI.
61. "District Officer of Tiv Division to the Resident of Benue Province," July 4, 1934, Yola ProF 12/1/646, NAK.
62. "Secretary of Northern Provinces to the Chief Secretary to the Government," November 25, 1933, Kano ProF 2184, NAK.
63. "Resident of Ilorin to the Chief Secretary to the Government," November 25, 1933, Kano ProF 2184, NAK.
64. H. Spottiswoode, "Game Preservation: Ambition or Achievement?," *Nigerian Field* 6, no. 3 (1937): 114–15.
65. "Summary of International Convention for 1933 Relative to the Preservation of Fauna and Flora in Africa in Their Natural State," FOR 12, NAK.
66. "Minutes of the First Meeting of the Northern Regional Game Preservation Committee Held in the Office of the Ministry of Natural Resources and Local Industries on the 28th September 1953," FOR 12, NAK.
67. For more about other game reserves in Africa that inspired the creation of the Yankari Game Reserve, see A. F. B. Bridges, "The Kruger National Park," *Nigerian Field* 6, no. 2 (1937): 53–57.
68. "D. R. Rosevear to the Chief Conservator of Forests," January 8, 1954, FOR 12, NAK.
69. "Inspector-General of Animal Health Services to the Director of Veterinary Services," September 5, 1953, GEN/TEC/6/S4, NAK.
70. "Minutes of the Second Meeting of the Northern Regional Game Preservation Committee Held in the Ministry of Natural Resources at Kaduna on the 30th March 1954," FOR 12, NAK.
71. "Minutes of Game Preservation Committee, 1955–1959," GEN/TEC/6/S vol. 3, NAK.
72. "Yankari Game Reserve: Rules and Regulations, 1957," GEN/TEC/6/S vol. 3, NAK.
73. "Yankari Game Reserve Is Progressing," WAP, September 9, 1959.
74. "Game Reserve Information, 1957," GEN/TEC/6, NAK.
75. "All-Nigeria Wildlife Preservation Conference, 18–19 February 1958," GEN/TEC/6, NAK.
76. P. E. N. Malafa, "Re-stocking London's Zoo," NDT, March 21, 1946.

77. "Mary and Loja," British Pathé, accessed August 9, 2019, https://www .britishpathe.com/video/mary-and-loja/query/Nigeria+lion+cubs.

78. "The Amir Visits the Zoo," *Daily Telegraph*, July 16, 1921.

79. Edmund M. Hogan, *Berengario Cermenati among the Ebira of Nigeria: A Study in Colonial, Missionary, and Local Politics, 1897–1925* (Ibadan: HEBN, 2011), 195–96.

80. F. de F. Daniel, "The Horse in Native Hands," *Nigerian Field* 5, no. 2 (1936): 54.

81. F. D. Golding, "Nigerian Pets V: 'Whiskers' the Palm Squirrel," *Nigerian Field* 7, no. 3 (1938): 121–23.

82. Dorothy H. Bostock, "Nigerian Pets IV: 'Tunde' the Potto," *Nigerian Field* 6, no. 2 (1937): 83–84.

83. Bostock, 83.

84. "News Notes and Comments," *Lagos Standard*, April 3, 1912.

85. "Lagosian on Dits," *Lagos Standard*, June 14, 1911.

86. "Monkey-Bite Case: Judgement Reserved," WAP, January 30, 1959.

87. Onuora Nzekwu, "Snake Charmer," *Nigeria Magazine*, no. 64 (March 1960): 18–27.

88. "Snake Charmer Bitten by Own Snake," WAP, September 10, 1956.

89. "Lagos RSPCA Members Paid Visits to the Zoos of Their Vice Patrons, Messrs W. H. Biney and A. F. Hooper at Surelere Yaba on July 26, 1947," ComCol 1136, NAI.

90. "Lion Worth £1,000 Due Lagos Soon," WAP, February 20, 1956.

91. Janheinz Jahn, *Through African Doors: Experiences and Encounters in West Africa*, trans. Oliver Coburn (New York: Grove, 1960), 82.

92. M. O. Okigie, "Biney's Zoo," NDT, May 13, 1946.

93. "All-Nigeria Wildlife Preservation Conference, 18–19 February 1958," GEN/TEC/6, NAK.

94. E. O. Iwobi, "Canary and Parrot," WAP, August 9, 1956; A. N. Druggo, "The Snake and Weaver," WAP, August 18, 1956; "King Tortoise Rides an Elephant," WAP, November 17, 1956.

95. Uncle Kebby, "Professor Benson Is a Charlatan," WAP, November 2, 1957.

96. "Charmer or Charlatan?," WAP, May 10, 1958.

97. "Charmer or Charlatan?"

98. Jahn, *Through African Doors*, 82.

99. "Mary and Loja."

100. "Acting Resident of Benue Province to C. L. Bowen," May 17, 1956, FOR 12, NAK.

101. "C. L. Bowen to the Resident of Benue Province," March 27, 1956, FOR 12, NAK.

CHAPTER 7: "LET US BE KIND TO OUR DUMB FRIENDS"

1. "Woman Is Arraigned and Fined in Court for Ill-Treating Dog," WAP, September 14, 1938. "Tortured with Red-Hot Iron," NDT, September 12, 1938.

2. "Man Is Arraigned for Cruelty to Animals," WAP, August 20, 1938.

3. "Bush Cat Bites Baby," WAP, March 20, 1956.

4. "Convicted of Cruelty to Animal," WAP, June 21, 1958.

5. "Convicted of Cruelty."

6. "Lady Is Jailed One Day for Cruelty," WAP, August 27, 1953.

7. "Prevention of Cruelty to Animals," 1950, Commissioner of the Colony Office, Lagos (hereafter cited as ComCol) 1136, National Archives of Nigeria, Ibadan (hereafter cited as NAI).

8. J. H. W. Vincent, "The Prevention of Cruelty to Animals," *Daily Service*, January 16, 1950; Jaiyeola, "Stop Cruelty to Rabid Dogs," WAP, June 14, 1950; R. A. Jaiyeola, the Acting General Secretary of the RSPCA, Nigeria, "Our Obligations towards the Lower Animals," WAP, October 30, 1950; Miss Banjoko Williams, "Society for the Prevention of Cruelty to Animals," WAP, July 24, 1954; "Cruelty to Animals" (editorial), WAP, May 26, 1941; "Cruelty to Animals" (editorial), WAP, December 10, 1942; "Government to Stop Cruelty to Horses," WAP, August 2, 1938.

9. "Resident of Kabba Province to the Secretary of the Northern Province," October 27, 1934, SNP K1385, National Archives of Nigeria, Kaduna (hereafter cited as NAK).

10. "Minutes of a Regional Conference Held on 23rd July 1951, in the Eastern Regional House of Assembly," OG ProF 2314, National Archives of Nigeria, Enugu (hereafter cited as NAE).

11. For the history of animal compassion in Britain, see Harriet Ritvo, *The Animal Estate: The English and Other Creatures in the Victorian Age* (London: Penguin, 1987), chaps. 3 and 4.

12. See children's columns in the WAP and the NDT.

13. "Animals Are Such Grateful Things," WAP, July 17, 1957.

14. Jay Gee, "Man's Inhumanity to Animals," WAP, April 13, 1938.

15. "Radio Talk Given by [G. L. Adebesin] the Secretary RSPCA, Kaduna Group on Wednesday September 28, 1949, at 6:15 P.M. to 6:30 P.M.," SNP K1385, NAK.

16. "Cruelty to Animals" (editorial), WAP, May 26, 1941.

17. Gee, "Man's Inhumanity to Animals."

18. Tolu Iwajowa, "The Kindness Animals Need," April 1942, ComCol 1136, NAI.

19. Vincent, "Prevention of Cruelty to Animals."

20. Vincent.

21. "Royal Society for the Prevention of Cruelty to Animals to the Governor of Nigeria," October 11, 1930, ComCol 1136, NAI.

22. "Administrator of the Colony to the Chief Secretary to the Government of Nigeria," December 2, 1930, ComCol 1136, NAI.

23. "The Governor of Nigeria to the Chief Secretary of the RSPCA," January 3, 1931, ComCol 1136, NAI.

24. *Extracts from Hadiths and Muslim Text Books on Subject of Treatment of Animals* (Kano: Emirate Printing Department, 1927).

25. "RSPCA to the Acting Chief Secretary to the Government of Nigeria," January 24, 1931, ComCol 1136, NAI.
26. "Enquire Whether the Issue of RSPCA Meritorious Service Medals to Certain Nigerian Rulers and Officers Is Approved," October 27, 1937, CO 583/223/11, National Archives of the United Kingdom (hereafter cited as NAUK).
27. "Enquire Whether the Issue."
28. "Resident of Niger Province to the Secretary of the Northern Province," June 28, 1937, Minna ProF A.B 402, NAK.
29. "Resident of Plateau Province to the Secretary of the Northern Province," July 28, 1937, Jos ProF 2226, NAK.
30. "Secretary of the RSPCA to the Secretary of State for the Colonies," October 27, 1937, CO 583/223/11, NAUK.
31. "Trap Holds Mouse: Chicken Is Ready Plucked in Nigeria's Open-Air Market," *Weekly Illustrated*, May 7, 1938.
32. "Colonial Office to the Officer Administering the Government of Nigeria," June 2, 1938, OG ProF 2314, NAE.
33. "Dr. Eric Sutherland to the Colonial Office," May 16, 1938, OG ProF 2314, NAE.
34. "Acting Secretary of Southern Provinces to the Chief Secretary to the Government," August 5, 1938, CSO 30229/S.1, NAI.
35. "The Nigerian Animal Aid Society," *NDT*, April 20, 1936.
36. "Nigerian Animal Aid Society."
37. "The Nigerian Animal Aid Society," 1936, ComCol 1136, NAI.
38. Gee, "Man's Inhumanity to Animals."
39. "Reverend S. Ade Oduwale to the Commissioner of the Colony," January 27, 1947, ComCol 1136, NAI.
40. "Oduwale to the Commissioner."
41. "Chief Secretary to the Government A. W. Moss to Public Relations Officer R. O. Daniel," October 3, 1947, ComCol 1136, NAI.
42. "Reverend S. Ade Oduwale to the Commissioner of the Colony," January 18, 1947, ComCol 1136, NAI; "Commissioner of the Colony to Reverend S. Ade Oduwale," February 1, 1947, ComCol 1136, NAI.
43. "Chief Secretary to the Government of Nigeria to the Royal Society for the Prevention of Cruelty to Animals," June 27, 1947, ComCol 1136, NAI.
44. "Animal Welfare Week," *WAP*, October 6, 1947.
45. "RSPCA Appeal to Moslems," *WAP*, May 20, 1960.
46. "RSPCA HQ to Be Opened Tomorrow," *WAP*, March 19, 1953.
47. *The A.B.C.: History, Policy, and Organisation of R.S.P.C.A* (London: RSPCA, 1949), 15.
48. "The Pets' PRO," *West Africa*, April 4, 1951.
49. "Commissioner of the Colony E. A. Carr to the Chief Secretary to the Government," August 5, 1947, ComCol 1136, NAI.
50. "Lagos RSPCA to Receive Sibly," *WAP*, January 18, 1956.
51. "Boys Told Not to Make Rams Fight," *WAP*, August 7, 1953.

52. "RSPCA Appeals Week," *WAP*, June 2, 1959.
53. "RSPCA General Secretary E. O. Daniel to the District Officer of Kano," June 30, 1951, SNP K1385, NAK.
54. S. B. Hogan, "Cruelty to Animals," *Daily Comet*, June 16, 1951.
55. "T. N. Douglas Okebugbu to the Acting Honorary General Secretary of the RSPCA," June 10, 1951, SNP K1385, NAK.
56. "Okebugbu to Acting Honorary General Secretary."
57. Quoted in "RSPCA General Secretary E. O. Daniel to the Senior Resident of Kano," June 7, 1950.
58. "District Officer D. A. Pott of Kano to M. A. Fashina, Secretary of the RSPCA," July 10, 1950, SNP K1385, NAK.
59. Wakilin Waje, "Prevention of Cruelty to Animals," July 20, 1950.
60. "Cruelty to Animals," *WAP*, December 10, 1942.
61. Assistant District Officer of Nsukka Mr. Milne, "Method of Slaughtering," 1939, OG ProF 2314, NAE.
62. Waje, "Prevention of Cruelty to Animals."
63. Waje.
64. "Slaughtering of Animals," *NDT*, March 1, 1933.
65. "Slaughter Place, Kano Market," *NDT*, February 18, 1933.
66. "Slaughter Place, Kano Market."
67. "Cruelty to Animals," *NDT*, March 1, 1933.
68. "Resident of Kano Province to the Secretary of the Northern Province," March 20, 1933, SNP K1385, NAK.
69. "Cruelty to Animals."
70. "The 'Humane Killer' Palaver," *WAP*, March 17, 1950.
71. "Humane Killer and Muslims," *Daily Service*, December 1, 1949.
72. "Humane Killer and Muslims."
73. "'Humane Killer' Palaver."
74. "Explaining 'Humane Killer,'" *WAP*, May 19, 1950.
75. "Explaining 'Humane Killer.'"
76. "Gold Coast Shows Nigeria How 'Humane Killer' Is Applied," *WAP*, May 31, 1950.
77. "Muslims Use 'Humane Killer' in Gold Coast," *Daily Service*, May 31, 1950.
78. "Govt. to Stop Cruelty to Horses," *WAP*, August 2, 1956.
79. "District Officer to the Veterinary Officer," June 10, 1943, OG ProF 2314, NAE.
80. "Note: Veterinary Office, Kano," September 1941, SNP K1385, NAK.
81. "Superintendent of Police of Northern Nigeria to the Veterinary Officer," June 22, 1944, ComCol 1136, NAI.
82. Jaiyeola, "Stop Cruelty to Rabid Dogs."
83. Jaiyeola.
84. "Secretary of the RSPCA to the District Officer of Ilorin," July 9, 1955, Ilorin ProF 1832B, NAK.

85. "Veterinary Development Officer to the District Officer of Ilorin," August 18, 1955, Ilorin ProF 1832B, NAK.
86. "Lt. Col. G. W. P. Thorn to the Secretary of the RSPCA Ibadan and the District Officer of Ibadan," January 16, 1953, Iba Div 1/1, 1344, NAI; "District Officer of Ibadan J. F. Hayley to the Chairman of the RSPCA Ibadan," January 24, 1953, Iba Div 1/1, 1344, NAI.
87. "Medical Officer of Health to the Secretary of the RSPCA," March 22, 1950, ComCol 1136, NAI.
88. Jubril Raji, "Rats and RSPCA," WAP, February 11, 1956; "Rats in Yaba Post Office Tear Parcel," WAP, September 3, 1951.
89. A. Omololu, "RSPCA in Nigeria," WAP, April 10, 1956.
90. Omololu.
91. "RSPCA President Says Overcrowding of Livestock Is Checked," *Daily Service*, December 4, 1956.

CHAPTER 8: "A GREAT EVIL RITUAL MURDER"

1. A. H. B. Kirkman, "Horses in Nigeria," *The Field*, February 2, 1952.
2. "A. H. B. Kirkman to Major Field," April 20, 1952, CO 554/530, National Archives of the United Kingdom (hereafter cited as NAUK).
3. Kirkman, "Horses in Nigeria."
4. "A. H. B. Kirkman to Major Field."
5. "L. R. Buxton to the Chief Registrar's Office," June 16, 1952, CO 554/530, NAUK.
6. C. S. Field, "Horses in Nigeria," *The Field*, March 22, 1952; R. A. Brown, "Horses in Nigeria," *The Field*, March 22, 1952; "Cruelty to Horses: Ritual Slaughter in Nigeria," *Times* (London), October 14, 1952; "RSPCA Secretary Investigates Horse Traffic," *Eastern Outlook*, August 14, 1952; Winifred Portland, vice president of the RSPCA, "Cruelty to Horses," *Times* (London), May 13, 1953.
7. "L. R. Buxton to the Chief Registrar's Office," May 27, 1952, CO 554/530, NAUK; "Secretary of State for the Colonies to Sir J. Macpherson of Nigeria," June 11, 1952, CO 554/530, NAUK.
8. "Cruelty to Horses: Ritual Slaughter in Nigeria"; "Secretary of the RSPCA to the Under Secretary of the Colonial Office," September 1, 1953, CO 554/530, NAUK.
9. Portland, "Cruelty to Horses."
10. "L. Rutledge to Winston Churchill," November 15, 1952, CO 554/530, NAUK.
11. "Faith Parsons to John Profumo," May 21, 1952, CO 554/530, NAUK.
12. "Letter from the Grove House," April 1, 1952, CO 554/530, NAUK.
13. "J. A. L. Duncan to Colonial Office," February 18, 1952, CO 554/530, NAUK; "Secretary of State for the Colonies to the Officer Administering the Government of Nigeria," November 25, 1952, CO 554/530, NAUK.

14. "Trap Holds Mouse: Chicken Is Ready Plucked in Nigeria's Open-Air Market," *Weekly Illustrated*, May 7, 1938.

15. "Horse Sacrifices in Nsukka Division, 1940," CSE 1/85/5172, National Archives of Nigeria, Enugu (hereafter cited as NAE).

16. "Mile Race Won by Eclipse: Two Accidents on the Course," *NDT*, October 10, 1945; "Tragedy on the Course on Christmas Day," *NDT*, December 27, 1944.

17. "Racing in Nigeria," *NDT*, February 19, 1942.

18. "Racing in Nigeria."

19. "Donations by the Lagos Race Club," *NDT*, February 4, 1943.

20. "Ibadan Race Club," *NDT*, November 8, 1941.

21. "Ibadan Easter Race Meeting: WF to the Editor," *NDT*, March 31, 1942.

22. "Victory Meeting 1946," *NDT*, June 4, 1946.

23. "Victory Meeting of the Lagos Race Club," June 24, 1946.

24. "Lagos Race Club Donates £100 to NEWA," *NDT*, February 27, 1947; "Kano Race Meeting in Aid of NEWA," *NDT*, March 17, 1947; "£300 Raised for NEWA at Ibadan," *NDT*, March 28, 1947.

25. "Racing in Lagos," *NDT*, March 6, 1944.

26. "Racing in Lagos."

27. "Racing in Lagos."

28. Turfist, "Handicapping of Horses," *NDT*, March 7, 1944.

29. "Horse-Owners and Jockeys Lodge Complaints," *Daily Service*, July 7, 1958.

30. Adeyemo Alakija, "Racing in Nigeria," *NDT*, March 14, 1944.

31. Alakija.

32. "Opening Day of Easter Race Meeting," *NDT*, April 3, 1944.

33. "Reported Arrival of Sick Horses in Lagos," *NDT*, March 21, 1946.

34. "Reported Arrival of Sick Horses."

35. "Medical Officer of Health to the Secretary of the Lagos Race Club," January 31, 1955, Commissioner of the Colony Office, Lagos (hereafter cited as ComCol) 2076, National Archives of Nigeria, Ibadan (hereafter cited as NAI).

36. "Medical Officer of Health."

37. Rex Niven, *Nigerian Kaleidoscope: Memoirs of a Colonial Servant* (London: C. Hurst, 1982), 94.

38. "Brilliant Performances at Kano Race Meeting," *NDT*, October 31, 1947.

39. "R. A. Denton to the Commissioner of the Colony," June 20, 1931, ComCol 1136, NAI.

40. A. Ade Adedokun, "Betting on a Horse," *WAP*, June 29, 1950.

41. Sportsman, "Campaign against Doping at Lagos Race," *Daily Service*, June 28, 1958.

42. Federal Department of Veterinary Research, *Annual Report for the Year 1959/1960* (Lagos: Government Printer, 1960), 54.

43. Federal Department of Veterinary Research; Sportsman, "Campaign against Doping."

44. "C. T. Lawrence Collection," CO 1069/66, NAUK.
45. "Senior Resident of Zaria E. H. B. Laing to the Secretary of the Northern Province," April 23, 1926, SNP K1385, National Archives of Nigeria, Kaduna (hereafter cited as NAK).
46. "Assistant Inspector General of Police of Northern Province to the Chief Veterinary Officer, Vom," April 19, 1932, SNP K1385, NAK.
47. "Senior Resident of Zaria E. H. B. Laing to the Managers and Agents of Niger Company, G. B. Ollivant, African Grown Cotton Company, W. Redfearn & Sons," February 24, 1926, SNP K1385, NAK.
48. "Chief Veterinary Officer to the Secretary of the Northern Provinces," February 26, 1926, SNP K1385, NAK.
49. "E. Figueredo Partner W. Redfearn & Sons to Senior Resident, Zaria," February 26, 1926, SNP K1385, NAK.
50. "Assistant Inspector-General of Police to the Secretary of the Northern Provinces," July 10, 1934, SNP K1385, NAK.
51. "Chief Veterinary Officer W. W. Henderson to the Assistant Inspector-General of Police," April 27, 1932, SNP K1385, NAK.
52. "Chief Veterinary Officer."
53. *Extracts from Hadiths and Muslim Text Books on Subject of Treatment of Animals* (Kano: Kano Emirate Printing Department, 1927).
54. Stephanie Zehnle, "War and Wilderness: The Sokoto Jihad and Its Animal Discourse," *Critical African Studies* 8, no. 2 (2016): 216–37.
55. "Resident of Plateau Province to the Secretary of the Northern Provinces," March 4, 1932, SNP K1385, NAK.
56. "Resident of Ilorin to the Secretary of the Northern Province," October 21, 1934, SNP K1385, NAK.
57. "From the Emir of Kano Abdullahi Bayero to the People of Kano," July 26, 1931, SNP K1385, NAK.
58. "Resident of Kano Province to the Secretary of Northern Provinces," October 26, 1932, SNP K1385, NAK.
59. "District Officer of Gombe to the Resident of Bauchi Province," October 27, 1934, Bauchi ProF 26754, NAK.
60. "From the Resident of Niger Province to the Secretary of the Northern Provinces," October 31, 1934, SNP K1385, NAK.
61. "Resident of Bornu Province to the Secretary of the Northern Provinces," November 12, 1934, SNP K1385, NAK.
62. "Resident of Plateau Province to the Secretary of the Northern Provinces," September 28, 1934, SNP K1385, NAK.
63. "R. F. P. Orme to the Residents of the Provinces," September 28, 1934, SNP K1385, NAK.
64. "Resident of Adamawa Province to the Secretary of the Northern Provinces," December 11, 1934, SNP K1385, NAK.
65. "Crown Counsel," January 7, 1935, SNP K1385, NAK.
66. "From the Resident of Niger Province to the Secretary of the Northern Provinces," October 31, 1934, SNP K1385, NAK.

67. "Resident of Bauchi Province to the Secretary of the Northern Province," November 12, 1934, Bauchi ProF 26754, NAK.
68. "District Officer of Gombe to the Resident of Bauchi," January 8, 1935, Bauchi ProF 26754, NAK.
69. C. K. Meek, *Law and Authority in a Nigerian Tribe* (Oxford: Oxford University Press, 1937), 166–68, 171–72, 316; "House Sacrifices in Nsukka Division, 1940," CSE 1/85/5172, NAE.
70. Simon Ottenberg, *Double Descent in an African Society: The Afikpo Village-Group* (Seattle: University of Washington Press, 1968), 198.
71. "Acting District Officer of Afikpo to the Resident of Ogoja Province," March 9, 1930, OG ProF 2314, NAE.
72. "Acting Resident of Bamenda Province to the Secretary of the Eastern Provinces," November 1, 1950, OG ProF 2314, NAE.
73. "District Officer of Obudu to the Resident of Ogoja Province," February 28, 1939, OG ProF 2314, NAE.
74. "Minutes of the 19th Regional Staff Meeting Held at Government Lodge on 7th April 1951 at 10 A.M.," OG ProF 2314, NAE.
75. "The Chief Commissioner of Eastern Provinces to the District Officers of Ikom, Afikpo, Obubra, Abakaliki," January 22, 1948, OG ProF 2314, NAE.
76. "Acting Resident of Bemenda Province to the Secretary of the Eastern Provinces," November 1, 1950, OG ProF 2314, NAE.
77. "District Officer of Calabar to the Senior Resident of Calabar," October 25, 1950, Cal ProF 7/1/2188, NAE.
78. "Resident of Ogoja Province to the Secretary of the Eastern Provinces," January 4, 1950, OG ProF 2314, NAE.
79. "Resident of the Ogoja Province to the Secretary of the Eastern Provinces," December 23, 1950, OG ProF 2314, NAE.
80. "District Officer of Abakaliki to the Resident of Ogoja Province," February 28, 1939, OG ProF 2314, NAE.
81. "Acting Principal Veterinary Officer to the Resident of Ogoja," November 20, 1951, OG ProF 2314, NAE.
82. "Secretary of the Eastern Provinces to the District Officers of Abakaliki, Afikpo, Ikom, Ogoja, Obubra, and Obudu," October 13, 1950, OG ProF 2314, NAE.
83. Director of Veterinary Services, "Traffic in Horses," November 4, 1950, OG ProF 2314, NAE.
84. "Ritual Slaughter of Horse in East Condemned," WAP, September 22, 1956.

CONCLUSION

1. "Osinbajo Distances Self from Ruga Settlement," *Guardian*, June 29, 2019, https://guardian.ng/news/osinbajo-distances-self-from-ruga-settlement/.
2. "Behold, the Yoruba Are Agonising and Organizing," *Guardian*, June 30, 2019, https://guardian.ng/opinion/columnists/behold-the-yoruba-are-agonising-and-organising/.

3. Kano Zoological Garden Facebook page, accessed September 16, 2021, https://www.facebook.com/Kano-Zoological-Garden-439915049799860/.

4. Bob Golding, "The Story of the Gorilla," Animals, Africa, and Other Secrets . . . , accessed August 12, 2019, https://www.bobgolding.co.uk/photo-gallery/the-story-of-the-gorillas/.

5. Robert R. Golding, "Can Gorillas Swim?," accessed on October 20, 2020, https://www.bobgolding.co.uk/wp-content/uploads/2019/06/Gorillas_Swim_v.12_June_2019_Bob.Golding.pdf.

6. Niels Bolwing, *From Mosquitoes to Elephants: A Life with Animals* (Cheltenham, UK: self-pub., 1983).

7. Robert R. Golding, "A Gorilla and Chimpanzee Exhibit at the University of Ibadan Zoo," *International Zoo Yearbook* 12 (1972): 71–77.

8. Golding, "Story of the Gorilla."

9. "Nigeria Has Lost 20 Rangers since 1991—National Park Service," PM News, July 30, 2019, https://www.pmnewsnigeria.com/2019/07/30/nigeria-has-lost-20-rangers-since-1991-national-park-service/.

10. A. A. Ogunjinmi, O. O. Oyeleke, A. A. Adewumi, and K. O. Ogunjinmi, "The Challenges to Nigeria National Parks Conservation Efforts: Key Informants Approach," *Nigerian Journal of Wildlife Management* 1, no. 1 (2017): 25–30.

11. Nachamada Geoffrey, *Yankari Game Reserve WCS Annual Report 2017* (Bauchi State, Nigeria: WCS, 2017).

12. Nigerian Field Society, accessed August 12, 2019, https://www.nigerianfield.org/.

13. Polo Sports in Nigeria, Nigerian Polo Federation, accessed August 14, 2019, http://polo.sitesng.com/en_Home.html.

14. "Ganduje Forbids Kano District Heads from Attending Emir Sanusi's Eid Durbar," *Punch*, August 11, 2019, https://punchng.com/ganduje-forbids-kano-district-heads-from-attending-emir-sanusis-eid-durbar/.

15. "Napri, Dspmean Differ on Bill to Stop Export, Killing of Donkeys," *Vanguard*, May 15, 2019, https://www.vanguardngr.com/2019/05/napri-dspmean-differ-on-bill-to-stop-export-killing-of-donkeys/.

16. "Group Faults NASS Bill on Donkey, Says Nigeria Loses $2bn Annually to Smuggling," *Daily Trust*, December 2, 2018, https://www.dailytrust.com.ng/group-faults-nass-bill-on-donkey-says-nigeria-loses-2bn-annually-to-smuggling.html.

17. "Hot Dispute on Donkey's Future," *Daily Trust*, May 19, 2019, https://www.dailytrust.com.ng/hot-dispute-on-donkeys-future.html/.

18. "Society Holds Send-Off for Dog, Urges Compassion for Animals," *Punch*, January 12, 2017, https://punchng.com/society-holds-send-off-dog-urges-compassion-animals/.

19. Diane Gifford-Gonzalez, "Introduction: Animal Genetics and African Archeology: Why It Matters," *African Archeological Review* 30, no. 1 (2013): 1–20.

20. H. Epstein, *The Origin of the Domestic Animals of Africa* (New York: African Publishing, 1971).

21. Pandrillus, accessed on December 31, 2021, https://www.pandrillus.org/.

22. "Fisheries Development in Nigeria," 1951, CO 554/218, National Archives of the United Kingdom.

23. Paula Ben-Amos, "Men and Animals in Benin Art," *Man* 11, no. 2 (1976): 243–52.

Bibliography

ARCHIVES

National Archives of Nigeria, Enugu
National Archives of Nigeria, Ibadan
National Archives of Nigeria, Kaduna
National Archives of the United Kingdom, London

NEWSPAPERS, PERIODICALS, AND MAGAZINES

Daily Service, 1940–50
Eastern Nigerian Guardian, 1941–50
The Field, 1952
Lagos Weekly Record, 1900–10
Nigeria Magazine, 1945–60
Nigerian Daily Times, 1930–60
Nigerian Field, 1933–60
Nigerian Pioneer, 1920–24
Southern Nigeria Defender, 1940–50
Times (London), 1952–53
Weekly Illustrated, 1930
West Africa, 1951
West African Pilot, 1938–60

PUBLISHED PRIMARY SOURCES

The A.B.C.: History, Policy, and Organisation of R.S.P.C.A. London: RSPCA, 1949.
Advice on Tsetse Surveys and Clearings. Kaduna: Government Printer, 1934.
Agriculture Ordinance (No. 4 of 1926). In *Annual Volume of the Laws of Nigeria Containing All Legislation Enacted during the Year 1936.* Lagos: Government Printer, 1937.
Annual Report of the Department of Veterinary Research of the Federation of Nigeria, 1954–1955. Lagos: Government Printer, 1957.
Diseases of Animals Ordinance. In *Annual Volume of the Laws of Nigeria Containing All Legislation Enacted during the Year 1917.* Lagos: Government Printer, 1918.

Dogs Ordinance (Chapter 98). In *Annual Volume of the Laws of Nigeria Containing All Legislation Enacted during the Year 1927.* Lagos: Government Printer, 1928.

Extracts from Hadiths and Muslim Text Books on Subject of Treatment of Animals. Kano: Emirate Printing Department, 1927.

Federal Department of Veterinary Research. *Annual Report for the Year 1959/1960.* Lagos: Government Printer, 1960.

Forestry Ordinance. In *Annual Volume of the Laws of Nigeria Containing All Legislation Enacted during the Year 1934.* Lagos: Government Printer, 1935.

Lagos Race Course, Management (Amendment). In *Annual Volume of the Laws of Nigeria Containing All Legislation Enacted during the Year 1934.* Lagos: Government Printer, 1935.

Nigeria: Legislative Council Debates. Lagos: Government Printer, 1940–50.

Report on Livestock Problems in Nigeria by P. J. Toit. Lagos: Government Secretariat, 1927.

Royal Society for the Prevention of Cruelty to Animal (Nigeria): Ibadan Auxiliary Branch. *Annual Report, 1952–53.* Ibadan: Nubi, 1954.

The Sleeping Sickness Ordinance. In *Annual Volume of the Laws of Nigeria Containing All Legislation Enacted during the Year 1936.* Lagos: Government Printer, 1937.

The Utilization of Animal By-products in the Colonial Empire. Lagos: Government Printer, 1938.

Wild Animals Preservation Ordinance. In *Annual Volume of the Laws of Nigeria Containing All Legislation Enacted during the Year 1936.* Lagos: Government Printer, 1937.

VIDEOS AND ONLINE PHOTO ARCHIVES

"Animals, Africa and Other Secrets. . . ." Accessed on August 12, 2019. https://www.bobgolding.co.uk/.

"Family History of Francis and Betty Humphreys." Accessed on August 5, 2019. http://www.mueller-humphreys.de/Humphreys/DicksonElizabeth/selbst/Nigeria/NigeriaFrankFoiE.html.

"Mary and Loja." British Pathé. 1925. https://www.britishpathe.com/video/mary-and-loja/query/Nigeria+lion+cubs.

"The Nigerian Field Society." Accessed August 12, 2019. https://www.nigerianfield.org/.

"The Nigerian Nostalgia 1960–1980 Project." Facebook. Accessed August 5, 2019. https://www.facebook.com/groups/nigeriannostalgiaproject/.

"Queen's 1956 Tour of Nigeria." British Pathé. Accessed January 20, 2018. https://www.britishpathe.com/workspaces/2e6592077f92958a84d91602b25fa58d/Queen-s-1956-Tour-of-Nigeria.

JOURNAL ARTICLES, BOOKS, AND UNPUBLISHED THESES

Abiodun, Rowland. *Yoruba Art and Language: Seeking the African in African Art.* Cambridge: Cambridge University Press, 2014.

Adams, E. C. (Adamu). *Lyra Nigeriae*. London: T. Fisher Unwin, 1911.

Adeboye, Babalola. *Akojopo alo Ijapa, Apa Kiini*. Ibadan: University Press, 1973.

Adeeko, Adeleke, and Akin Adesokan, eds. *Celebrating D. O. Fágúnwà: Aspects of African and World Literary History*. Ibadan: Bookcraft, 2017.

Aderinto, Saheed. "Empire Day in Africa: Patriotic Colonial Childhood, Imperial Spectacle, and Nationalism in Nigeria, 1905–1960." *Journal of Imperial and Commonwealth History* 46, no. 4 (2018): 731–57.

——. *Guns and Society in Colonial Nigeria: Firearms, Culture, and Public Order*. Bloomington: Indiana University Press, 2018.

——. "Modernizing Love: Gender, Romantic Passion, and Youth Literary Culture in Colonial Nigeria." *Africa: The Journal of the International African Institute* 85, no. 3 (2015): 478–500.

——. *When Sex Threatened the State: Illicit Sexuality, Nationalism, and Politics in Colonial Nigeria, 1900–1958*. Urbana: University of Illinois Press, 2015.

Adesanya, Aderonke. *Carving Wood, Making History: The Fakeye Family, Modernity, and Yoruba Woodcarving*. Trenton, NJ: Africa World, 2012.

Afigbo, A. E. *The Warrant Chiefs: Indirect Rule in Southeastern Nigeria, 1891–1929*. London: Longman, 1972.

Akpang, Clement. "Nigerian Modernism(s) 1900–1960 and the Cultural Ramifications of the Found Object." Doctoral thesis, University of Bedfordshire, 2016.

Anderson, Benedict. *Imagined Communities: Reflections on the Origin and Spread of Nationalism*. London: Verso, 1983.

Apter, Andrew. "On Imperial Spectacle: The Dialectics of Seeing in Colonial Nigeria." *Comparative Studies in Society and History* 44, no. 3 (2002): 564–96.

——. *The Pan-African Nation: Oil and the Spectacle of Culture in Nigeria*. Chicago: University of Chicago Press, 2005.

Awolowo, Obafemi. *Awo: The Autobiography of Chief Obafemi Awolowo*. Cambridge: Cambridge University Press, 1960.

Azikiwe, Nnamdi. *My Odyssey: An Autobiography*. New York: Praeger, 1970.

Banerjee, A. K., and S. O. Elegbe. "The Incidence and Diagnosis of Rabies in Nigeria." *Bulletin of Epizootic Diseases of Africa* 18 (1970): 53–56.

Barnes, Sandra T., ed. *Africa's Ogun: Old World and New*. Bloomington: Indiana University Press, 1989.

——. *Patrons and Power: Creating a Political Community in Metropolitan Lagos*. Bloomington: Indiana University Press, 1986.

Barth, Henry. *Travels and Discoveries in North and Central Africa*. 3 vols. New York: Drallop, 1890.

Basden, G. T. *Among the Ibos of Nigeria*. London: Seeley, Service, 1921.

Begho, Mason. *The Dog-Bite Magistrate: His Struggles*. Lagos: Daily Times, 1988.

Beier, Ulli. *The Hunter Thinks the Monkey Is Not Wise . . . The Monkey Is Wise, but He Has His Own Logic: A Selection of Essays*. Edited by

Wale Ogundele. African Studies 59. Bayreuth, Germany: Bayreuth University, 2001.

——. "Yoruba Attitude to Dogs." *Odu* 7 (1959): 31–37.

Beinart, William. "African History and Environmental History." *African Affairs* 99, no. 395 (2000): 269–302.

——. *The Rise of Conservation in South Africa*. Cambridge: Cambridge University Press, 2003.

Beinart, William, and Lotte Hughes. *Environment and Empire*. Oxford: Oxford University Press, 2007.

Bello, Ahmadu. *My Life*. Cambridge: Cambridge University Press, 1962.

Ben-Amos, Paula. "Men and Animals in Benin Art." *Man* 11, no. 2 (1976): 243–52.

Blench, Roger M. "A History of Domestic Animals in Northeastern Nigeria." *Cahiers des Sciences Humaines* 31, no. 1 (1995): 181–237.

Blench, Roger M., and Kevin C. Macdonald. *The Origins and Development of African Livestock: Archeology, Genetics, Linguistics and Ethnography*. New York: Routledge, 2000.

Bolwing, Niels. *From Mosquitoes to Elephants: A Life with Animals*. Cheltenham, UK: Self-published, 1983.

Bond, Jennifer, and Kennedy Mkutu. "Exploring the Hidden Costs of Human-Wildlife Conflict in Northern Kenya." *African Studies Review* 61, no. 1 (2018): 33–54.

Boulger, L. R., and J. S. Porterfield, "Isolation of a Virus from Nigerian Fruit Bats." *Transactions of the Royal Society of Tropical Medicine and Hygiene* 52, no. 5 (1958): 421–24.

Boulger, L. R., and J. Hardy. "Rabies in Nigeria." *West African Medical Journal* 11, no. 6 (1960): 223–34.

Brown, Frederick L. *The City Is More than Human: An Animal History of Seattle*. Seattle: University of Washington Press, 2016.

Brown, Karen. *Mad Dogs and Meerkats: A History of Resurgent Rabies in Southern Africa*. Athens: Ohio University Press, 2011.

——. "Political Entomology: The Insectile Challenge to Agricultural Development in the Cape Colony, 1895 to 1910." *Journal of Southern African Studies* 29, no. 2 (2003): 529–49.

Bryant, Kenneth J. "30 Years On." In *Advancing in Good Order: Northern Nigeria Attains Independence*. Zaria, Nigeria: Gaskiya Corp., 1959.

Callaway, Helen. *Gender, Culture, and Empire: European Women in Colonial Nigeria*. Urbana: University of Illinois Press, 1987.

Campbell, Dugald. *On the Trail of the Veiled Tuareg*. Philadelphia: J. B. Lippincott, 1928.

Carruthers, Jane. *The Kruger National Park: A Social and Political History*. Pietermaritzburg, SA: UKZN, 1995.

——. *National Park Science: A Century of Research in South Africa*. Cambridge: Cambridge University Press, 2017.

———. *Wildlife and Warfare: The Life of James Steven-Hamilton.* Pietermaritz-burg, SA: University of Natal Press, 2001.

Coker, Increase H. E. *Landmarks of the Nigerian Press: An Outline of the Origins and Development of the Newspaper Press in Nigeria, 1859 to 1965.* Lagos: Daily Times, 1968.

Coleman, James S. *Nigeria: Background to Nationalism.* Berkeley: University of California Press, 1958.

Crocker, W. R. *Nigeria: A Critique of British Colonial Administration.* London: George Allen & Unwin, 1936.

Crosby, Alfred W. *Ecological Imperialism: The Biological Expansion of Europe, 900–1900.* Cambridge: Cambridge University Press, 1986.

Davies, Howell. *Tsetse Flies in Nigeria: A Handbook for Junior Control Staff.* Ibadan: Oxford University Press, 1977.

Darnton, Robert. *The Great Cat Massacre and Other Episodes in French Cultural History.* New York: Basic Books, 1984.

Denham, Dixon, and Hugh Clapperton. *Narrative of Travels and Discoveries in Northern and Central Africa.* Vol. 1. London: John Murray, 1826.

Dlamini, Jacob S. T. *Safari Nation: A Social History of the Kruger National Park.* Athens: Ohio University Press, 2020.

Donovan, Tristan. *Feral Cities: Adventures with Animals in the Urban Jungle.* Chicago: Chicago Review, 2015.

Drewal, Henry John. *African Artistry: Techniques and Aesthetics in Yoruba Sculpture.* Atlanta: High Museum of Art, 1980.

Epstein, H. *The Origin of the Domestic Animals of Africa.* New York: African Publishing, 1971.

Equiano, Olaudah. *The Interesting Narrative of the Life of Olaudah Equiano or Gustavus Vassa the African, Written by Himself.* 1789. Edited and with notes by Shelly Eversley. New York: Modern Library, 2004.

Fagunwa, D. O. *Ogbójú Ode Nínú Igbó Irúnmalè.* 1938. Edinburgh: Thomas Nelson, 1983.

Falconer, J. D. *On Horseback through Nigeria.* London: T. Fisher Unwin, 1911.

Few, Martha, and Zeb Tortorici. *Centering Animals in Latin American History.* Durham, NC: Duke University Press, 2013.

Field, H. I. "The Development of Veterinary Education in Nigeria." *Veterinary History* 2, no. 3 (1982): 112–23.

Fitz-Henry, Lassie. *African Dust.* London: Macmillan, 1959.

Feldmann, Susan, ed. *African Myths and Tales.* New York: Dell, 1963.

Freund, Bill. *Capital and Labour in the Nigerian Tin Mines.* London: Longman, 1981.

Fuller, Harcourt. *Building the Ghanaian Nation-State: Kwame Nkrumah's Symbolic Nationalism.* New York: Palgrave Macmillan, 2014.

Gbadegesin, O. A. "The Intersection of Modern Art, Anthropology, and International Politics in Colonial Nigeria, 1910–1914." Master's thesis, Emory University, 2007.

Gibson, Abraham H. *Feral Animals in the American South: An Evolutionary History.* Cambridge: Cambridge University Press, 2016.

Gifford-Gonzalez, Diane. "Introduction: Animal Genetics and African Archeology: Why It Matters." *African Archeological Review* 30, no. 1 (2013): 1–20.

Gnindlingh, Albert. "'Gone to the Dogs': The Cultural Politics of Gambling—the Rise and Fall of British Greyhound Racing on the Witwatersrand, 1932–1949." *South African Historical Journal* 48 (2003): 174–89.

Goody, Jack. *Technology, Tradition and the State in Africa.* Cambridge: Cambridge University Press, 1980.

Griswold, Wendy, and Muhammed Bhadmus. "The Kano Durbar: Political Aesthetics in the Bowel of the Elephant." *American Journal of Cultural Sociology* 1, no. 1 (2013): 125–51.

Hall, Herbert C. (Johnny). *Barrack and Bush in Northern Nigeria.* London: George Allen & Unwin, 1923.

Henninget-Voss, Maty J., ed. *Animals in Human Histories: The Mirror of Nature and Culture.* Rochester, NY: University of Rochester Press, 2002.

Hogan, Edmund M. *Berengario Cermenati among the Ebira of Nigeria: A Study in Colonial, Missionary, and Local Politics, 1897–1925.* Ibadan: HEBN, 2011.

Isichei, Elizabeth. *Igbo Worlds: An Anthology of Oral Histories and Historical Descriptions.* London: Macmillan, 1977.

Jacobs, Nancy. *Birders of Africa: History of a Network.* New Haven, CT: Yale University Press, 2016.

——. "The Great Bophuthatswana Donkey Massacre: Discourse on the Ass and the Politics of Class and Grass." *American Historical Review* 106 (2001): 485–507.

Jahn, Janheinz. *Through African Doors: Experiences and Encounters in West Africa.* Translated by Oliver Coburn. New York: Grove, 1960.

Jegede, Dele. "Art in Contemporary Africa." In *Africa*, vol. 5, *Contemporary Africa*, edited by Toyin Falola, 705–34. Durham, NC: Carolina Academic, 2003.

Johnson, Carolyn, ed. *Harmattan, a Wind of Change: Life and Letters from Northern Nigeria at the End of Empire.* London: Radcliffe, 2010.

Johnson-Odim, Cheryl, and Nina Emma Mba. *For Women and the Nation: Funmilayo Ransome-Kuti of Nigeria.* Urbana: University of Illinois Press, 1997.

Kean, Hilda. *Animal Rights: Political and Social Change in Britain since 1800.* London: Reaktion Books, 1998.

Kete, Kathleen, ed. *A Cultural History of Animals in the Age of Empire.* New York: Bloomsbury, 2007.

Ki-Zerbo, J., ed. *General History of Africa.* Vol. 1, *Methodology and African Prehistory.* Paris: UNESCO: 1981.

Kirk-Greene, Anthony. "Breath-Taking Durbars." In *Advancing in Good Order: Northern Nigeria Attains Independence.* Zaria: Gaskiya Corp., 1959.

——. *Hausa Ba Dabo Ba Ne: A Collection of 500 Proverbs*. Ibadan: Oxford University Press, 1966.

——. *Symbol of Authority: The British District Officer in Africa*. London: I. B. Tauris, 2006.

Kisch, Martin. *Letters and Sketches from Northern Nigeria*. London: Chatto & Windus, 1910.

Kwashirai, Vimbai. "Environmental Change, Control, and Management in Africa." *Global Environment* 6, no. 2 (2013): 166–96.

Lander, Richard. *Records of Captain Clapperton's Last Expedition to Africa*. 2 vols. London: Henry Colburn & Richard Bentley, 1830.

Langa, Langa [H. B. Hermon-Hodge]. *Up against It in Nigeria*. London: George Allen & Unwin, 1922.

Lansbury, Carol. *The Old Brown Dog: Women, Workers, and Vivisection in Edwardian England*. Madison: University of Wisconsin Press, 1985.

Larymore, Constance. *A Resident's Wife in Nigeria*. London: George Routledge, 1908.

Lasekan, Akinola. *Nigeria in Cartoons*. Lagos: Ijaiye, 1944.

Law, Robin. *The Horse in West African History: The Role of the Horse in the Societies of Pre-colonial West Africa*. Oxford: Oxford University Press, 1980.

——. "Horses, Firearms, and Political Power in Pre-colonial West Africa." *Past and Present* 72 (1976): 112–32.

——. "A West African Cavalry State: The Kingdom of Oyo." *Journal of African History* 16, no. 1 (1975): 1–15.

Lawal, Babatunde. *The Gelede Spectacle: Art, Gelede and Social Harmony in an African Culture*. Seattle: University of Washington Press, 1996.

Lent, John A., ed. *Cartooning in Africa*. Cresskill, NJ: Hampton, 2009.

Leonard, Arthur. *The Lower Niger and Its Tribes*. London: Macmillan, 1906.

Lucas, J. Olumide. *The Religion of the Yorubas*. Lagos: CMS Bookshop, 1948.

Lugard, Frederick. *The Diaries of Lord Lugard*. Edited by Margery Perham and Mary Bull. 4 vols. Evanston, IL: Northwestern University Press, 1959.

Lugga, Sani Abubakar. *Dikko Dynasty: 100 Years of the Sallubawa Ruling House of Katsina, 1906–2006*. Kaduna: Lugga, 2006.

Mabogunje, Akin L. *Urbanization in Nigeria*. London: University of London Press, 1968.

MacGregor, Arthur. *Animal Encounters: Human and Animal Interaction in Britain from the Norman Conquest to World War One*. London: Reaktion Books, 2012.

Mamdani, Mahmood. *Citizen and Subject: Contemporary Africa and the Legacy of Late Colonialism*. Princeton, NJ: Princeton University Press, 1996.

Mavhunga, Clapperton Chakanetsa. "Mobility and the Making of Animal Meaning: The Kinetics of 'Vermin' and 'Wildlife' in Southern Africa." In *Making Animal Meaning*, edited by Georgina Montgomery and Linda Kalof, 17–43. East Lansing: Michigan State University Press, 2011.

Mba, Nina Emma. *Nigerian Women Mobilized: Women's Political Activity in Southern Nigeria, 1900–1965.* Berkeley: University of California Press, 1982.

McCaskie, T. C. "People and Animals: Constru(ct)ing the Asante Experience." *Africa* 62 (1992): 221–47.

Meek, C. K. *Law and Authority in a Nigerian Tribe.* Oxford: Oxford University Press, 1937.

———. *The Northern Tribes of Nigeria.* 2 vols. New York: Negro Universities Press, 1925.

———. *A Sudanese Kingdom: An Ethnographical Study of the Jukun-Speaking Peoples of Nigeria.* London: Kegan Paul, 1931.

Mikhail, Alan. *The Animal in Ottoman Egypt.* Oxford: Oxford University Press, 2013.

Mokhtar, G., ed. *General History of Africa.* Vol. 2, *Ancient Civilizations of Africa.* Paris: UNESCO: 1981.

Mullin, Molly H. "Mittots and Windows: Sociocultural Studies of Human-Animal Relationships." *Annual Review of Anthropology* 28 (1999): 201–24.

Mwangi, Evan Maina. *The Postcolonial Animal: African Literature and Posthuman Ethics.* Ann Arbor: University of Michigan Press, 2019.

Niven, Rex. *Nigerian Kaleidoscope: Memoirs of a Colonial Servant.* London: C. Hurst, 1982.

Nuru, S., and H. J. Barnes. "Bovine Rabies in Kano State, Nigeria." *Bulletin of Epizootic Diseases of Africa* 22, no. 3 (1974): 211–15.

Nzegwu, Nkiru. "The Concept of Modernity in Contemporary African Art." In *African Diaspora: African Origins and New World Identities,* edited by Isidore Okpewho, Carole Boyce Davies, and Ali Al'Amin Mazrui, 391–427. Bloomington: Indiana University Press, 1999.

Oduntan, Oluwatoyin. *Power, Culture, and Modernity in Nigeria: Beyond the Colony.* New York: Routledge, 2018.

Ogbechie, Sylvester. *Ben Enwonwu: The Making of an African Modernist.* Rochester, NY: University of Rochester Press, 2008.

———. "Portrait of the Artist in the Shadow of Discourse: Narrating Modern African Art in 20th-Century Art History." *Critical Interventions: Journal of African Art History and Visual Culture* 1, no. 1 (2007): 14–27.

Oguibe, Olu. "Appropriation as Nationalism in Modern African Art." *Third Text* 16, no. 3 (2002): 243–59.

Ogunjinmi, A. A., O. O. Oyeleke, A. A. Adewumi, and K. O. Ogunjinmi. "The Challenges to Nigeria National Parks Conservation Efforts: Key Informants Approach." *Nigerian Journal of Wildlife Management* 1, no. 1 (2017): 25–30.

Ogunremi, Gabriel Ogundeji. *Counting the Camels: The Economics of Transportation in Pre-industrial Nigeria.* New York: NOK, 1982.

Ojo, M. O., and A. Adeoye. "Rabies in a Nigerian Dwarf Goat." *Bulletin of Epizootic Diseases of Africa* 15 (1967): 409–10.

Ojoade, J. Olowo. "Nigerian Cultural Attitudes to the Dog." In *Signifying Animals: Human Meaning in the Natural World*, edited by Roy Willis, 214–21. London: Routledge, 1994.

Okediji, Moyo. *African Renaissance: Old Forms, New Images in Yoruba Art*. Boulder: University of Colorado Press, 2002.

———. *Western Frontiers of African Art*. Rochester, NY: University of Rochester Press, 2011.

Okeke-Agulu, Chika. "Nationalism and the Rhetoric of Modernism in Nigeria: The Art of Uche Okeke and Demas Nwoko, 1960–1968." *African Arts* 39, no. 1 (2006): 26–37.

———. *Postcolonial Modernism: Art and Decolonization in Twentieth-Century Nigeria*. Durham, NC: Duke University Press, 2015.

Okonkwo, Rina. *Protest Movements in Lagos, 1908–1930*. Lewiston, NY: E. Mellen, 1995.

Ola, Abayomi. *Satires of Power in Yoruba Visual Culture*. Durham, NC: Carolina Academic, 2013.

Olaniyan, Tejumola. "Cartooning Nigerian Anticolonial Nationalism." In *Images and Empires: Visuality in Colonial and Postcolonial Africa*, edited by Paul Stuart Landau, 124–40. Berkeley: University of California Press, 2002.

Olmstead, Alan. *Arresting Contagion: Science, Policy, and Conflicts over Animal Disease Control*. Cambridge, MA: Harvard University Press, 2015.

Oloidi, Ola. "Art and Nationalism in Colonial Nigeria." *Nsukka Journal of History* 1, no. 1 (1989): 92–110.

Olusanya, G. O. "Olaniwun Adunni Oluwole." In *Nigerian Women in Historical Perspective*, edited by Bolanle Awe, 122–31. Ibadan: Bookcraft, 1992.

Ottenberg, Simon. *Double Descent in an African Society: The Afikpo Village-Group*. Seattle: University of Washington Press, 1968.

Peffer, John. "Becoming Animal: The Tortured Body during Apartheid." In *Art and the End of Apartheid*, edited by John Peffer, 41–72. Minneapolis: University of Minnesota Press, 2009.

Pratten, David. *The Man-Leopard Murders: History and Society in Colonial Nigeria*. Edinburgh: Edinburgh University Press, 2007.

Ritvo, Harriet. *The Animal Estate: The English and Other Creatures in the Victorian Age*. London: Penguin, 1987.

Robbins, Louise E. *Elephant Slaves and Pampered Parrots: Exotic Animals in Eighteenth-Century Paris*. Baltimore: Johns Hopkins University Press, 2012.

Ross, Doran H., ed. *Elephant: The Animal and Its Ivory in African Culture*. Berkeley: University of California Press, 1992.

Savage, R. G. A. "A Case of Human Rabies." *West African Medical Journal* 7 (1934): 125–35.

Schauer, Jeff. "The Elephant Problem: Science, Bureaucracy, and Kenya's National Parks, 1955–1975." *African Studies Review* 58, no. 1 (2015): 177–98.

Schroeder, Richard A. "Moving Targets: The 'Canned' Hunting of Captive-Bred Lions in South Africa." *African Studies Review* 61, no. 1 (2018): 8–32.

Shadle, Brett. "Cruelty and Empathy, Animals and Race, in Colonial Kenya." *Journal of Social History* 45, no. 4 (2012): 1097–116.

Sharwood-Smith, Joan. *Diary of a Colonial Wife: An African Experience.* London: I. B. Tauris, 1992.

Sklar, Richard L. *Nigerian Political Parties: Power in an Emergent African Nation.* Princeton, NJ: Princeton University Press, 1963.

Smaldone, Joseph P. *Warfare in the Sokoto Caliphate: Historical and Sociological Perspectives.* Cambridge: Cambridge University Press, 1977.

Smith, E. C. "Canine Rabies in Nigeria." *West African Medical Journal* 2 (1928): 120–25.

Smith, John. *Colonial Cadet in Nigeria.* Durham, NC: Duke University Press, 1968.

Smith, Robert S. *Warfare and Diplomacy in Pre-colonial West Africa.* Madison: University of Wisconsin Press, 1989.

Somolu, Olujide. *Olumo: The Mystique of an Alluring Symbol: The Memoirs of the Honourable Justice Olujide Somolu, Chief Justice of the Western State, 1967–1971.* Edited by Kayode Somolu, Femi Somolu, and Seke Somolu. Lagos: Florence & Lambard, 2011.

Steinhart, Edward L. *Black Poachers, White Hunters: A Social History of Hunting in Colonial Kenya.* Athens: Ohio University Press, 2006.

Swart, Sandra. *Riding High: Horses, Humans and History in South Africa.* Johannesburg: Wits University Press, 2010.

———. "Writing Animals into African History." *Critical African Studies* 8, no. 2 (2016): 95–108.

Taiwo, Olufemi. *How Colonialism Preempted Modernity in Africa.* Bloomington: Indiana University Press, 2010.

Talbot, P. Amaury. *In the Shadow of the Bush.* New York: George H. Doran, 1912.

———. *Life in Southern Nigeria: The Magic, Beliefs and Customs of the Ibibio Tribe.* London: Macmillan, 1923.

———. *The Peoples of Southern Nigeria.* 4 vols. London: Frank Cass, 1969.

———. *Tribes of the Niger Delta: Their Religions and Customs.* London: Frank Cass, 1932.

———. *Woman's Mysteries of a Primitive People: The Ibibio of Southern Nigeria.* London: Cassell, 1915.

Temple, O. *Tribes, Provinces, Emirates and States of the Northern Provinces of Nigeria.* Cape Town: Argus, 1919.

Thorne, A. L. C. "The Problem of Rabies in Nigeria." *Bulletin of Epizootic Diseases of Africa* 2 (1954): 265–67.

Tlili, Sarra. *Animals in the Qur'an.* Cambridge: Cambridge University Press, 2015.

Tremearne, A. J. N. *The Tailed Head-Hunters of Nigeria.* Philadelphia: J. B. Lippincott, 1912.

Tutnet, James. *Reckoning with the Beast: Animals, Pain, and Humanity in the Victorian Mind*. Baltimore: Johns Hopkins University Press, 1980.

Tutuola, Amos. *My Life in the Bush of Ghosts*. London: Faber & Faber, 1954.

Umeasiegbu, R. N. *The Way We Lived*. London: Heinemann, 1969.

Umoh, Jarlath, and E. D. Belino. "Rabies in Nigeria: A Historical Review." *International Journal of Zoonoses* 6 (1979): 41–48.

Van Sittert, Lance, and Sandra Swart, eds. *Canis Africanis: A Dog History of Southern Africa*. Leiden: Brill, 2008.

———. "*Canis Familiaris*: A Dog History of Southern Africa." In *Canis Africanis: A Dog History of Southern Africa*, edited by Lance Van Sittert and Sandra Swart, 1–34. Leiden: Brill, 2008.

Von Hellermann, Pauline. *Things Fall Apart? The Political Ecology of Forest Governance in Southern Nigeria*. New York: Berghahn, 2013.

Wischermann, Clemens, Aline Steinbrecher, and Philip Howell, eds. *Animal History in the Modern City: Exploring Liminality*. London: Bloomsbury, 2018.

Zehnle, Stephanie. "War and Wilderness: The Sokoto Jihad and Its Animal Discourse." *Critical African Studies* 8, no. 2 (2016): 216–37.

Index

Page numbers in italics refer to figures and tables.

game: animals, 39; law, 182, 187; licenses, 183
gastrointestinal problems, 60
geology, 23
George (grass monkey), 99
Gidado, Muhammad Dikko dan, 74, 175–76, 193
Gilmore, Francis, 161
giraffe, 175–76, 187, 190
Goat and Sheep Bye Law, 43, 46
Gogo (dog), 99
Gold Coast, 38, 138, 149, 163, 196, 222, 232
Gombe, Inua, 107, 244
Government Reservation Area, 160
Greening, Derek Miles, 100, 101, 102
Gregory, Alexander, 106–8, 161
Griffiths, J. A., 157–58
guinea pig, 150, 196
guns, xiii, 13, 20, 117, 169, 179, 180, 204, 256. *See also* rifle shooting
Gurara Waterfalls, 102

habitat, 7, 11–14, 19, 26, 39, 176, 179, 187, 200, 256
hadiths, 210, 239–40
harpoon, 186
Hausa-Fulani, 7, 69, 129, 219, 242, 253
hawk, 140, 196
"heart of the North," 65–71
Henderson, W. W., 239
Hercules (bicycle brand), 69, 181, 181
Hermon-Hodge, H. B. *See* Langa Langa
hippopotamus, 180–82, 187–88, 190
Hooper's zoo, 196, 197
Horace (goat), 99
horse: accident, 230; breeders, 81; care, 71; ceremonies, 85; horsemanship, 70; horse-riding culture, 243; lover, 84; military, 66; owners, 76; racing, 64, 71, 72, 78, 188, 257; ritual, 24, 244–48; trade, 246. *See also* Association of Race Horse Owners; Barb (horse ancestry); cruelty: to the horse and donkey; Dongola (horse ancestry); horse and donkey; horsemanship; indigenous: horse riding; *jahi* (royal horse greeting); movement: of horses and donkeys; racehorses; save-the-Nigerian-horse-and-donkey campaign; war horses; *and specific names of horses*
horse and donkey, 8, 65, 90, 248
horsemanship, 242–44
horticulture, 23, 45

human-animal relations, 18, 96, 141, 171; encounters, 11; entanglement, 4; human-dog life, 101; human-dog relations, 26, 27
humane killer, 220, 221, 222, 223
hydrophobia, 147, 150, 152–54, 157–58

Ibadan, xv, 19–20, 48, 180, 236
Ibrahima (*Atta* of the Igbirra), 193
ichthyology, 23
Idoma, 7
Igala Division, 185
Igbo, 7, 94, 97, 129, 147, 172, 183, 227, 244, 246
Igbosere High Court, xiv, 23
Ijebu Province, 45
Ijebu Review, 45
Ikoli, Ernest, 124
Ikoyi, 13, 107, 110, 154, 161, 167
Ilorin, 13, 48, 188, 224, 242
Imade, 20, 253, 255, 255
immunization, 56
Imoudu, Michael, 130
imperialism: aesthetics, 176; capitalism, 26; hunting, 5; ideology, 94; male author-ity, 84; power, 22, 35; science, 147, 157
indigenous: African knowledge systems, 5; conceptions of nature, 194; dog population, 93; faiths, 59; horse riding, 244; law and custom, 203; racing, 65; therapy, 55
indirect rule, 7
industry, 36, 41, 42, 43, 47, 52, 106, 135, 204, 234, 235
infantry battalions, 51, 66, 67, 72, 73–74
inflation of animal prices, 47
infrastructure, 11, 15, 36, 44, 71, 115, 117, 183, 206, 252, 258
Inter-African Bureau for Epizootic Diseases, 38
Irede Village, 173
Ironsi, Aguiyi, 121
Islam: civilization, 240; festivals, 75, 86
ivory, 176–77, 180, 184

Jacobs, Nancy, 5
jaguar, 70
Jahan (Shah), 85
jahi (royal horse greeting), 83, 88
Jahn, Janheinz, 98
Jane (dog), 107–8
Jibowu, Olumuyiwa, 107
jockeys, 13, 76, 78, 79–80, 82, 230. *See also* racehorses

John (chimpanzee), 196
John Holt & Company, 62, 158, 162–63
Johnson, W. B., 158
Jos, 171
Jubilee (horse), 63, 64, 76
Juno (horse), 77

Kabba Division, 100, 185
Kaduna, 102, 109, 157–58, 168, 171, 173, 191, 208, 218, 258
Kafanchan, 112, 116, 186
Kano, Halilu, 87
Kano: abattoir, 40; Kano Township Advisory Board, 170; Kano Veterinary Department, 163; race clubs, 75
Kano Emirate, 40
Kano Township Advisory Board, 170
Kano Veterinary Department, 163
kennel, 152, 154, 161–62, 165, 172–73
King's Church, 214
Kirk-Greene, Anthony, 65, 69, 70, 72, 74, 86
Kisch, Martin, 73
Kishi, 185
kraals, 55

labor: carton, 130–34; strikes, 41; taxation, 7; union, 120, 125, 128
laboratory, 152, 155, 157, 235
Lagos: Colony Butchers' Union, 37; dog gas chamber, 171; race club, 75, 76, 110, 231; racecourse, 78
Lagos and Colony Butchers' Union, 37
Lagos Daily News, 44
Lagos High Court, 119
Lagos Race Club (LRC), 76, 77, 78, 79, 81, 231–34
Lagos Standard, 72, 194
Lagos Town Council (LTC), 37, 46, 60, 107, 145, 153, 161, 165, 172–73, 225, 233; dogcatchers, 161
Lagos Weekly Record, 75, 77
lamb, 127, 130, 132
land: animals, 19; sequestration, 17, 34; tenure, 38; use and the ecosystem, 18
Langa Langa (H. B. Hermon-Hodge), 72, 99, 102–4, 108
Larymore, Constance, 66, 71, 85, 94, 99, 101–4
Lasekan, Akinola, 82, 119, 120, 121, 129, 136, 139
Law, Robin, 5
Lawani, Safuratu, 201–2

Lawrence, C. T., 102, 256
Lebanese, 76, 99
Legislative Council, 139
Lékèéwògbé (dog), xiv, 92
Lekki Poultry Industry, 47
leopard, 176, 177, 184–85, 187, 190, 194–96, 199, 202, 204
Liberal Party, 84
Liberia, 38
lion, 104, 119, 124, 128, 131, 133, 136, 140, 175, 177, 181, 184, 187, 190, 192–94, 196
lioness, 119, 129, 131–32
livestock: accident caused by, 45, 46; disease, 37, 41, 47; as food, 33–36; modern, 36; population, 37; slaughtering of, 26, 61; taxes, 253; urban, 43–44, 45, 46, 62
Loja (lion), 193, 199
Lokoja, 15, 67, 70, 73, 193
London Zoological Garden, 15, 193, 198
Lube (dog), 97
Lucky (monkey), 203
Lugard, Frederick, 24, 51, 67, 99, 148

Macaulay, Herbert, 44, 124
Macpherson Constitution, 141
Madigbolesu (dog), 97
Maiduguri, 72, 148, 167, 171
Mamdani, Mahmood, 7
mammalogy, 23
Manchester Guardian, 225, 226, 247
marriage, 7, 206
Mary (lion), 193
masculinity, 24, 71, 78, 82–83, 142
Mastaf Dauro (horse), 88
Mbari Club, 91
medical pluralism, 55
memoir, 99
menageries, 104, 195–97, 216
Meritorious Service Medal, 210–11
meteorology, 23
metropolitan horse breeders, 81
metropolitan livestock and plants, 33
military: barracks, 74; coup, 121, 253; forces, 74; horses, 66; recreation, 73
Miss Silva, 197
Mobo (festival), 97
modern: abattoirs, 59; animals, 10, 13, 14, 15, 19, 93; colonial subjects, 177; conceptions of animals, 15; dog, 14, 93, 94; livestock, 36; racing, 65; vessels, 180; veterinary therapy, 55; zoo and animal exhibition, 192–200

Moss, A. W., 215
motor drivers, 46, 116
movement: of animals, 55, 116; of dogs, 160; of horses and donkeys, 65
Mughal emperor, 85
mule, 55, 68, 247
Mumani, T. A., 161
Murray, A. E. F., 212
Mushin, 117, 172
Muslims, 19, 43, 44–47, 59, 220–22, 226, 240, 258
mutton, 36

Nagogo, Usman, 74
National Council of Nigeria and the Cameroons (NCNC), 83, 119–20, 121, 125, 127, 130–31, 132–33, 134–36, 137, 140, 141, 142
National Ex-Servicemen's Welfare Association, 232
National Park Service, 256
naturalists, 13, 22, 124, 177, 182, 187, 188–89, 190, 192, 196, 198
Negri bodies, 146, 152
newspaper: cartoons, 120; headlines, 80
New Star (horse), 76
Nguru, 167
Ngwa Clan Union, 217
Niamey, 38
Niger Company, 162, 180, 238
Nigeria Cold Storage Company, 15
Nigeria Commoners Liberal Party, 84
Nigerian Animal Aid Society (NAAS), 212, 214
Nigerian Citizen, 51, 86
Nigerian Council of Ministers, 183
Nigerian Daily Times (NDT), 42, 43, 46, 47, 52, 61, 62, 63, 75, 77, 78, 79, 80, 82, 118, 154, 155, 159, 164, 165, 214, 220, 231, 232, 233
Nigerian Field, 22–23, 194, 196, 256
Nigerian Field Society, 23, 196
Nigerian Ivory Trading Company, 180
Nigerian Nostalgia Project, xv, 23
Nigerian Pioneer, 96
Nigerian Youth Movement (NYM), 47, 124, 130, 131, 132, 134, 135, 136
Nigeria Royal Society for the Prevention of Cruelty to Animals (NRSPCA), 28, 145, 164–65, 167, 196, 198, 208, 214–26
Niger River, 19, 48, 48
Niger River delta, 37
Niven, Rex, 87, 234

Nnewi, 115
nomadic pastoralism, 42
Normal College of Art, 124
Northern Elements Progressive Union (NEPU), 131, 140
Northern Regional Game Preservation Committee, 189
Nsukka Division, 115, 219, 244, 246

Obisesan, Akinpelu, 112
Obudu Cattle Ranch, 43, 54
Oduwale, S. Ade, 214
Ogun (Yoruba god), 97, 98
Ogunmola, Basorun, 19
Ogunnaike, J. S. O., 173
Ojikutu, A. Y., 37
Okediji, Moyo, xv, 123
Okeke, Uche, 123
Okigwi, 167
Olagbegi, Oba Olateru, II, 178
Ollivant, G. B., 238
olowondabira, 110
Olusanya, G. O., 84
Oluwagbohun, Babatunde, 202
Oluwole, Adunni, xi, 84, 84
Oluwole, I. Ladipo, 59, 154, 214
Omidunsin (dog), 97
Onabolu, Aina, 123–24
Ondo Province, 117
Onitsha Province, 115
Onobrakpeya, Bruce, 123
Orimolusi (king) of Ijebu Igbo, 183
ornithology, 22
Oturkpo, 99
oxen, 68

Panama (horse), 232
Pasteur Institute, 149, 150
pastoralism, 5, 37, 42
pasture, 37, 41, 44, 49, 50, 256
Pax Britannica, 185
Peggy (dog), 99, 108
Penyam Forest Reserve, 51
Periwinkle (horse), 76
Phillip, Susuana, 201
photograph, 10, 23
photojournalism, 40
photophobia, 156
physiology, 14, 177, 206, 233
Piccin (dog), 108, 196
pigs, 6, 25, 33, 39, 41, 44–46, 150, 184
polo, 24, 65, 72, 102, 150, 230, 251, 257
Poppy (dog), 100, 108
porcupine, 196